The Cambridge Companion to Singing

Ranging from medieval music to Madonna and beyond, this is the only book to cover in detail so many aspects of the voice. The volume is divided into four broad areas. Popular Traditions begins with an overview of singing traditions in world music and continues with aspects of rock, rap, and jazz. The Voice in the Theatre includes both opera singing from the beginnings to the present day and twentieth-century stage and screen entertainers. Choral Music and Song features a history of the art song, essential hints on singing in a larger choir, the English cathedral tradition and a history of the choral movement in the United States. The final substantial section on performance practices ranges from the voice in the Middle Ages and the interpretation of early singing treatises to contemporary vocal techniques, ensemble singing, the teaching of singing, children's choirs, and a comprehensive exposition of vocal acoustics.

JOHN POTTER is a member of the internationally renowned vocal groups The Hilliard Ensemble and Red Byrd. He is lecturer in music at the University of York and author of *Vocal Authority: Singing Style and Ideology* (1998).

The Cambridge Companions to Music

The Cambridge Companion to Brass Instruments
Edited by Trevor Herbert and John Wallace

The Cambridge Companion to the Cello
Edited by Robin Stowell

The Cambridge Companion to the Clarinet
Edited by Colin Lawson

The Cambridge Companion to the Organ
Edited by Nicholas Thistlethwaite and Geoffrey Webber

The Cambridge Companion to the Piano
Edited by David Rowland

The Cambridge Companion to the Recorder
Edited by John Mansfield Thomson

The Cambridge Companion to the Saxophone
Edited by Richard Ingham

The Cambridge Companion to Singing
Edited by John Potter

The Cambridge Companion to the Violin
Edited by Robin Stowell

The Cambridge Companion to Bach
Edited by John Butt

The Cambridge Companion to Beethoven
Edited by Glen Stanley

The Cambridge Companion to Berg
Edited by Anthony Pople

The Cambridge Companion to Brahms
Edited by Michael Musgrave

The Cambridge Companion to Benjamin Britten
Edited by Mervyn Cooke

The Cambridge Companion to Chopin
Edited by Jim Samson

The Cambridge Companion to Handel
Edited by Donald Burrows

The Cambridge Companion to Schubert
Edited by Christopher Gibbs

The Cambridge Companion to

SINGING

EDITED BY
John Potter
University of York

CAMBRIDGE
UNIVERSITY PRESS

PUBLISHED BY THE PRESS SYNDICATE OF THE UNIVERSITY OF CAMBRIDGE
The Pitt Building, Trumpington Street, Cambridge, United Kingdom

CAMBRIDGE UNIVERSITY PRESS
The Edinburgh Building, Cambridge CB2 2RU, UK
40th West 20th Street, New York NY 10011–4211, USA
10 Stamford Road, Oakleigh, VIC 3166, Australia
Ruiz de Alarcón 13, 28014 Madrid, Spain
Dock House, The Waterfront, Cape Town 8001, South Africa

http://www.cambridge.org

First published 2000

Printed in the United Kingdom at the University Press, Cambridge

Typeset in Adobe Minion 10.75/14 pt, in QuarkXpress™ [SE]

A catalogue record for this book is available from the British Library

Library of Congress Cataloguing in Publication data
The Cambridge Companion to singing / edited by John Potter.
    p.   cm. – (The Cambridge companions to music)
Includes bibliographical references and index.
Contents: Popular traditions – The voice in the theatre – Choral
music and song – Performance practices.
ISBN 0 521 62225 5 (hardback) – ISBN 0 521 62709 5 (paperback)
1. Singing–History. 2. Choral singing–History. 3. Vocal music–
History and criticism. 4. Performance practice (Music)
I. Potter, John, tenor.   II. Series.
ML1460.C28   2000
782′.009–dc21   99–32948   CIP

ISBN 0 521 62225 5 hardback
ISBN 0 521 62709 5 paperback

Contents

Illustrations

Notes on the contributors

Stephen Banfield is Elgar Professor of Music at the University of Birmingham. He is the author of *Sensibility and English Song* (1985), the award-winning *Sondheim's Broadway Musicals* (1993) and *Gerald Finzi: An English composer* (1997) and is editor of the twentieth-century volume of *The Blackwell History of Music in Britain* (1995).

Neely Bruce is Professor of Music and American Studies, Director of Choral Activities, and former chair of the Music Department at Wesleyan University. He is a composer, conductor, pianist and scholar of American music. He was on the Editorial Committee of New World Records and was the first chairman of the New England Sacred Harp Singing. He has long been associated with the works of John Cage, Henry Brant and Anthony Philip Heinrich, 'The Beethoven of America'.

Timothy Day was educated at Oxford University, where he was organ scholar at St John's College. He joined the staff of the National Sound Archive in London in 1978, and since 1980 has been Curator of Western Art Music. He is currently writing a study of one hundred years of recorded music for Yale University Press.

Joseph Dyer teaches music history at the University of Massachusetts, Boston. He is also an organist and has been a performer on historic wind instruments. He has published articles on performance practice, medieval music theory, liturgy and liturgical music, especially Old Roman chant. His special interest is the history of chant and liturgy at Rome during the Middle Ages.

Linda Hirst was a Swingle Singer and a founder member of Electric Phoenix. With both groups she toured the world, leading to an enormously varied solo career which included operatic roles, large-scale new works with symphony orchestras (Osborne, Rands, Sciarrino, Ferneyhough), and many premières by Holt, Muldowney, Knussen, Weir, Harvey, Ambrosini, Lachenmann and others. She has been active in education since 1973 and has taught at Dartington International Summer School since 1978. In 1995 she was appointed Head of Vocal Studies at Trinity College of Music, London, and in 1998 she became a Fellow of Dartington College.

Felicity Laurence was born in New Zealand and is a children's choir specialist and composer. Her publications include *Birds, Balloons and Shining Stars: A Teacher's Guide to Singing with Children* (1994); the children's choral works *African Madonna* (1990 and 1997); *My Place* (1992); *Frugvin Margareta* (1993); *Moder Jords drömmar* (1998) and *Friendship – The International Children's Choir Festival for Friendship* (1997). She currently teaches at the Staatliche Hochschule für Musik, Trossingen, Germany.

Heikki Liimola studied singing and conducting at the Sibelius Academy, Helsinki, where he is now teacher of choir conducting. He conducts the Tampere Philharmonic Choir, Harju Chamber Choir, Tampere Opera Choir and Chorus

Cantorum Finlandie. He is also artistic director of the Tampere International Choral Festival and has run courses for choirs both in Finland and the rest of Europe.

David Mason is a pianist and teaches singing at Trinity College of Music, London, and has private studios in London and Madrid. He is voice teacher to the Rundfunkchor Berlin. His students have performed in all the important concert halls and opera houses nationally and internationally. He has contributed to the *New Oxford Companion to Music* and to the magazines *The Singer* and *Opera Now*.

Richard Middleton is Professor of Music at the University of Newcastle upon Tyne. Previously he taught for twenty-five years at the Open University. He is the author of *Pop Music and the Blues* (1972), *Studying Popular Music* (1990), *Reading Pop* (1999), and numerous articles on popular music topics. He is also a founding editor of the journal *Popular Music*.

John Potter is Lecturer in Music at the University of York. He has been a member of the Hilliard Ensemble since 1984 and is a co-founder of the ensemble Red Byrd. He has made more than a hundred CDs ranging from Leonin to Led Zeppelin and has contributed articles to the revised *New Grove* and *Popular Music* among many other publications. He is the author of *Vocal Authority: Singing Style and Ideology* (1998).

John Rosselli, until 1989 Reader in History in the University of Sussex, has worked for the past twenty years on the social history of opera. He is the author of *The Opera Industry from Cimarosa to Verdi: The Role of the Impresario* (1984), *Singers of Italian Opera: The History of a Profession* (1992), and *The Life of Mozart* (1998).

John Schaefer is the author of *New Sounds: A Listener's Guide to New Music* (1986; 1990), and a former contributing editor for *Spin* and *EAR* magazines. He has written numerous articles and CD booklets, as well as the biography of composer La Monte Young (*Sound and Light*, 1997). In 1982 he created the nightly radio program 'New Sounds', devoted to new and unusual musics from around the world, on WNYC, where he has been director of programming since 1991.

Johan Sundberg has a personal chair in Music Acoustics at the Speech Music Hearing Department at KTH (Royal Institute of Technology), Stockholm. He has published extensively on many aspects of singing and summarised research in this area in *Röstlära* (2nd ed. 1986, translations: *The Science of the Singing Voice* (1987) and *Die Wissenschaft von der Singstimme* (1997)). As the President of the Music Acoustics Committee of the Royal Swedish Academy of Music (1975–91) he edited or co-edited eleven volumes in a series of *Proceedings* of public seminars on music acoustic themes arranged in Stockholm since 1975, and he is the author of *The Science of Musical Sounds*. A singer himself, he is a member of the Royal Swedish Academy of Music, the Swedish Acoustical Society (President 1976–81) and a fellow of the Acoustical Society of America.

David Toop is a musician and author. He has published three books – *Rap Attack* (first published in 1984, now in its third edition), *Ocean Of Sound* and *Exotica* – and released three solo albums – *Screen Ceremonies*, *Pink Noir* and *Spirit World*. As a journalist he has contributed to *The Times*, *The Face*, *The Sunday Times*, *The Wire*, *The Observer* and many other publications.

Stephen Varcoe is known world wide as a concert and opera singer, with a repertoire stretching from the early Baroque to the latest contemporary works. His discography of more than one hundred recordings includes songs by Schubert, Fauré, Hahn, Parry, Bridge, Grainger, Butterworth and Finzi. He has given master classes on Lieder, French and English song at many universities and music colleges.

Richard Wistreich is a professional singer who specialises in the performance of pre-nineteenth-century and contemporary Western classical music. He is co-founder of the ensemble Red Byrd and appears throughout the world in concerts and operas. He is Professor of Singing at the Staatliche Hochschule für Musik, Trossingen, Germany, and is doing doctoral research into the social history of singing in sixteenth-century Italy.

David Wright is a musicologist working on aspects of twentieth-century music, including a range of contemporary British composers and concert life in London since 1945. He has written an outline history of Faber Music and entries for the revised *New Grove* and the *Dictionnaire de l'Art vocal*, as well as articles for *The Listener*, *Musical Times and Tempo*. He is Head of Postgraduate Programmes at the Royal College of Music.

Acknowledgements

It would not have been possible to put such a comprehensive volume together without the help of a large number of people. Among these I should especially like to thank Stephen Banfield, William Duckworth, Christopher Page, John Schaefer, John Snelson and Robert White, who were generous with their advice and time. I should also like to record my gratitude to the contributors, who all responded with great enthusiasm. My son Edward Potter assisted in the compilation of the bibliography and the music examples for Chapter 12 were transcribed on Finale by Gerard Power. Penny Souster at Cambridge University Press has been tremendously supportive throughout, and I am very grateful for the sharp eyes of copy editor Ann Lewis.

A note on pitch: the Helmholtz system is used throughout: c^1 is middle C.

1 Introduction: singing at the turn of the century

JOHN POTTER

Singing moves and excites people, often in very large numbers. Thousands turn out for the Three Tenors or rock concerts, millions mourned Frank Sinatra and the Berber singer Lounès Matoub; every week in Europe millions more sing their hearts out at football matches. We are born into a babble of voices and the clamour continues, if we're lucky, for the rest of our lives: our voices *are* us, directly expressive of our personalities and emotions. A voice is not like an oboe or violin, something you can take out of its case and put away, an instrument with hundreds of years of technical development behind it. You don't have to be a virtuoso to express your own emotions. Everyone can speak, and everyone can sing, so we all have our own idea of what singing actually is. This is one reason that the *Cambridge Companion to Singing* is different from its instrumental predecessors: in the end a choice has to be made about which aspects of singing can be usefully explored in the space available. Like the other Companions, this one deals almost exclusively with the music we experience in the industrialised West. At the beginning of a new century, with artistic ideas and activities expanding in all directions, it seems appropriate to begin with 'world music'. The term is a Western concept, involving the incorporation of singing outside the Western tradition into the stream of possibilities that are available to us today. If I had to predict where significant developments in singing will come in the future, I would hazard a guess that what we now call world music is the well-spring from which new forms of vocal expression will flow. Many, but by no means all, varieties of singing are to be found between these covers, and how the authors dealt with their subjects has been left broadly up to them. Significant omissions include folk music (a very large and nebulous subject) as well as anything more than a passing glance at more abstract issues of sociology, semiotics and meaning. A balance has been struck between 'classical' and 'popular' singing, and the final list of topics was arrived at with a great deal of agonising over the weighting given to each one.

At almost any other time in recent history a singing Companion would probably have meant an anthology of writing about fairly narrowly defined 'classical' singing.[1] Looking backwards to the latter part of the twentieth century and forwards to the twenty-first, it is possible to see a

major and continuing change in our perception of what singing is, to the
extent that it is no longer possible to come up with any single meaningful
definition. The classical variety, as used in opera, still has a significant
place in our culture after hundreds of years, but it is no longer automatically thought of as being *the* authoritative way to sing. There are not only
many varieties of singing that might be called 'classical' – the re-envisag-
ing of 'lost' styles by early music singers, for example, or new vocal techniques for contemporary repertoires – but for very large numbers of
people in the USA and Europe there is real cultural significance in the
myriad varieties of popular music that pour from our radios, televisions
and CD players every day. This encompasses not only Afro-American
varieties but singers from all of the earth's continents. It is a major perceptive shift, and one that the *Cambridge Companion to Singing* embraces
wholeheartedly. Frank Sinatra was regarded by many as one of the greatest voices of the twentieth century, and in many ways is a symbol of the
cultural value that we now assign to singers of popular music.

Singing has a peculiarly awkward, shifting relationship with econom-
ics, art and status. Most singers are very happy to ignore this and simply
get on with whatever they like to sing. But there is undeniably a sociological dimension to the way singing is perceived by listeners (non-singers,
perhaps): societies (particularly governments and institutions) make
value judgements about artistic worth. So at the turn of the century we
find in England, for example, that opera and jazz have similar numbers of
fans who go to concerts, yet jazz, a vibrant art form with perhaps increasing relevance to the twenty-first century, receives roughly one hundredth
of the funding available to opera, which seems to lurch from crisis to crisis
and always to have at least one foot in the nineteenth century. Western
classical singing still has a unique world status: Japanese music colleges
turn out fine singers of the classical Western canon, but very few Western
conservatories teach Japanese singing. The classical song recital is in
decline (perhaps terminally so, Stephen Varcoe hints) but opera is still
seen as the vocal summit. John Rosselli's two chapters in this volume
recognise a clear division between a dynamic past and a more traditional
present, and he offers an interesting French correction to the conventional Italian bias of many early opera histories. Most major American
and European cities have music colleges, and each year these institutions
prepare for the profession a much larger number of singers than can actually earn a living in it. A lot of classical singers certainly make successful
careers (some gloriously so) but many more end up as teachers (where
they rejoin the production cycle at a different level) or leave the profession
altogether. Jazz and pop music are increasingly seen as having pedagogical
value, but singers suffer from the same lack of opportunity once they get

out into the market place. The market that classical singers enter is often not subject to the usual laws of supply and demand. At the very top, opera singers can earn fantastic sums of money, often far more than can be covered by box office receipts alone. The shortfall is made up from government subsidies or institutional or commercial sponsorship, which enables opera houses to run up huge paper losses even when admission prices are extremely high and every seat sold. These structural absurdities often seem to have a debilitating effect on both audiences and opera companies (the demands of corporate entertainment are not easy to reconcile with imaginative programme planning) and it will be interesting to see how far into the twenty-first century this situation can continue. Singers of popular music have a much more precarious existence. A small number make huge sums and some performers are able to make a very good living playing major festivals (which are often heavily sponsored), but many are subject to the market cruelty which ensures that they sing for very little reward at all.

One of the consequences of the stylistic fragmentation of classical music has been the proliferation of singing styles associated with early music. Early music is unlike any other variety in that it purports to work within a stylistic framework that does not belong to the present, and cannot (yet?) be part of a living tradition in the sense that, say, opera or rock music are. Some aspects of early music singing have seemed anachronistic, such as the muddled attempts to re-create Baroque gesture or the strange coupling of highly researched instrumental playing with academically under-nourished singers. Nevertheless, some early music singers have often found themselves closer to the cutting edge than their more heavyweight colleagues. The record industry has supported a great variety of singers: the wave of small British and American ensembles that became successful in the 1970s has been joined by new groups from Italy, France, Germany and Scandinavia. Few of these until recently have had much time for serious investigation into the *sound* of pre-twentieth-century singing, but several performers on both sides of the Atlantic are taking more risks in this direction. The sources are there for singers to construct their own techniques, whether they be medieval or Renaissance, Romantic or modern, and Joseph Dyer, Richard Wistreich and David Mason in this volume provide a good starting point for singers to do just that. There are also signs that singers are having the courage to break away from slavish adherence to musicological dogma and are beginning to think more like their medieval and Renaissance predecessors (who, the evidence suggests, generally preferred the delights of emotional self indulgence to the musicology of their own day). Of course historical texts should be respected, but as a means to an end in the present. There is more willingness to admit that if early music is to be relevant to the present, certain aspects of it are perhaps better left un-revived or engaged with critically (anti-Semitism in medieval and Renaissance motets, for example, or the casual sexism of much secular music). The further back you go, the less evidence there is: the improvising traditions of the medieval period are almost entirely lost to us, for example. Increasingly this is seen as a chance to be creative and not to worry too much about what is not known, offering the possibility for a new dynamism in early music.

Early music singers have living examples which could point the way to at least a partial recovery of lost techniques: Middle Eastern and north African singers may hold clues to a medieval sound; jazz and improvised music certainly offer clues to understanding something of what was not written down. As John Schaefer's chapter shows, we are increasingly open to the huge variety of singing from outside the Euro-American axis. Many strands of twentieth-century popular music have been driven by Afro-American innovations, and towards the end of the century we have seen African, Indian and Arabic singers making a serious impact in the West. Many of these singers come from improvising or non-literate traditions and have interacted with both mainstream popular music and jazz. This northwards and westward movement of southern and oriental singing styles has a curious and timely historical parallel: a similar process may have been happening at the end of the first millennium.[2] It will not be lost on students of ethnomusicology that most of the 'alternative' sounds discussed in Linda Hirst's and David Wright's chapter are perfectly normal in a global context. Popular music has benefited from periodic injections of Afro-American influences which have enabled it to reinvent itself, as Richard Middleton implies (and as I point out in my contribution on jazz singing). David Toop's chapter on hip-hop shows that the capacity of Afro-American culture to take popular music by the scruff of the neck knows no bounds. Not that all American music is African influenced: Stephen Banfield draws our attention to the remarkable Jewish contribution to the American musical.

Choral singing flourishes throughout Europe and North America, though in England there is still a big divide between the elite Oxbridge singers and the amateurs who form the backbone of the choral movement. Timothy Day explains the origins of the 'English' choral sound, pointing out that this is far from the monolithic phenomenon that it sometimes appears to be. Heikki Liimola describes how to make the best of singing in an amateur choir, a very different tradition but one which in his native Scandinavia has produced some of the very best singing of recent times. A North American perspective is provided by Neely Bruce, whose chapter outlines the long and fascinating history of choral singing in black, white and native American communities. The two final, but by no means least important, chapters in this anthology are about children's singing and vocal acoustics. In some ways these are actually the most important topics dealt with here: we would all benefit from the all-singing childhoods envisioned by Felicity Laurence, and a knowledge of how the voice actually works can solve technical mysteries without compromising its imaginative and artistic use.

The shape of this Companion is designed to link the various topics, beginning with John Schaefer's world music chapter and ending with Johan Sundberg's exposition of vocal acoustics. There are many possible routes through the material, and I hope that interested readers will be tempted by more than just the chapter associated with their own interests, perhaps moving outwards via adjacent chapters. The final selection of topics and authors was mine and obviously reflects my own interests and biases, but I have tried to cover as many aspects as possible within the series format. Another editor could easily have come up with a very different collection, and he or she would inevitably have had to deal with the question of what to leave out. Looking back over the second half of the twentieth century, it seems to me that singing is a sign of the enormous social diversity encompassed by musical activity, whether it is the blatantly commercial or the shamelessly subsidised, the church choir or the urban rapper. If there is one identifiable characteristic associated with singing and singers as we move into the new millennium, it is a move away from the closed introspection of an earlier generation, towards an open-endedness, a generosity of spirit that can bring together musicians and listeners from creeds and cultures all over the planet.

PART ONE

Popular traditions

2 'Songlines': vocal traditions in world music

JOHN SCHAEFER

Ten years ago, the death of a Pakistani singer, no matter how talented, would have gone unnoticed by most of the world. But when Nusrat Fateh Ali Khan (see Fig. 1) died in August 1997, at the age of forty-eight, even America's notoriously parochial television news programs carried the story. Khan was not just one of the world's greatest singers, he was emblematic of a startling rise of interest in non-Western music, especially within the last quarter of the twentieth century. The late Pakistani singer, along with such world-wide sensations as Youssou N'Dour of Senegal and the globe-trotting choirs of Tibet and Bulgaria, came to represent a musical genre known by the informal and somewhat loosely defined term 'world music'. This chapter provides an armchair traveller's guide to the world's increasingly miscegenated music. Nusrat Fateh Ali Khan, for example, was a master of the infectious, rhythmically charged Sufi devotional music known as *qawwali*. Lionised by such rock musicians as Peter Gabriel, The Who's Pete Townsend, and Pearl Jam singer Eddie Vedder, he also proved himself a thoroughly modern fellow, eagerly embracing his unexpected musical allies and moulding their Western pop styles to suit his own needs.

While it was probably an unintended result of the twentieth-century revolution in communications technology, with hindsight it seems unavoidable that people in the West would find themselves, for the first time since the Crusades, becoming keenly aware of non-Western systems of music and singing. Modern Western listeners have had the unique experience of hearing their own popular music styles refracted through the prism of a hundred different cultures and returning as a brood of musical changelings – for example, in the form of African or Asian cross-cultural pop. And, of course, listeners in contemporary America or Europe have had the opportunity to hear live performances and recordings by some of the greatest singers in the classical, folk and popular styles of the world.

The Indian subcontinent

India and Pakistan are a veritable Disneyland of vocal traditions: classical raga singing, semi-classical *ghazals* (sacred poems) and *bhajans*

Figure 1 Nusrat Fateh Ali Khan

(love sonnets), and various folk and pop styles. India's contributions to world music include the most recorded voice in human history: Lata Mangeshkar maintained an iron grip for many decades on India's popular music, the hybrid style known as *filmi*. Scarcely a film soundtrack came out between the 1950s and 1980s that did not have her distinctively pinched, nasal voice soaring over some combination of orchestral strings, traditional Indian instruments, and, later, Western pop sounds. The classical raga singing of the Indian subcontinent is another major contribution. The raga, a carefully prescribed yet infinitely elastic form of song, is generally constructed around sacred, often mystical, texts. Even an instrumental raga performance aims at an almost vocal effect. 'Our tradition is absolutely a vocal tradition', says the sitarist Ravi Shankar, 'first you must learn the songs, because it's all based on song; only then, after some years, (do) you learn to play them on sitar, or *sarod* or flute'.[1] It is rare to find a classical Indian musician who is not also an able singer; Shankar himself has recorded several albums of crossover music in which he sings. Another of India's great sitarists, Vilayat Khan, from a family of famous singers, has become an important teacher of both instrumentalists and singers, and, in the case of his son Shujaat Khan, has taught both disciplines to one artist.

Indian singing has been misunderstood: it is microtonal, but Western writings that refer to a tuning system of twenty-two notes to the octave are somewhat misleading. Classical Indian scales are based on a series of scale-forms – the particular scale-form will give the raga its name – and these forms are generally built on a series of seven notes. But as Vilayat Khan explains, 'there are many ways of pronouncing these notes. Some notes can be slightly lower, or slightly higher. The same note is used in so many ways and each way brings out a different colour.'[2]

It is not within the scope of this chapter to explore the many musical and extra-musical concerns of the Indian raga. Suffice it to say that regardless of style and region, the classical singer of India attempts to operate on two levels, or to inhabit two worlds at once. The strict rules of raga govern every aspect of performance: the scale-form, the acceptable inflections of the notes, the shape of both the ascending and descending scales (they need not be the same), and the grace notes that the singer may use are just a few examples of an art that demands years of concentrated practice. And yet, the performance must transcend musical rules and flashy display. 'One of the things Pandit Pran Nath used to tell us about raga', recalled the composer La Monte Young, 'is that you practice it for twenty years, until you can do it in your sleep; then you go on stage and you don't think. You forget everything you know and you just let it happen. That's called *uppaj*. It means imagination, or flying like a bird.'[3] The late Pandit Pran Nath was a major force in bringing Hindustani singing to the West. His students included such acclaimed Western composers and musicians as La Monte Young, Terry Riley, Jon Hassell, and many others.

Qawwali, the devotional music of Pakistani Sufism, takes ornate embroidery and celebratory spirituality to the extreme. Full of extraordinary flights of song, *qawwali* is propelled by a battery of singers, hand claps, tabla, and often a harmonium or *sarangi* (box cello). Leading

performers include Abida Parveen and the Sabri Brothers, and of course
Nusrat Fateh Ali Khan. Khan's Qawwali Party, with its slightly faster
tempos, did indeed have a good-time, dance-party sound, but the singer
himself never lost sight of what the music meant. 'It is not party music', he
said, 'it is based on the poetry of the Sufi saints, and its purpose is to praise
God, and Ali. It *is* music for dance, but for a sacred dance. When we sing
and dance, we are praying.'[4] *Qawwali*, especially as practised by Khan and
his Party (mostly members of his family), is some of the most overtly
ecstatic music in the world.

The Indian and Pakistani diaspora has brought the vocal traditions of
the subcontinent to the West, especially to the United Kingdom, the
United States and the Caribbean. The disco-influenced *bhangra* music of
the London clubs and the unusual marriage of Afro-Caribbean and *filmi*
styles in the Guyanese neighbourhoods of New York are just two of the
contemporary step-children of Indian music. In the UK, two women have
had a notable impact on the world music stage with their own distinctive
blends of Indian vocal styles and Western technology. Najma Akhtar (or
simply Najma) learned the *ghazal* repertoire by listening to records, and
has used Western instruments and technology to create songs that clearly
grow from that tradition. 'The tradition in India or Pakistan is that the
poet writes the verses and the singer composes the melody', she points
out; 'I've done that too. So it's the traditional idea; it's the instrumentation that's quite different.'[5] That instrumentation includes vocal harmonies, which are unknown in classical or semi-classical Indian music, as
well as saxophone, violin and electronics. Sheila Chandra has also developed a style that finds threads connecting apparently disparate traditions.
'It's actually been very easy', she says, 'and something that occurred to me
through the experiments I was making with my voice rather than any
clever intellectual exercise. The challenge was to produce the fusion in a
single vocal line.'[6] Chandra found that many vocal gestures, such as trills
and arpeggios, remain the same through many traditions. 'Because of this
crossover, I think I can no longer draw the line between the British folk
tradition and the Indian tradition, or the Islamic tradition and American
soul, because things just become so similar and my voice slips so easily
between (them).' Her 1993 recording *Weaving My Ancestors' Voices*
demonstrated this by moving effortlessly, if not authentically, between
the song techniques of the British Isles, the Islamic world and India. Over
the course of the next four years, Chandra began to pursue one thread in
particular: drones are the basis of the music of the Indian subcontinent, as
they are for virtually every major tradition in Central Asia, as well as
Gaelic pipe music, Eastern Orthodox sacred music, and Australian aboriginal music. 'We drone', Chandra claims; 'as long as we're alive, we emit

frequency – from the stapes bone in the middle ear, for example. So I'm not surprised that a lot of musical cultures honour that fact.'[7] In Chandra's CD *ABoneCroneDrone*, several layers of vocal and instrumental drones give rise to brief modal fragments that reinforce the harmonics of the drones. 'Drones are so deceptive. They are a wonderful rich tapestry of harmonic sparkles and cyclic riffs, which are ever-changing even if you play the same drone ten times. I really wanted to evoke this sense of being in a cauldron of sound – in a melting pot – where there is apparently nothing, and yet there is everything.' Chandra, interestingly, has also recorded a number of vocal exercises under the title *Speaking In Tongues*. These pieces are a personal extension of the mnemonic syllables learned by Indian drummers. Chandra has taken this pedagogical device and put it to purely musical use. The sound of this thoroughly unorthodox and modern approach to an ancient teaching device is, paradoxically, reminiscent not only of the ubiquitous digital sampling of modern pop, but also of Vedic chant, the oldest form of Indian vocal music.

Central Asia

Music has proven herself a delightfully indiscriminate mistress in Central Asia, and the ancestry of the various regional styles is difficult to establish. It is clear that Tibetan chant, which has become increasingly familiar to Western listeners, has roots in ancient Indian chant. The chanting of the Vedic scriptures, which survives to this day (most notably in the chanting of South Indian singer M. S. Subbulakshmi), was probably brought into Tibet with the spread of Buddhism, and certainly had an impact on the development of the Tibetan style. Both types of chant are highly metric, and shaped by the stressed syllables and the length of the vowels of the sacred text. Melodically constrained, such chants are, at their most basic, barely more than a drone.

The chanting of the Buddhist monks of Tibet has enjoyed surprising popularity in the West, with the monks of the Gyütö college especially maintaining a high profile through their collaborations with such Western musicians as Philip Glass and Grateful Dead percussionist Mickey Hart. Their chant represents one of the most distinctive forms of prayer in the world. Along with the traditional chanting of the Qur'an, the chanting of the Tibetan monks is, strictly speaking, not music at all. For this reason, any discussion of Tibetan chant from a purely musical standpoint is bound to be unsatiefactory. 'This is something we have little personal history with here in the West', observed Philip Glass. The American composer is a practising Buddhist and has toured with, and occasionally acted as spokesman for, the Gyütö monks. 'It's a tradition where the musical and spiritual inheritances of the community are really identical. A tradition of singing like this, which is a high art form, is also a part of their spiritual life.'[8] A deep fundamental note is chanted by the monks, and from the overtone series of that fundamental, at least one and occasionally two of the component harmonics are separated out and made audible. In effect, each monk is singing two or three notes. The techniques of overtone chant are considered by many Tibetan colleges to be part of the practice not of music, but of Tantric Buddhism itself. Like Tibet itself, Tibetan music has developed in isolation and has been slow to warm to Western influences. But the chanting of young singers such as Yungchen Lhamo, Choying Drolma and Lama Gyurme have begun to appear in decidedly Western settings. Lhamo and Drolma are young women whose performance style is closer to the folk style of Tibet. Gyurme's recording *The Lama's Chant*, with French keyboard player Jean-Phillippe Rykiel, uses the characteristic deep tones of Tibetan sacred music; but his performances are genuine songs, short on overtone effects and long on melodic invention. David Hykes, founder of the Harmonic Choir, has studied both Tibetan and Mongolian overtone techniques intensively. Hykes feels Tibetan chant represents something that is not foreign to the West, but simply lost or hidden. 'Some documents from medieval Europe suggest that Christian monks would occasionally notice a harmonic moving in parallel with their chant', Hykes notes; 'and they apparently thought this meant that the angels were pleased with the chant, and were singing along.'[9] It may not be too fanciful to suggest that the Tibetan chant techniques developed from a desire to consistently reach such divine heights. However, at least some singers in more northern regions of Central Asia claim that Tibetans adapted the technique of overtone chant from them. Alexander Cheparukin, translating for the gifted Tuvan singer Kaigal Ool and his now well-known ensemble Huun-Huur-Tu (see Fig. 2), relates the theory that Tibetans returned home with overtone chants after bringing Buddhism to Tuva, a Russian province. 'Tuva is probably the only region where this is really widespread tradition, where thousands of ordinary people practise it. In Tibet, it's an esoteric art restricted to a few monasteries. It's natural to think they took it from the area where it's widespread.'[10]

Tuvan singing has developed not as an attempt to reach or to engage the spiritual world, but as a way to evoke the sights and sounds of this one. Unlike Tibetan chant, which is generally slow and melodically restricted, Tuvan songs usually move along at a good clip, and often sport catchy melodies. Tibetan vocal production involves the use of the throat as a resonator tube and a loose, vibrating larynx as a kind of sounding board,

Figure 2 Tuvan throat singers Huun-Huur-Tu

especially for the production of the low fundamental notes so prized by the monks. The Tuvan singer typically uses a whole range of techniques, including several that involve forcing the air through a tightly constricted throat to produce a series of whistling harmonics that recall the wind on the steppes or the sounds of the forest. Tuvan/Mongolian singing is highly virtuosic; it is possible for the overtones to serve as either a melody or an accompaniment, and for a single performer to sing both simultaneously. Not surprisingly, Tuvan singers are by and large solo artists. Tuvan throat singing, known generally and somewhat inaccurately as *hoomi* (actually just one of three or four major techniques of overtone singing in Tuva), is traditionally the province of men, and of the rural spaces where those men herded and rode. But Western music has had a powerful impact on this region: industrial punk, rap, even country music have spawned a decidedly contemporary, urban breed of *hoomi* singers. A gifted female singer, Sainkho Namtchylak, has appeared in a number of settings with leading new music figures in both the United States and

Europe, employing the vocal techniques long forbidden to women in traditional Tuvan and Mongolian society.

The Near East

Islam is the single biggest defining factor in the music of the Arabic world, Turkey and Iran. Orthodox Islam has historically looked upon music with suspicion, and only a few carefully delimited forms have been accepted. These include the *ezan*, the calls to prayer sung by muezzins throughout the Islamic world, and the chanting of the Qur'an. This chant inhabits the same plane as Tibetan and Vedic chant, but the vocal techniques can often be quite musical and are related to the rich vocal legacies that have grown up throughout the Near East. It is no accident that the two great centres of Koranic chant – Egypt and Turkey – are also home to some of the Near East's greatest vocal traditions. It is certainly possible to listen to the chanting of the Qur'an for its musical content – although Islamic orthodoxy has long sought to avoid this. If one is not listening intently for the proper pronunciations of the Arabic texts, then one's attention is immediately drawn to such musical concerns as the use of vibrato, precise placement of microtonal pitches, and subtleties such as holding notes briefly on the letters 'n' and 'm' as well as on vowels. Sometimes, especially in the *ezan* where the chanter has considerably more latitude, the performance blurs the distinction between speech and song.

The mystical branch of Islam, Sufism, has provided some of the Near East's greatest musical treasures. As with the chanting of the Qur'an, the music of the Islamic mystics draws its inspiration from the text, and its structure from a sophisticated set of modes, rhythms and traditional forms. It is in vocal practice that the impact of each of these elements is most clearly felt. In general, solo vocal lines are considerably more elaborate and melismatic; choral songs have a simple, almost chant-like approach to the syllables of the text. That said, specific songs vary widely: some employ melismatic phrases on key syllables only; in extreme cases, single syllables are stretched out to such an extent that they begin to lose their semantic context in favour of a purely musical one, much like medieval European organum. According to Nail Kesova, vocalist and leader of the Galata Mevlevi Dervish Ensemble in Istanbul, this is a matter of tradition. A composer will write directions or notate in the written score how to approach the texts, but the actual performance choices, including when to use vibrato and how wide to make it, are a result of the singer's studies with a particular lineage of teachers.[11]

Like the music of Central Asia, music in the Near East exists in two worlds: its unusually strong mystic tradition has grown up alongside more popular/folk styles, and has dramatically influenced some of the region's most popular music. Styles vary widely, but a few singers have transcended regional differences and become international superstars. These include the Lebanese singer Fairuz, and the great Egyptian vocalist Oum Kalthoum, a woman of such immense stature in the Arabic world that her funeral in 1975 was attended by heads of state from almost every Arabic country and effectively shut down Egypt for four days. Both Oum Kalthoum and Fairuz cross over between sacred and secular song. Oum Kalthoum took her inspiration from classical Arabic poetry and chant, and was as adept as any of the great mystic singers of the Sufi tradition at singing a text and developing the melody. Legend has it that, as a young girl, she dressed as a boy in order to chant the sacred texts in public. Her training in the art of sacred chant left her with both a technical facility astounding in a popular singer, and the endurance to create songs that could evolve over the course of an hour or more. But her popularity rested with her voice – a rich, well-rounded instrument that was both sophisticated and raw, as emotive as the greatest blues or flamenco singers. To connoisseurs, Oum Kalthoum's mastery of the *maqamat*, the scale-forms of classical Islamic music, is the basis of her legend. Indeed, she is revered today throughout the Arabic world as the greatest traditional singer. This of course is nonsense. In her day Oum Kalthoum was every bit as revolutionary as she was talented. Her great recordings, including the groundbreaking 'Enta Omri', and suites like *Ya Msahnri, El Hob Kollo* and *Hagartak*, caused consternation among purists with their use of Western orchestral strings and, in 'Enta Omri', an electric guitar. Much of this music was made in collaboration with the great Egyptian composer Mohammed Abdel Wahab. Similarly, the Lebanese singer Fairuz has collaborated for many years with the Rahbani Brothers, also a progressive source of Western influences from the Baroque to reggae. These great singers are hardly traditionalists, yet their success in blending a uniquely Arabic style of song with influences from around the world has ensured that the Arabic tradition would be relevant to listeners well into the late twentieth century. Nor was this an accident, as both singers were keenly aware of their places in a musical continuum that stretched back to the eighth century.

Contemporary Arabic music has taken the stylistic liberties of Oum Kalthoum and Fairuz to the extreme. Now splintered into many styles, this music is often closely modelled on Western pop – highly amplified, with steady backbeats and lyrics that speak to a younger, perhaps more rebellious, generation. Nowhere is this more apparent than in Algerian *rai*, the popular music that grew out of the rough streets and houses of ill-repute in Oran, Algeria. Modern *rai* is a blend of Arabic song with rock, funk and disco; the 'King of Rai', the fiery singer known as Khaled, lists among his influences both Oum Kalthoum and Bob Marley. This style gained flavour-of-the-month notoriety in rock clubs around Europe during the 1980s, and paid the price when a handful of record producers seemed to corner the market with homogenised dance mixes of *rai* songs.

Sub-Saharan Africa

It makes sense that West Africa would be such a hotbed of world music. After all, it is the wellspring from which American blues – and therefore American pop, jazz and soul – had sprung. Similarly, Cuban, Brazilian and other Latin American styles would be unthinkable without the influence of Central African slaves. When Western rock and Cuban popular dances began to find their way to the radio stations of West and Central Africa, respectively, they were enthusiastically adopted by musicians who often had no idea that they were in fact embracing long-lost musical relatives. Music is integral to the daily life of much of sub-Saharan Africa. Even more than in Asia and the Near East, African songs often have an extra-musical purpose. This heritage has continued to affect the contemporary music of Africa as well. Renowned figures like Salif Keita, the remarkable albino singer from Mali, and Youssou N'Dour or Baaba Maal, leading singers from the rich Senegalese tradition, tour the world with electrified, pop-inflected songs – both traditional and original – which stay true to music's role in West Africa as a storytelling, history-recording, patron-flattering art. 'Music doesn't really exist by itself in traditional black African culture', says singer/guitarist/composer Francis Bebey of Cameroon. 'Actually, we do not even have a word for music in our languages. When we talked about music we used the same word as dance. As we came in contact with Western music, we had to borrow the word *musiki* from the West.'[12] Bebey came to international attention as one of the first leaders of the Central African style called *makossa*; his own work, though, reflects the wide diversity of the region's music. His 1984 recording *Akwaaba* is a veritable catalogue of vocal styles – head and chest voices, singing while inhaling, and a kind of deep moaning or groaning voice rich in harmonics – 'a kind of double voice', as Bebey explains. 'You see, we use the voice as an instrument. These techniques are common across the continent and are very old.' A distinguishing feature of Bebey's music is the use of pygmy hockets and yodels. 'Having learned some of the pygmy vocal techniques, I can't sing now without using them; they come by themselves.'[13] In the East, the jaunty, Asian-influenced wedding music, or *taarab*, of Zanzibar has begun to attract world music fans. Here too, performers continue to sing about age-old themes like behaving correctly and making sure your man is doing the same.

In countries throughout the continent, politics informs the music to a degree that might be hard to appreciate in the West. Political music is an age-old tradition everywhere, but for those chafing under colonial or military rule, writing political songs carried a deeper message than the one in the text: such songs could be a powerful assertion of cultural pride and defiance. Perhaps nowhere is this truer than in the *chimurenga*, the so-called 'Music of Resistance', created by the great singer Thomas Mapfumo in Zimbabwe. Fed up with singing Western pop songs and with a white Rhodesian government that taught the Shona people to view anything indigenous as inferior, Mapfumo began in the 1970s to write songs in Shona – a brave and risky thing to do at the time. His music was based almost exclusively on the sound of the *mbira*, the sacred instrument of the Shona people. Until recently, the *mbira* itself was not used in the ensemble (the melding of spiritual and decidedly secular meant that Mapfumo was treading on uncertain cultural ground); Mapfumo's innovation was to transfer the patterns and rhythms of the instrument to a pair of electric guitars.

Thanks to Paul Simon's *Graceland* (1986), the music of South Africa has become more familiar in the West. One might think that Simon had single-handedly plucked the vocal group Ladysmith Black Mambazo (see Fig. 3) and South African music in general out of obscurity, but in fact South Africa boasts one of the world's biggest and most durable music industries. South Africa is home to a bewildering diversity of musical styles, including a distinctive jazz tradition, Western-derived soul and rhythm-and-blues acts, and at least two major musical genres that have now circled the world countless times. The first is the *a cappella* choral music of such bands as Ladysmith Black Mambazo, whose music evolved from the confluence of communal Zulu call-and-response forms and the Christian hymns and Gospel music introduced by Europeans. The second is the so-called Township Jive, or *mbaqanga*, a high-octane mix of Western pop and distinctly Africanised vocal harmonies. This style's best known proponents are Mahlathini and the Mahotella Queens.

Vocal music in South Africa is characterised by extremes. The course of South African music was altered and shaped by a male soprano, Solomon Linda. In 1939, Linda wrote 'Mbube' ('The Lion'), which not only shattered sales records in Africa but came to define a whole style of music. His main innovation was to set his startlingly high soprano against a four-part, bass-heavy vocal ensemble. The effect was both immediate

Figure 3 Ladysmith Black Mambazo

and enduring. A whole host of imitators sprang up, and the song reached the West when the folk group the Weavers recorded it as 'Wimoweh' in 1950. It achieved international fame in 1961 under the name 'The Lion Sleeps Tonight' in a version appropriated by the doo-wop group The Tokens.

The *mbube* style got a shot in the arm when producer/saxophonist West Nkosi began working with Joseph Shabalala and his formidable vocal ensemble, Ladysmith Black Mambazo, in the 1970s. Singing original songs on traditional Zulu themes and religious songs with Zulu lyrics, Shabalala's group quickly created a popular style that updated Solomon Linda's sound with richer, more subtle harmonies. They used sophisticated, often softly sung, harmonies, and an unusual array of clicks and other percussive effects (unusual to Western ears, that is; the sounds are part of several southern African language families).

If Solomon Linda's high soprano represented one extreme, the voice of Simon Nkabinde, better known as Mahlathini, occupies the other. Although several African vocal styles require a deep bass voice, Mahlathini's voice is almost unnaturally deep. A perhaps apocryphal story claims that Mahlathini's own family, fearing demonic causes, considered exorcism as his voice continued to deepen. As a young man in the

1960s, Mahlathini was recruited by West Nkosi, who felt his deep, 'groaning' vocals were the perfect foil for a female *a cappella* group – the exact opposite of the *mbube* style. Nkosi's electric, Western-sounding band, paired with the unusual combination of three- to five-part female harmonies and Mahlathini's basement vocals, came to define the style known as *mbaqanga*. '*Mbaqanga* is a type of food', explains Nkosi; 'it has lots of vegetables all mixed up – and in this music are many styles mixed together: traditional rhythms, rock'n'roll, even reggae'.[14] 'But our harmonies are absolutely different from those in the West', adds Hilda Buthelezi, one of the Mahotella Queens; 'they are specifically South African'.[15] Buthelezi also notes that a generation of South African youth ruined their voices with whisky and cigarettes attempting to imitate the low growl of Mahlathini. To this day, though, no one has succeeded in duplicating his musical or popular success.

Latin America and the *nueva canción*

Music in Central and South America reflects the influence of the African slave trade and European colonialism. Indigenous music continues to exist in the altiplano (the remote highlands of the Andes) and among the aboriginal tribes of the Amazon river basin. But while singers like the remarkable Brazilian Marlui Miranda have adapted traditional Indian songs and brought them to a wider audience, much of the music in Central and South America, and in the Caribbean, developed out of the confluence of the European and African traditions. Much of this music is relatively young, at least by the standards of world music. One of the most important recent developments in Latin American music, and perhaps the most important in terms of vocal music, is the style known as *nueva canción*, or 'new song'. It is a style that crosses political boundaries and now extends throughout the Spanish-speaking parts of the Western hemisphere.

Nueva canción grew out of developments in Argentina in the early 1960s and first took hold in Chile. Victor Jara may not have been the founder of the *nueva canción*, but he was certainly its first superstar. A poetic songwriter and fearless singer through dangerous and turbulent times, he was tortured and murdered by the Chilean authorities in 1973. His passion infected a generation and inspired a host of later singers: Jara's influence can be heard in the great Cuban singer Silvio Rodriguez, and in one of South America's earliest and still most active proponents of *nueva canción*, the Chilean band Inti-Illimani. Oddly enough, the group first made a name for itself by performing Andean and Andean-inspired music on indigenous instruments. (Inti-Illimani is a Quechua name meaning 'Holy Mountain of the Sun God'.) Sent to Europe as a kind of cultural ambassador of the Allende government in 1973, the group was in Italy when the Pinochet coup occurred. Finding themselves in exile for fifteen years, the group's songwriting and vocal performances blossomed.

Despite its political implications, Horacio Salinas of Inti-Illimani points out that 'the *nueva canción* is not so much political as social. Across South America, it represents how we think about our lives today. At one time, it was dangerous to think, and especially to think about democracy. But we began to say, we are Latin Americans, we have a tradition. We have roots to build our tree.'[16] 'It is political only because we have a concept,' adds fellow band member Jose Seves: 'we would like a certain kind of society. So it's not necessarily *political*, but maybe it is *useful*.'[17]

Other Latin American vocal contributions to world music include the Cuban *son*, Puerto Rican *bomba* and *plena*, with their obvious West African roots, and *salsa*, a style that grew up in the 1960s among New York musicians like Willie Colon. Colon explains that 'because of all the different Latino communities here, they all started mixing together into a kind of pan-American folklore, and then jazz and rock started creeping in'.[18] Originally based in Afro-Cuban styles, it was not called *salsa* until the early 1970s. 'It refers to music with an African beat but that speaks about city life. It has a social connotation – it's more spicy, I guess.' (*Salsa* means 'sauce'.) Colon led the prototypical *salsa* band, with its electric, dance-orientated sound, and its call-and-response vocals. The group also became a proving ground for future superstars, most notably singer Ruben Blades. Colon's band also formed much of the backing ensemble for David Byrne's dynamic world music effort *Rei Momo* in 1989. Along the way, Colon enjoyed some success of his own, including the chart-topping Latin American hit 'El Gran Varon' in 1989. This lament on the Latino response to AIDS was none the less typically upbeat musical fare. As Colon points out, 'that's those African roots. There's no contradiction in dancing your sorrows away.'

The Caucasus and south-eastern Europe

World music implies music outside Europe and North America; but even in Europe, there are vocal traditions that fit in this brief survey. A cursory glance at a map would show why the striking choral music of Armenia and Georgia could reasonably be viewed as world music: these countries occupy the crossroads between continents, sitting at the edge of Europe but strongly influenced by the music of the Near East. Armenia and

Georgia were the first countries to adopt Christianity as their official religion, and choral music in both countries draws on the distinctly eastern version of Christianity practised in the Caucasus. Both countries also possess a fertile bardic tradition, and the influence of epic folk song, ploughing and other work songs have given the choirs of this region some of their most striking music.

Armenian choirs draw heavily on both sacred and secular traditions. A single figure is largely responsible for much of the revived interest in both forms of choral music: Komitas (occasionally transliterated as Gomidas) was a composer, priest, and apparently indefatigable transcriber and arranger of Armenian song. Komitas travelled the Armenian countryside in the late nineteenth and early twentieth centuries, collecting folk songs, harmonising old hymns and writing his own sacred works. Much of the repertoire sung by such choirs as the Haissmavourk Choir or the Yerevan Women's Choir consists of Komitas arrangements or compositions. Komitas was a composer trained in the Western classical tradition, and although he arranged many songs for solo voice and piano, it is his choral arrangements, freed from the constraints of the piano's equal-tempered scale, that capture the spirit and the sound of this ancient and ill-starred people. Armenian sacred songs represent arguably the oldest Christian music extant, and, especially in the unaccompanied vocal solos, one often hears the same exotic, modal quality found in Islamic or Hebraic chant – a powerful example of parallel development in the three great religions of the area.

Unlike Armenian music, where harmonisation is a relatively recent addition, Georgian singing is traditionally polyphonic. 'There is a strong tradition of songs with three parts', explains Alan Gasser, part of the American trio Kavkasia, who have spent several years studying, recording and performing Georgian songs. 'You have what almost sounds like a stand-alone melody, and another voice that is very steady and still, just one or perhaps two notes. The third part sounds like it's drawn from the overtone series of the first part.' Some Georgian songs have such distinctive parts that they demand to be sung by a trio rather than by a choir. 'The parts can be somewhat . . . wayward', Gasser says, 'and these songs would not really work for a choir, because it would be hard for two or more basses, for example, to sing that wayward part in the same way.' Nevertheless, Georgian choirs, led by the Rustavi and Tsinandali Choirs, are gaining popularity through their Western recordings. Like their Armenian counterparts, they are trained professionals performing carefully crafted arrangements.

It was a similar marriage of a grassroots vocal tradition with a sophisticated, almost classical, approach that unleashed upon the world one of the most surprising and successful phenomena in world music: the Bulgarian Women's Choir. The Bulgarian State Radio and Television Female Vocal Choir, as it was formally known, grew out of composer/arranger Philip Koutev's attempts in the 1950s to create a modern choral music that would be true to the sounds of Bulgarian folk song, with its curiously close harmonies, its penetrating, tight-throated vocal production, and its occasional drone or bell-like effects. The landmark recording *Le Mystere des Voix Bulgares* was the first international evidence of his success, and although Koutev died in 1982, his work led to several other volumes before the ensemble split into two choirs in the mid-1990s. Three of Bulgaria's most renowned soloists have also recorded and toured widely as the Trio Bulgarka. The women of the Bulgarian choirs have proven themselves adept world travellers, touring frequently and turning up in some startling contexts: in the Norwegian band Farmers Market, on recordings by rock singer Kate Bush, in collaboration with operatic singers in Belgian composer Nicholas Lens' music, and even in an arrangement of a Palestrina mass by Hungarian composer/arranger Ivan Lantos. The sound of Bulgarian singing is immediately identifiable. By forcing air through a tightly constricted throat (similar to the technique used in Tuvan/Mongolian singing), the women of Bulgaria have developed a keening, nasal sound that clearly reflects the outdoors roots of some of their songs. And while Bulgarian singing varies from region to region, diaphonic songs have helped define 'that Bulgarian sound'. Instead of the usual consonant harmonies heard in the West, Bulgarians have an affinity for more allegedly dissonant intervals: seconds, sevenths and ninths. However, identifying these harmonies with precision can be a tricky thing: the Koutev arrangements are true to the Bulgarian tradition of whoops and slides that can often obscure the actual interval being sung.

Unusual harmonies are also the rule on the island of Corsica. In some ways Corsican song is the exact opposite of the Bulgarian music: often sacred in character, and, traditionally at least, exclusively male. In two important aspects, though, the two unrelated traditions are similar. The men of Corsica, whether singing in full choir or in the preferred format of a small (usually three- or four-voice) ensemble, are capable of prodigious volume, and their choice of harmonies can be utterly foreign to ears raised on Western classical singing. Favourite intervals include both major and minor sevenths and various species of seconds. A typical Corsican quartet might feature a deep, droning bass, a pair of middle voices producing a sound not unlike the groaning style of some African music, and an upper voice which usually carries the melody and may often have a curiously nasal quality. Harmonic movement is often slow and in folk songs sometimes restricted to only two or three chords. Like their Bulgarian counterparts, Corsican singers have an appealing repertoire of bell-like songs as well. The use of audible overtones varies widely according to the ability of the singers, but can be quite striking.

'Oceania'

We have by no means exhausted world music's capacity for surprise. Take, for example, the unexpected success of the Tahitian Choir in the early 1990s. Their eponymous CD was released first in Europe and had most of its success there, but it attracted enough attention in North America to make possible several further recordings of Polynesian choral music. The Tahitian Choir performs a combination of Christian hymns and indigenous songs, some with lyrics old enough to be untranslatable even to modern Tahitians. Their most striking sound is a flattening of the notes at the end of a phrase or sequence. This is not a function of amateur inability, but a deliberate, highly unorthodox form of cadence. The effect sounds like the choir collectively 'running out of gas', or a record player running down. It does not, however, seem to be a general practice, and is not heard in some of the other choirs of the region that have appeared recently on recordings. Some, in fact, have a decidedly Western sound. Stewart Copeland, former drummer of the rock band The Police and now a successful composer of soundtrack music, uses the Keali'i O Nalani Choir, an ensemble of Polynesian singers based in California, to great effect in his score to the film *Rapa Nui*. The tuning of the ensemble blends perfectly with the sounds of the Western orchestral instruments.

The largest island in the South Pacific is, of course, Australia. It is also home to mankind's oldest song tradition. To even sketch what song has meant to the aborigines of Australia over the past 50,000 years would require a substantial chapter on its own. Song in aboriginal culture traditionally went beyond recounting the people and deeds of the past, or spinning a creation myth, or reflecting the landscape: it did all of these things, and actually brought listeners in contact with the ongoing process of creation known as the Dreamtime. (The aboriginal creation story tells of the Dreamtime, when mythic beings or totems called the world into existence through song.) Of course, the usual songs of love, gossip, games and war are part of the aboriginal tradition too, but song could be viewed as a truly sacred act. The most important songs are those that describe a songline – one of the tracks left by the creators, marked by both physical signposts in the landscape and musical ones in the song.[19] A good song will describe, both in text and in its musical shape, the sights and sounds of the important flora and fauna and physical features of the land.

Although this volume is specifically devoted to the human voice, the aboriginal instrument known as the *didgeridoo* is worth mentioning because it occupies a curious place somewhere between the voice and the rest of the instrumental world. (Also, it is far more frequently heard than actual aboriginal singing.) Traditionally made from a eucalyptus branch, the didgeridoo is played as an extension of the human voice, and is considered a sacred extension of those songs that intersect with the Dreamtime. In fact, the instrument was forbidden to all but a few initiates in many aboriginal lands. The technique of playing it involves circular breathing and a fascinating array of yells, whoops and grunts that clearly represent the sounds of the totemic creatures important to the people of a given region. As the Australian didgeridoo player Adam Plack notes, 'it's pitched on one note, and any differentiation comes from harmonic chanting, if you will, like that in Tibetan music. So you're using your vocal chords.'[20] A good didgeridoo player, according to Plack, can tell a story as easily as a singer. 'To show the kookaburra, for example, you create the bird's laughing sound – by actually having a good laugh through the instrument. You learn to play out in bush, watching a lizard or watching an eagle, and trying to interpret the character or spirit of that creature.'

In recent years, the aborigines have begun to make their presence felt in the modern world. The aboriginal rock band Yothu Yindi has spearheaded the thrust of native culture into the pop charts in Australia and beyond. The 'instrumental vocals' of the didgeridoo have become a part of late twentieth-century music through the work of artists like David Hudson Dwura (whose recording *Rainbow Serpent* is perhaps the first genuinely modern didgeridoo recording, combining traditional Dreamtime totems and gestures with modern studio production techniques and electronic processing) and Alan Dargin (whose rare bloodwood didgeridoo can be heard on recordings by aboriginal and white Australian artists alike). The songline – the idea that a song can access a different place and time – may be particularly Australian, but even a casual look at song traditions around the world reveals an intricate web of songlines between apparently disparate cultures. These similarities and connections suggest that something fundamental and universal, something that affects people regardless of their specific place and time, lies at the heart of all musical impulse. The aborigines of Australia believe that the world was sung into existence. Among them, and in many other parts of the world, the art of song retains an importance and a power that goes far beyond questions of number of units sold and chart position. The vocal styles of the West have justifiably established themselves on the world stage; but Western technology has given them disproportionately large exposure. Now that same technology is bringing us traditions of equal sophistication and far greater antiquity in return.

3 Rock singing

RICHARD MIDDLETON

Types of singing

> He hunches into the microphone and croons, growls and then screams from the pit of his stomach.... As Cobain circles round the lyrical repetitions, his voice becomes more and more racked ... and he pushes the words so hard it's as though he's trying to vomit them out.[1]

Rock singing[2] – as in this description of Nirvana lead singer, Kurt Cobain – is typically thought of in terms of its extreme emotive and dramatic qualities, its physical presence, its originary authenticity, at times so insistent as to occasion pain. It is, so to speak, a *natural* expression – by comparison (implicit or explicit) with the trained, disciplined technique, the pure tone, the objectifying control associated with classical singing. It is certainly true that in much rock singing the absence of low-larynx technique and of diaphragm-orientated breath-control lead to relatively speech-like voice production; that *individuality* of voice quality tends to be at a premium; and that the resulting *directness* of utterance is often taken to be a mark of expressive truth. This flouting of the rules of 'good singing' lies at the root of many responses to rock – both approving (it is breaking the rules that makes emotional authenticity possible) and dismissive (breaking the rules proves incompetence, indiscipline and even immorality). Nevertheless, it does not take a great deal of acquaintance with the rock repertoire to suggest that this picture of rock singing is over-simple. Elvis Presley's rich, sustained baritone and soaring, long-breathed tenor, especially marked in his ballad performances, are matched for control and lyricism by a whole string of female 'divas', from Dionne Warwick to Celine Dion; Billy Joel singing 'Just the Way You Are' reminds us of the earlier jazz-influenced tradition personified by Frank Sinatra, rather than what Sinatra himself described (in 1958) as the 'brutal, ugly, desperate, vicious' form of rock 'n' roll, sung 'for the most part by cretinous goons';[3] Marvin Gaye's eloquent head-voice summons memories of classical countertenors; while Ian Dury sounds as much like a music hall singer as a stereotypical rocker. The *range* of vocal techniques and timbres employed by Annie Lennox, Kate Bush or Björk suggests, within even an individual style, a capacity to *portray* heterogeneous voices quite at odds with any monological definition of rock vocalism, or the aesthetic of expressive realism that generally underpins such definitions.

In fact, just as rock as a whole did not overthrow the previous musical system so much as renegotiate it, so the best way to conceive rock singing is as a spectrum of approaches working within a territory structured through a triangulating intersection of traditions. First, there is the 'natural' technique already described, deriving mostly from neo-folk styles originating in the American South – country music and, above all, African-American blues and gospel – and with something of a pre-rock popular music history attributable to the influence of jazz. Constantly interplaying with this, perhaps predominant, lineage, we find approaches indebted to the vernacular derivatives of *bel canto*, transmitted mostly through traditions of 'light' music, Romantic operetta and sentimental ballad. Each of these models, in its own way, is founded on a concept of 'authenticity', the first based on the emotional integrity of the performer, the second on the aesthetic integrity of technique. The third side of the triangle, however, puts such authenticity in question through techniques of *stylisation*, derived from traditions of theatre, cabaret and carnival-esque role-play. Here – where star image, performative 'show' and the protagonistic 'voices' of song texts meet up, overlap and compete – is the sphere of *persona*, rendered all the more powerful by the mediatory roles of recording studio, film and video.

As in virtually all song, the role and effect of words are crucial. But the strength of the 'naturalistic' tendency is such that a para-linguistic dimension is often as important as direct verbal meanings. Another way of putting this is to say that 'it is not just what they sing, but the way they sing it, that determines what singers mean to us'; 'song words work . . . as structures of sound that are direct signs of emotion and marks of character'.[4] Indeed, there is research to suggest that some listeners to rock pay little attention to verbal meaning.[5] A more typical situation, perhaps, is where a vocal 'hook' works by bundling together the meaning, resonances and sound-shapes of the words together with the melodic, rhythmic, timbral and articulatory dimensions of their sung performance, encapsulating that particular semantic-affective field which will come to be associated with the song.

A second triangulation offers a useful way to model the relationships of words and music in rock singing – but, because of complications in this relationship of the sort just described, this triangulation maps on to the first only in a partial, skewed and fluid manner. At one extreme, words govern the musical flow, working as *narrative*; the voice tends towards speech. Bob Dylan's 'Masters of War' or 'Subterranean Homesick Blues' are examples. At the other extreme, words are absorbed into the musical flow, working as *sound* or *gesture*; the voice becomes an instrument. Little Richard's 'Tutti Frutti', with its rhythmicised 'non-sense' ('Awopbopaloobop Alopbamboom') and rhyming musical parallelisms ('Rock to the east, rock to the west, She's the girl that I love best'), is a good example. In between, words merge with melody, result-ing in *intoned expression*. This is the sphere where, above all, the sub-clas-sical strand in rock singing makes its home (especially in ballads); but a more 'natural' vocal approach can flourish here too (as it does, for example, in a good deal of soul music). And this 'natural' approach can also accommodate not only the para-linguistic sound-gestures of 'Tutti Frutti' but also the 'narrative' drive of Dylan's 'talking blues' or of rap. The technique of stylisation can potentially place any word–music rela-tionship in quotation marks.

Sources

The common perception that rock 'n' roll originated from a coming together of country music and rhythm-and-blues is broadly correct – though in this ancestry the dominant parentage was black, its inheritance passed on both directly and through previous African-American influences on country. The literature on African-American singing is copious.[6] There is general agreement on the core tendencies: short phrases, often falling or circling in shape, usually pentatonic or modal but with much microtonal inflection, pitch bending and glissando, the phrases often much repeated; call-and-response (antiphonal) relation-ships between performers; off-beat accent, syncopation and rhythmically flexible phrasing; a huge variety of register (including falsetto) and of timbre (including shouts, whoops, yells, growls, humming and wordless moans). Overriding characteristics are the permeable boundary between 'song' and 'speech' modes (perhaps deriving from African tonal lan-guages), the insistence on 'distortion', inflection and constant variation, and the love of heterogeneity of sound (rather than a single sustained timbre). Of course, 'dirty' tone, para-linguistic effects and 'blue notes' have high expressive potential, fully exploited in jazz singing as well as in blues and gospel, but they are also symptoms of a 'playful' attitude to the voice, conceived as a species of musical instrument – just the body using its own resources to make sound (the 'vocalised tone' of many African-American instrumentalists comprises the other side of this equation).

This said, the *variety* of African-American singing types is immense – from Louis Armstrong's gravelly scat to Howling Wolf's cold-eyed aggres-sion, from Bessie Smith's majestic growl to B. B. King's honeyed melis-mata. Voice-production is usually 'relaxed'; this is particularly clear in the ecstatic flights of gospel singing, passed on subsequently to soul music (compare Rosetta Tharpe or Mahalia Jackson with Aretha Franklin). However, there is a blues strand where emotional tension tightens the throat: Robert Johnson is the central figure, and the influence of his celebrated 1930s recordings permeates the post-War Chicago blues of Wolf, Muddy Waters, Elmore James and others. This strand can then be identified as the single most important source for the 'standard rock voice' – the straining, strutting macho lead – of the 1960s and 1970s (and indeed, Johnson was an iconic figure for Mick Jagger of the Rolling Stones, Led Zeppelin's Robert Plant, and many heavy metal singers). At the same time, the warmer, more projected style of the 'blues shouters' deriving from the Kansas City tradition (Jimmy Rushing, Joe Turner) and the Memphis school (B. B. King) offered an alternative approach, taken up, for example, by rock 'n' rollers such as Elvis Presley.

A second source for the tightened rock throat can be found in country music. A singing style characterised by high pitch, tense control and nasal tone can be traced back to the folk origins of country in the southern mountains (and from there, maybe, back to British traditions). Though equally 'speech-like', this is far more formalised than typical African-American approaches; while it was subsequently often modified as a result of the influence of black singing, the tension can be heard in the recordings of the first great solo singer, Jimmie Rodgers, and, still, in those of the greatest country proto rock 'n' roller, Hank Williams. Coming through into rock, such an approach sometimes also brings with it characteristic country vocal harmonies (open fourths and fifths; high-pitched close voicing; parallel movement: from the Everly Brothers to the Beatles and beyond), and the square phrasing, regular rhythmic tread and steady narrative pull of folk-ballad story-telling; the latter flows most obviously through the networks of folkish singer-songwriters, and most influentially via the lineage leading from Woody Guthrie to Bob Dylan and radiating out from the early 1960s folk-revival and folk-protest milieu within which Dylan's career began.

Within the repertoires of country music and R & B themselves, the occasional assimilation of sentimental pop ballads brought with it an invitation to pursue a more classical singing technique. Stemming initially from late Victorian domestic song on the one side, contemporary Tin Pan Alley on the other, this trajectory features so strongly in a few cases – from Vernon Dalhart to Jim Reeves, from Lonnie Johnson to Johnny Ace – as to place them in the margins between 'ethnic' and 'mainstream' categories, as well as preserving the manners of nineteenth-century bourgeois song for adaptation in rock. More broadly, the work of early classical recording stars – notably Enrico Caruso – and 'light classic' singers – such as John McCormack – together with related styles in the musical theatres of Broadway, London and other European cities, maintained a presence in the culture for this tradition, which on the one hand continued to inform mainstream popular singing (the coming of the electric microphone enabled crooners from Bing Crosby onwards to approximate the effect without the need for a full-scale trained technique), and on the other ensured that rock music would not eclipse it. In the rock ballad at its best, rhythmic focus is added to what might otherwise be bland sentiment, but at the same time the thread connecting Elton John, Barry Manilow, Barbra Streisand and Lisa Stansfield to Al Jolson and even Clara Butt is palpable. It becomes possible to understand how heavy rockers Meat Loaf and Freddie Mercury (of Queen) could perform with Luciano Pavarotti and Montserrat Caballé, respectively.

Naturally, the theatre is also the biggest single source of *stylisation* techniques. The music hall approach to the portrayal of character and scene through musico-dramatic performance and demotic accent – preserved in the years between the wars by Gracie Fields and George Formby – informs a segment of British rock, from the Kinks through Madness to Blur. Similarly, it may not be too fanciful to link the exaggerated generic stereotyping so important in American vaudeville and the performance of early Tin Pan Alley song (Irving Berlin, for example) with the over-the-top presentation common in heavy metal concerts. Arguably, there is a specific 'blackface connection' – evident in both sung and gestural mannerism, and originating in nineteenth-century minstrelsy – running from Al Jolson through Elvis Presley to Michael Jackson. At the same time, it seems true that stylisation as an approach has been under some pressure in twentieth-century popular song from the rising strength of an aesthetic of sincerity. But the increasing importance of video, TV and film (including musical film), joined with the continued effects of existing traditions of avant-garde theatre (Brecht/Weill, for instance), cabaret and nightclub, has ensured a significant presence in the rock repertoire for techniques of vocal masking, irony and role-play, which can be found in genres as varied as indie music (Talking Heads, Björk), singer-songwriters (Randy Newman), art rock (Roxy Music, David Bowie), proto-punk (Alice Cooper, New York Dolls, Iggy Pop) and mainstream pop (Eurythmics, Madonna). Moreover, pressure on the ideology of 'authenticity' itself in the 1990s may signal that stylisation is set to increase.

Some examples

In influence and historical impact, Elvis Presley's position at the head of rock genealogy is unchallenged,[7] both in relation to musical style and to the image of the male rock star – rebellious, sexy, hedonistic, living life on the edge – that he constructed. Yet Presley's singing style is not entirely congruent with this image; and it is the *mixture* of elements brought together in his vocalism that makes him prototypical for a whole strand of development in rock singing. From the start, he sang not only rockers but also ballads – and he sang them with full, rich, well-produced tone, smooth phrasing and legitimate tuning ('I'll Never Let You Go', 'Blue Moon', recorded in 1955 and 1954, respectively). But this approach was carried over into up-tempo numbers too – though here it is generally modified, *energised,* by the application of techniques which have been called 'boogification' (off-beat accenting, usually in boogie-woogie-like triplet rhythms, and often breaking up words and even syllables), 'gospelisation' (analogous inflections applied to pitch) and 'vocal orchestration' (mixing between registers, simulation of physical effort).[8] This can be heard as early as Presley's first record release (1954), where the R & B song, 'That's All Right Mama' – given a notably lyrical, romanticised treatment – is coupled with a speeded-up version of the country tune 'Blue Moon of Kentucky', which is 'boogified' into rock. But the mixture is given classic shape in his first national hit, 'Heartbreak Hotel' (1956), where Elvis's full repertoire of vocal tactics is on display.

From the start, Presley's skilful *control* of these varied strands suggested, as would become clear in his later output, that he was above all a self-aware *performer.* In 'Don't Be Cruel' (1956), 'All Shook Up' (1957) and similar later songs, boogification was exaggerated, perhaps even parodied, into mannerism; but this tendency – a refusal to take rock too seriously – can be heard in his earliest records: 'Baby Let's Play House' (1955), for instance. His expanding repertoire displays an 'authentic multiplicity'[9] of genres and approaches, and, rather than treat the later focus on slick film performances and schmaltzy ballads as a decline, it is better to see him, throughout his career, as pioneering one important response to the challenge of being a rock singer: Elvis constructed his persona as that of the romantic hero, updated for a modern consumer society; and, while he no doubt believed in it (at least at first), he also knew full well the techniques of stylisation that would produce its effects, enabling other singers (Cliff Richard, John Lennon, Tom Jones) to try them on for size.

Presley's debt to blues singing derives mostly from the controlled projection of the 'jump' blues vocalists and big-band shouters. The more 'downhome' style which came up from Mississippi to Chicago R & B did not really feature in white popular music before the sixties – but its tight-throated rasping timbres, its melodramatic outpourings of desire and self-assertion, then became central to a whole strand of 'hard' rock. The link between this vocal tradition and the obsessive, often narcissistic, and (for women) oppressive male sexual expression that has been so crucial in rock ideology has been drawn often enough. But, while a notable feature of rock culture, this tradition – from Jagger to Cobain, via Jimi Hendrix, Rod Stewart, Bruce Springsteen, Axl Rose and many more – is easily traced. At least as interesting is what its prominence means for *women* singers. One effect is to reserve for them a *different* vocal sphere – the supportive or available feminine Other, delineated through 'warm' and 'nurturing' soft-rock and rock-ballad tones. An alternative is to attempt to *appropriate* the macho style – as exemplified in the work of Janis Joplin.[10]

If Joplin's 'favorite metaphors – singing as fucking (a first principle of rock and roll) and fucking as liberation (a first principle of the cultural revolution)'[11] – were taken over from her late sixties male contemporaries, their gender inversion was equally hard to live and to sing. Joplin's expressions of thrusting desire and lusty hedonism, in varied guises, can be heard in 'Move Over', a fusion of Chicago R & B and the heavy rock of such bands as Cream; in her Bessie Smith imitation 'Turtle Blues'; or in the exhilarating 'Down on Me', where her highly coloured vocal line shades imperceptibly into a feedback-rich guitar solo. Even in these recordings, though, erotic energy is always threatening to shift into that underside awaiting any woman playing the role of 'one of the boys': a throat-tightening apprehension of rejection, loss and suffering. It is this dialectic – dependence victimised, subject forced into submissive objectification – that dominates many of Joplin's most celebrated performances – 'Cry Baby', 'Get It While You Can', 'Ball and Chain' – where lyrics, apart from the occasional emblematic phrase, disappear into streams of fragmentary emotive outpourings, lacerating shrieks, and strangulated moans. The characteristic timbre at these moments is of nails on flesh. Thus, although she actually possessed a remarkable range of 'voices' – listen, for example, to the rich melismata, warm phrasing and floated head-voice effects of 'Try (Just a Little Bit Harder)', almost like soul singer Aretha Franklin's – what is most striking is how the focus almost always ends up on the worn-raw vocal chords of hard-living, passionate victimhood. Ellen Willis points out, perceptively, that Joplin 'used blues conventions to reject blues sensibility'.[12] Blues catharsis – self-protecting 'distance' – giving way to self-centred expressionistic angst is altogether a defining quality of hard rock, but inevitably struck harder at a woman; and Joplin's untimely death, certainly a symptom of unsatisfied need, echoed the music's message.

Vocal soul-baring (replacing the soul-sharing typical of blues – a cultural performance which aids the art of living) represents the attempted conflation of art and life, a core element of the rock myth. But of course, it depends on effective performance (and listener interpretation) of the appropriate style conventions (lived-in voice, cracked notes, etc.). Nowhere is this contradiction between 'style' and 'spontaneity' better exposed than in punk rock. Punk's mission to *provoke* – to offer a conduit for the expression of 'street' anger in the most extreme forms possible – was at the same time the product of careful (and equally extreme) aesthetic construction and marketing hype – especially in the hands of Sex Pistols manager, Malcolm McClaren. Moreover, the object of the attacks was not only mainstream society but established rock as well: its perceived elevation of style over substance, certainly, but also its apparent self-regard – its reification of musical skill, its commodification of 'feeling'. By pushing through the limits, punk revealed the cracks in this aesthetic and commercial 'conspiracy'; 'by its very unnaturalness, punk made the host culture [including existing rock music] seem like a trick'.[13]

In the Sex Pistols' most celebrated recordings – 'Anarchy in the UK', 'God Save the Queen', 'Pretty Vacant', 'Holidays in the Sun'[14] – Johnny Rotten's basic singing mode is one of narrative declamation; all appeal of musical technique seems to be refused. Yet on closer acquaintance, the 'naturalism' here is revealed as so exaggerated, so distorted, as to be mannered. The punched-out, mechanical rhythms, together with the grating timbres, alienate the listener – just as the performance tactic of 'gobbing' was designed to do; comparison with the performance tradition developed in Brechtian music theatre is apt. Rotten's accenting and pitch-contours are often radically at odds with the natural shapes of the verbal phrases, a technique especially marked in his bizarre and typical upward-curving pitch-bend on the final syllable of a phrase. The ends of words are also often given a lengthy '. . . er' extension ('. . . anarchy-errrr'), suggesting the rhetorical address (and the duplicity?) both of political speech and the street trader. The exaggerated 'estuary English' diction – most dramatic in artificially prolonged diphthongs – might suggest street realism, but actually – against the mid-atlantic norm of the rock music culture – comes over as intensely *stylised*. Rotten's tendency to switch between different vocal modes – conversational gabbling, public declamation, brief bursts of pitched song – rejects any attempt at listener identification, just as shifts between subjects in the lyrics often refuse clear indications of who is addressing whom.[15] Transfixed by this *performance*, we find the words sliding past in a blur, an effect intensified when the voice (as most memorably in 'Holidays in the Sun') disappears into the mix. The Pistols' overall rhetorical thrust is confirmed in the cover of 'My Way' (made famous by Frank Sinatra a decade before), when Sid Vicious, taking over the singing and many of Rotten's mannerisms with it, brings down the curtain on punk rock, demolishes the pretensions of vocal 'self-expression' in his up-tempo, punked-up version of the song, and prefaces this with a wicked parody of 'proper' singing which manages to conflate the pop ballad tradition and the classical heritage lying behind it. As Greil Marcus writes, the Sex Pistols made it necessary to ask, 'Can rock and roll ever be taken at face value?'[16]

While white rock (especially in its core period of *c*. 1963–1980) exercised itself over issues of 'expression', contemporary black pop music – even though it had, in blues, a lineage that in its own way also foregrounded emotional truth – rarely tried to hide its status as *performance*. The larger-than-life personae of the great singers, from Wilson Pickett and Aretha Franklin down to Prince and Michael Jackson; the centrality of performance gesture, drama and dance; the importance of interaction with audiences; the hyperbolic sentiments of many lyrics: all these characteristics testify to a conception of musical activity as consciously pursued cultural work, a conception fully infusing singing styles as well. Nowhere is this clearer than in the music of James Brown, famed for the emotional intensity of his shows, the dramatic structures of which were carefully choreographed by the 'hardest working man in show business'.[17] In the mid-1950s, Brown, along with Ray Charles, was largely responsible for introducing the call-and-response patterns and the ecstatic timbres and phrasing of gospel music into R & B (soon to be renamed soul music). But already in his first hit, 'Please, Please, Please' (1956), the lyrical lines start to fragment through the extravagantly melismatic treatment – varied in detail each time – of keywords (especially 'please'). A characteristic ascending whoop on a final syllable, often into falsetto, points towards the para-linguistic extremes that were to come. By the time of the ground-breaking 'Papa's Got a Brand New Bag' (1965), the descending melismata often cover an octave, with partly indeterminate pitches, and Brown's vocal – with its harsh timbre; internally referential lyrics; punchy, percussive rhythms and construction through semi-improvised variation of short, repeating phrases – functions more like an instrument in the texture than like a conventionally sung tune. All the ingredients of what would become known as 'funk' were signposted here; and in a series of subsequent classics – 'Cold Sweat', 'I Can't Stand Myself' (1967), 'Say It Loud – I'm Black and I'm Proud' (1968), 'Sex Machine', 'Superbad' (1970) – they were paradigmatically laid out: varied repetition of short units (what has been termed 'signifyin'[18]), often over lengthy single-chord passages; a wide spectrum of often extreme para-linguistic effects (Brown's grunt and almost incredibly high-pitched shriek being widely sampled by later black musicians); absorption of the vocal into a dense, polyrhythmic texture of interlocking riffs. The tendency to 'instrumentalise' the voice results in recordings that are virtually instrumentals ('Funky Drummer' (1969)), and in 'Get Up, Get into It, and Get Involved' (1970) and 'Soul

Power' (1971) the band is mixed so high and the vocal call-and-response between Brown and a supporting singer so low (relatively) that the latter becomes part of what is in effect a percussion ensemble; the words, even though they tend at times to rap-like narrativism, register only sub-liminally.

There were many strands of black music in the 1960s and 1970s, and James Brown represents the 'hardest', most rhythmically orientated, most 'musicalised' vocal tendencies; yet he foreshadows many subsequent developments – in funk, hip-hop and white as well as black dance music of the 1990s. In his music we hear a quite different concept of vocalisation from that current in white rock: not so much 'personal feeling' translated into song, more the exertions of a 'vocal body'. There is no lack of emotion – indeed, the extreme use of the voice constantly produces signifiers of intense feeling; but, rather than this being treated as a focus in itself, it is put into the domain of public action – corporealised, socialised.

Within the rock/pop mainstream of the 1980s and 1990s, wherever the lessons of punk were learned and those of black music (soul, funk, disco and then hip-hop) registered, the rock aesthetic of 'self-expression' could be sustained only with difficulty (as in the case of Kurt Cobain, for instance, or U2's Bono); or – as it were – at a distance, through self-aware 'framing' techniques (the approach in much indie music: listen to Morrissey, or Michael Stipe of REM); or else – even more dramatic – in quotation marks: through irony, or at least through explicit modes of self-presentation. The last strategy is exemplified particularly clearly by Madonna.[19]

Madonna's early hits – 'Holiday' (1983), 'Lucky Star' (1984) – are in a soft-soul, disco-influenced style; but she herself is recorded with so much reverb and double-tracking as to be, so to speak, 'de-personalised'. By the time of the 1985 album *Like a Virgin*, she is consciously constructing 'characters' – a coquettish sex-kitten in the breathy, simpering title-song; a sexually ruthless woman-of-the-world in 'Material Girl', with its hard, polished timbre and tight, rather mechanical rhythms. This is a lineage continued in some later songs, for example through the *femme fatale* persona and semi-spoken, soft porn-ish vocal of 'Justify My Love' (1990). 'Crazy for You' (1985), from the film *Vision Quest*, demonstrates through its warmer timbre and ballad-style lyricism that Madonna can construct herself into the more traditional role of torch-song protagonist; and the *True Blue* album (1986) builds on this more 'mature' persona – for instance, in the full-voiced ballad 'Open Your Heart', the dramatic 'Papa Don't Preach', with its soundtrack-like backing, and the atmospheric 'Live to Tell', where Madonna's lower tessitura, 'lived-in' timbre and 'sophisti-cated' phrasing (more off-beat, with little swoops and mordents) signal

'experience'. By the time of 'Don't Cry for Me Argentina', from the musical
Evita (1996), a connection with the traditions of opera (mediated by the
American musical) is explicit.[20]

Madonna as actress – an identity consummated in one way, of course,
in her film roles, for instance in the private-eye spoof *Dick Tracey* (1990)
as well as in *Evita* – emerges musically in perhaps the clearest form in
songs presenting her through multiple voices.[21] 'Rescue Me' (1990), in
addition to the backing vocals, features both Madonna's semi-speaking
and soul-like styles, and also breathy interpolations; 'Like a Prayer' (1989)
is structured round a contrast between pure-toned lyricism in the verses
and syncopated, gospel-influenced R & B in the choruses, creating diver-
gent modes of quasi-religious eroticism.[22] In the introduction to 'Vogue'
(a 1990 hit from the *Dick Tracey*-derived album *I'm Breathless*), we hear
Madonna ask 'What are you looking at?' and instruct us to 'strike the
pose!'; and in the song's bridge she raps a roll-call of Hollywood greats –
from Astaire to Monroe – connecting herself to a historical semiotics of
star gesture. The alignment of screen fantasy and dance-floor pose (the
star as object of desire; the dance as setting for erotic display) provides the
context for the dialogue in Madonna's performances between mainstream musico-dramatic traditions on the one hand (ballad, musical,
Hollywood), and black music and youth subculture on the other. Like
Elvis Presley (who also brought together rock, bodily gesture and cine-
matic image), she constructs herself as a 'romantic hero' – one appealing
especially to girls and women, but multi-faceted, bridging cultures, connecting histories.

Aesthetics

The aesthetic of 'authenticity' dominates mainstream rock vocalism: 'real
experience', expressed with 'sincerity', is regarded as the indispensable
basis of good (that is, 'honest') singing. The tendency to autobiography
(or an illusion of autobiography) towards which this pushes performers is
illustrated at its most extreme by the work of 'confessional' singer-songwriters, from Joni Mitchell and Leonard Cohen down to Tracy Chapman
and P. J. Harvey. As Dave Laing has pointed out,[23] what happens here is
that two distinct semiotic levels – that of the 'text' and that of the 'utterance' – are conflated; thus the subject of the song's lyric (of the *énoncé*, as
literary theorists call it) is identified with that of the performance-act (the
énonciation). When Janis Joplin sings about 'me and Bobby McGhee' in
her famous recording of the Kris Kristofferson song with that title, most
listeners probably identify the 'me' as Joplin, and, similarly, when Elvis

Presley sings 'that's all right mama, that's all right with me', the 'me' is heard as being Elvis. But such elision is by no means universal. In 'Heartbreak Hotel', Elvis identifies the 'broken-hearted lovers' variously as 'they' and 'you' as well as 'I', opening up a gap between *énoncé* and *énonciation*; and when James Brown boasts that 'papa's got a brand new bag', it would seem that we hear Brown, the performer, looking at and describing himself as 'papa'. When Johnny Rotten, in 'Holidays in the Sun', admits that 'I don't understand this bit at all', the gap is consciously manipulated.

Obviously, such divergences complicate patterns of relationship between listeners and singers. But it needs to be remembered that the rock voice not only carries a grammatical position; it is of course also a *singing* voice, working in a genre where it is almost always texturally dominant. According to Sean Cubitt, the trail left by this acoustic trace itself acts as the focus of listeners' identification, empathy and desire.[24] Yet, as Cubitt points out, this trace also (and inevitably) marks an *absence* – that of the real person, the real *body*, whom we can never possess. This gap is, one might suppose, only intensified by the way that the recording process detaches the sound from any sight of the singer – though, arguably, such 'disembodiment' can stimulate the imagination too, an activity amply encouraged not only by cultural knowledge (for example, of voice types and their associations) but also by exponential growth in the surrounding visual apparatus (film, TV, video, publicity photos). Moreover, the recording process also can be used to amplify and manipulate vocal personality (through mixing, double-tracking, echo and other electronic techniques), creating larger-than-life effects and bringing the star 'closer' to the listener. Given that rock was the first musical genre to be created for and through recording, this is clearly important. But the potentials of such techniques and contexts are manifold and varied, and smooth patterns of connection can never be guaranteed. Furthermore, while the rock vocal may often possess a stylistic coherence, this is, as we found earlier, not always the case: Elvis Presley's vocal orchestration and boogifying hiccups, James Brown's para-linguistic extremes, Madonna's multiple characterisations, Johnny Rotten's self-exploding mannerisms – all fragment the singing subject, and, with it, the positions of response available to listeners. Arguably, it is within this whole multi-faceted nexus of incongruities that the play of the unconscious on the construction of 'vocal subjectivity' is to be located.

This play has been theorised by Roland Barthes through his notion of the 'geno-song'. By contrast with the 'pheno-song' – which covers 'everything in the performance which is in the service of communication, representation, expression' – the geno-song, or 'grain of the voice', concerns that semiotic dimension where the voice's 'very materiality . . . the voluptuousness of its sound-signifiers' invites the listener to an erotic pleasure that disrupts the boundaries of the conscious subject.[25] Barthes's theory has been much discussed within rock studies, but seldom applied analytically – and with reason, perhaps, since his image of a de-personalised material body is just as much a product of romantic wishful thinking as its apparent obverse, the all-conquering pheno-song beloved of the ideologists of authenticity. This is not to deny the centrality of the 'vocal body' to rock music effects. Indeed, rock might be described, in its most typical forms, as overwhelmingly a 'voice music' – not only in its domination, culturally and texturally, by singers, but also in its takeover from African-American music of ways of treating instruments as would-be voices, a tendency often amplified by electronic technology (pitch-bends, vibrato, wah-wah, etc.). This suggests that it might be better to construe the processes of desire and identity surrounding rock in terms not so much of 'lack' as of *plenitude*: drawing on the 'dialogical' account of semiotics and subjectivity offered by the Russian theorist Mikhail Bakhtin, we might then describe the ever-present *intertextuality* of rock singing – its multiple references to other songs, other voices, a variety of vocal traditions, a range of vocalising techniques – as a symptom of a state of, so to speak, *over*-completion.

Needless to say, much of the argument in this section is pertinent to all singing. However, it seems especially relevant to rock because this is a genre which almost always presents itself as *performance*. (While, admittedly, performers in concert strive to imitate their pre-existing recordings, the records offer themselves, aesthetically, as 'performances', even if they have taken many studio hours to produce.) Generally, performers create, or participate in creating, their own material; 'composition' takes place through performance, or performance-like processes; the actual delivery of the songs is integral to their aesthetic status. Thus the roles of singers and other performers, as protagonists relating both to their material and to their listeners, are critical. Simon Frith argues[26] that three dimensions of the singer's role should be distinguished. First, the singer plays the role required by the song (which may relate to a first-person position in the lyric or may not); second, he or she plays the role of star, and must relate the performance to their pre-existing star persona; and third, the singer enacts the gestures of a real person, physically present (visually, tangibly, aurally), a site of audience desire. As a rule these dimensions partly, or sometimes wholly, overlap – the different protagonists move together and map on to each other; at times, though, they may be held apart – by performance techniques or by listening strategies.

In its mainstream tradition, rock singing, under the sign of 'authenticity', strives for conflation. But, as we have seen, this tendency is surrounded by a variety of other tactics, and is always under threat. One way of reading the history is in terms of an attempt to impose on this multifariousness an elision of role differences – to sing what is lived, live what is sung, to 'have it all', and offer this, as a single ethico-aesthetic package, to a 'rock community' – followed by a slow, partial rediscovery of limits which, ironically, had been widely taken for granted in rock's own beginnings: when, for instance, Elvis Presley sang that he was 'all shook up' with a tone, style and phrasing that said, unmistakably, 'know what I mean?'

4 The evolving language of rap

DAVID TOOP

In 1979, the American release of two unusual records heralded the early stages of a new musical movement that would develop into a multi-million-dollar industry. Produced by New York City based labels (Spring and Sugarhill, respectively) during the sunset of the disco era, The Fatback Band's 'King Tim III (Personality Jock)' and The Sugarhill Gang's 'Rapper's Delight' were typified by loosely structured rhymes spoken with speed, cadence, syncopation and boastful humour over funk backing tracks.

Although the second of these records turned out to be a substantial commercial success, there was little contemporary awareness of the indigenous rap scene that inspired the releases, let alone the tremendous impact that this new style of 'hip-hop' (or rap, as it came to be known) would have on the mainstream recording industry in the future. As for the deep historical roots of this innovative form of musical expression, the prevailing prejudice against popular music at the time, particularly a youthful black dance music, ensured a generally dismissive response, an assumption that the music was transient, a juvenile fad with no ties to any community or body of tradition. The artistry essential to success in rapping – an ability to use the voice, to write, retain in memory and spontaneously embellish rhymes that might be rapped for hours at a stretch in highly competitive, if not combative, environments – was awarded scant value until a combination of overwhelming commercial success, critical attention and academic interest offered redemption.

Yet within a small circle of performers and entrepreneurs in New York's Harlem and Bronx districts, the motivation that lay behind the release of many early rap records stemmed from an awareness that the music was linked to forms of expressive music-speech-song hybrids that predated disco. Older entrepreneurs who had experienced the disco era of the mid- to late1970s as a time of musical alienation and financial setback greeted the emergent genre of hip-hop with some ambivalence. On the one hand, this was music they heard at home; their children were writing rhymes, attending the block parties that were the crucible for rap, aspiring to make their own records, teaching their parents. The music used in conjunction with these rhymes was played by DJs on record decks rather than by musicians on conventional instruments. It tended to be retrogressive, at least in its source material, and more closely connected than disco to a lineage of African-American musical tradition. This dated from the blues: either soul tracks from the 1960s, raw funk records from the early 1970s or drum breaks lifted from music of many different persuasions, whether heavy metal, jazz, electronic, pop, even disco itself.

Any empathy and familiarity that these paternal and maternal figures might feel was offset, however, by a feeling of *déjà vu*. The experienced Harlem record producer Paul Winley, notorious for sharp practice with his Winley Records label, claimed 'Rapping goes back. Rapping is an old thing. Like a lot of black singers couldn't sing but they could talk. My brother is singing now with a group called The Inkspots. If you go back to that era, the part my brother does is the bass 'cos he was bass with The Clovers, so now he talks. James Brown did rapping, Isaac Hayes did rapping, Millie Jackson did rapping. Rapping is nothing new.'[1]

At the most basic level, hip-hop was amateur music-making accomplished with severely restricted means, an approach to creativity that sounded nostalgic echoes of the street corner doo-wop vocal style that had flourished in American cities such as New York during the 1950s. In either form, a complete performance could be given with the voice alone, though as both doo-wop and hip-hop developed in sophistication during their respective eras, the fascinating potential of *a cappella* vocalising came to be regarded as a curiosity or gimmick, divorced from the mainstream. According to Bobby Robinson, an important producer of the period,

> Doo-wop originally started out as the black teenage expression of the '50s and rap emerged as the black teenage ghetto expression of the '70s. Same identical thing that started it – the doo-wop groups down the street, in hallways, in alleys and on the corner. They'd gather anywhere and, you know, doo-wop doo wah da da da da. You'd hear it everywhere. So the same thing started with rap groups around '76 or so. All of a sudden, everywhere you turned you'd hear kids rapping. In the summertime, they'd have these little parties in the park. They used to go out and play at night and kids would be out there dancing. All of a sudden, all you could hear was, hip-hop hit the top don't stop. It's kids – to a great extent mixed-up and confused – reaching out to express themselves. They were trying to express themselves and they made up in fantasy what they missed in reality.[2]

Winley along with Joe and Sylvia Robinson at their newly founded Sugarhill Records label and Bobby Robinson (not related to the Sugarhill Robinsons) at his Enjoy label were veterans of many black music styles. The main focus of their releases during the 1950s had been rhythm-and-blues, though they had also dabbled with spoken word in a variety of forms, including comedy routines, 'blue' party records, prison narrations and comic monologues, political oratory and 'message' poetry read over funk and jazz backings. Paul Winley's LP releases of speeches by Dr Martin Luther King and Malcolm X underlined important connections between the speech-making of the civil rights movement, black nationalism and the ecstatic sermonising of the African-American Christian church. This move, for Winley and the Robinsons, in late middle age, into releasing examples of yet another passing teenage street trend (as hip-hop was viewed at the time) was perhaps not surprising. Rap was perceived by them, correctly if somewhat grudgingly, as an evolutionary offshoot from the rich and diverse oratorical background stretching back through Harlem glories to distant folklore. Inevitably, such folkloric forms connected to the slave trade and the African cultures that were dislocated, transplanted and transformed by that trade. Living and working in close proximity to Harlem's legendary Apollo Theatre, or the Audubon Ballroom, where Malcolm X was shot dead, the record producers who launched rap at its initial underground level were conversant with every historical precedent of the youthful rappers they exploited.

Though his analysis of the motivations of rappers simplifies the story, Bobby Robinson's conclusion – 'they made up in fantasy what they missed in reality' – touches upon an important element in the African-American oral tradition. In its earliest days, hip-hop evolved as a multiple form of expression: somebody attending a party on one day might become a 'performer' on the next, either with dancing, graffiti painting, rapping or DJ skills. Eventually, these large parties – held in school gymnasiums, parks, unoccupied buildings and similar public spaces – needed focus. The first step was taken by hip-hop's pioneering DJ, Kool Herc, who used rappers to shout slogans as he played records. These simple slogans traded upon the territorial nature of the parties, with its roots in the defence of gangland turf. Other early DJs discovered that their virtuosity in manipulating record decks and montaging sound at high speed could be detrimental to the party spirit. As Grandmaster Flash has explained,

> At that time, with my mixing ability, once I warmed up and really got into it, the crowd would stop dancing and just gather round as if it was a seminar. This was what I didn't want. This wasn't school – it was time to shake your ass. From there I knew it was important to have vocal entertainment. There were quite a few MCs, as we called it before the industry called it rap, that tried out for the job to rap with me and the first member of the crew to really pass the test was Keith Wiggins, known as Cowboy.[3]

The nickname taken by the late Keith Wiggins – Cowboy – is an indication of the style in which these early MCs presented themselves. As Bobby Robinson suggests, they were filling an absence with fantasy. So in their stage personae and their self-written rhymes they were champagne-drinking superheroes, fabulously rich, sexual conquerors, owners of fine clothes and status-enhancing fast cars, even though the reality might fall far short of these imaginative constructs. This form of boasting, known as toasts, had enjoyed a long and fairly secret tradition in male African-American culture. As one source puts it,

> toasts are a form of poetry recited by certain blacks – really a performance medium, widely known within a small (and probably disappearing) community and virtually unknown of outside it. They are like jokes: no one knows who creates them, and everyone has his own versions. But toasts, like any other form of stylised expression, have their own conventions of form and content. Furthermore, they come from a clearly defined subculture and meet all the standard criteria of folk literature: dispersion and longevity as well as anonymity and mutability. Though most toasts are pure boast or precept, the most common type is narrative – stories ranging from simple anecdote to highly elaborate, almost epic tales.[4]

Toasts such as 'Signifying Monkey', 'Stackolee', 'Titanic' and the gleefully macabre, obscene 'Dance of the Freaks' were frequently collected in prisons, an environment whose enforced intimacy and boredom encouraged a facility in the dramatic delivery of stories. Like Marlow, the narrator at the centre of a number of Joseph Conrad's novels and short stories, the storyteller was licensed to be controversial, obscure, nostalgic, surreal, a dispassionate observer of moral dilemmas or the vicissitudes of fate, so long as his tale was absorbing. 'As much evidence as there is for viewing toasts as the poetic literature of the street or partying black man', wrote Bruce Jackson,

> there is evidence to consider it, along with the worksongs of the black convict in the South, as his jailhouse testament. It is in jail that these poems are recited as much as ever and more than elsewhere, and it is just those street roles of badman, pimp, hustler, and junkie described in so many of the poems that get those jailhouse tellers and auditors in jail in the first place.[5]

Toasts take their place, then, in the undergrowth of literature, shared and taken for granted among working class, criminalised black men, studied by anthropologists, yet otherwise obscure. Sylvia and Joe Robinson had released such material on their All Platinum label, prior to the launch of the rap-orientated Sugarhill label. With a *Rated XXX Adults Only* warning printed on its front cover, *The Tramp Is Funky* by Billy Guy featured unsanitised (and frankly obscene) renditions of well-known toasts such as 'Call of the Freaks' and 'Stackolee', performed as if in a nightclub. Absorption of the wild and amoral Stackolee, a character of myth who flamboyantly revels in sexual violence and gunplay, into the subject matter of rhythm-and-blues songs of the 1950s and 1960s was perhaps inevitable. His celebration in African-American toasts and ballads had established him as an important fictional locus of much repressed rage. In *Deep Down In the Jungle: Negro Narrative Folklore from the Streets of Philadelphia,* Roger D. Abrahams links Stackolee to a type of personality once found in Southern black communities. 'The bully is not responsive or responsible to white laws or society', he writes, 'his modern urban counterpoint is the gang leader'.[6]

A tame version of Stackolee surfaces in 'Jack That Cat Was Clean', recorded by Dr Horse for the Sue label during the 1960s. Less rare than the Dr Horse recording was James Brown's 'King Heroin', released in 1972. Similarly recited over a repeated, though less jaunty, riff, the story begins with what Roger Abrahams calls a 'discovery' stanza. In a dream, Brown sees 'a real strange weird object standing up talking to the people'. The object turns out to be heroin. 'Make haste, mount the steed', Brown rasps, 'and ride him well, for the white horse of heroin will ride you to hell . . . to hell . . . will ride you to hell until you are dead . . . dead, brother . . . dead . . .' This version of 'King Heroin' was released during the era of so-called Blaxploitation cinema, a brief period of action films made by black directors, starring black actors, scored by black musicians and set in an urban black milieu. The genre was initiated, obliquely and unintentionally, by vocalist, actor and director Melvin Van Peebles with his 1971 film *Sweet Sweetback's Badasssss Song* and followed by more mainstream Hollywood examples of the genre such as *Shaft* and *Superfly.* Again, there is the undercurrent of subversive, marginalised (so essentially clandestine) oral culture, emerging into the spotlight of mainstream entertainment. 'Any genre should include among its subgenres some form of the heroic epic', wrote Thomas Cripps in *Black Film As Genre.*

> But black film has been characterised by an absence of the hero in the tradition of El Cid, King Arthur, or even King Chaka of the Zulus. Instead, black heroic tradition, at least in the movies, has borrowed from older Afro-American traditional folk heroes, among the most influential the trickster modelled after Br'er Rabbit or the 'bad nigger' modelled after Staggerlee, the sexual outlaw of black urban folklore.[7]

As if cinema had shown the way, Lightnin' Rod's *Hustler's Convention* album presented the narrative form and content of the toast as an aural drama, complete with music and sound effects, spanning both sides of a long-playing record. Released in 1973, effectively the final year for the Blaxploitation craze, the record was devised by Jalaluddin Mansur Nuriddin, originally a member of the Harlem-based East Wind poetry collective, a group that transformed itself during the late 1960s into the

more celebrated antecedents of rap: The Last Poets. The album was conceived shortly after an impromptu recording session during which
Nuriddin, Jimi Hendrix and drummer Buddy Miles improvised a driving
funk-rock version of *Doriella Du Fontain*, a toast popular in Harlem.
Hustler's Convention was released by producer Alan Douglas on his
Douglas label. As Douglas told *The Wire* magazine, 'Every one of those
characters [on the record] came out of the jail toasts. I felt this was more
like a film, so I had Kool And The Gang and another band called Full
Moon, and we scored it like a film.'[8] So folk art and the experiences of life
collided with Hollywood as the aesthetics of cinema were fused with an
intrinsically dramatic branch of African-American storytelling. The
impact of these examples on the first rappers is clear, since *Hustler's
Convention* was adapted and recorded by Melle Mel (a member of
Grandmaster Flash and The Furious Five) and a version of 'King Heroin'
was recorded by one of the very first rap groups, Funky Four. Both adaptations were released by Sugarhill Records. This direct link between generations revealed further connections. Though toasts were important to
hip-hop at its earliest stages, the full significance of this aspect of African-
American oral culture did not become apparent until the emergence of
so-called Gangsta Rap in the late 1980s, a sub-genre that thrived on
stories of the violence and sexual rapaciousness of outlaws.

The prolific rhyming skills of rapping tapped into other aspects of
verbalisation that had developed, without acknowledgement, as serious
cultural expression. Roger Abrahams collected tape recordings of toasts,
jokes and verbal contests such as 'the dozens' in the predominantly black
area of Camingerly, Philadelphia, during the late 1950s and early 1960s.
He described the adept of talk, as a 'man of words' to whom rhyming is
vital. 'He not only uses traditional rhymes as part of his entertainment
repertoire', Abrahams wrote,

> but uses his abilities to insert rhymes that may entertain into any social situation
> ... Words are power to him in a very real way ... The men of Camingerly use this
> inherent power in their most important battles, their verbal contests. Verbal
> contest accounts for a large portion of the talk between members of this group.
> Proverbs, turns of phrase, jokes, almost any manner of discourse is used, not for
> purposes of discursive communication but as weapons in verbal battle. Any
> gathering of the men customarily turns into 'sounding', a teasing or boasting
> session.[9]

Abrahams made clear the connection between the verbal battles he could
witness in his own neighbourhood and their historical origins. 'I have
found through fieldwork in the British West Indies', he wrote, 'that the
approach to words and word use and creative performance is shared
throughout the two culture areas. Further, recent ethnographic works on

Negro groups throughout Africa and the New World give indications that this attitude and pattern is an African cultural retention in its New World situations, subject to reinterpretations'.[10]

Studies of West African oral culture have noted the social importance of similar verbal battles. In *Oral Literature In Africa*, Ruth Finnegan finds instances of poetry and music used as instruments of power:

> Lampoons are not only used between groups but can also be a means of communicating and expressing personal enmity between hostile individuals. We hear of Galla abusive poems, for instance, while among the Yoruba when two women have quarrelled they sometimes vent their enmity by singing at each other, especially in situations – like the laundry place – where other women will hear. Abusive songs against ordinary individuals are also sometimes directly used as a means of social pressure, enforcing the will of public opinion.[11]

Abusive songs that exert social pressure and influence, if not enforce, the will of public opinion have become the backbone of a lucrative industry. In the mid-1990s, two American rap stars – Tupac Shakur and Biggie Smalls – became notorious for trading vindictive, highly personal insults against each other, using best-selling record releases as the vehicle for their abuse. Both were shot dead in circumstances that remain entangled in conjecture, thus demonstrating the degree to which violence, financial fortunes and verbal abuse have become entwined.

Though the precise details are impossible to determine, we know that hip-hop began in New York's South Bronx during the mid-1970s. The three most important figures in this early history – the so-called 'old school' – were all DJs: Kool DJ Herc, Grandmaster Flash and Afrika Bambaataa. All three were record collectors who reacted against the prevailing music industry trends of the time by playing an eclectic mix of records, old and new, often playing only the percussion 'break downs' of funk or rock tracks; these breaks would be punctuated by 'scratching' – a percussive noise produced by a combination technique of scratching the stylus in a record groove and synchronising the punch-in of a turntable fader. Isolated from greater public awareness or the attentions of record companies for three or four years, these DJs and their peers developed their abilities to extremely high levels of originality and virtuosity.

Rapping began as a simple form of MC announcement, a cheerleading support for the DJ, and quickly developed into an elaborate art in its own right. If the rappers, the MCs, fulfilled a familiar entertainment function, using well-established traditions of oral literature as a basis for their creations, the DJs were embarking on a far less familiar journey. Their work entailed a rapid montage of fragments and rhythmic noise from preexisting material, cut together by switching between two or more record turntables to make a seamless flow that was inspiring for dancers, absorbing for listeners, sufficiently consistent for the rappers and dauntingly impressive to potential competitors.

But the symbiotic relationship of DJ and MC inevitably provoked formal changes in both activities. As the MCs learned to tailor their rhymes to increasing audience sophistication and the venal pragmatism of record companies looking for hits, so the DJs were pressured into applying more conventional song structuring to their otherwise continuous beat-driven streams of montaged fragments. As for the DJs, their expertise lay in the art of creating a flowing motion of rhythm, differentiated by peaks of intensity which might fall away to provide respite for the more romantic sectors of the audience, then build again at the peak of the night. The MC had to be capable of rhyming at great length, maintaining metric equilibrium despite the fragmentation within the DJ's flow. As Grandmaster Flash has said,

> The particular MC I was looking for was somebody who could complement scratching. This person had to be able to talk with all the obscure scratching I was doing. I'm doing all this but I'm doing it all on time so you have to have the ear to really know. Even now, I might walk into a club and if I'm cutting and keeping it going they rap, but if I stop on time to the beat they get lost. There's some that can't really catch on to it when the music's being phased in and out to the beat.[12]

Hip-hop's formative history was characterised by a shared culture of dancers, graffiti painters, DJs, rappers and musicians. Inevitably, as this culture became absorbed within mainstream entertainment, the focus narrowed to the vocalists who stood at the front of the stage, or whose contributions were most prominent on recordings. In other words, financial reward and celebrity has gone to the rappers, though many DJs learned to apply their musicality, technological aptitude and encyclopaedic knowledge of records to the influential backroom of recording studio production, so accruing rewards of their own. The first DJ stars – Grandmaster Flash and Afrika Bambaataa – were the most widely known, although from the mid-1990s a slight shift away from individual star rappers was perceptible with the emergence of the Wu-Tang Clan, a shifting collective of rappers and producers, and DJs such as DJ Shadow, whose predominantly instrumental soundscapes of digital sample fragments and montaged beats have been profoundly influenced by the early history of hip-hop. But in the public eye, rap is equivalent to singing, and this development is one of the most fascinating aspects of popular music's recent history. Most attempts to match spoken poetry with jazz, soul or rock have failed to appeal beyond a 'cult' audience (for example Gil Scott-Heron or Ivor Cutler), yet some of the best-selling pop artists of the past ten years have been rappers such as Snoop Doggy Dog and Tupac Shakur.

Though few rappers (thankfully) attempt to sing, rap has matured into a form of speech delivery that can be described as lyrical speech. The pitching does not conform to melodic demands but rather rolls off the tongue with an actor's sense of drama, a comedian's grasp of timing and a saxophonist's appreciation of the precision and fluidity that can be expressed within musical time. The earliest hip-hop styles owed much of their vocal delivery to the circumstances of performance. At parties held in the open air or an echoing gymnasium, amplified by inadequate public address systems, raps had to be shouted over remorseless, often disconnected, music tracks supplied by the DJs. Some rap originals – for example DJ Hollywood, Eddie Cheeba and Kurtis Blow – were clearly influenced by the radio disc jockey style popular in the 1940s and 1950s, a fluent stream of jive talk made famous by Jocko Henderson, 'Your Ace From Outer Space' on his '1280 Rocket' show. This mode of performance speech was strongly stressed on the offbeats, giving simple rhyming couplets a rubbery feel that challenged intelligibility. Verging on self-parody, this stereotypical approach to rap was soon regarded as dated and rather 'showbiz', the kind of smoothly professional patter delivered by an older music business personality like radio DJ Frankie 'Loveman' Crocker. Though the first wave of MCs would still revive the style for recordings, where backing tracks might be inappropriate anyway, live party tapes from the period reveal a tendency to flatten the delivery to a monotone, with the values of stamina, fluency and invention replacing R & B radio clichés.

Rap began as a party music, but with the 1982 release of Grandmaster Flash and The Furious Five's 'The Message', the first rap to deliver a coherent narrative fired by injustice, the scope broadened in both subject matter and variations in vocal texture. As Furious Five rapper Danny 'Kid Creole' Glover has said, explaining his first reservations on seeing the lyrics: 'It talked about problems and it ended in death. Who the hell wants to hear some shit like that?' As for Grandmaster Flash himself, he rationalised their initial reluctance to record the song as a resistance to change. 'There was a raw tape', he recalled.

> Duke Bootee had wrote the major parts of the record and Miss [Sylvia] Robinson, every now and then, she would play this tape for us. We used to snap on this song. That song! At that time, the form of rap was braggadocio: I got six girls, I got diamond rings. If you could talk about what you got the most, then you was the most.[13]

Written by an outsider, 'The Message' initiated a more considered, literary and self-conscious approach to rap. The immediate effect of its success, both artistically and commercially, was to split the group. Melle

Mel, the lead voice on 'The Message', stayed with Sugarhill to develop as a solo artist, while Grandmaster Flash entered a period of litigation and artistic uncertainty. Danny Glover blamed Sylvia Robinson: 'I guess she must have thought that in every group there's one guy who really is the group. I guess that's the way she saw us. The norm is one guy carrying the whole show but it wasn't like that.'[14] The truth of his analysis is evident. This is common practice in the record industry. One or, at the most, two highlighted individuals within a band are easier to market to media that demand simple, quick packages and a public that is prone to confusion. With hindsight, it is possible to see an artistic component to the split. With a few notable exceptions, such as Spoonie Gee and Lovebug Starski, the majority of early rappers worked in groups, alternating lines, adding comment to solos, contrasting individual vocal styles and personality traits, using call and response, all rapping together for choruses. While the individual soloed, the rest of the group gave support. Through this method, a collective idealism that permeated the culture of hip-hop, rappers evolved a means of structuring their music. For better or worse, 'The Message' put forward a strong case for the dissolution of this democratic approach (though many groups have since developed rap's collective approach in extremely interesting directions, e.g. Public Enemy, Beastie Boys, NWA, Wu-Tang Clan). As the possibilities of a more focused form of self-expression became apparent, a number of influential stylists emerged. Melle Mel was one of these, along with L L Cool J, Rammelzee, Rakim, Roxanne Shante and Ice Cube. Since the individual rapper did not have to answer to the group, or squeeze personally meaningful and carefully crafted lyrics into unsympathetic, overcrowded texts, personal idiosyncrasies and literary influences could be explored more fully in this new context. In the ascendant Los Angeles scene, for example, Ice-T claimed that his lyrics were influenced not only by his own early delinquency but by the autobiographical writings of Robert Beck, better known as Iceberg Slim, and the black crime fiction of Donald Goines, author of *Street Players, Dope Fiend, Daddy Cool* and *Black Gangster* . The legacy of this approach can be heard in so-called Gangsta rap recordings like Snoop Doggy Dog's 'Murder Was the Case', which depict incidents of violence with the methodology of crime fiction and cinema: sound effects, quasi-film music. It surfaces in lyrics such as 'Pumping on my chest and I'm screaming, I stop breathing, damn, I see demons, dear God, I wonder can you save me, I can't die, my woman's 'bout to have my baby'.

Opponents of the content of Gangsta rap lyrics have argued that they inspire violent crime, misogyny and profane language. Although this debate lies outside the scope of this essay, being a broader question of the effects of art on behaviour, the controversy of language usage in rap is directly relevant. As John Baugh observed in *Black Street Speech,*

> My years of recording in Los Angeles, Philadelphia, Chicago, and Texas have taught me that many people are emotionally involved with the topic of black American dialects. Some people argue that a non-standard dialect is essential to cultural identity, while others see vernacular black speech as an impediment to success. A few even argue for both positions at the same time – as being complementary.[15]

The origins of hip-hop, prior to 1979 when the first rap singles were released, lay outside the conventions and strictures of entertainment industry practice. Rap language reflected the speech patterns and aspirational imagery of youthful writers with few resources other than their own creativity and drive to succeed. From this perspective, hip-hop has played a significant role in the general acceptance of black dialect and African-American oral culture. Appreciated as a rich and diverse, if highly controversial, means of expression, rap now communicates meaning on a global, rather than local, scale. What was once specific (ironically an expression of increasing American cultural dominance throughout much of the world yet, within America, a marginalised aspect of that same culture) had become a vehicle for translation. It is to be found not only in countries that accepted varying degrees of Americanisation and shared language fluency, such as Britain, Germany and Holland, but, more surprisingly, in Japan, Thailand, Africa, Hong Kong and all points north, south, east and west.[16]

5 Jazz singing: the first hundred years

JOHN POTTER

Most jazz historians begin with an attempt to define the subject, and just as you think you have stumbled on an author who has finally got it right, you realise that there are so many exceptions that the exercise is futile. There is no general agreement on the derivation of the term and even jazz singers find it very hard to define the word except in terms of itself ('I am a jazz singer. I sing jazz. I am a jazz singer.').[1] Jazz means a certain sort of repertoire: the historical accretion of songs and tunes over the course of the twentieth century has created a body of musical material that is categorised loosely as jazz. Jazz is also a particular set of expressive skills and styles that are brought to bear on this repertoire, a feeling and a freedom to create as well as simply to interpret. A significant element of this is, or may be, improvisation. Although for many improvisation is a defining characteristic of the music, it is perfectly possible to have a kind of jazz without it. Frank Sinatra and Ella Fitzgerald, among others, sang and recorded swathes of what has come to be called the Great American Songbook, often faithfully reproducing the composers' and arrangers' scores with little or no improvisation. Swing is another element that many would consider crucial to most jazz, yet some singers found under 'jazz' in record shops (Astrud Gilberto comes to mind) are not usually associated with the term. Dave Brubeck's definition comes closer than some:

> What is jazz? When there is not complete freedom of the soloist, it ceases to be jazz. Jazz is about the only form of art existing today in which there is this freedom of the individual without the loss of group contact.[2]

This is only a partial definition, but Brubeck has articulated one of the great jazz truths: soloists (when playing a jazz repertoire) can take what freedoms they want and expect to be backed up by their fellow musicians. So Ella Fitzgerald *can* sing Cole Porter, Gershwin and Arlen straight, but she doesn't *have* to. At its most serious, jazz is musicians' music, that can happen whether people want to listen to it or not. As Branford Marsalis eloquently put it, 'I'm used to playin' music no one wants to hear . . .'.[3]

Jazz histories are often lists of great performers, stories of who was influenced by whom, huge and colourful personalities who left behind recorded remnants of themselves for us to ruminate over.[4] Like all popular music forms, jazz changes over time as a result of a complicated interaction of musical and sociological factors. Seen with the broad sweep of hindsight, the beginnings of jazz seem inextricably linked to the musical expression of the social realities created by racial inequality in the USA. This is of course only background noise to the actual music, which was largely to do with escapism, dance and generally having a good time, often against the odds. For the musicians it was a secret world in which they could freely interact with each other, bypassing the often grim practicalities of real life, creating improvised forms within given song structures. The commercial success of the late 1920s and 1930s meant that jazz never really established a socio-political agenda, and there is something fundamentally escapist about the concept of 'swing', that intangible ingredient that separates off jazz musicians from other members of the human race. Swing is both of the body and of the mind: for singers it means a uniquely vibrant way of enunciating text, a way of obliquely relating syllables to underlying pulse in an almost physical way while communicating in a purely cerebral fashion with fellow musicians.[5] For audiences it can produce compulsive dance rhythms or maudlin sentimentality and introspection. It tends not to be a good vehicle for the more obvious expression of serious subjects (and many jazz instrumentalists are often reluctant to communicate directly with an audience at all).

In this short essay it is not possible to give more than a flavour of a fascinating and complex subject. Jazz made it into the mainstream thanks to Armstrong and Crosby, and evolved in several distinct but overlapping phases to become the most vital force in popular music in the first half of the twentieth century. Post-Crosby, the bands of the swing era provided opportunities for a generation of women singers. Parallel with this came the male 'crooners', culminating in Frank Sinatra. Even as Sinatra was taking this music to its apogee, post-War uncertainty and the urgent radicalism of hard bop were questioning its very roots. Both the traditional and avant-garde were rejected by the rock 'n' roll generation, and only in recent years has jazz singing begun to find a new incarnation for itself, drawing elemental historical threads together to begin a new synthesis. But it all began with Louis Armstrong...

Louis Armstrong's position as one of the foremost trumpeters of the twentieth century, together with his success late in life with some very ordinary pop tunes, has tended to overshadow his essential contribution to the evolution of jazz singing. By the end of the 1920s Armstrong had integrated his trumpet playing and his singing into one creative medium, and listening to the recordings it is often impossible to say whether he is 'singing like a horn' or playing like a singer. Out of the multitude of musics (especially instrumental music) that coalesced into jazz, he was able to fashion a singing that was very close to his speech. Some of the early blues singers used a similar technique but many more were 'shouters' who, before the widespread use of amplification, depended on what were in effect elements of conventional 'classical' singing technique to make themselves heard. The so-called 'Classic Blues singers' – Ma Rainey, Bessie Smith, Ida Cox and Ada Brown, for example – had powerful voices characterised by plenty of vibrato and a solid breathing technique. If they looked to vocal role models, it was presumably something of European origin that they had in mind. Louis had no use for these conventions, and his singing removed any residual 'classical' tendencies from popular singing, making it ultimately susceptible to swing in the same way as instrumental music. Swing is a manipulation of tempo, working between the beats. A speech-like shaping of syllables, words and phrases is far more likely to facilitate it than the sustained and cultured tone of a conventional singer. There is a subtle flexibility in everything Armstrong sang, which gives life to the lyrics while grounding the vocals in the instrumental rhythmic texture surrounding them. He showed that being a horn player or a singer were not so very different from each other, and that the basic requirements of singing were to do with feel and personality.

Armstrong's legacy is not simply a technical one, of course. His early recorded repertoire ranges from comic songs that are probably best forgotten, to some powerful blues singing ('I'm not rough') and his strangely liquid scat. He probably did not invent scat singing, as has sometimes been claimed, but his 'Heebie Jeebies' of 1926 is the first recorded example. Armstrong said he resorted to wordless vocalising because he dropped the music during the recording, and the great stir 'Heebie Jeebies' caused among his contemporaries suggests that scatting was at least unusual at this time.[6] He developed the style further with the 1928 'Basin Street Blues' and 'Squeeze me', allowing himself the same improvisational freedom as if he were playing his instrument. Many singers took up scatting, and it became the major opportunity for them to improvise as though they were horns without simply being pastiche instruments. Leo Watson took the art to a new level when he introduced quotation and even spontaneous story-telling into his scat breaks, before Ella Fitzgerald took the world by storm with her dazzling vocal gymnastics. Louis Armstrong first brought scat into the public domain, and as with his basic singing style, made it possible for others to take it somewhere else.[7]

An equally significant aspect of Louis Armstrong's singing is the influence it had on Bing Crosby. Crosby is today better known for his film roles and his middle of the road crooning than for the revolutionary impact he, too, had on the early history of jazz singing. Crosby's first recordings with the Whiteman band during the 1920s reveal his singing to be little different from the mannered and superficial style of his (white) contemporaries. By the early 1930s the stylised vibrato was gone, as he learned to apply the 'natural' Armstrong technique to his relationship with the microphone. The result was a harder, more committed sound which demonstrated that you did not have to be a black man to sing authentic jazz. Crosby could improvise effortless scat ('Sweet Georgia Brown') and deliver an authoritative blues ('St Louis Blues'), refining the Armstrong spontaneity into something both more astringent and smooth. Crosby's stylistic development and his friendship with Armstrong were crucial factors in creating the jazz vocal sound that would be exploited commercially beyond the black community, and which is in essence still with us today.[8] Popular singing style moved in the space of a generation from sub-classical to speech-related jazz, a 'race music', which Crosby converted to the natural style for popular song regardless of the colour of singers or audiences. Without a clear break from the vestiges of nineteenth-century singing, the history of vocal jazz might have taken a completely different turn (perhaps giving us 'classical crossover artistes' several generations ahead of time).

Crosby continued to dominate jazz singing well into the post-War period, with successful singers such as Dean Martin, Mel Tormé, Billy Eckstine and Perry Como very much in the same mould. One of the few to be inspired by Crosby, but to use his style as a basis for one of his own, was Frank Sinatra, who began life as a big band singer with Harry James and Tommy Dorsey but quickly outgrew them to become the outstanding jazz voice of the century. Sinatra's singing is different from Crosby's both in style and in technique. He irons out Crosby's bending syncopations to produce a legato line that classical singers would be perfectly familiar with. This requires a 'classical' breathing technique to sustain it, and Sinatra was known to refer to his technique as *bel canto*. What prevents Sinatra from crossing the border that separates him from a classical light baritone is the relationship of tone-colour to text. Sinatra rarely tries to make a beautiful sound for its own sake (he just leaves that to his 'natural' voice): delivering the lyrics is always his first priority. Although keen for people to know that there was considerable craft behind his art he had little time for classical music (listen to his 1947 *Don Giovanni* duet), yet more than any other singer (except perhaps Ella Fitzgerald) he was responsible for a canon of work that he recycled in much the same way as a classical Lieder singer homes in on a fairly limited repertoire. A great deal of Sinatra's repertoire dates from the decade before the Second World War, songs such as 'Night and Day' and 'My Funny Valentine' becoming standards during the 1950s.

If Armstrong, Crosby and Sinatra provided models for male jazz singers to follow, then many female singers even as late as the 1960s looked to Billie Holiday as their major influence. The big band era produced scores of 'canaries' who followed in the footsteps of Mildred Bailey, Connee Boswell and Lee Wiley after their initial success in the early 1930s. Holiday, too, probably expected to become a big band singer, but her early experiences with Count Basie and Artie Shaw in 1937 and 1938 were not happy (especially being the only black person in the all-white Shaw band). Her image from the start was the very epitome of human frailty and her singing seems to have an umbilical connection to the curious public intimacy of the club. The deprivations of her background became synonymous with her songs, early experience of orphanages, prison, rape and prostitution, alcohol and drug abuse fuelling the legend from which the singer emerged. Her early influences were Armstrong, Bessie Smith and Ethel Waters,[9] yet like all truly great singers she seems to have sprung from nowhere. Her collaboration with saxophonist Lester Young produced only a few hours of recorded material, but is recognised as one of the most remarkable musical relationships in jazz. These songs have been pored over at length by every writer on the music of this period, and there is little point in adding to the thousands of words that attempt to express the inexpressible; the recordings are there for all to hear. For Billie Holiday the lyrics and the emotions underlying them were equal to the music. In fact, one of her trademarks was a spontaneous rewriting of the tune if she felt that by doing so her mood could better serve the meanings of the text. 'My last affair', recorded in 1937, is a good example, with only the remnants of the melody surviving her rhetoric.

The sheer musicianship of Billie Holiday, together, perhaps, with the mystique that went with the legend, inspired generations of great female singers. Some, such as Peggy Lee and Sarah Vaughan, operated on the fringes of what was accepted as jazz, others such as Anita O'Day, Abbey Lincoln, Carmen McRae and Betty Carter were centred in the jazz idiom. This is certainly not an exclusive list, and jazz fans will argue at length about their favourite singers. Perhaps the most significant of all post-Holiday singers is Ella Fitzgerald. She not only took on the American Songbook, but she also took scatting into realms that would have been unimaginable to her predecessors. The famous 'Flying Home', which first appeared in 1945, became a vehicle for extended improvisation and quotation, with snatches of a dozen or more different songs dovetailing in and out. Ella very rarely sang the same thing twice, and each of the many versions of 'Flying Home', though they share a similar tempo, is a unique mini-anthology. Her control over her material is almost miraculous and matches that of the best instrumentalists, a staggering achievement considering that the equivalent of the instrumentalist's finger dexterity, embouchure and articulation happen virtually invisibly in the few centimetres between larynx and lips. Unsurprisingly, she was one of the few singers from the swing era to grapple with bebop, with an unmatched understanding of high-speed chord changes.

The other area of virtuosity in vocal jazz is the movement known as vocalese. This is the practice of putting words to a pre-existing instrumental improvisation, which began in the 1940s but became fashionable after King Pleasure had a hit with his texted version of Charlie Parker's 'Parker's Mood' in 1952. The art of vocalese is in matching syllables to notes in such a way that what was an improvisation becomes a coherent narrative. It is often very clever, but the creativity is limited to devising lyrics to fit existing tunes and often appears to be simply cleverness for its own sake. Nevertheless, the recordings by Lambert, Hendricks and Ross from the mid-1950s onwards are undoubtedly impressive, and the more recent Manhattan Transfer version of 'Birdland' at least gives the singers a chance to have a go at a great tune that would otherwise be denied them.

Jazz fans will argue indefinitely about who swings and who doesn't, and will often write off singers who are not thought to possess the magic ingredient. But the exclusiveness of swing can cocoon jazz (and its fans) in a ghetto of its own making, discouraging singers from directly addressing topics outside a narrow agenda. The vocalese movement dealt on the whole with fairly trivial subjects, concerned with the projection of sheer speed, text as scat, virtuosity as narrative. A lot of it certainly swings. Virtuosity can be put to much more serious use, as in Cleo Laine's singing of John Dankworth's settings of Shakespeare and a host of other literary figures. There have been singers who have happily sacrificed swing for directness. Nina Simone is a case in point. Her connection with the civil rights movement is well-known. She undoubtedly *can* swing a love song or dance tune with the best of them (try 'My baby just cares for me', from her first Bethlehem album) but her enormous reserves of passion and technique can also express feelings that take her audiences way beyond the conventional jazz habitat. In 'Black is the colour', a folk song popularised by Joan Baez in the 1960s, Simone accompanies herself on the piano sounding alternately like Baez and the fruity mezzo of Janet Baker. The significance of the word 'black' is entirely new in this context, and her rendering insists on the kind of attention listeners give to a classical song recital. She can be less subtle, as in her civil rights anthems ('The king of love is dead'). These are not exactly swinging stuff, but involve a careful measuring of each word to get her point across. One of her most moving recorded performances is 'Strange fruit'. This was originally written for Billie Holiday in 1939, and is a graphic account of the sights and smells of burning flesh after a night of klan lynchings. In Holiday's canon it is unusually forthright (and actually led to her contract with Commodore, ARC having refused to record it). Holiday generally sang it accompanied only by a piano (irritating arpeggios from a compulsive doodler on the live album) where it sat uneasily beside even her autobiographically introspective numbers. She often said that some songs were impossible to sing, and perhaps 'Strange Fruit' was one of those. Nina Simone's version hits you in the face. It sounds as though she is actually looking at the scene; Holiday, despite her belief in the song and her attempts to engage with the horror of it, never leaves the jazz club (where we've heard too many songs about her own problems, perhaps). Simone's piano playing is sparse, as though she can hardly bring herself to touch the instrument, but her singing is among the most powerful performances of her entire output (and for me, her performance of this song, with its searingly passionate treatment of almost unbearable subject matter, is one of the most moving performances on record of anything). Nina Simone did not like to think of her music as jazz (a 'white' term), and the many facets to her music certainly make categorising it even more pointless than usual.

Cassandra Wilson's 'Strange fruit' begins with the chilling striking of a match. She presumably knew the paradigms, but there is no sign of any influence in her totally original version. De-tuned guitar and bi-tonal trumpet stab at each other over an agitated double-time bass. She outlines the text with an ironic coolness, and the instrumentation fills in the detail. Cassandra Wilson's singing actually swings, and you are left with the feeling that this too is ironic, an incredibly sophisticated rhetorical device which could commit the history of jazz singing to a very serious future. The album of which this is the first track, *New Moon Daughter,* is full of such reinventions, taking a huge range of styles as source material, ranging from the blues of Son House to such apparently unpromising songs as the Monkees 'Last Train to Clarksville'. The singer transforms them all, intimating that no past or present popular music need be outside the jazz frame. A similarly dynamic approach to renewal is found in the work of Dianne Reeves. Her background, growing up amid the racial upheavals of 1960s Denver listening to Sarah Vaughan, Nina Simone and Stevie Wonder, gave her something to sing about. Later exposure to Harry Belafonte and Joan Armatrading, rock and fusion, enabled her to incorporate even more diverse elements into her maturing style. The live album *New Morning*, recorded at the Parisian jazz club of that name in 1997, shows her at her best. She has an obvious command of her material, teasing the audience à la Betty Carter with hints at what is to come before setting off on something that may not have originated in the jazz canon at all (Joni Mitchell's 'Both sides now', for example).

There are noticeably fewer male jazz singers with anything new to say. The industry has exercised itself from time to time over a successor to Sinatra (Harry Connick, for example, a fine singer and pianist who seems destined to remain in the dead master's shadow). The one really original male voice to emerge in the 1980s was that of Bobby McFerrin. McFerrin's first appearance on record was on Vocal Summit's *Sorrow is Not For Ever – Love Is* of 1982. This is remarkable for McFerrin's duetting with himself and with Polish virtuosa Urszula Dudziak (not to mention the contributions of Jeanne Lee, Jan Clayton and Lauren Newton). On his subsequent solo albums he achieves multi-layered textures by rapid switching in and out of falsetto, and using his chest as a resonator, supporting an inventory of mouth sounds that manages to avoid the banal (mostly) and even to swing.

The new *fin-de-siècle* generation of jazz singers is very much a female, post-feminist one, singers born to a far more comfortable life than many of their predecessors. No one would want to experience Billie Holiday's childhood in order to become a jazz singer, and it is no longer possible to live the jazz life in the sense that Charlie Parker meant when he famously said 'If you don't live it, it won't come out of your horn'.[10] But just as novelists can write intuitively about things they have never experienced, so it should be possible for the music to evolve without actually killing those who do it. There are probably two evolutionary paths that jazz singing can take. One is a sentimental one, a continuous return to the legitimising songbook of old, a fantasy land where the smoke and the drink achieve a kind of retrospective sanitised glamour. The other is the path of reinvention. This means not only new original material but also the incorporation of existing music into the jazz habitat, a process similar to that which happened with the great songs of the past but bypassing the period sentimentality. It also gives to jazz the possibility of a kind of timelessness commentary or discourse. The maturing and fragmenting of rock has left a space for jazz singers to explore, and this is the world inhabited by Cassandra Wilson, Dianne Reeves, Bobby McFerrin, and even those on the periphery of jazz such as Meredith Monk and the various unclassifiable singers to be found on labels such as ECM. Both pathways have, of course, been fundamental to jazz since soon after its beginnings. There will probably never again be a mass market for this enthralling music, but for singers there will still be expressive possibilities that go beyond the immediacy of rock or the constraints of opera for a long time to come.

PART TWO

The voice in the theatre

6 Stage and screen entertainers in the twentieth century

STEPHEN BANFIELD

The field and the evidence

The performance practice of the twentieth century's singing entertainers is a vital component of the mass culture of its period, and it cries out to be analysed and interpreted. How should it be categorised alongside other types of singing, and how and why has it undergone such enormous changes? There is almost no literature on the subject. Pleasants[1] deals with the rise of modern popular singing from one particular standpoint, that of its opposition to classical singing, and Osborne[2] takes a sustained critical look at the Broadway 'belt', again from the same viewpoint, though, unlike Pleasants, with negative rather than positive intent. Yet neither author has the opportunity to develop a more neutral historical investigation comprehensively based on evidence from primary and secondary source material, in other words in the 'early music' terms that Robert Philip[3] pioneered for classical orchestral music of the first half of the twentieth century.

Three types of source material constitute the evidence for performance practice, its identity and changes. The first and most important is recordings. The second is film (plus TV and video footage), for although the musical content of a film can be isolated as its soundtrack recording, the visual element is also significant in analysing a singer's performance practice (though this is beyond the scope of this chapter). The third type of evidence is that of written and spoken documentation: correspondence, production files and promptbooks, published and unpublished memoirs and other monographs, interviews, press reviews, song manuscripts and dance plots.

In the Discography at the end of this chapter a sample of historical recordings has been chosen in the form of a sheaf of current CD anthologies. It has its limitations. The top stars – Sinatra, Madonna – are not anthologised on CD, no doubt for contractual reasons. It is also a bit thin on Hollywood and the more recent musical stage, and correspondingly top-heavy on the early side, including every known recording for the New York musical stage up to 1920 [NYS].[4] Still, the earlier the recording, the more valuable it is, potentially, in terms of pointing us towards the reconstruction of a lost past, not just of its own period.

Many of those early musical stage recordings were made by Broadway artists in London, and the first American original cast recording of a show is generally taken to be that of *Oklahoma!* (1943). Thus we have documentation of how the original *Show Boat* sounded in London in 1928 [OCR/SB/1–9 or DL/5–7] rather than in New York in 1927. This is just one example of the limitations of the evidence; another is the possible disjunction between what a song sounded like on the stage and what it sounded like in the recording studio. Before the advent of electrical recording around 1925 this disjunction is serious. The sound of theatre orchestration, generally reduced in the primitive studio (even in early musical film) to a wheezy, raucous band of winds (for example, with tuba on the bass line); the balance between singer and accompaniment; the enunciation of the text; the interdisciplinary element of movement; the tempo and energy of the song: none of these can be relied upon to tell the theatrical whole truth on disc, though one can, and must, extrapolate conclusions none the less. The same disjunction does not apply to singing on film and television, of course, where the soundtrack *is* the performance, aurally speaking. A radio broadcast from a ballroom or auditorium lies somewhere between the two (where mixing, balance and visual presence are concerned).

The first shift

If one looks for a simple model for the changes in the way English-language stage and screen entertainers sing in the course of the twentieth century, the answer must be that there are two traditions or considerations in opposition and that one gives way to the other for specific reasons, at particular nodal points, and in precise ways as time goes on. Exactly what is in opposition to what, the identity of the combatant that ultimately loses out, is less easy to assert, however. For Osborne it is the technically pure, secure, trained, 'integrated' use of the singing voice giving way to the Broadway belt. He hinges his argument on the female show voice and locates the shift in the 1940s, with Ethel Merman's Annie Oakley in *Annie Get Your Gun* (1946), and Celeste Holm's Ado Annie in the 1943 *Oklahoma!* (once again). Pleasants sees the shift as being from classical to popular singing, the latter closer to opera's original expressive premises, swinging back towards the primacy of text as classical singing had moved too far away from it in the nineteenth century. Popular singing, he argues, is propelled by an African-American model already present as parody in much nineteenth-century song and dance, thereafter at face (rather than blackface) value rapidly dominating the USA

entertainment industry from the early 1920s onwards because of successful black musical theatre (*Shuffle Along*, 1921), the invention of radio and
the rise of 'race' records.

Both theories involve replacing an elite with a vernacular or folk voice,
but for them to be reconciled necessitates a deeper layer of distinction,
not just between (culturally) 'high' and 'low' musical voices but between
the actorly truth of speech and the singerly enchantment of song. The fact
that this last distinction is obvious even on the earliest batch of musical
theatre recordings suggests that there had long before 1890 been a bipolar
field of allure, profession and technique on the musical stage. The vast
bulk of the NYS recordings points between 1890 and 1920 to only two
types of musical entertainer: comedians and singers. The subsequent
accommodation between the two has been an attempt to replace or
underpin parody with wit, affection, and the rhetoric and sentiment of
the bourgeois comedy of manners, perhaps because opera lost its hold on
these from Rossini onwards. Neither Pleasants nor Osborne deals with
the further shift in the musical theatre to the modern show voice with pop
or rock component, but this second, late twentieth-century shift might be
attributable to a reverse move to exit the bourgeois field of comedy and
sentiment and re-enter the realms of melodrama, raw parody and bur-
lesque with an admixture of agitprop.

The female belt and its precursors

Osborne's 'belt' thesis acts as a useful initial pivot. He writes, of the
mythology of Holm's *Oklahoma!* audition, 'how, with a background of
traditional vocal training',

> she sang . . . Schubert's 'To music' . . . how excited [Richard Rodgers was] to
> discover Holm's trained voice; how he then asked her if she could sing
> something in a 'completely untrained voice, like a kid'; how Holm allowed as
> how she could hog-call, and did . . . and how Rodgers thought that was terrific
> and forthwith cast her (though with constant admonitions of 'louder!' during
> the rehearsal period) as Ado Annie.[5]

He proceeds to analyse the 'extremely uncomplicated' sound that resulted
in 'I cain't say no' [OCR/O/5]:

> It has no audible vibrato . . . and does not alter in texture over the song's
> restricted compass. It grows weak at the bottom and loud toward the top, and
> does not give the impression that the singer has any choice in this matter.
> Though the tops of the higher phrases give the impression of being 'high', we
> note that they fall only in the area of B and C above middle C – high for a male

voice, but only in the very center of a developed female one. The technique preserves the phonetically open vowels and constrictive diphthongs of the character's dialect, without any of the rounding that a 'cultivated' singer would observe above the register break around E [e^1] or F [f^1]. Indeed, we observe that a thin but definite chest co-ordination has been made to stretch upward (with the expectable impression of an impending 'snap' toward the top) for the entire compass of the song, which lies between comfortable tenor and contralto tessituras, but is closer to the former.

And that is precisely the nature of the belt: it is an attempt to extend the normally 'short' female chest register upward. A fifth or sixth can be incorporated in this fashion, by driving the co-ordination at a high intensity and in a shallow adjustment . . . When secure, the belt produces an edgy, driving sound. Because of the tension involved in holding the position, vocal qualities associated with relaxation (vibrato, ability to sing at less than full intensity), as well as all those associated with the integrated head register it sends packing (sweetness of tone, ductility in phrasing, flexibility of movement), are closed out. There is no such thing as a quiet belt, or a beautiful one.[6]

Osborne exaggerates his argument about register, for Holm's basic compass in 'I cain't say no' is c^1 to c^2, with an upward chromatic extension to $c\#^2$ and d^2 at the climax, skilfully if tensely engineered by both Rodgers and Hammerstein (whose words at that point in the second refrain are 'something inside of me snaps'). Yet he is right about how high the belt sounds and how low it really is.

Slightly earlier Judy Garland pioneered a film belt. It is closer to a male croon in its intimacy (because it is able to rely on the microphone where theatrical performers were still managing without it), and certainly does not eschew vibrato, which is wider, slower, more continuous and more sensuous than that of most, if not all, of the recorded female entertainers who preceded her. But it still sounds brazen and climactic as low as a^1. She goes above this to b^1 in 'Texas tornado' of 1936 [SSR/II/9] but not in 'The trolley song' of 1944 [SSR/II/16], where her range, perfectly catered for in Roger Edens's arrangement, is $g\#–a^1$.

As for Merman, her belting 'top' C (i.e. c^2), well privileged in 'Some people' (1959 [SSR/III/14]), was famous as early as 1930, when it was held as a dominant pedal for six bars at a time in the second refrain of 'I got rhythm' from *Girl Crazy* (recorded in 1947 on AMT/I/18). The publication of this song a fourth higher, in B♭ major, may well indicate that Gershwin wrote it expecting a lyric soprano or mezzo rendition, standard into the 1930s even for sultry diegetic spots in Broadway shows (compare Helen Morgan's fragile, rapid-vibrato 'Can't help lovin' dat man' recording of 1928 [SSR/I/16, AMT/I/14], soaring effortlessly to g^2 but failing on the low $c♭^1$; Lonette McKee's 1994 recording [SSR/IV/18] is pitched as much as a fifth lower). Merman's legendary vocal power tailed off rapidly above c^2, like that of Bernadette Peters above b^1, and Irving Berlin expertly fused dramatic situation and expediency in leaving her out of the reckoning on the solo d^2s in the third refrain of 'There's no business like show business' [AMT/II/20 (1966 revival)], even with a ten-note scale up to them. Her brassy tone was not unprecedented even in 1930, and minus the vibrato, of which she uses a fair amount, something similarly forward may be heard from white singers over at least the preceding decade, but in the context of female close-harmony groups such as the Duncan Sisters and the Boswell Sisters, the former acting and sounding southern, the latter genuinely so. To trace the belt back to the pseudo-southern may be to uncover the original appearance of an American accent in the sung voice, which seems therefore to have entered vernacular performance practice (it is still not acceptable for art music performance) as a matter of regional parody. It was not only a matter of regional parody, however, but of racial parody too: with the pseudo-southern went the pseudo-black, often in blackface make-up. This is to say that the belt originated in the coon song as sung by the coon shouter, a type of white female vaudeville star (such as May Irwin). The touchstone of this historical moment is superbly preserved: Stella Mayhew's show-stopping 'Fifty-seven ways to catch a man', recorded in 1910 [NYS/I/iii/3]. Her advice is couched in a parlando strophic frame, forcefully enunciated and with a crystal-clear diction that is still largely Anglicised (with hard 't's) but not entirely so, for her plagal[7] F major range (c^1–c^2), of a coarse contralto quality on the low dominants but rising to squeaks for some of the more spoken rhetoric, privileges a southern diphthong mouthing of 'plan' and 'man' on the long a^1s. These southern-belt moments foreshadow the first of her two virtuosic ethnic cameos in the song, an episode in which, although entirely spoken, the stance and vocality of the southern black mama capturing her feckless dandy are fixed. Presumably there is a female transference of minstrelsy humour at work here, but any attempt to project its performance style backwards to the unrecorded hinterland of the all-male minstrel show would be risky.

The male comic

If the female comedy stars found ways of singing when they needed or wished to, the male ones avoided the attempt as much as possible, drawing attention instead either to dandified charm or uncoordinated eccentricity, or a mixture of the two. This meant vast swathes of parlando, or the carrying of a melodic line, somewhere between baritone and tenor in range, with flattened tone, no sostenuto and very little vibrato, an approach probably meant to demonstrate that a dandy need not be effeminate, and evident as late as Fred Astaire's films of the 1930s and 1940s before descending to the mid twentieth-century baritone of Professor Higgins and King Arthur – that is, of Rex Harrison in 'I've grown accustomed to her face' [UB/I/11, 1956] and Richard Burton in 'Camelot' [UB/I/19, 1960]. Harrison's performance is almost entirely spoken, Burton's sung to a surprising extent but still founded on parlando, not for the notes, which both can sing when they want to, but for the phrasing, since neither has a singer's breath control and uses, instead, the more flexible rhetoric of speech for rubato and the inflection of just a few syllables at a time.

David Van Leer[8] correctly points out that Harrison's and Burton's stage appearances in 'book' musicals were the result of pop music and dramatic entertainment having gone their separate ways with the rock revolution of the 1950s: musicals could no longer, by and large, incorporate the current singing stars and had to make their money by billing 'straight' actors and filmstars instead, in plausibly well-made book roles. But his historical reasoning is applied to the women as well as the men – 'King Arthur and Sally Bowles [in *Cabaret*, 1966] need only serviceable voices' – whereas Ethan Mordden's observation, in a well-focused study of the Broadway 'star comic' in the 1920s, that 'there were no singing male stars in the musical then, except . . . Chauncey Olcott',[9] implies as corollary that the erotic attraction of male singing had in any case long been a cultural liability and could only be channelled for mass consumption under certain conditions. Comics and dandies, conversely, there would always be.

However, almost all of the male comedians – from George Grossmith junior and Joseph Coyne to Noël Coward and including Astaire in his early partnership with his older sister Adele – were paired with real sopranos. Two examples of this are furnished by Coyne's 'I want to be happy' [AMI/I/11] and Jack Hulbert's 'Here in your arms' [OCR/LL/21, 1927], the former with Binnie Hale, the latter with Phyllis Dare, both sporting pure, piercing, quick-vibrato tone warbling up to g^2, trained breath control, faultless English pronunciation, and excellent intonation. So the allure of verbal romantic comedy in the one sex was complementary to the allure of enchantment – in its literal sense of singing – in the other. It was not, however, a gender relation easily reversed, at this or any later point in the history of singing entertainment, for belters' moments have tended to be commanding, and perhaps that is one of the things that makes the culminatory duet of Dot and George (Bernadette Peters and Mandy Patinkin), 'Move on', in Sondheim's *Sunday in the Park with George* [OCR/SPG/15, 1984] such a big deal, when a singing male and a belting female achieve fusion in moments of parallel thirds and canon at the unison rather than the octave and the melodic climax goes to the man (Patinkin's octave leap to g^1).

Cantorial singing

Patinkin can sing his heart out because he represents one of four oppressed, exiled or manufactured male types permitted and indeed expected to do so when the dominating twentieth-century culture requires of it a song: the Jew, the Negro, the crooning toyboy, and the sentimental Irish tenor. This last died out shortly after Olcott, for whatever reason, and need not concern us further. The Negro voice, however, exacts a look at Bert Williams. Operating earlier in his career with George Walker, he was a phenomenally successful black vaudeville comedian. The resonance of his lugubrious speaking voice, with its impeccably clear diction, should have allowed a deeper emotional level to shine through the shiftless, hen-pecked stereotype at which he excelled. But he undercut this possibility, in four ways. First, his performances were 90 per cent parlando, at least on record. Nevertheless, it was his command of this – with a very modern sense of rubato phrasing, casual breathing and general timing – that made him outstanding and, presumably, influential on later modes of confidential song, whether spoken, crooned or belted. Second, when he did choose to modulate his broad range of pitch inflection into singing, it was at the upper, acoustically shallower, end of his voice, heady and jerky and of a caricature personality with 'coon' vowels (this can be heard in the final stanza of 'Borrow from me' [NYS/II/iii/21], 1913). Third, he avoided any hint of vibrato in the bulk of his recordings. Finally, he employed, and imitated, glissando trombone in his orchestral accompaniments (hear his signature tune, 'Nobody', recorded in 1906 [NYS/I/iii/14], or 'Constantly' [NYS/II/ii/6]). Thus he was never quite linked with the profound nobility of Paul Robeson. If Williams leads anywhere, it is to Sportin' Life rather than Porgy, to Cab Calloway and Armstrong in their personae that many felt still to be demeaning to the African-American. Nor does Noble Sissle, joint creator of *Shuffle Along*, appear to hold the key to continuity and development when he sings: one of his contemporary recorded numbers from the show, 'Love will find a way' [SSR/I/13], has nothing aurally black about it at all, but perpetuates old-fashioned parlour baritone decorum, curiously riding Eubie Blake's novelty piano accompaniment. Another, 'Baltimore buzz' [AMT/I/8], does replicate Williams's interactive portamento but lacks his southern drawl and sports a rather clipped northern American accent, closer to the white dandy's cultural space.

It is therefore not immediately clear how black, as opposed to black-face, singing transforms the sound and meaning of stage entertainment. Much clearer is the fact that (male) cantorial singing does so on a massive scale and in a permanent way. The parable is headlined by Jolson's first talking film, *The Jazz Singer* of 1927: Jewish cantor's son turns his God-given singing talent to secular stage entertainment. Three recorded Jewish singers epitomise the cantorial stage tradition that Patinkin perpetuates: Irving Berlin, Eddie Cantor and Jolson himself. The model is a voice on the pitch border between baritone and tenor, highly flexible in register and rhetoric but unifying these by maintaining an intimate lyrical intensity over a concentrated tessitura rather than by long-line phrasing and disguising of breaks. Legato is achieved in short spans but all trace of Italianate articulation has gone. Parlando is still frequently resorted to but as a wise-cracking respite from singing, not vice versa as with Williams, whose lazy, shambling instrumental accompaniment is replaced by the ragtime rhythms that drive the whole performance into a more frenetic gear.

All three men were of Russian parentage, Berlin and Jolson being born in the old country. Jolson, whose own story was the *Jazz Singer* plot, and Berlin had fathers who were cantors, while Eddie Cantor took the word for the deed when, like the other two, he changed his name. In the synagogue the cantorial voice weeps to God. In the theatre it cries tears of sorrow or laughter to its mother, its lover, its fellows; deprecatingly or challengingly to itself. Thus emerged a new, direct emotionality on the entertainment stage and screen, arguably the single most important factor in defining the modern musical when, in tandem with and as an emotional model for the female belt, it finally managed to throw off the comedian's motley and with the help of the auditorium microphone usurped the operatic voice, hitherto the only way of singing 'seriously' on the biggest scale.

Berlin and Cantor could never cease to be comedians when they sang, but Jolson's melodrama, doubtless borrowed from the spoken main-stream, stormed his audiences. All three voices shared certain features, Berlin's notably like Cantor's. Cantor was influenced by Jolson in his later recordings. Jolson's superstar status, and therefore the significance of what he did with his voice, can hardly be exaggerated, and two separate and highly indicative phenomena might be taken as a starting point for explanation. One is the pervasive use of the portamento upper $\hat{3}$–$\hat{1}$ vocal cadence[10] in major keys, on the downbeat, the other is the mobility of mouth, tongue and lips.

The former is as pervasive, standard and unnotated a feature of performance practice with these three singers as was the telescoped 4–3 cadence in Baroque opera recitative. Berlin can be heard doing it at the end of 'Follow the crowd' [NYS/III/i/15 (1914)]; it is not in the score. If Bert Williams perfected the humour of the title refrain, this cliché rubber-stamps its inevitability, and like Berlin with 'Follow the crowd' Cantor slurs a $\hat{3}$–$\hat{1}$ title phrase at the end of 'You'd be surprised' [SSR/I/9 (1919)], as does Jolson in 'That haunting melody' (therefore with false accentuation) [NYS/II/iii/11 (1911)] and countless other songs. The idiom is used in a limited range of keys that keeps the listener buttonholed by the voice in its upper, most eager range – C major being the most common. This major third ambit is often the basic set of pitch coordinates for the engagingly sung portions of the song. It lends a chant-like quality to an emotionally charged vocal line, and Dick Powell's high minor-key version of it (a^1–$f\sharp^1$) as he holds up a glass ritualistically in the last solo vocal notes of the film (and song) *42nd Street* is unforgettable. Sometimes Jolson similarly incorporates a portamento $\hat{7}$–$\hat{5}$, for instance at a dominant mid-point, and this is exactly what he does with the sixth and seventh notes of the 'Kol nidre' when singing real Jewish chant in the final scene of *The Jazz Singer*.

This scene also enables us to study Jolson's mouth and body language, though the results are implicit in the sound of his recordings. If you are in blackface and your mouth is a white painted ring, the expressive mobility of that ring is crucial, as with the white-gloved hands that greatly increase demonstrativeness. The mouth must be able to flatten to a smile or a frown and pass in flux from that to an open sigh or cry; there is no scope for the flattened larynx or fixed mouth, low tongue and wide throat position of the opera singer. The flexible lip shapes mean moving both the vowels and consonants around in the front of the mouth constantly, and with that seems to go a fairly constant, slower but wider vibrato than warblers of the time used, a high, forward tongue position, flattened colloquial vowels (henceforward standard for American vernacular song: 'jab' for 'job', 'dants' for 'dahnce' in 'Follow the crowd'). This is associated with a rubato approach that can bring initial consonants in early or late, thus greatly increasing the urgency of communication through vocal timing, because they are sung through in time, as are the diphthongs, rather than treated, à la *bel canto*, as points of articulation *between* time events. Try singing through the 'm' and 'n' consonants as Jolson does in 'mammy mine' and 'north' in 'Rock-a-bye your baby' [NYS/IV/ii/1 (1918)], and a resonance is set up between the nose and the throat, behind the tongue, that produces Jolson's reedy plumminess that is not vastly different in the latter-day Patinkin. And as the mouth moves, so do the hands: again the final scene of *The Jazz Singer* demonstrates the connections, for it is not afraid to show the Jewish stereotype. First we see the mother's anguished gesticulation, reaching out to God, as her husband dies; the camera cuts directly to Jolson's similar hand positions, movements and angle in the shot as he sings the 'Kol nidre'; then we have him reaching out to 'mammy' in the famous closing sequence, the outstretched hands underlining his mordents just as in the synagogue chant and furnishing the show singer's basic cue for applause ever since.

Thus it took a male Jew to liberate body language in serious singing on the entertainment stage and transform a moribund genre, the minstrel song, into a lasting model. Of course the point about the blackface mouth should also apply to female lipstick, but photographic evidence suggests that lipstick was first applied to make the musical comedy mouth demure and petite – more the visual corollary of the warbling soubrette than the belter – and that the transformation into rounded, mobile sensuousness came later. This is especially evident in the sound-film close-up and eventually in the overtly osculatory (or worse) relationship between lips and microphone that now pertains in pop singing, having passed through variety, cabaret and musical in what is essentially a mid-twentieth-century phenomenon, if one calls to mind Judy Garland, Ethel Waters and Carol Channing. You can almost *hear* Channing's lipstick in 'Before the parade passes by' [SSR/III/18, (1964)], and her 'Hello, Dolly' [UB/I/21] represents the apotheosis of Jolson's $\hat{3}$–$\hat{1}$ cadence, arguably of musical comedy presentation altogether. Singing an octave below the score, her whisky baritone belt if anything lower than Jolson's (in places the chorus boys are an octave above her), she slurs the low $\hat{3}$–$\hat{1}$ on the third and fourth notes of the tune but refrains from doing so on the high one to which the entire number repeatedly builds: the band's playout cliché has its own way of doing that.

Crooning

The male crooning tradition was established with radio in the 1920s. We have the gas shells of the First World War to thank for it if it is true that 'Whispering' Jack Smith whispered because one of them damaged a lung. A crooning pioneer, along with Rudy Vallee, his initial technique was to separate very light, heady baritone singing from an extremely low speaking growl, quite without precedent because he alternated parlando and singing, not between verses or periods, but between notes, even syllables, sliding up to singing tone from a gargle, and, as with more modern extended vocal techniques, could do so only with the agility the microphone afforded. In place by 1925–6, Smith's style can be heard in 'Miss Annabelle Lee' [GTS/5 (1928)].

Vallee's light baritone was nothing special and, unlike Smith's, involved a strongly American, rather laddish enunciation of consonants and cocky smirk on the vowels similar to Fred Astaire's (for instance, in 'This is the missus' [BBR/17, 1931]). Something in the post-War youth culture called for this new vernacular regardless of what the microphone could achieve, for Astaire began on unamplified Broadway and Vallee used a megaphone at first. Nevertheless, it was a dashing young gentleman's vocal image, the dandy finally separated from the comic because he could now whisper in your ear, and it brought a new premium to classy British tones, perhaps via Coward. Smith almost sounds British, but more suavely so than Al Bowlly (actually a South African), who retains a touch of music hall in 'The pied piper of Hamelin' [CCF/17 (1931)].

Bing Crosby's early recordings take their frivolous place in the 1920s dance band, but by 1931 he had deepened and foregrounded the crooner's expressivity and spearheaded a permanent singing revolution:

> [he] evolved a style of singing appropriate to the microphone, using it to emphasize the text rather than the tune ... and as the most popular singer of his generation prompted the definite separation of classical from popular singing. His way of seeming to talk or whisper to a melody involved singing less forcefully, passing into the head voice lower than art-song performers, singing on consonants (a practice of black singers shunned by classical artists) and the discreet use of appoggiaturas, mordents and slurs to emphasize the text.[11]

Pleasants does acknowledge Jolson's influence on Crosby, but the consonants and decorations probably come more from that specific stable than he thinks. The sound of Crosby's voice is so familiar that it is almost impossible to analyse its components, but clearly he found just the right amount of baritone resonance, initial portamento, nasal consonant, overtone-rich vibrato and sentimental rhythmic licence for remaining persuasive but not overbearing, manly but romantic, conversational yet musical, rich-toned yet not classical. The first sixteen bars of his Christmas Day 1946 broadcast of 'White Christmas' [AAWS/I/9] are a cornucopia of his performance practice. The tessitura is low, A major, a minor third below the score, its rich G♯ leading notes lower than anyone's range so far discussed in this chapter except Robeson's. The first four-bar phrase is split into one- and two-note groups, while the second, for contrast, is sung through in one breath. Berlin's plethora of evocative downbeat bisyllables ('Christmas', 'treetops', 'glisten', 'children', 'listen') is motivically unified by altering the written rhythm in each case to a Lombardic. A few syllables begin portamento ('I'm' and 'where', marking the eight-bar beginnings), but only one note is dropped altogether for a residual parlando, the $\hat{4}$ on 'to' (of 'to hear'); this is at the four-bar subdivision. The melodic climax, on b, is shaded by singing through the 'n' consonant ('onnnes'), by dotting all the rhythms of the phrase, and by adding a nonchalant triplet mordent immediately after it (there is another, connotatively, on the 'sleigh' of 'sleigh bells'). Only one rhythm is syncopated for effect, at 'in the snow'.

This was never a live theatre sound, and it created, and long sustained, a tension between the packaged croon performance and the operatic or vaudeville thrill of musical theatre. From their inception in 1934 until the mid-1960s, almost all the Oscar-winning songs in the AAWS collection [I, II and III/1–6] are presented in croon performances, largely in the glossy spirit of the film itself. Bob Hope ('Thanks for the memory' [AAWS/I/5, 1938]), Dick Haymes, Judy Garland and Johnny Mercer join Crosby as leading lights of the genre; as their successors, we might list Sinatra (analysed by Potter[12]), Mel Tormé, and many others, shading off into Ella Fitzgerald and jazz. Disney has of course traded in a comparable visual gloss from the 1930s to the present, and whether sung by a cartoon bear or as at the award ceremony by Mercer, a performance such as that of 'Zip-a-dee-doo-dah' from *Song of the South* [AAWS/II/2 (1946)] offers us the aural equivalent of the Disney characters' reassuring grins and feel-good eyes.

Classical singing

We have so far largely skirted the role of classical or operatic singing in the world of twentieth-century entertainment; yet musical theatre singing in both America and Britain was surprisingly operatic for surprisingly long. Throughout the first half of the twentieth century there was never any problem with a low- or middlebrow audience accepting a 'pure' soprano voice, though because of its lightness the operetta or musical comedy soprano, best thought of as soubrette, tended to sound higher than it was. At this point it is worth noting Rastall's formula[13] for establishing the tessitura of a vocal part by ascertaining its pitch centre of gravity (PCG). A soprano in *Show Boat* is not the same thing as a soprano in *Porgy and Bess*, for the latter, despite the weighty associations its female roles may produce, deals with real (i.e. high) operatic registers: the first solo vocal note in the score, Clara's in 'Summertime', is $f\sharp^2$. An entry would never be this high in a musical, and despite ranging higher (to g^2), Magnolia's tessitura in 'Make-believe' is lower, its PCG, b^1, nearly a tone below 'Summertime''s ($c\sharp^2$).

Old-fashioned English-language operetta singing remained popular and accepted both on Broadway and in the West End until well after the Second World War. *Show Boat* itself in the 1928 London recordings sounds like a heady confection from old Vienna, and only four years before *Oklahoma!*, Kern and Hammerstein in *Very Warm for May* were purveying an Epicurean schmaltz, however satirically, that makes Ivor Novello's contemporaneous Drury Lane extravaganzas sound restrained by comparison. (Compare the coloratura soprano Hollace Shaw's 'All the things you are' [OCR/VWM/2] with Mary Ellis's 'Fold your wings' or Olive Gilbert's superb 'Why is there ever goodbye?' [DL/15 and 18].) Nevertheless, the taste watershed of the Second World War demanded a purge of camp. Preceded as this was in America by the New Deal's and Hollywood's growing dictates of folk realism, it is easy to see where *Oklahoma!* came from; yet, Holm's belt apart, most of the singing in *Oklahoma!* and its successor *Carousel* (1945) represents no more than what happens when an American accent is added to classical voices – acceptably mundane voices, that is, namely baritone and mezzo soprano. Alfred Drake in *Oklahoma!* and John Raitt in *Carousel* are giants of American musical theatre singing because of their command of this juncture. Both sing throughout with sufficient by way of American consonants and vowels to sound vernacular yet without sacrificing depth of chest tone. The greatest dividend paid is in the perfectly smooth transition from speech to song achieved by Raitt in the *Carousel* bench scene, famous for its compositional fluidity in this regard. (The moment to study comes at 2′07″ in 'If I loved you' [OCR/C/3 or UB/I/2].) Previous stage performers, unless they were comedians, are unlikely to have been able to master this technique, any more than most opera singers can today. The opening of Drake's 'The surrey with the fringe on top' [OCR/O/3] illustrates different issues. He tends to classicise his performance of the verse in order to enter firmly on the initial e^1; by the time he gets to Rodgers's more conversational repeated-note refrain melody, an octave lower, he can afford to relax into vernacular pronunciation ('whennnItak' you owdinth'surri') and tone (more nasal, non-vibrato, with a touch of country whine). Curly's plagal A major baritone range in 'The surrey with the fringe on top' is nicely followed and foiled by Will Parker's, colourless in tone and mixing something of comedian, coon shout, music-hall mutter and croon, a tone lower in 'Kansas City' (sung by Lee Dixon in G major [OCR/O/4]). A simple octave equivalent of range and tone between Curly and Laurey sends them both up to F (f^1, f^2) for the climax of 'People will say we're in love', though Joan Roberts's light soprano has more difficulties than Drake's baritone in moving between registers in 'Out of my dreams' [OCR/O/8, 11]. Meanwhile a third baritone has been added in the shape of Jud Fry (though Drake sings his solo on the recording). The fourth male role, that of Ali Hakim, is despatched parlando.

Amplification and accommodation

The golden age of the American musical, roughly from *Oklahoma!* to *Cabaret* (1966), was short but brilliant. It was clearly thereby also a golden age for the stage entertainer, and since a professional life lasts longer than, in these cases, a generic one, it is worth seeing how the canonic musical of this period[14] accommodated specific stars' voices as well as the types that it had inherited. Two representative original cast recordings for assessment and comparison are *Gypsy* [OCR/G (1959)] and *Hello, Dolly!* [OCR/HD (1964)].

Both showcase a belter *extraordinaire*, as we have already seen – Merman in *Gypsy*, Channing, a good deal lower, in *Hello, Dolly!* (Merman's range is g to c^2, with extensions to $d\flat^2$. Channing's is c to g^1, though she fakes a b^1 in 'Dancing'; the score sometimes has her part written at pitch, sometimes an octave higher.) Behind women like these the men need no musical command and must not overshadow them, though they must still be prominent character or comic actors, often from non-musical film, as here – remnants of the leading comics studied earlier. Thus neither Jack Klugman as Herbie in *Gypsy* nor David Burns as Horace Vandergelder in *Hello, Dolly!* does more than croak his way insecurely through the odd baritone refrain.

The younger female leads, two in each case, parallel a 'legit' mezzo soprano with a girlie belter. Eileen Brennan as Irene Molloy in *Hello, Dolly!* has to have pure old-fashioned tones to represent her Irish charm, and she sinks to g and rises to f^2 (in 'Elegance') with secure ease and a well-integrated range that by now has lost most, if not all, of its soubrette warble. Sandra Church as Louise in *Gypsy* is much the same until she demonstrates the belt in the historical making, emblematically on behalf of the whole world of the show voice graduating from innocence to experience at the crux of the plot when she is transformed from a vaudeville juvenile into a stripper. Their younger sidekicks, Baby June (Jacqueline Mayro) in *Gypsy* and Minnie (Sondra Lee) in *Hello, Dolly!*, can only create character with a piercing infantile belt of the sort rightly lambasted by Osborne.

Their male partners in *Hello, Dolly!* are representative in Barnaby's case (Jerry Dodge) of very little at all and in Cornelius's of the cantorial baritone/tenor (sung by Charles Nelson Reilly) that by now is the male lead show voice, its vibrato highly emotional in an attempt to create vocal richness but again relying on the microphone, though hardly exploiting it. Tulsa in *Gypsy*, however (Paul Wallace), represents a new phenomenon, for he does exploit – and need – the intimacy of the microphone, yet is not exactly a crooner. His young, husky and rather breathless baritone sexiness suggests a man with strong body language, a dancer who can lead you straight into the bedroom, and this must be among the first fruits, on the bourgeois Broadway stage, of the black-inspired rock revolution.

The implication is that microphone amplification was slow to have a fundamental effect on the vocal production and characterisation of the musical theatre stage. There were surely (fixed) microphones in front of a musical theatre cast before 1957, but the development appears not to have been chronicled, and Hal Prince's statement that 'we didn't . . . use micro-phones until *West Side Story*'[15] must for the time being stand.[16] Before amplification, if Vivian Ellis's autobiography is to be believed, the problem was less one of melodic power than of verbal audibility – 'the perennial Battle of Words' in rehearsals,[17] solved by compromise all round and various musical sacrifices. After it, verbal audibility without musical sacrifice was just one of the very much increased multi-disciplinary demands made on show performers.

Prince describes how Michael Bennett, as choreographer/director in the Jerome Robbins tradition, solved the inhuman expectations of simultaneous dancing and singing in *Follies* (1971): 'He recorded the company in rehearsal and had them sing in sync with their own voices in performance; otherwise they would have been too winded to achieve any volume'. His view of this in 1974 was as follows:

> Ordinarily I abhor this sort of thing . . . But performers aren't trained to project their singing voices and rarely do they know how to protect them. Audiences, meanwhile, aren't trained to listen. The advent of television and electronic instruments has pushed the audience back in its seats. I remember when I first went to theatre, having to adjust for perhaps five minutes to the sounds of the actors. I would sit forward in my seat and the connection that I made with the stage was an investment in the experience. Had I taken away the amplification at *A Little Night Music* [1973], which is a show that could have survived without it, it would have made the audience reach out to the stage. I wish I'd had the courage to do it. Do we not run the risk of mechanizing the theatre until it becomes so slick it loses its 'liveness'?[18]

Prince blames TV, but the *cul de sac* of slickness was fully implicit in the musical film. If Fred Astaire and Gene Kelly had ever gone back on to the stage after working in film, something would have had to be done about those *Gesamtkunstwerk* audience expectations of multidisciplinary slick-ness much earlier than *West Side Story*, where they came to a head because it was the next phase of musical theatre production's greedy assimilation of means and media. In the vaudeville days this had been a series of separ-ate acts – comic, lyrical, balletic, gymnastic, erotic – though all with music, the art ultimately to be blamed for making us, in the last third of the twentieth century, want it all in one performer at one moment on the stage as well as the screen. Robbins and others had brought modern ballet fully into the musical from the late 1930s onwards; ballet brought with it erotic youth and, up to a point, modern mimetic music; now Robbins demanded all that and the inarticulate but melodramatic vernacular heroics of Brando-type method acting as well. The musical had to accommodate this, for James Dean in film and Elvis Presley in rock 'n' roll had already set new styles for stardom. But what did it do to singing?

It fundamentally changed, even destroyed, the acoustic equation between effort and reward, between vocal energy and meaning. Crooning had already disarmed vocal effort but had found lyrical modes and representations appropriate to the new pacific state – the sugar-daddy reassurance of Crosby or Hope and the jolly down-home 1950s virginity of Doris Day. But Larry Kert as Tony in *West Side Story* is different, and 'Maria' [UB/I/13] gives us the new shift in a nutshell. The method actor in him – in the musical character, that is – internalises his powerful emotions, for he does not have the verbal education to rhyme and be witty and construct thirty-two-bar quatrains and persuasive, clear sentences. The one word he is comfortable with, 'Maria', takes him all over the stage as he sings it to the buildings, twenty-nine times. He knows his body and the power of its aggressive youthful energy, but this is the first time he has ever discovered 'how wonderful a sound can be'. So he will 'say it loud' and 'say it soft', but the last thing we must believe is that he knows how to sing. His erotic triumph needs a tenor, and Bernstein wrote for one (with a $b\flat^1$ climax – Kert does the lower *ossia* – and much dynamic marking), but slim, handsome young dancers are not tenors, any more than uneducated white West Side kids would have been in the 1950s, and Robbins and Prince had to cast the part for a baritone. The tenor range remains, for its cantorial urgency requires it, and the song is still a cruel feat today (it has a range of almost two octaves, up to a^1 but with a PCG as low as $b\flat$), while the microphone makes the notes possible – just: Kert wavers and sharpens on the final cadence. What is lost in the effort is the reward of any integrated tone or identity of register. The voice at the beginning of the $E\flat$ major main section sounds like that of a different person from the opening. The character is no longer presenting his voice to the audience as the stage act, and Michael Crawford of 'The music of the night' [UB/II/16 (1991)] can be explained almost entirely in terms of what has already happened in this recording. Yet it is an impressive and powerfully seductive performance, and there could be no looking back from it.

The second shift

A different way of looking at the two twentieth-century shifts in entertainment singing would be to argue that if the first was about class, the second was about age and gender. That is, the first shift elided or redefined distinctions between black and white, Jew and Gentile, American and British, folk and opera, south and north, comic and serious, ordinary and special, above all between the vernacular of speech and the enchantment of singing, by fusing both in the same performer, with or without the aid of the microphone. The second wanted youth to have the resources of age, innocence to have experience, purity to have grit, agility to have authority, evanescent beauty to have the permanence of soul, always and only with the aid of the microphone. And as the microphone increasingly took care of the sound, the performer in a visual age focused audience attention on sight and movement: the acting singer became the singing actor. The shift was also about gender because previously one of the terms of these distinctions had tended to play opposite the other between the sexes. Rakish dandy comedians had been paired with innocent sopranos, crooning youths (or choruses) with croaking belters, reassuring and reliable older baritones with younger mezzos. Now one sex should be able to represent, and have, everything. The microphone became the holy grail bringing power to the individual's quest, not to the complementary couple.

There were two predominant manifestations of the second shift. One was the accessing of male adolescence into a world of sexual authority previously denied to it, as with the cartoon Aladdin, drawn to look like Tom Cruise and recorded with close enough miking that Brad Kane's singing in 'One jump ahead' [CD/II/4 (1992)] becomes the pillow talk of the bedroom pop idol, absolutely effortless amid his marketplace chase: the epitome of cool. The other was the combination of girlie and woman, of purity and passion (either way round), in what Osborne calls the female 'belt with legit', of which he defines two forms: 'One attempts to simply stack a soprano block on top of a belt block. The other tries to alternate belt and legit sounds in the same range'.[19] He devotes some space and detail to assessing the achievement of a female 'belt mix' in Barbra Streisand and Mary Martin and the retention of a soprano voice in Barbara Cook and Julie Andrews.

The natural and inevitable destination of Tony's ecstasy in 'Maria', and of the second shift in male terms, was the rock scream. Analysis of the rock voice is beyond the scope of this chapter, but its use on the entertainment stage and screen must be acknowledged as both vastly liberating and eventually deadening. The aggressive, hysterical youthful anger of Jesus and Judas in Lloyd Webber's *Jesus Christ Superstar* (1970–2) and Che in his *Evita* (1976–8) has elicited extraordinary rock, heavy metal and soul performances, on initial concept album or subsequent stage, from the likes of Murray Head, David Essex and, perhaps most astounding of all,

Clive Rowe (well on the way to James Brown), pushing what is essentially an integrated baritone rhetoric without a head voice, let alone falsetto, break right up to a^1 and c^2 in the score, improvised d^2 in performance, in 'Heaven on their minds', 'I only want to say', and the overpowering 'Judas' death' [JCS/I/2, II/2 and 7]. It was shocking for the male voice to accept this degree of pain – the exact pitch equivalent of the belt that females had been subjected to for decades – but the intensity could not last. The rock voice, still today the voice of youth's self-expression and empowerment for the majority of the globe's population, remains a major factor in the changing show sounds of the late twentieth century. Its effect in the theatre, however, particularly in conjunction with the current paraphernalia of contact mikes, mixing desk, speaker stacks and feedback loops, has quickly gone from political urgency to the sarcastic hectoring of *Les Misérables* and *Miss Saigon*. Even in *Evita* Che becomes a bore, and rock's opening of the doors to recitative and arioso in the musical was a Pandora's box of cliché well before *Rent*, which cannot redeem it through Adam Pascal's desperate earnestness, a late twentieth-century show voice mix of cantorial crying and rock rasping which comes to a head in 'Goodbye love' [OCR/R/II/12 (1996)].

Nowadays amplification has the same levelling effect on the presentation of show voices in non-rock contexts. So how is difference, this casualty of the second shift, to be re-established? Lloyd Webber was smart enough to present heavy rock as one of several pastiches in *Jesus Christ Superstar* by foiling it with the showbiz of Herod. Rock as one of a spectrum of voices on the musical stage or screen means that all of them are increasingly heard in inverted commas as camp re-emerges from the dead end of sincerity and postmodernism makes its liberating mark. Disney's recent cartoon successes offer one of those semiotic transactions beloved of the twentieth century when they use well-known stars' voices of various sounds and periods as fixed points of character recognition in their figural mythologies. They go further by parodying voice types and scenes of the past as witness to the ever more accessible heritage of films, recordings and shows that constitutes our museum culture. They go further still, and complete a circle of reference, in returning these mimetic items to the metropolitan stage, as they have now begun doing.

The Jungle Book and *The Lion King* trade a good deal in pop and rock voices, but in *Beauty and the Beast* the vocality and stance of operetta and the classic musical are back with a vengeance, however wry the inverted commas. Mrs Potts has the voice of an old belter, Angela Lansbury. Lumière is Jerry Orbach, but Orbach imitating Maurice Chevalier. Belle is an operetta soprano, her historicism built in by having her sung by

Paige O'Hara, who has made her name on 'authentic' recordings of old shows. She sounds and acts like Julie Andrews as Maria in *The Sound of Music*, twirling her way across a hilly meadow, arms outstretched. Gaston, sung by Richard White, replicates Howard Keel, Alfred Drake, John Raitt, Dennis King and above all, in his eighteenth-century costume, Nelson Eddy in *New Moon*, whose 'Stout-hearted men' from the film is parodied in 'The mob song'. Both leads therefore gather up the heritage of complementary vocal genres; but they do not marry each other, so the genres and the voices have been subverted. Instead, Belle's Beast (Robby Benson) adds a little rasp, croon and baritone to a gruff parlando and thus offers a new amalgam of old signals which Belle must figure out for herself.

Discography

[AAWS] *The Envelope Please . . . : Academy Award Winning Songs (1934–1993)* (5 CDs, Rhino Records, 1995)

[AL] *Americans in London* (3 CDs) and [MB] *The Music of Broadway: 1939* (2 CDs) (Box Office Recordings, 1991–2)

[AMT] *American Musical Theater: Shows, Songs, and Stars* (4 CDs, Smithsonian Collection of Recordings, Washington DC, 1989)

[BBR] *The Best of Broadway – The Revues* (CD, Pavilion Records, Wadhurst, 1997)

[B20s] *Bands of the '20s*, [B30s] *Bands of the '30s* (2 CDs, Intersound, Roswell, GA, 1996)

[CD] *Classic Disney* (5 CDs, Walt Disney Records, Burbank, CA, 1995–8)

[DL] *Theatre Royal, Drury Lane: The Great Musicals* (CD, Conifer Records, West Drayton, 1994)

[GIGH] *George and Ira Gershwin in Hollywood* (2 CDs, Turner Classic Movies Music, 1997)

[GMH] *The Glory of the Music Hall* (3 CDs, Pavilion Records, Wadhurst, 1991)

[JCS] *Jesus Christ Superstar* (2 CDs, TER Records, London, 1995)

[NYS] *Music from the New York Stage: 1890–1920* (4 vols., 12 CDs, Pavilion Records, Wadhurst, 1993)

[OCR/] Original Cast Recordings: [/C] *Carousel* (1945, CD, MCA Records, Universal City, CA, 1993); [/G] *Gypsy* (1959, CD, CBS, New York, 1973); [/HD] *Hello, Dolly!* (1964, CD, RCA Records, New York, 1989); [/O] *Oklahoma!* (1943/44, CD, MCA Records, Universal City, CA, 1993); [/R] *Rent* (2 CDs, SKG Music, 1996); [/SB] *Show Boat*, [/S] *Sunny* and [/LL] *Lido Lady* (1928, 1926 and 1927, 1 CD, Original Cast Series, Pavilion Records, Wadhurst, 1994); [/SPG] *Sunday in the Park with George* (CD, RCA Records, New York, 1984); [/VWM] *Very Warm for May* (CD, AEI Records, Los Angeles, 1985)

[SSR] *Star Spangled Rhythm: Voices of Broadway and Hollywood* (4 CDs, Smithsonian Collection of Recordings, Washington DC, 1997)

[TVT] *Television's Greatest Hits* (3 CDs) and *The Commercials* (1 CD) (TeeVee
    Toons, New York, 1986–9)
[UB] *Ultimate Broadway* (2 CDs, Arista Records, New York, 1998)
You Must Remember This . . . [CCF] *Classic Children's Favourites*; [GFS] *Great Film
    Songs*; [GLS] *The Great Love Songs*; [GTS] *Great Theatre Songs*; [HA] *The Happy
    Album*; [VCS] *Vintage Comedy Songs* (6 CDs, Conifer Records, London, 1996).

7 Song into theatre: the beginnings of opera

JOHN ROSSELLI

And their singing! Good Lord! Let me never hear a Frenchwoman singing Italian arias. I can
forgive her if she screeches out her French trash, but not if she ruins good music! It's simply
unbearable.

So Mozart wrote from Paris in 1778.[1] A few years earlier, the British musicologist Charles Burney heard the soprano and high tenor in the main
Paris concert series 'screaming' and 'bellowing'. At the Académie Royale
de Musique, the home of serious opera, things were little better: voices 'in
themselves really good and well toned' but, in their expression, 'detestable
and unnatural'. At the other main house, the Opéra-Comique, 'bravura
songs' were 'so ill performed that no one used to true Italian singing can
like anything but the words and action'. It was 'hardly too much to say,
[good singing] is never to be heard at the theatres'.[2]

Mozart and Burney were among many who, into the early nineteenth
century, dismissed French opera singing out of hand because it was unlike
Italian. By the 1770s the two operatic traditions had been established for
over a century; between them they dominated Europe. The Italian tradition ruled from Lisbon to St Petersburg by way of London and Berlin; it
was *the* way to sing in the theatre, just as Italian opera was *the* opera and
Italian or Italian-trained singers appeared on stage everywhere – but not
in France. There, occasional visits by Italian companies – from the 1640s
to the 1750s – set off debate; their methods found champions, yet every
time the French public went back to its own composers and singers and to
their performing style, however 'detestable' to outsiders. Though the
tradition must have pleased the bulk of the home audience, in Europe it
was isolated.

This needs explaining. France was the dominant country in Europe.
From the reign of Louis XIV (1661–1715) French culture held sway. The
educated followed the literature and thought of France; they used its language as their means of exchange, internationally and, often, among
themselves. Italy still sent out architects, painters and sculptors, but
France exported the so-called minor arts of decoration, furniture making
and fashion; it was the headquarters of journalism and gossip. Only in
music was it unheeded. Yet if the theoreticians had had their way – Italians
foremost among them – opera should by rights have developed everywhere as it did in France. The practice of Italian opera had triumphed

against the advice of all the best people. A counterfactual analysis – 'what if. . . ?' – might try to discover what opera singing would have been like if performers and audiences had taken that advice to heart.

What came to be known from the 1630s as opera, an all-sung dramatic entertainment, undoubtedly began in Italy. From the opera houses of Venice, the first to draw a paying audience, singers and (just as important) scene designers took it to the rest of Italy and to Paris.[3] But the strands from which opera grew were many; of these, many originated, as early as 1600, in the courts of rulers and great nobles, the cardinals of the Church included; throughout the seventeenth century – in many places throughout the eighteenth as well – most opera singers depended on those rulers and nobles and their successors, at once paymasters and audience.

'Opera singer' is, however, a modern notion. Around 1600, singing, acting, dancing, composing and playing an instrument were not distinct callings; many who appeared in early opera excelled at more than one. Composers sang (not often on stage), hence taught singing, and were to go on doing so down to Rossini; actors sang and danced; some early singers could accompany themselves on a stringed instrument; singers who appeared in opera might be called 'musicians' or 'actors'; in Italy what they did was at first called 'acting in song' (*recitar cantando*). The entertainments from which opera grew, both there and in France, likewise mixed what we think of as distinct genres.

In both countries one important strand leading towards opera was the 'interlude' or 'ballet', given at court as part of a grand performance to mark a royal event: it provided, between parts of a spoken drama, a separate allegorical sung drama heightened by dances and mobile scenery ('flying machines'). Another was the Italian *commedia dell'arte*, a semi-improvised play given by a professional troupe and interspersed with songs; it reached France and influenced Molière's and Lully's *comédies-ballets* (comic or pastoral interludes). Of Monteverdi's court operas, *Orfeo* (1607) reflected the interlude in its madrigals and dances; in *Arianna* (1608) the title role went in an emergency to Virginia Andreini, leading lady of a *commedia dell'arte* troupe.[4]

The search in court entertainments for the astonishing, the 'marvellous' in both visual and vocal display, shaped early opera far more than did the high-minded experiments, limited to sung declamation, of a group of Florentine intellectuals who harked back to the supposed methods of ancient Greek tragedy; yet – intellectuals being as usual concerned with each other – Italian critics of opera time and again upheld the standards of this Florentine group, above all the precedence given to words and drama over music, and decried singers and composers who ignored them. Throughout the seventeenth and eighteenth centuries these critics, though 'appalled', had to admit 'the overwhelming, almost daily success of this hybrid and, indeed, "abnormal" form of entertainment' that degraded poetry for the sake of music and flouted the academic rules of drama; they called for reform and regeneration.[5] Some looked enviously at France, where the native form of opera upheld their ideals as, after the early experiments, Italian opera never did.

Why should the actors of a drama sing at all? Verisimilitude bothered early critics both in Venice and in Paris, though after the first few years only Parisian makers of opera did anything about it. What specially bothered the critics was that actors should sing self-contained patterned melodies, that is, arias; sung declamation (recitative) troubled them much less or not at all, presumably because Greek drama was thought to sanction it. Should patterned song be allowed only when the drama showed a character to be singing one? Should gods, mythological figures, and maybe shepherds enjoy such licence, rather than ordinary men and women? (We do not know how the Olympian gods communicated; shepherds, by convention, have all the time in the world to sing and dance.)

These speculations shaped the way French opera singers performed. *Tragédie-lyrique* (as French serious opera of the late seventeenth and eighteenth centuries was called) moved in real time. Patterned songs – *airs* – did not, as in Italian opera of the same period, stop the action to dwell on an 'affect' or emotional state for seven or eight minutes; they were generally short; word-setting was largely syllabic and repetition used chiefly for dramatic emphasis. Often the move from recitative to *air* was marked by heightened intensity and more broken rhythm rather than by distinct pattern making; recitative itself was more inflected, through changes in time signature, than the Italian equivalent. True, French audiences wanted the 'marvellous' in opera as much as anyone else, but they got it through visual means – ballet and spectacle, plausibly cued by the twists of a fantastic plot; now and again a more elaborate Italian-style aria would creep in under the apologetic name *ariette*.

What all this meant for singers we can guess from a treatise by Bénigne de Bacilly, written alongside Lully's formative *comédies-ballets* and early operas. Much of it was to be parroted by authors writing almost a hundred years later.[6] Bacilly gave over two-thirds of his work to the articulation and musical setting of words; the bee in his bonnet was the proper treatment of quantities in French syllables, a notion drawn from Latin verse which he rather speciously applied to the unaccented French language. Singers, he wrote, must study literature if they were not be scorned as mere 'minstrels'; in a good *air* words and music ought to show equal merit, but the words must embody 'good sense' and be fully intelligible, unlike the words of many Italian arias which were at once 'barbarous' in themselves and deployed, through endless repetitions, without an eye to keeping their syllables distinct.[7]

By 1755 the most authoritative treatise of the mid-eighteenth century, by Jean-Antoine Bérard, brought some new ideas but still opined that song was a 'more embellished' form of declamation, and must therefore 'submit to the yoke of French prosody'.[8] He distinguished between 'articulation' (bringing out the words clearly) and 'pronunciation' (giving them expression). Like Bacilly, he was concerned with problems set by the French language: nasal vowels (the nasal twang should be merely touched in at the last possible moment), many mute 'e's at the end of words (to be sounded as French 'eu'), and single or double consonants (to be sounded or not according to the emotional import of the passage). Even a critic of 1780 who set out to overthrow Bérard in the name of changed taste thought French opera had grown tedious for lack of good libretti: it could 'more easily do without perfect music than without interesting words'.[9]

By the mid-eighteenth century native critics could praise French opera singing as 'simple, innocent, firm, and vigorous' or – if, like Rousseau, they upheld Italian methods – write it off as 'dragging' and 'mournful'.[10] They were responding to a tradition, by then entrenched, that prized diction, clarity and emotional expression, all aimed at putting across a coherent drama written in choice French words. This may help to explain why foreigners who knew French but not intimately, like Mozart and Burney, talked of screeching and bellowing.

Burney's further complaint that 'the French voice never comes further than from the throat' – singers never used the chest voice[11] – could be rephrased to say that the French language is spoken forward in the mouth ('dans le masque') and that, in taking care to 'articulate', French opera singers did without some of the possible placements of the voice. Bérard remarked that Italians were more used than French people to singing high notes with a small thread of voice.[12] French singers, we may guess, were too impressed with the need for 'pronunciation' – for getting the drama across – to deliver emotional phrases in other than full voice, all the more if (as seems likely) the thread-spinning reported of Italians meant barely touching in vital consonants.

French priorities might conceivably have been exported to the rest of Europe, together with French operas set to French words. Why were they not? Some have argued that Louis XIV's 'cultural mercantilism', his concentration of opera in Paris and Versailles as a monopoly run by Frenchmen, isolated French musical life from the rest of Europe and choked off creativity, so that a few operas by Lully were repeated over as much as a century – a phenomenon unique in this period.[13]

Another possible explanation is that the concern with words and drama rooted in French high culture was not shared by people outside France; they responded to the singing voice far more than to the words it had to sing, and they accordingly welcomed Italian opera. It is difficult to imagine a late eighteenth-century singer outside France enjoying the position of Sophie Arnould, a friend of *philosophes* known for her diction and acting rather than for quality of voice, whose witty sayings were collected and published; Burney heard her and, of course, disliked her. In Italy, contemporaries of the philosophes met not in the drawing room but at the opera house; a few intelligent and socially presentable singers are recorded, like Arnould's contemporary Caterina Gabrielli, but no one thought to take down what they said. Even in the street outside, according to the German composer-teacher J. A. Hiller, untrained Italians sang better than most trained Germans; Burney too heard pairs who sang duets 'very agreeably', 'very well in tune'.[14] Italy thus seemed the fount of vocal music, a reputation it would not earn on present-day evidence.

What Italian street singers and their professional colleagues sounded like is as hard to establish as are all musical sounds before the age of recording. Fashion in the performance of early music has changed over the past thirty years or so: vibrato, for instance, used to be unthinkable, but, as Robert Donington wrote in 1988, we can now acknowledge 'a wide range of gradual variability all the way through from complete trills or even mordents down to minimal vibrato . . . The last quality appropriate for baroque music in general is the spectral quality of vibrato-less playing' or, we might add, singing.[15]

Just as theoretical works might make one think that Italian opera ought to resemble French in the subordination of music to words and drama, so early treatises on singing give the impression that the singers of both nations ought to sound much alike. Neither is true; yet we have to rely on treatises because descriptions of actual singing, in the seventeenth century in particular, are vague. Italian treatises almost as much as French stressed the importance of words and suitable expression and acting; French authors as much as Italian dwelt on ornaments, their number and variety and the right and wrong way to perform them.

The reason for concentrating on ornaments was that, in opera as in the forms that led up to it, singers were expected to decorate the vocal line with additional notes which were not written down. This was the more necessary when the aria or *air* included repeats of whole sections, as in French *couplets*, in arias with stanzas separated by ritornellos, and, from about 1680, in *da capo* arias. The most influential and endlessly copied Italian author, Pier Francesco Tosi (whose 1723 treatise itself codified what earlier authors had written), told singers to work out their own ornaments: it was a weakness of many women singers that they needed to have theirs written out for them.[16] Bacilly put it elegantly: the first stanza in *couplets*, which the singer might ornament discreetly, was the drawing; fuller ornamentation of the second stanza coloured it in.[17]

Such was the cult of ornamentation that at least two teachers, Ludovico Zacconi (in 1592) and Ottavio Durante (in 1608), warned singers against embellishing the start of a phrase: let ornaments come in the middle, so that a burst of coloratura at the end has been prepared for.[18] Zacconi – like Bacilly and Tosi after him – recommended a well-controlled 'trembling voice' in passage-work. Just what this meant is hard to interpret, because the same authors decried excessive tremolo, but it suggests a line almost as serpentine, bar upon bar, as that to be heard from an astonishing Bengali male singer in Satyajit Ray's film *The Goddess*.

Authors of treatises listed as many as fifteen distinct ornaments (Raparlier, 1772), a number of them varieties of appoggiatura. Bacilly and Tosi both recommended portamento or *port de voix*, another term hard to interpret: to them it meant approaching a note through one or more other notes or 'commas' (the nine microtones between the tones of the untempered scale), though Tosi also talked of 'sliding' or 'dragging' as against staccato in passage-work. They and other authors had much to say about varieties of trill. Only in 1775 would Vincenzo Manfredini write that trills were fine in cadenzas but otherwise inessential next to 'singing from the heart'; he voiced a dislike, common since mid-century, of over-ornamentation – 'appoggiaturas taking up half a bar', as a singer-critic put it – though his advice in general was much like Tosi's.[19] All authors, for that matter, warned singers against over-ornamentation, though what that meant is again a riddle.

Zacconi could not, in 1592, envisage opera; Bacilly and Tosi wrote for those who might sing not only in the theatre but in church or in a great man's chamber, where (fugal church music apart) the ornaments they detailed would be as welcome. Besides readiness to ornament, early opera called for vocal expressiveness and perhaps for acting ability; it did not call for a particular kind of voice, still less for a size of voice far outclassing that needed in chamber or church. In the grandest theatres, those of Paris, Naples and Turin, orchestral numbers grew to sixty or so by 1790, but those were nearly all gut strings and woodwind, softer than their modern equivalents; brass was for special effects. A light voice well focused would come through.

Most of the earliest opera singers had behind them the practice of madrigal singing. This had developed around the turn of the sixteenth and seventeenth centuries from polyphony voiced by a small group of male singers for their own enjoyment to dramatic utterance for a single voice, male or female, at times still within a piece written for a group, at times a solo, either way brandished at an audience that sat ready to marvel and applaud but not to join in.[20] When we hear these late madrigals, for example those composed in the 1580s by Luzzaschi for the 'concert of ladies' who sang in private for the Duke of Ferrara – a famous threesome imitated by other courts[21] – the emotional range of any one piece may strike us as narrow, but the singers are undoubtedly playing on an audience's feelings. Monteverdi's madrigals from the 1590s to the 1620s included snatches of opera, virtual or adapted (the famous lament from his *Arianna*), as well as a miniature opera like *Il combattimento di Tancredi e Clorinda*. The mercurial handling of emotional expression shows that the new dramatic form has found a master; the singer needs to catch every sudden shift of feeling. [22]

Others who appeared in seventeenth-century Italian opera had experience mainly of singing in church. These included most of the castrati. Boys – nearly all Italians – with promising treble voices were, from about 1550, castrated and trained for a career as professional musicians; they worked mainly in church choirs, where a ban on women and a new dislike of boys' voices and falsettists made for a steady demand.[23] They did not at once jump to the forefront of the new theatrical genre. In Monteverdi's *Orfeo* a castrato sang three episodic parts, but the all-important lead went to the tenor Francesco Rasi; his late Venice opera *Il ritorno d'Ulisse in patria* (1640) had no part obviously requiring a castrato; the lead was a baritone. Soon afterwards, however, the castrato as *primo uomo* – 'first man', the juvenile lead as hero or lover – became a requirement of Italian opera. When, about 1700, comic opera split off from what had been an undifferentiated courtly-erotic-heroic-comic entertainment, he remained the focal point of Italian serious opera, matched only at times by the *prima donna*.

Understanding of castrati in opera has been hindered by the film *Farinelli* (1995). It repeats and embroiders all the myths that have clustered, understandably enough, round a disconcerting custom. The evidence shows that only in the period of decline, from about 1740, did most Italians regard castration for musical ends as shameful. Until then it was virtually a routine matter, provided for in apprenticeship contracts and now and then subsidised by the ruler. At a time when impoverished Italy held vast numbers of monks, a castrato appears to have been thought of as a specialised monk whose family could hope for a regular income. Most castrati – often, as members of church choirs, on lifetime appointments – sang opera only now and then, in local Italian seasons; the best sang in oratorio at least as much as in opera; as trained musicians many became apt teachers. Only in France were they barred from the stage; even there a visiting star castrato might sing in concert, while humbler ones were on the strength of the royal chapel at Versailles. Their lives, where we can observe them, were often lonely and quiet.[24]

The reason for the triumph of the most accomplished castrati in Italian serious opera is bound up with the aesthetics of the genre. It was highly artificial. The often conventional but more realistic Italian comic opera – it prevailed increasingly from about 1740 – used castrati only now and then, as a rule in minor parts; its simpler music called for natural voices, looks and verve rather than for extraordinary vocal feats. Serious opera, however, consisted for most of the period 1680–1780 of a string of arias each embodying an emotion or 'affect'; while it lasted, the action was suspended. After the original production the recitative leading up to the aria – often beautifully written by Metastasio, the chief librettist of the eighteenth century – might be cut or rewritten. The aria was the thing the audience had come for. It was not necessarily a burst of coloratura fireworks: pathetic *cantabile* singing was highly prized; Gasparo Pacchierotti, one of the last famous castrati, specialised in it and was said to have reduced a theatre orchestra, of all people, to tears; but it too demanded great control of such devices as *messa di voce* (gradual swelling and diminishing of tone).

Castrati further suited early Italian opera because the genre depended a good deal on sexual ambiguity. Plots often turned, as in Shakespearean comedy, on women disguised as men or vice versa. A castrato playing a hero added a fresh touch: a voice powerful as a man's natural tones (thanks to a highly developed thoracic cavity and undeveloped vocal cords), hence far more brilliant than a falsettist's, yet as high as a woman's; often his part would be deliberately written higher than that of the *prima donna* he sang opposite. A few castrati like Farinelli (see Fig. 4) heightened the ambiguity by mastering an extraordinary range; his was said to go over three octaves, from C to D *in altissimo*, though it was more usual for a castrato to start his career as a soprano and end as an alto. Since the typical cast of an Italian serious opera came to be two castrati, two women and a tenor (with perhaps a bass as well), the vocal palette was prevailingly light.

In French opera, however, the *haute-contre* who sang many leading parts was – rather than a countertenor such as we now hear – a tenor with an unusual high extension, able, like two who sang leads in Rameau's works, Pierre de Jélyotte and François Poirier, to sing freely up to high D or even E; a few present-day tenors can match them.[25] *Haute-contres* might sing the part of a fury or some other mythological being, like the frog-nymph in Rameau's *Platée*, originally sung by Jélyotte. Human cross-dressing was thought against 'good taste', but for an old convention whereby tenors could sing the parts of comic old women (just as an older

Figure 4 Farinelli, drawn by Antonio Zanetti

actor had played such parts in Molière's company, which included actresses).

In Italian serious opera, tenors – their range somewhat lower than we are used to – had limited scope: they sang the parts of fathers and rulers, might earn a ration of display arias, but, with a few exceptions such as Anton Raaff (Mozart's Idomeneo), were esteemed and paid less than the castrato and the *prima donna*. Only at the very end of the eighteenth century did they start to outdo the castrato in both prestige and fee. In keeping with the artificiality of the genre, the commonest male voice, the bass, was almost nowhere, unless an outstanding singer inspired a composer as Antonio Montagnana and Giuseppe Maria Boschi inspired Handel; the bass part would then be as highly ornamented as anybody's.

Women in Italian serious opera made for ambiguity as much as did castrati. Their appearance on a public stage struck many as titillating or scandalous: at a time when respectable women kept to home and church – even there flanked by male relatives – they exposed themselves to hundreds of male eyes, not to mention encounters behind the scenes. Mid-seventeenth-century Venetian opera – its themes by and large erotic – exploited the beauty, costuming and allure of women singers at least as much as their voices. It harked back to the Venetian institution of the courtesan, who might be a distinguished poet, chamber singer and composer as well as a high-class prostitute.[26] Some of the women who sang in Italian opera down to about 1690 were as notorious but far less distinguished; the others needed male guarantors to proclaim their respectability, as did the men who compiled a book in praise of Anna Renzi, the original Ottavia in Monteverdi's *L'incoronazione di Poppea* (1643).[27] In Rome the papal government forbade women to appear on stage, a ban kept up until 1798, though women sang in the semi-privacy of noblemen's palaces; in public theatres, young castrati sang women's parts.

The height of ambiguity was for a woman to put on breeches and act a man's part – at a time when in everyday life no woman dare show herself in other than a full-length skirt – better still the part of a woman disguised as a man, or a man disguised as a woman, like Achilles trying to avoid the Trojan War. Here and there a woman sang the hero's part that would normally have gone to a castrato. The duty to appear 'as a man' figured in some women singers' contracts, as the duty to appear nude (or the right to decline such scenes) now figures in those of actresses; the stress involved was probably much the same.

The development of the aria in Italian serious opera did much to redeem women singers from being automatically written off as courtesans. Arias, which had come to be many but short, from about 1700 grew longer, fewer and much more elaborate. A beautiful woman with a limited voice and technique would no longer do. An incidental cause may have been the cost of the wars that distracted most of Europe, with only a short break, from 1689 to 1713. Rulers cut down or dismissed their chamber musicians; for women, church music was out (except here and there, as in Vienna); public opera, on the other hand, grew, especially in Italy where several petty rulers developed a 'ducal circuit'. In these years a number of women singers, though billed as 'virtuosa' in the service of one or other ruler, in practice ran their own careers and went round the main Italian public theatres as star attractions.

In Paris during those same years the ageing and increasingly pious Louis XIV's loss of interest in opera meant that women – employed, like their male colleagues, on an annual salary – became, in effect, specialised government servants. True, a woman member of a Paris state theatre or opera company might have an influential lover-protector at court – a habit kept up, with republican ministers taking over from courtiers, down to the early twentieth century – but that was a discreet arrangement, quite unlike being labelled a prostitute.

Women's new professionalism in serious opera was at times belittled on the grounds that their sex prevented them from studying to become accomplished musicians, as a number of castrati did in the famous Naples schools (*conservatorii*, originally orphanages). For fear of scandal or worse, parents and guardians would not let them see men other than relatives. There is something in this, but less than authors of treatises made out. Many singers, women as well as men, were the children of musicians; many castrati studied privately; teachers in the schools often blurred the line between private and institutional teaching. Some women singers had to learn their parts by ear, but so did some men, and in any event illiteracy was common; we hear of an apprentice male singer who could read notes but not words.[28] Some musicians specialised in teaching women singers in their homes. Flavia Muzzillo, a Neapolitan beginner living with her married sister, in 1737 had one teacher, a minor composer, for music and singing in general; an engagement at Corfu prompted her to call in another for special embellishments.[29] By doing so Muzzillo probably intended to qualify herself for serious opera. In comic opera, a genre then beginning to flourish, arias were closer to folk song (and in turn influenced Neapolitan folk song; the two can be hard to disentangle). The soubrettes (who sang young women's parts) were still treated by the Naples authorities as virtual prostitutes; one was packed off to a convent after she had had a rival in song and love shot dead in the street, as, again and again (with the alternative of expulsion), were others when they tried to marry a well-born young man. Besides the soubrette, the reigning figure in the genre was the comic bass; he might have a mediocre voice but neat patter and irresistible comic verve.

From about 1760 the frontier between the Italian genres grew increasingly blurred. Comic opera developed 'serious roles' that called for more elaborate singing (examples are Donna Anna and Don Ottavio in *Don Giovanni*). Serious opera, influenced partly by French examples, partly by audiences bored with old formulas, took to greater use of ensembles and choruses, in particular to a climactic ensemble with chorus as the first-half finale, a device pioneered by comic opera; some short, simple numbers could now be inserted among the display arias. An intermediate genre of 'semi-serious' opera took shape, inspired by the sentimental bourgeois comedies popular in the spoken theatre. In French comic opera too – a various genre, defined by spoken dialogue and no ballet – the late eighteenth century and especially the Revolution brought vast changes: serious, historical, on occasion tragic subjects now came in, as did spectacular stage effects such as avalanches. The genre was exportable, for instance to Germany, Britain and Russia. French all-sung opera itself began to take on, under Napoleon, the historical and educative pretensions that would mark nineteenth-century grand opera.

All this reflected larger changes in society, away from the unquestioned domination of aristocratic and religious ideals. For kindred reasons, castrati dwindled in numbers and – a few star singers apart – in prestige; after 1800 only one famous castrato appeared in opera, G. B. Velluti. In the latter half of the eighteenth century many European cities built new theatres and started regular opera seasons; the Revolution for a time broke all the old monopolies, setting off a burst of opera performances in all French cities. In Europe as a whole, far more singers were active in 1800 than in 1740, many of them modestly employed in comic opera, though the craze for the Italian variety had only another twenty years or so to run.

We are scarcely aware of the period of transition between the death of Mozart in 1791 and the first overwhelming success of Rossini in 1813, because the operas that dominated it – by Cimarosa, Paisiello and Mayr in Italy, by Grétry, Cherubini, Méhul and Spontini in France, by Salieri in Vienna – rarely take the stage.[30] Rossini therefore gets the credit for changes that were gradually worked out by all those composers and others, and then triumphantly codified by himself. One change was the speeding up of opera. This had to do as much with the military band music ever-present through another virtual quarter-century of European war, from 1792 to 1815, as with deliberate artistic choice. Audiences became attuned to quick, effervescent march tunes and loud effects; the soft, melancholy singing in which Pacchierotti had shone was no longer enough on its own. Rossini's Italian serious operas, culminating in *Semiramide* (1823), peppered grand ensembles and solo coloratura displays with brisk military-style crescendos and headlong codas. In these works the basic structure of an aria or scene was now a slow, meditative *cantabile* section, usually followed (after some startling piece of news or other turn in the action) by a faster section, the *cabaletta*. This made for excitement, decoration (of the second stanza), and resolution in a slam-bang ending.

Another change came of the gradual merging of the serious and comic traditions. Italian comic opera might now require as much virtuoso singing as did serious, at any rate from the lead tenor and *prima donna*. There were still comic opera specialists, but Marietta Marcolini, Ester Mombelli, the tenor Giovanni David and the bass Filippo Galli, who created roles in several of Rossini's Italian operas, excelled at both genres. Rossini's habit of writing down ornamentation does not mean that singers stopped devising their own – rather that he gave first place in opera to vocal music of ideal beauty and wished to set a clear framework for performance.[31]

In France by the 1820s the distinction between all-sung opera and comic opera with spoken dialogue still held good, though comic opera in the many theatres that gave it – all over the French-speaking area and beyond – required 'sopranos à roulades', able to cope with Italian-style arias, as well as more traditional light, expressive singers named after the famous Louise-Rosalie Dugazon (1755–1821). Her long career meant that there were openings for 'matronly' as well as for 'young' *dugazons*. In Paris, Italian opera was at last established, with its own theatre the most fashionable place to be seen in. With the European craze for Rossini's music at its height, the composer in 1824 moved to Paris and, with great care, set about making himself the presiding deity of both the Italian and the French serious opera. His work there culminated in *Guillaume Tell* (1829), which virtually invented nineteenth-century grand opera while summing up and unifying a great deal of past practice, both French and Italian. It coincided with the high tide of Romanticism, a movement alien to Rossini's outlook; after this mighty effort he fell silent as opera composer. He had none the less codified and launched what were to be the dominant traditions of opera in both Italy and France, hence in the world: singers trained in his works would carry forward opera into the mid-nineteenth century.

8 Grand opera: nineteenth-century revolution and twentieth-century tradition

JOHN ROSSELLI

Rossini's *Guillaume Tell*, first performed in 1829, defined the new genre of Parisian grand opera. This was grand indeed. Divided as a rule into five acts, with a ballet spatchcocked into at least two acts; on a historical subject, freely interpreted for maximum spectacle (in Berlioz's *Benvenuto Cellini* of 1838 the Pope and the College of Cardinals enter Cellini's studio just as the furnace explodes and the brand-new statue of Perseus rises from the smoke); educative intent built into the plot so as to show great historical forces arrayed in conflict – it all suited a bourgeois audience that welcomed notions of liberty and progress. Tyranny might win for the moment, yet the march of civilisation would prevail, helped on its way by sacrificial love: Halévy's *La Juive* (1835), Meyerbeer's *Les Huguenots* (1836) and *Le Prophète* (1849) hinted at freedom of worship, *Tell* and Verdi's *Les Vêpres siciliennes* (1855) at national independence, Verdi's *Don Carlos* (1867) at political liberty; each gave one plenty to look at, ballerinas' legs included. The whole thing took five hours or more and called for months of rehearsal to drill the hundred-strong chorus and get the vast, historically accurate sets right.

Rossini had carefully led up to *Tell* by adapting for Paris three of his Italian operas. Though his music had already taken Europe by storm, he altered it to meet French taste: he cut down ornamentation, allowed for more dramatic singing, and brought forward the chorus. The outcome each time was a great success. The tenor and soprano leads in *Tell*, Alphonse Nourrit and Laure Cinti, had sung in those earlier adaptations and, under Rossini's guidance, had worked out a vocal technique that combined some features of the French and Italian schools; Cinti, a Frenchwoman, showed the new outlook by Italianising as her stage name her second Christian name, Cinthie, and when she taught at the Paris Conservatoire she inculcated her own largely Italianate practice while in theory upholding all the old French saws about the primacy of the word.[1]

At the Opéra-Comique, which Rossini left alone, older French ways persisted: when the younger composer Bellini came along in 1833–5 he complained, like Mozart, that the theatre's singers 'shouted senselessly' and indulged in 'killing roulades'.[2] That kind of French singing was to go on in comic opera, in vaudeville, and later in operetta – forward in the mouth, to the outside ear perhaps thin or acid or nasal-sounding, at its best soothing the French ear with words given their right expression. The singer-composer Reynaldo Hahn, in influential lectures of 1913–14, was yet again to describe the singing voice as 'speech made more beautiful'.[3]

Serious opera of the 1830s and 1840s, meanwhile, dwelt more and more on the violent emotion conjured by Romantic writers: *Tell*, itself an elevated work marked by a neo-classical aesthetic of dignity and restraint, coincided with the high tide of Paris Romantic melodrama in the works of Victor Hugo and others, and with early influences from the more fantastic Romanticism of Germany. Opera would not remain immune, whether in France or in Italy.

What was the old Italian vocal style that would shortly have to meet the Romantic demand for extreme, immediate emotional impact? We do not of course know by direct experience: recorded sound allows us to hear only voices active from about 1900. We therefore have to rely largely on treatises. One scholar who has made a thorough survey of them concludes that 'purely technical vocal emission' remained unchanged from 1550 to about 1836.[4] Italian treatises throughout that period did inculcate pretty much the same virtues. For a description of the actual sound aimed at, we can go to an intelligent amateur, the Highland lady Elizabeth Grant of Rothiemurchus, who studied about 1818 with Mrs Bianchi Lacey, a retired Italian singer, widow and former pupil of the composer Francesco Bianchi. Her teacher's voice – Mrs Grant recalled – was 'round and true and sweet in the upper notes, and the finish of her whole song, the neat-ness of every [coloratura] passage, the perfect expression she gave to both music and words . . . gave to me a different notion of the art.' Her stress was on meaning, true intonation, even emission, few but neat graces, 'the whole got up so perfectly as to be poured forth with ease, any effort, such as straining or forcing the voice or unduly emphasising a passage, being altogether so much out of taste as to produce pain instead of pleasure'.[5]

Mrs Bianchi Lacey, it seems, reflected the taste of her late husband's generation, already in part overtaken by Rossini. The castrato Girolamo Crescentini, whose delicately shaded pathos had made him a star from the 1780s to the 1800s, like other Italian critics blamed Rossini for drowning the voice in 'a pile-up of a great many notes and of excessive noise' from wind instruments: by the 1820s a singer had to 'shout' rather than 'smoothly emit' his voice.[6] 'Shouting' is relative: what horrified Crescentini would pass us by. Without it, the elegant, rounded, effortless emission he and Mrs Bianchi Lacey aimed at had allowed the finest eigh-teenth-century singers to be heard even in a very large theatre like the San Carlo, Naples: Metastasio had thought the tenor Anton Raaff's 'inimitable graces and extraordinary agility' would be lost in that 'enormous mass of air', but as it turned out Raaff scored a success.[7] Crescentini specially disliked the *cabaletta*, the last part of a Rossinian aria: it discharged the emotion built up in the earlier, often meditative part; it might show a vocal line at once jagged and rapid, ending in a volley of loud chords underlined by brass and drums. French and German opera composers of the 1830s might use different means, but they too wrote vocal lines spikier than their predecessors' and thickened the instrumentation of key moments: Romantic plots – once summed up by Bernard Shaw as 'passion, poison, and petrifaction' – called for no less.

Legend has it that one singer found the answer: the French tenor Gilbert-Louis Duprez returned to Paris from a successful career in Italy and in 1837 astounded everybody by singing Nourrit's old part in *Tell* with a 'chest high C', by pushing his chest voice into a range where tenors till then had sung in gentler head voice. The powerful tenor or *tenore di forza* was born and, from then on, became indispensable. Duprez did astonish the Paris audience; the legend, however, collapses into one episode a change that took place over thirty or forty years. The tenor voice does seem to have led the change. Confined in eighteenth-century Italian serious opera to the decorative and near-baritonal, it branched out – both into more heroic tone and into a higher range – as the castrato voice declined. Was the change helped forward by the influence of the French *haute-contre* voice which Italians so despised? The question has not been studied. The earliest Italian heroic tenor, Matteo Babbini, spent time in Paris during the Revolution and later impressed audiences with his dramatic ability and vocal power in 'republican' parts such as the merciless Roman patriot in Cimarosa's *Gli Orazi e i Curiazi* (1796); unlike the *haute-contre*'s, however, his range was short – a mere octave.[8]

The foray into a higher range was led by Giacomo and especially Giovanni David, father and son. Giovanni – who created Rodrigo in Rossini's *Otello* (1816) – carried into heroic parts the extraordinary three-octave range he had previously used in the lovers' parts of comic opera. He and other tenors of his day are reported to have sung in chest voice up to G or A, at most up to B flat; above that they sang in head voice, known in Italy (to the confusion of English speakers) as falsetto. Yet David, according to a reliable source – his mistress, also a singer – in 1814 was acquiring greater power and looked to be 'even more successful because he has almost completely forgotten his head notes'.[9] It sounds as though he was trying to please the audience (if not the critics) by pushing up his chest register, something that was reported also of a slightly later, more baritonal, tenor, Domenico Donzelli, who created Pollione in Bellini's *Norma* (1831). The account of Donzelli dwelt on his ability to join the chest and head registers so that the shift was imperceptible – a skill commended by Italian teachers from Monteverdi on – but added that in runs he would go up too high in chest voice and therefore became too loud.[10]

Several tenors, it may be, were feeling for a heroic ring in upper notes; Duprez's chest high C was only the most publicised breakthrough. In 1838 the wife of Duprez's predecessor Alphonse Nourrit – who had gone to Italy in a doomed attempt to match the younger man's feat – wrote that over the previous fifteen years the emission of Italian tenors had gone from 'flute' to 'horn'.[11] An exceptional tenor like G. B. Rubini – known, like Donzelli, for moving from one register to the other with no detectable join – went on singing in head-voice notes otherwise out of reach, like the high F Bellini wrote for him in *I puritani* (1835), but by the time he retired in 1845 the tenors for whom Berlioz, Meyerbeer, and the young Verdi and Wagner wrote seem all to have been cultivating power rather than smoothness. They had also come to monopolise the part of the lover-hero: by 1838, when Mercadante made a baritone the lover in *Elena da Feltre*, he saw this piece of casting as a 'defect' to be explained by the peculiarities of the tenor engaged for the season.[12]

A little earlier, the male romantic lead could have gone to a woman. The disappearance of castrati meant that from about 1800 Italian serious opera cast as the lover a female contralto in breeches, not now exceptionally but as a matter of routine; she was known by the old euphemism for a castrato – *musico*. In 1830 Donizetti and Bellini wrote the last well-known *musico* parts (in *Anna Bolena* and *I Capuleti e i Montecchi*). The practice lingered on for a decade or so, with the *musico* now in the subsidiary part of the hero's or heroine's friend, but it was on the way out; by 1844 Verdi would not hear of a female bandit-lover in *Ernani*. Rossini had composed a number of leading parts, both male and female, for a voice then known as a contralto, which he said was the normal Italian woman's speaking voice; we might sometimes call it a mezzo. In Paris, where verisimilitude still ruled, he took to a local habit of casting a female soprano as a boy, typically a page: his Isolier and Jemmy (in *Le Comte Ory* and *Tell*) followed Mozart's Cherubino in *The Marriage of Figaro*. More such adolescents would carol through operas by Berlioz, Verdi (exceptionally in the French-influenced *Un ballo in maschera*), Gounod, and Massenet among others, showing off their legs to an audience unused to seeing them in public.

For forty years or so contraltos thus had an unusual chance – after a period around 1770–80 when soprano mania ruled, perhaps thanks to the phenomenal high soprano Lucrezia Agujari.[13] Yet even the finest contralto of the 1840s and 1850s, Marietta Alboni, 'never drew such a big audience as a soprano of the same merit would have done',[14] while the greatest French singer in this range, Pauline Viardot, did best in a handful of parts, especially Meyerbeer's Fidès (in *Le Prophète*) and Gluck's *Orphée*. The operatic contralto from then on would as a rule be paid less than the soprano and tenor leads. Likewise the baritone, who emerged about 1840 as a distinct operatic voice, often cast in the part of a villain or ruler; until then he had been known as a 'singing bass', that is, one able to sing coloratura, as against the comic bass and the occasional deep bass, typically cast as a priest or heavy father. High voices still had power to excite, though in all operatic genres they were now sexually differentiated.

In opera of the high Romantic period, from about 1825 to 1850, the most important and, as a rule, highest paid figure was the soprano who could deliver poignant drama as well as coloratura. No one term described this vocal type, though in France Cornélie Falcon bequeathed her surname to the kind of voice in which she had sung Meyerbeer's dramatic parts, Alice in *Robert le Diable* and Valentine in *Les Huguenots*. Sopranos were not yet clearly distinct from mezzos, and the most famous prima donnas of the age, Giuditta Pasta and Maria Malibran as well as Falcon, were a bit of both. Malibran, like the leading German dramatic soprano Wilhelmine Schröder-Devrient, sang Bellini parts requiring coloratura display as well as Beethoven's *Fidelio* (but only Malibran dared sing both on the same night). All four women faced technical vocal difficulties, which – for a time – they overcame to astound their audiences. After six years on the stage Falcon lost her voice; after twice as many Pasta was apt to sing out of tune; Schröder-Devrient, always undertrained, grew wild; death caught the twenty-eight-year-old Malibran still at her peak. Romantic opera, then, made new demands; in meeting them the best singers could rouse audiences to a pitch of emotion most likely unprecedented, but with difficulty – perhaps the result of having to master both old and new styles, to be, as Bellini said of Pasta, 'encyclopaedic'.[15] Opera would make still greater demands from about mid-century; these amounted to something of a revolution in theatre singing. From then on, only an extraordinary artist – Rosa Ponselle or Maria Callas – could beat all comers at more than one kind of singing, even then not usually at the same time.

After about 1840 the demand for power spread from tenors to other singers. The heroines of Verdi's early operas, like Abigaille in *Nabucco* (1842), sang a line at once fast, vehement and spiky; Verdi, even more popular across the world than Rossini, led Italian composers in cutting down recitative, speeding up the action, and doubling the vocal line at times with brass. Crescentini and his like had blamed Rossini for making singers shout; in 1849 the London conductor Michael Costa complained that the newly dominant Verdian school 'ruins voices, and singing now consists . . . in mere *shouting*. . . . [W]here have those days gone when we heard intimations of paradise?'[16] Well into the late nineteenth century teachers and critics echoed his complaints and his harking back to the idyllic days of Rossini; a little later still, Wagner would be denounced as wrecker. As late as 1907 tenors at the Paris Conservatoire were being made to sing in head voice.[17] The effortless ideal of Mrs Bianchi Lacey was, all the same, a thing of the past.

The change came together with a singing technique described as new, though the description was perhaps newer than the result. Manuel García the younger, the teacher mainly responsible for propagating the technique from about 1840, was the first to claim not only that it rested on scientific knowledge of the vocal organs but that pupils must acquire that knowledge for themselves, in full physiological detail; he shared the general mid-nineteenth-century belief in exact science. García stressed the role of the larynx (as scientific explorer he had once looked into his own, thanks to a small mirror attached to a pencil): lowering or raising it controlled the registers, while the pharynx determined the timbre. Bérard in 1755 had preceded him in urging control of the larynx as a means to producing high or low notes, and in taking an interest in anatomy – inspired by the 'enlightened' authors of the *Encyclopédie* – but García was the first of many who made students learn about sushyoidian muscles and the like.[18] In the late nineteenth century his pupil Mathilde Marchesi trained many women opera singers; one, Emma Eames, reported that Marchesi's notion of dropping the larynx and avoiding clear pronunciation of words above middle F gave 'the impression of ventriloquism'.[19]

For all García's quirks – he decreed three registers instead of the usual two, and a much argued over *coup de glotte* or click in attacking a note – he kept faith by and large with the tenets of the old Italian school, as did Marchesi. What really made for a new kind of singing in opera was, besides the onrush of Romantic feeling, a new set of working conditions. The Paris grand operas of Meyerbeer, from about 1840 to 1890 almost as popular as Verdi's and more highly regarded, made orchestras in all the chief opera houses grow to eighty or a hundred players. Because opera now drew a rising audience from middle and lower middle classes themselves on the increase, new theatres were built to hold 2000 or 3000 – here and there in the Americas, 4000 or even 5000; some were arenas for open-air performance. Volume was now called for. At the same time, opera as a genre embodied in new or very recent works began to dry up in all the countries that supported it. The term 'repertoire opera' can be traced back to 1845 and the actuality – twenty or thirty familiar works endlessly repeated, some a hundred years old or more – soon became the pabulum of opera houses. Finally, the growth of self-conscious national schools of opera, especially in Germany and Russia, led some singers to keep to their own school and develop a characteristic style even as the profession at large became more and more internationalised. In the new large theatres with large orchestras, where Verdi and Meyerbeer dominated a now scant repertoire, 'shouting' might be welcome: in 1877 an agent was asked to provide, for a season at Bilbao in Spain, a singer 'who can shout well'; he would have to take on all the leading tenor parts, a dozen or so including those in *La sonnambula* and *I puritani*, both originally created by the smooth, lyrical Rubini and calling for anything but a shout.[20] The omni-competence demanded in opera houses that could afford only one lot of soloists often had dire results, at their worst early in the twentieth century, when verismo (the Italian form of naturalism, in *Cavalleria rusticana* and its progeny) gave mediocre singers an excuse to bawl.

True, the tenors who created Wagner's Tannhäuser (in 1845) and Tristan (in 1865), Joseph Tichatschek and Ludwig Schnorr von Carolsfeld, had sung Bellini and Mozart. The soprano Lilli Lehmann excelled about 1880–1900 as both Norma and Brünnhilde as, slightly later, did the contralto Ernestine Schumann-Heink in both Wagner and Donizetti. In the 1920s Frida Leider sang Donna Anna as well as Isolde and Rosa Ponselle sang Norma as well as late Verdi. Taking on a wide range of parts remained for many years the average singer's lot. Increasingly, however, for an artist in the top flight to do so would seem extraordinary if not rash.

Repertoire opera given in late nineteenth-century conditions – at the shortest notice, without a producer of modern type – encouraged singers to have 'their' own parts which they could step into with one piano rehearsal or none, often bringing their own costumes and even their own stage business. At one extreme, the bass Vittorio Arimondi agreed, on a tour of South America in 1903, to undertake any of 'his' thirty-nine parts.[21] In contrast, a type of soprano developed who specialised in a few Italian coloratura parts as the creators of those parts had not: Lucia di Lammermoor, Rosina in *The Barber of Seville*, and one or two more, joined by a few French or German ones specially written (Philine in *Mignon*, Lakmé, Adèle in *Die Fledermaus*). Such parts had come to seem decorative, even tinkling: you could now guy the *prima donna* as a 'canary'. The Italian ones, and with them a whole forgotten repertoire, would be rescued for musical drama only about 1950, by Maria Callas.

Meanwhile comic opera, in decline through the earnest Romantic period, split off about 1860 into operetta. In Paris, together with Vienna the fount of the new genre, some like Hortense Schneider (who created Offenbach's Belle Hélène and Grande-Duchesse) dispensed its seductive cheek and little else. This was a new use for the light voices that had earlier moved between comic opera and vaudeville, as, in the British Isles, they moved from comic opera to ballad opera and pantomime. While the vogue for operetta lasted – down to the 1930s – minor opera houses in France and the German-speaking countries expected singers to tackle it along with everything else; Italy, where the comic tradition was worst obscured, had separate, disreputable operetta troupes.

National schools of singing grew alongside national opera in countries such as Germany, Russia and Bohemia-Moravia (later the Czech Republic), which until the mid-nineteenth century had been content to put on an international repertoire, chiefly Italian and French. In Russia from the mid-eighteenth century, native singers had been trained to sing in Italian without leaving St Petersburg or perhaps learning the language – a compliment returned only in the past twenty years by those Western singers who have taken to singing in Russian.[22]

The German national school inevitably came to be identified with Wagner, not because the composer wanted it – he preferred to have his operas sung by artists trained in the old Italian school, like Lilli Lehmann and the Austrian bass Emil Scaria – but because by the 1880s Wagner's works dominated German-language opera. Down to 1914 a high-minded craze for them ruled leading opera houses everywhere. Outside Germany they were not – as now – the preserve of German or Scandinavian singers or kindred Americans who sing little else: the French bass Marcel Journet and three tenors, the Pole Jean de Reszke, the Italian Giuseppe Borgatti, and the Belgian Ernest van Dyck, all triumphed in Wagner parts. Many of their countrymen and women sang *Lohengrin,* the *Ring, Meistersinger* and *Tristan und Isolde* along with other composers' works, often in their own language. Within Germany, however, the Bayreuth Festival under Wagner's widow Cosima established a tradition too often characterised by the 'Bayreuth bark'. At the height of the Wagner craze a cosmopolitan singer wrote a perceptive account of the festival's weaknesses and strengths. The distinguished baritone Giuseppe Kaschmann came from Istria, a region of mixed Croat, Italian and German-speaking population; he was Italian-trained but sang in all three languages, and in 1894 he was singing Amfortas at Bayreuth in Wagner's own production of *Parsifal,* which he thought far superior to Cosima's later work. The trouble with Bayreuth, he wrote in a private letter, was the many German singers who 'seek expression not in the intonation of the note but in exaggeratedly vehement diction of the word, with a dessert of consonants purposely made harsh and overstressed'; they had not been properly trained, were unaware of it, and could not make feeling 'vibrate in the soul' of the listener as Wagner had intended.[23] Despite special pleading – 'heart' and 'soul', Kaschmann wrote, were the privilege of Italy – this brought up in a new context Mozart's old objection to singers who 'shrieked' and 'bellowed' to put the words across. The difference was perhaps that, at the greater volume needed to sing Wagner rather than eighteenth-century French opera, the actual note of the 'bark' could be hard to make out. Standards have almost certainly improved since 1894, but in the operas of Wagner, Richard Strauss and other German composers one can still on occasion hear the musically indeterminate 'bark'.

The growth of a Russian school kept pace from the mid-nineteenth century with that of Russian opera. Nationalist dislike of foreign opera encouraged it, while the supposed difficulty of mastering the language for many years kept non-Russians out of the new repertoire. What struck Western audiences when they heard Russian companies were the powerful deep basses; the most famous, Fyodor Shalyapin (at his peak in the first quarter of the twentieth century), was as much actor as singer. Excellent Russian singers of all vocal types made an international mark from the very late nineteenth century in different kinds of opera, as they do again today; only the fortress policy of the Stalinist period (about 1930–80) kept them from our ears.

Though a number of singers clung to their own schools and seldom ventured abroad, internationalisation from the mid-nineteenth century tended to blur differences within the profession. This has gone on until in our own day Italian operas put on in Italy, German operas in Germany, and French operas in France may be sung by an array of singers most of them from abroad, often from the United States. What set off the trend was the coming of modern industry and with it of steam technology; fast railway and ocean travel opened up vast spaces in the Americas and Australasia, as well as other unlooked for opera dates such as Cairo, Macao and the Azores. Jet travel from the 1950s merely speeded up changes a century old. Late nineteenth-century mass migration from opera-loving countries provided a 'national' audience for low-cost opera in the New World – Italian in Buenos Aires, New York and San Francisco, German in New York and Chicago; since the 1790s an earlier migration had provided an audience for French companies in New Orleans. At the same time the newly peopled United States, Argentina and Australia made both a source of singers uncommitted to any national repertoire and a well-off public eager to consume European opera. In Europe itself the growth of cities and of a vast lower middle class meant that even minor towns in France, Italy and the German-speaking countries now had an opera season.

One result was the downfall of the Italian language as the medium of all opera – and of Italian or Italian-trained men and women to sing it – in cities where the upper classes had equated it with the genre. Italian-language performances of such works as *Faust*, *Mignon* and *Les Huguenots* (in London of *Der Freischütz* and *Lohengrin* as well) vanished from the Vienna Opera between 1876 and 1884, from St Petersburg after 1885, from Covent Garden after 1887. A strongly Italian-influenced city like Buenos Aires held out till the First World War, and its opera chorus went on singing everything in Italian till 1961, whatever language the principals might be using. French companies stopped playing New Orleans after 1914; they had vanished, half a century earlier, from Latin America, earlier still from St Petersburg. At the Metropolitan Opera in New York, which had veered between all-German and all-Italian opera (with such results as *Carmen* in German and *Fidelio* in Italian), multilingualism began in the 1890s.[24]

For Italian singers the change was at first disguised by the immense popularity of a few tenors (Enrico Caruso, Fernando De Lucia) and baritones (Titta Ruffo, Giuseppe De Luca) who could get away – chiefly in the Americas – with performing in their own language not just Italian opera but certain French or German works (*Martha*, *L'Africaine*, *Hamlet*, *Carmen*, *Les Pêcheurs de perles*). Italian women singers were increasingly confined to their own country's repertoire, though that was so wide that they and their male colleagues felt little need to branch out. French singers (some of whom, like Duprez, Henriette Méric-Lalande, the baritone Paul Barroilhet, and the bass Prosper Dérivis, had created important roles in Italian Romantic opera) likewise started to withdraw into their own repertoire and, more and more as the twentieth century went on, their own country.

Wherever opera singing was cultivated, the number of men and women entering the profession peaked somewhere between 1860 and 1918. The range of possible careers and earnings was now enormous. At one extreme, Adelina Patti, whose operatic career flourished from about 1860 to 1890, became in real terms almost certainly the highest paid singer ever. Through careful management of her voice and health, added to great gifts, she broke box-office records wherever she went. On her United States tours she had her own railway coach, with a saloon furnished in monogrammed blue plush, a satinwood bedroom, a bath, a piano, and her own chef, and after a Buenos Aires season the management posted her receipt for £36,000 – well over £1 million at present values. At the other extreme, a struggling singer was paid a few francs or shillings a night to perform a leading part in a small Italian town like Assisi. In the French town of Béziers, a typical late nineteenth-century season running from September to June included about 115 performances of eighty-five distinct programmes – a play and an opera, or two plays; the operas numbered about thirty-five, between four and ten of them newly put on that season, and the singers performed in nearly all – with help from the prompter, no doubt. In both countries, a common hazard was the manager who went bankrupt or disappeared, leaving the company in the lurch. It did not help that aspiring singers from the New World, women especially, were now ready to sing in Europe for nothing or even to pay for the experience and the advertisement back home.[25]

Between these two levels, singers developed who could, at short notice, step into almost any feasible part. The diminutive Mathilde Bauermeister became a pillar of both Covent Garden and the Metropolitan Opera by knowing everyone's part – besides 'her' one hundred or so – and taking over, if need be, in mid-performance.[26] Between 1874 and 1897 Rosina Aimo sang in fourteen countries in four continents (a tour of Colombia had her singing twenty-four operas) but never in a front-rank theatre at home in Italy. At a very large Genoa theatre she sang 'night after night for weeks on end'. We know nothing of her quality, but such conditions encouraged the development of a voice that would not have been tolerated before 1840–50 – large, brazen, unfaltering at most times but with a wide vibrato not far from a wobble. Loud high notes from such voices excited some in the audience; they still do.

Aimo's 'night after night' meant that she was singing five times a week – a practice unremarked in eighteenth-century theatres with their generally smaller size and lighter orchestral sound, but resisted by leading singers from the age of Rossini on. Unavoidable in minor theatres, it was worst abused in some leading opera houses of the New World, out of a blend of commercial pressure and scant regard for the discrimination of the audience. At the Metropolitan in seven days of March 1889 Lilli Lehmann sang five performances, including four Brünnhildes (in all three *Ring* operas, two of them in the most taxing, *Götterdämmerung*). Mary Garden, at the rival Manhattan Opera in 1909, sang two operas in one day. She was not the only one to do so: when Félia Litvinne refused, the general manager of the Met brought his fist down on the piano, saying 'all the great artists have done it'; Litvinne replied 'I am not yet a great artist'.[27]

At all levels, singers attained a new social respectability. The theatre as a whole made this gradual climb during the nineteenth century – capped in Britain by the knighthood conferred on Henry Irving in 1895. The first opera-singer knight (thirty years retired from opera) seems to have been the baritone Charles Santley in 1907; Dames Emma Albani (a Canadian) and Nellie Melba (an Australian) would follow. Women were most affected by the change. In mid-Victorian Britain, revulsion from all theatre made the 'Swedish nightingale' Jenny Lind withdraw early from opera; so, perhaps on similar religious or moral grounds, did the leading soprano Helen Lemmens-Sherrington. Both then did well in oratorio and concert. Later singers worried less. On the Continent some leading singers were welcomed as they married into the nobility, with their past earnings as dowry. The old courtesan-singer was long gone – not that her disappearance stopped the cliché of the capricious, extravagant *prima donna* from feeding the popular press down to our own time. Opera singing easily makes people seem larger than life.

After the First World War, opera as an entertainment for most urban classes shrank, beaten back by the cinema. Numbers in the profession fell; with minor seasons on the way out and opera houses once again confined to the main cities, the general standard of attainment almost certainly rose. The growth since 1945 of regional opera companies in countries – Britain and France – where they had never existed or had withered away has added only marginally to this smaller but choicer trade.

Competition within this reduced group – teachers have often alleged – leads modern singers to rush their fences and burn themselves up too soon. They have said it again and again, at least since G. B. Mancini in 1774.[28] The complaint is probably as valid or invalid now as then: whether in the eighteenth or the late twentieth century, some singers have managed their careers prudently, some not, some have lasted a long time, some not; no concrete evidence suggests a decline at any one point.

The chief influences on opera singing in the twentieth century have been, first, the growth of recording and broadcasting; secondly, the shift from a genre ruled by singers to an integrated form of musical theatre where conductors, producers and designers matter at least as much, and where all opera house staff are unionised and paid a decent wage. From about 1900, records meant large earnings and world-wide renown for a few stars like Caruso. In the early days, voices recorded better than orchestral music, and some voices better than others: hence the triumph on records of the coloratura soprano Amelita Galli-Curci, who might disappoint admirers (like Uncle Matthew in Nancy Mitford's novel *The Pursuit of Love*) when heard in the flesh. Until about 1950, far more records were sold in rich countries, particularly Britain and the United States, than in a poor one such as Italy then was: the singers who found a new audience through records were those who had done well in the English-speaking world. The coming of long-playing records and CDs, and the enrichment of countries like Italy and Spain, has not ended the domination of the market by the United States. Radio made singers known to a wide audience, some of them, like the British coloratura soprano Gwen Catley, with few opportunities in the theatre; but such fame was limited to home ground.

Television, when it came in the 1950s, followed three decades later by video, made less difference than one might have expected. A small screen distances a larger-than-life genre twice over. Figures published early in 1998 showed that televised operas in Britain drew 'only' 200,000 or so – disastrous for this medium; true, it means a hundred times the audience at Covent Garden, but scarcely a hundred times the attention or pleasure. On Italian state television in December 1997 Verdi's *Macbeth*, opening the La Scala season amid vast publicity, drew 'only' a million; the same network injured the memory of Maria Callas by holding a 'Callas Day' dependent on her few, often inadequate, film clips. The singers who have benefited most from the new medium are probably those stars who have 'packaged' themselves for it outside the opera house, like the 'three tenors' Luciano Pavarotti, Placido Domingo and José Carreras.

Sometime between 1920 and 1970 opera singers changed, in J. B. Steane's words, from 'star' to 'musician'; the shift in the balance of power towards managers, conductors and producers left them with new responsibilities, a new dignity and greater professional respect.[29] Since the beginnings of opera, principals' fees had accounted for roughly half the cost of putting on an opera; by the 1980s this had come down to one-fifth. True, they could make money on the side from records (but they had once made it from concerts in private houses). They were now artists working alongside others rather than 'sacred monsters'. It is no coincidence that two of the finest singers of the century, Rosa Ponselle and Maria Callas, were accomplished musicians. With help from a conductor (Tullio Serafin) and a producer (Luchino Visconti) as well as from the long-playing record and the spirit of the age, Callas brought off what Ponselle could only begin – the rescue of Italian Romantic opera from oblivion and canary-fancying. A group of mainly Vienna-based singers and conductors – some in exile during the Nazi period – had the musicianship to rescue Mozart's Italian comic operas from daintiness, and his *Idomeneo* from the library; here the singing of Sena Jurinac and Cesare Siepi remains a touchstone. Other singers and conductors have brought Monteverdi's operas back to life.

Though opera is now largely a museum art enshrining a tradition, new operas from time to time reach the stage. Some – perhaps almost as old as the twentieth century itself, like Schoenberg's monodrama *Erwartung* of 1909 – even now share the avant-garde characteristic of striking many hearers as difficult. Marie Gutheil-Schoder, who originally performed *Erwartung* (in 1924), sang many parts from Mozart to Strauss; her accuracy in atonal music, though, tends now to be the preserve of specialists who sing in concert rather than in the opera house. There, not only *Erwartung* but Berg's masterpieces *Wozzeck* and *Lulu* may be left to singers some of them with doubtful intonation, made up for – or not – by dramatic punch.

PART THREE

Choral music and song

9 European art song

STEPHEN VARCOE

My involvement with this subject started in earnest at university, where I would take volumes of songs out of the library and read through them by the hundred. If I was in luck, a friendly pianist would help out for an hour or two, but more often than not I was on my own with my horrible piano playing. As a result I came to know much of the repertoire from within, as a performer, rather than from the point of view of a scholar or historian. The present chapter necessarily has a historical basis, but I would like to emphasise that this is not how I discovered the treasures of European song. Nothing can replace the experience of singing them for yourself (in a sound-proofed room if necessary), and I very much hope that readers of these pages will want to explore some of the highways and byways of this wonderful musical heritage.

What is an art song? First of all, it was intended to be accompanied by a keyboard, originally perhaps a harpsichord or fortepiano, later a pianoforte. Secondly, the poem (or sometimes a prose text) should have been chosen not only for its suitability as a song, but also for the composer's ability to identify with it and to express its meaning in an individual manner. Lastly, the intentions of the composer and the question of taste and discrimination have to be considered.

The development of the song out of Italian monody is discussed elsewhere in this book, and Italian forms held sway into the eighteenth century. It was in Germany in the 1730s that the first reaction to Italian dominance took place, led by Sperontes (1705–50), whose collection *Singende Muse an der Pleisse* sprang from a desire to re-create songs in a traditional German manner. Through what became known as the Berlin Lied school, Glück (1714–87), Zelter (1758–1832) and Reichardt (1752–1814) developed a simple Classical style of song. This, then, is the beginning of the art song – the Lied – and it is important to recognise that it was essentially a German invention, a fact which colours the whole of our subsequent appreciation of song writing.

At first, the accompaniment consisted of the melody and a figured bass, as in the songs of C. P. E. Bach (1714–88), and was intended for the harpsichord or clavichord. A crucial step forward came with the invention and rapid improvement of the fortepiano, an instrument capable of greater expression and dynamic range than its predecessors. In fact, this was really the reinvention of the fortepiano, since the first instrument was built in Italy by Cristofori in 1620. This had a complicated mechanism which told against its general adoption, and with its thin strings and hard hammers it sounded rather like a loud harpsichord. Silbermann's forte-pianos of the 1730s were criticised by J. S. Bach for their heavy touch and weak treble, but by 1747 Bach was able to admire the improved versions. A further step came in the 1770s with Stein's escapement, which prevented the hammers restriking the strings with a stuttering effect. Fully realised accompaniments were now appearing, though as with many of Haydn's songs, for example, they were not always independent of the vocal line, with the vocal melody often being doubled in the right hand.

The rise of the Lied is firmly linked with the Romantic movement and the poets Goethe (a close friend of Zelter and Reichardt) and Schiller, who knew both Reichardt and the south German composer Zumsteeg (1760–1802). Goethe held that his poems should be set strophically; through-composition was for him 'thoroughly reprehensible, since the general lyrical character is thereby completely destroyed and a false inter-est in detail is demanded and aroused'.[1] Fortunately Zumsteeg was not of this opinion, preferring melody, changing mood and expression of feeling. The stage was now set for the most important development of all, the work of Franz Schubert (1797–1828).

Robert Schumann wrote, 'No music except Schubert's is so psycholog-ically remarkable for the development and association of ideas and the impression of logical transition that it conveys; moreover, very few composers have been so successful in imprinting a single individuality upon such a variety of tone-pictures, and fewer still have written so much for themselves and their own heart'.[2] Here was an Austrian whose songs were nevertheless rooted in the German renaissance and more particu-larly in Zumsteeg's work, many of whose song texts Schubert sub-sequently set himself. Zumsteeg used a form quite new to German literature: the ballad, an imitation of English and Scottish prototypes. These were often long poems containing dialogue, narrative and super-natural events, which offered great possibilities for imaginative song writing. Carl Loewe (1796–1869) specialised in this form, and though Schubert wrote relatively few ballads, one of them, *Erlkönig*, became the most celebrated song of all.

Schubert's taste in poetry, though wide-ranging, was always fastidi-ous, especially in relation to its suitability for setting to music. After all, great poetry may not necessarily lend itself to being made into song, while lesser poetry may be raised to the heights thereby. For him there was no desire for religious piety, for moral expressions or pastoral sentiments. The simplicity he sought came, not from the German folk tradition (from the *Knaben Wunderhorn*, for instance), but from Goethe. This was poetry that was deeply felt, passionate, drawn from nature rather than being merely decorative. In Walter Scott and in Macpherson's *Ossian* there was a more powerful evocation of the past than in Germanic literature, and in Schiller there was the philosophical and the Classical combined. His immediate and large circle of friends included many whose poems he set to music, among them Mayrhofer, Schober, Seidl and Spaun. These friends regularly gathered for what became known as *Schubertiads*, informal concerts of his music in which songs played an important part. The small size of the room was matched by the relatively small sound of the fortepiano, and any student of the songs of this period will gain great insight by performing or listening to them with the appropriate fortepiano accompaniment.

Although Schubert's friends and admirers were largely of the middle class, and although he was virtually unknown outside Vienna during his lifetime, his influence as a song composer was colossal. Beethoven (1770–1827) on the other hand – patronised by the upper classes, famous throughout Europe, the revolutionary mind that changed the course of music – had a far smaller impact as a writer of songs. Beethoven, Haydn (1732–1809) and Mozart (1756–91) had generally written songs in the Classical Italianate style, often to commission. Haydn produced arrangements of over four hundred British airs for various English publishers, Beethoven more than one hundred. In one respect at least Beethoven did make a significant contribution to song writing, and that was with *An die ferne Geliebte*, the first German song cycle. The songs of Mendelssohn (1809–47) betrayed the influence of his teacher, Carl Friedrich Zelter, by being generally strophic. But as his *Lieder ohne Worte* for piano showed, his primary preoccupation lay with melody rather than with text.

The next truly great Lieder writer after Schubert is Schumann (1810–56), who was fully steeped in the Romantic ideal. Classicism had been exemplified by order, equilibrium and control; Romanticism reached out for freedom, passion and a longing for what was far off, fantastic and unattainable. Schumann, with an introverted poetic nature, was deeply interested in literature. He chose poets such as Heine, Eichendorff, Kerner and Byron to express his most profound feelings. In 1840, the year of his marriage to Clara, he wrote more than one hundred songs – ardent, tender, yearning, fearful – an outpouring of many of the greatest songs in the canon. One of his major contributions to the development of the Lied was his use of the piano: a rhapsodic style with preludes and postludes which extended the instrument's role as a partner in the depiction of emotional context. The lightly strung instruments of 1800 had grown from five to as much as six-and-a-half octaves in the

1820s. Streicher's use of iron bars in 1835, and Hoxa's full iron frame in 1839, permitted heavier stringing and greatly increased the dynamic range. Listen to Schubert's *Der Sänger* and Schumann's *Ballade des Harfners* (settings of the same Goethe text), one with a wooden-framed piano, the other with a big iron-framed instrument of the 1840s; one with a charming Haydnesque introduction, the other with a brilliant array of spread chords. The contrast is almost shocking.

The German composer most obviously associated with the political, intellectual and artistic ferment of the middle of the century was Wagner (1813–83). And yet for all his monumental impact on the world of drama, art, philosophy, on music generally and vocal music particularly, his song writing was confined to his *Wesendonck Lieder* with orchestral accompaniment; it was left to his successors to carry his ideas into the Lieder tradition. As a composer of songs it was the conservative Brahms (1833–97) who now held the foremost position. Qualities which pervade his music are controlled seriousness and introspection. Even his most moving and passionate songs, such as *Wie bist du, meine Königin*, exhibit this restraint. It is as though he were a Romantic writer expressing himself in a Classical idiom. He devoted enormous efforts to studying the style and technique of the composers of the past, and this fashioned his approach to the form and structure of his songs and their accompaniments. The simplicity of folk song was for him a kind of ideal, which manifested itself not only in his straightforward settings of traditional songs, but also in many of his original Lieder.

Brahms was highly self-critical, and open and honest in his criticism of others. One young composer who was subjected to this criticism was Hugo Wolf (1860–1903); he never forgot the hurt it caused, and placed himself firmly in the Wagnerian camp. Wolf's great gift to the Lieder repertoire was in the declamation of the text; the strophe had vanished to be entirely replaced by through-composition, where melody was always subservient to the needs of poetic inflexion. The role of the piano was now at least equal to that of the voice, carrying through in miniature the ideals expressed in Wagner's music. Whereas in traditional opera the dramatic impulse was in the singing line, Wagner's music drama was a unified art form. He saw drama as having an inner and an outer expression: the inner carried by the orchestra, and the outer, the momentary unfolding of the narrative, carried by the voice. The orchestra was the primary factor in the music, with the vocal line woven into it, and this was the principle behind Wolf's songs, with the piano taking the orchestral role. Like all his great forerunners in the Lied he had a finely formed taste in poetry and an instinctive grasp of the needs of lyrical expression. His six main collections were devoted to one poet at a time, with the poet's name above his own, and the emphasis on equality between words and music. Most of his songs are miracles of clear understanding and economy of means. What could surpass *Anakreons Grab* for limpid conciseness? While songs can reduce the multiple layers of meaning inherent in a poem to those few highlighted by melody and harmonic framework, this song, as with so many of his others, enhances and deepens one's understanding of the text. Many writers have concluded that these songs represent the highest point of the Lieder tradition. Just as the Schubertiads had provided a platform for Schubert's songs, so the Wolf Society performed the same function for his. The *Liederabend* had become an established part of the concert scene, with Schumann's and Brahms's songs enjoying especial success. This success was based upon the enthusiasm of amateur singers for the genre; but by the end of the century that enthusiasm was beginning to wane.

The earliest songs of Mahler (1860–1911) were for voice and piano, but the later sets were with piano or orchestra, or orchestra alone. The power and originality of his music shines through in some of the greatest vocal writing ever achieved. *Das Lied von der Erde* may not be art song in the narrow terms of our definition, but as song in a wider sense it is unequalled. Richard Strauss (1864–1949) likewise produced orchestrations of his songs, though, unlike almost all of the great song writers, he claimed not to have been unduly fastidious about the text he chose; just so long as it fitted the general idea of the song that was welling up inside him. Strangely, this process proved successful: so much so that some of the finest Lieder resulted from it. His *Vier letzte Lieder* for soprano and orchestra, a sublimely inspired creation, signals the end of the long *Liederreise* which Schubert began.

Meanwhile, what of the rest of Europe? In Italy, vocal music remained firmly in the grip of the Church and the theatre. Opera was deeply rooted in the popular mind, appealing to prince and beggar alike: *bel canto* was in the blood. Opera-lovers came from all walks of life, a phenomenon unique to Italy. The enthusiasm of its followers stimulated an unbroken stream of rehashed or ridiculous plots stringing together seemingly impossible feats of vocal gymnastics. The recitative, which was central to the early operas of Monteverdi, became merely a means of moving the story on between the really important items, the arias. Rossini and Verdi became national heroes, symbols indeed of Italian nationality. Even the drawing room songs were essentially simplified operatic arias, designed primarily for 'a good sing'.

France was a different matter. During the late eighteenth century the *romance* developed, turning away from the affectation of the earlier *chanson* and adopting a simple archaic style. The beginnings of a Romantic sensibility can be found here and there, notably in Jadin's setting of Goethe's *La mort de Werther*, yet the compositional style is still French-Italian in the manner of Mozart's *Dans un bois solitaire*. Berlioz's (1803–69) *Neuf Mélodies* of 1829, based on texts from Moore's *Irish Melodies*, showed a new depth of emotional expressiveness. His *Les nuits d'Eté* of 1841, later orchestrated, stands alone as an astonishing artistic achievement which had no precedent and no immediate successor. Apart from this bolt of Romantic lightning the *romance* underwent a slow evolution into the true French art song, the *mélodie*.

The early years of the nineteenth century saw the birth of French Romantic poetry – Hugo, de Lamartine and Gautier among many others. The songs of Schubert, which became known in France in the 1830s, offered a model for composers to attempt this new literature, but it took time for musical techniques to catch up and express it fully, which is perhaps why Berlioz's example was an isolated phenomenon. Gounod (1818–93) achieved fame as an opera composer, but he also wrote more than 150 songs. Some of these are 'undeveloped' *romances*, sentimental drawing room songs, many of which he wrote for the English market. But the simplest, least pretentious ones stand as true early *mélodies*. Lalo (1823–92) and Bizet (1838–75) were more consistent in their output, producing *mélodies* with the traditional charm of the *romance*.

Saint-Saëns (1835–1921) holds a key position in the developments of this time. He was a man of prodigious gifts, not only in music but also in the classics, philosophy and science. His knowledge of, and enthusiasm for, composers of the past was very unusual for his day. Many of his more than 150 songs are highly imaginative and harmonically interesting, mostly to his own or contemporary writers' texts. Outside the world of opera, music had come to be regarded more and more as a German art form: if Beethoven was the earthquake then Wagner was the tidal wave. The Franco-Prussian war of 1870–71 helped to precipitate some action against this foreign musical domination, and in 1871 Saint-Saëns founded the *Société Nationale de Musique* to promote new music by French composers. On the board of this body was one of his pupils, Fauré (1845–1924), with whom the *mélodie* can be said to have come of age. The earliest of Fauré's songs still showed their *romance* roots, but those of his middle period (1880s) and, even more, his late period (after 1890) show the authentic clarity, subtlety and textual understanding of French art song. Fauré's reticence and avoidance of showy effects are not dryly academic: coupled with his harmonic inventiveness and originality they reveal the true nature of the meaning within the poetry.

Whereas Fauré fought shy of the influence of Wagner and pursued his individual path right up to the final *L'horizon chimérique* of 1921, Henri Duparc absorbed it and gave it French colour. Duparc (1848–1933) left just thirteen songs, all written before 1885, by which time a nervous condition prevented him from composing anything more. His studies under César Franck had been based upon the German heritage in music, and the strength of that tradition, coupled with his French sensitivity to the texts of Verlaine and Baudelaire, created songs of unique power.

In other countries composers were seeking a national identity in their folk music: in France they followed a different course. Music for them was essentially intellectual in character, emphasising refinement of taste and technique, and the obvious 'Frenchness' of their works sprang from this aesthetic. For this reason Debussy (1862–1918) is the most French of them all, and a pivotal figure in the history of Western music. In literature, the Symbolist poets (Mallarmé, Verlaine, Baudelaire) considered music to be the primary force behind all art. In painting, the Impressionists' theories of the refraction of light and the blurring of outline offered musicians a new way of approaching composition. These two strands of artistic theorising met in Debussy's harmonic view of music. 'The harmonic density, tonal vagueness, and the erotic undertow in the music of Debussy are what matters; and, in the best sense, its artificiality. Its derivation from the arts of its time rather than from nature or more personal emotions is a significant prophetic factor, one that points to the aesthetic of our time.'[3] Melody emerges from within the shifting harmonies, creating songs that are both uniquely beautiful and extraordinarily expressive.

Apparent similarities between the music of Debussy and of Ravel (1875–1937) are superficial. Ravel was by nature highly reserved, a quality which led him to adopt a detachment in his music and a fastidiousness in everything. His tonal harmony was combined with melodies that had a modal flavour, possibly stemming from his Basque-French heritage. Chabrier's (1841–94) *Six Mélodies* of 1890 are probably the pattern for his *Histoires Naturelles* of 1906. Of these, *Le Grillon* displays most clearly Ravel's fascination with the artificial and the miniature, overlaid with a wry humour.

Erik Satie (1866–1925), an extraordinary and eccentric character, holds an influential position in French musical history. His small-scale works with their comical instructions possessed a seriousness of intention which pointed to the future, especially the future of his protégés, Les Six. One of these, Poulenc (1899–1963), proved to be the last great writer of *mélodies*. Like the man, his music is charming, witty and urbane, with flowing melodic lines and pleasing, quirky harmonies. The songs could be frivolous (*Fêtes galantes*) or deeply serious (*Sanglots*). They could be amorous (*Violon*), all but obscene (*Chansons gaillardes*) or heart-rending (*C*). Throughout all of them run those supreme French qualities of discernment and taste which have always been the hallmark of the great *mélodies.*

In England during the early eighteenth century the craze for Italian opera did not last long. In 1728 John Gay's *Beggar's Opera* ushered in a new era of ballad operas, satirising contemporary politics and parodying the Italian style, using popular tunes as their basis. The broadside ballad became an enormously successful genre, being turned out by the thousand during the next 150 years. With the increase in wealth and influence of the middle classes came a greater demand for music of all kinds. Music of quality was generally provided by foreigners, 'mostly Germans and then French, for the English are not much better musicians than the Dutch, and they are fairly bad'.[4] In 1729 Daniel Defoe proposed an academy 'to prevent the expensive importation of foreign musicians',[5] but nothing came of it. Much of London's musical life centred on the pleasure gardens, especially those of Ranelagh, Vauxhall and Sadler's Wells, which were imitated elsewhere in the country. Collections of pleasure garden songs for home use were published to satisfy a voracious public appetite, with nothing too challenging for amateur taste or technique.

The presence in England of German refugee piano makers in the 1760s, and the rise of the firm of Broadwood, meant that pianos were becoming more and more available to an avid public. After the Napoleonic wars French composers provided charming lightweight pieces for players of limited technique. Chopin wrote in 1848: '[Englishwomen] all look at their hands and play wrong notes with sentiment'.[6] To complement this army of talentless pianists an enormous production of bland stereotypical songs took place, and those composers who were writing serious songs were using Austrian and German models. Attwood (1756–1838), Samuel Wesley (1766–1837) and the tragically short-lived Pinto (1785–1806) wrote in the manner of Haydn, who had a large influence on English musical life. Later Sterndale Bennett (1816–75) was held in high esteem in Germany for his Mendelssohnian works. Indeed, on the old Guildhall School of Music in John Carpenter Street, his name was included amongst those of the great composers carved in stone. Song writing was not regarded as a very serious craft, however, especially since the field was flooded by an incessant outpouring of popular balladry.

British culture, which since Henry Purcell's time had lacked a native musical tradition capable of comparison with others, was at its lowest musical ebb during the nineteenth century. Standards of musical education were at last being raised by the founding of the London conservatories, but the syllabus was unrelentingly German. The most influential of the late Victorians, Stanford (1852–1924) and Parry (1848–1918), were staunchly conservative in their approach to composition, preferring Brahmsian technique and restraint to the exciting developments taking place through the works of Wagner and his followers. Stanford's early work, *Twelve Songs by Heine*, clearly shows the Brahmsian influence, though his wonderful *La belle dame sans merci* from the same period displays a passionate intensity rare in English music of the time. Parry's twelve sets of *English Lyrics* generally have a quality and refinement which raise them from the simply lyrical to something worthy to be called art songs, showing a finely crafted technique and poetic sensibility. Somervell (1863–1937) and Quilter (1877–1953) produced many attractive songs, effectively using an old-fashioned style. But it was nearly always the lyric element in English poetry which appealed to composers rather than the more challenging forms of epic verse or Romanticism. 'The lyrical tradition was the enemy of invention',[7] so often making for insipid unoriginality.

The man who was to produce music of a passion and grandeur not hitherto associated with the English was the working-class, self-educated Elgar (1857–1934). He helped to raise standards of British music-making generally and of orchestral playing in particular. Of his songs, the most important are *Sea Pictures* (1899), for contralto and orchestra, which do not strictly belong here. Elgar was not part of any 'movement' as such, but was a kind of bomb under the musical establishment of the time, and the herald of the English musical renaissance. For a 'movement', we have to look to the folk-song revival which came at the turn of the century. Here was a music not associated with continental ideas and academic dogmas, but which had a different kind of tonality, modal in nature, offering a means of escape from chromaticism and the diatonic scale. It harked back to a pastoral golden age before the industrial revolution had scarred the landscape, and provided, for a while, a specifically English solution to the problems posed by the musical developments of the time.

The composers most associated with this revival were Vaughan Williams (1872–1958), Holst (1874–1934), Grainger (1882–1961) and Butterworth (1885–1916). Outside this folk-influenced group were the significant figures of Bridge (1879–1941), Bax (1883–1953), Ireland (1879–1962) and, most important, Delius (1862–1934). Notwithstanding Delius's famous setting of *Brigg Fair*, his use of folk themes was sparing, and always decorative rather than structural. He was a figure isolated from his contemporaries, forging a personal and unmistakably 'English' style. Gurney (1890–1937) also remained apart from the folk revival. He was a poet of considerable gifts, whose sensitivity to poetry is clearly shown in his songs.

A major event in the history of English song was the publication in

1896 of A. E. Housman's *A Shropshire Lad*: sixty-three poems of youth, love, death, nostalgia and bitterness set in a rural landscape with country folk at the centre, and in a form which seemed to invite composers to set them to music. Many did, and one of the most successful was Vaughan Williams with *On Wenlock Edge* – six songs for tenor, string quartet and piano. Somervell was another, with a fine set of ten songs. Ireland and Moeran produced their own settings, altogether tougher and darker than Somervell's, reflecting the turmoil not only in music (through Schoenberg and Stravinsky, for example), but also, through the Great War, in the world itself. The reputation of Butterworth, who was killed in that war, relies almost entirely on his Housman songs, which have a haunting, spare quality about them that reaches to the true inner nature of the poetry in a way that no one else achieved. Yet another element in the musical ferment of the early twentieth century was the rediscovery and reassessment of Renaissance and Baroque music, and a renewed interest in the instruments of the period led by Arnold Dolmetsch. One who admired and studied this early music was Warlock (1894–1930), whose songs have a complex and interesting harmony within a diatonic framework.

The long association of Britten (1913–1976) with the tenor Peter Pears bore fruit in many fine songs, the instrumentally accompanied *Serenade* and *Nocturne*, and the Michelangelo and John Donne *Sonnets* among them. His skill at word painting places him in the highest category of song maker. *Winter Words* is a group of Thomas Hardy settings, a poet whom most composers seem to have found uncongenial as a source for songs, possibly because his poems possess an inner music of their own, with unusual metres and rhyme-schemes, as Hardy himself maintained. They clearly appealed to Finzi (1901–56), however, whose mental cast resembled Hardy's in his distrust of religion and his sense of the evanescence of life. Many of the forty-seven poems which he used were treated in a form of syllabic recitative, carefully calculated to correspond with the ebb and flow of the text. Indeed, they call to mind Peri's description at the end of the sixteenth century of the basis of his compositional style. One could almost say that Finzi had rediscovered the principles of Italian monody in the last days of English song.

German domination of music during the nineteenth century was not confined to France and England, but was felt throughout Europe. In Russia the preferred model for song was the French *romance*, which held sway no doubt because French was the language of fashionable Russian society. As far as the German academic tradition was concerned, it was the 'mighty handful' who led the revolt, and of these Mussorgsky (1839–81) had the greatest impact on the world of music, especially on account of the modal folk-song elements he used. His songs, for example the cycles *Sunless* (1874) and *Songs and Dances of Death* (1875), show his concern with the natural rhythms of Russian speech, rather than with the imposed rhythms of a melodic pattern. Out of this renaissance came the twentieth-century giants: Stravinsky, Prokofiev and Shostakovitch. It was the revival of folk music which lay at the heart of musical renewal in other countries also. The Hungarian Liszt (1811–86), a citizen of the world, wrote both *mélodies* and Lieder. It was for Kodály (1882–1967) and Bartók (1881–1945) to create a musical identity for Hungary. Similar roles were played in Bohemia by Smetana (1824–84), Dvořák (1841–1904) and Janáček (1854–1928); in Spain by de Falla (1876–1946); and in Norway by Grieg (1843–1907), whose example served as one of the models for the English folk revivalists.

The developments of the twentieth century opened a gulf between the connoisseurs of contemporary art music and the wider popular taste. The songs of Schoenberg (1874–1951), Webern (1883–1945) and Berg (1885–1935) maintained a link with the past even as they redefined the future. Composers who, at least in part, remained in the land of tonality like Poulenc, Britten, Eisler (1898–1962) and Tippett (1905–98) could produce songs of originality and power. But new literature and new music were exploring the disintegration of old forms, undertaking a Freudian analysis of the human psyche in their own terms. The melody and harmony of the past had no place in this new world, and that is what popular taste craved. Hindemith (1895–1963) wrote, 'The performing amateur who seriously concerns himself with musical matters is quite as important a member of our musical life as the professional'.[8] Yet he found that there was little desire amongst amateurs for contemporary Lieder.

The nineteenth-century Lieder tradition in Austria and Germany was based upon a bedrock of amateur involvement. Song recitals by professional singers were a kind of showcase, a pinnacle of achievement. In England the showcase was the Royalty Ballad concert, the first of which took place in 1866. Here, programmes of works from one publisher's catalogue were performed with the object of selling copies to the public, leading to an output that was largely sentimental and undemanding. The first professional Lieder recital in England was given by Raimund von Zur Mühlen in 1882. In 1903 the newly opened Bechstein Hall (later the Wigmore Hall) still had just five song-only programmes; in 1912 there were more than thirty. The old mixed programmes of songs and instrumental pieces were beginning to disappear, and by the 1930s the song recital had settled into a form which it still largely retains: unrelated groups of songs offered up by a performer who, if male, usually wears a costume that was old-fashioned in the Edwardian era.

Imaginative programming (such as the themed programmes of the Songmakers' Almanac) can help to attract people to take an interest in song, but they need more than that. They need to be encouraged to sing for themselves, to experience the process directly, and this is clearly the province of musical education in schools. Yet 'serious' music, like so much of art, is today often seen as elitist and unapproachable, and of the songs now being written, most are inaccessible to the amateur because of the demands of vocal technique and the instrumental forces usually required.[9] Altering this is clearly the province of composers, though how they can achieve it is so far an unanswered question.

10 English cathedral choirs in the twentieth century

TIMOTHY DAY

In the twentieth century the English cathedral and collegiate choir has consisted typically of about sixteen trebles – boys with unbroken voices, aged between about eight and thirteen (often with four additional 'probationers') – and at least six men taking the three lower parts. Numbers have varied from time to time in any particular choral foundation; in recent times York, Durham and Winchester Cathedral choirs have all used twelve men, as have Magdalen College, New College and Christ Church Cathedral in Oxford. King's College and St John's College in Cambridge have both used fourteen men's voices, each with six basses. St Paul's is the largest establishment of all, with thirty-eight boys and eighteen men.[1]

Historians, journalists, critics and cathedral musicians themselves have been sure they can identify a style of singing peculiar to these choirs which they define by reference to purity of tone, accuracy in intonation, precision in ensemble, and an absence of rhetoric. The 'essence' of the cathedral choir said one authority is 'the boy's voice', and its men are 'at their best when they blend with that clean white tone'.[2] Again and again throughout the century the same epithets have been used to characterise the singing, 'pure', 'otherworldly', 'ethereal', 'impersonal'; writers who do not admire the style refer to its 'coldness', its lack of 'passion' or 'personality', to the cultivation of beauty of sound at the expense of any real expressiveness, to 'under-interpretation', to rather barren meticulousness; a French critic writes about 'performances that are *millimetrées*, as if they were mathematical exercises'.[3]

When did this style appear? How was it formed? Why was it cultivated? Choirs of men and boys have after all been adorning the 'cool and ancient'[4] Offices of the church for hundreds of years, and not a few pieces in their repertories – by Byrd and Tallis, for example, by Purcell, Boyce, Greene, Battishill and by S. S. Wesley – have been sung almost continuously since the day they were first heard in these venerable buildings. Recordings, though, have shown how dangerous it is to make any assumptions about unchanging performing styles. With English cathedral music there is a particular danger in extrapolating back even into earlier decades of the nineteenth century for there is clear evidence that towards the end of the last century there were real changes in the music of cathedral and college chapels. 'In respect of performance, of demeanour, and of general efficiency', as a former organist of Trinity College, Cambridge, put it in 1914, there had been 'an immense advance' as he considered it, 'upon the conditions that prevailed' three or four decades earlier.[5] This was not just a question of higher standards; in the 1880s the Dean of Windsor listened to his choir under the new organist, Walter Parratt, and thought that he detected 'a new spirit in Church music . . . a revelation of new things in prayer and praise'.[6] Even those who did not altogether approve of these 'new things', who considered that the last quarter of the last century marked a high point in the history of English choral singing and that subsequent developments have represented an aberration or an unfortunate departure from a noble tradition, have agreed that this was a defining moment when new ideals were being consciously forged.[7] The particular qualities of the boy's voice which were so prized in the decades round 1900 appear not to have been especially valued earlier in the nineteenth century. S. S. Wesley, the most famous cathedral organist of the nineteenth century, for example, regretted that he had to use what he considered a 'poor substitute for the vastly superior quality and power of those of women'.[8]

Early in 1900 the organist and choirmaster of Old St Paul's Church, Baltimore, visited seventeen of the English cathedrals and heard sixty choral services and commented on what he found in a letter to *The Musical Times*: 'Without doubt the finest choir in England is that at Magdalen College, Oxford. And in the same breath one must also mention St Paul's Cathedral, London, and King's College, Cambridge. These three afford the best examples in the world of the possibilities, the beauty, the perfection of vested choirs of men and boys.'[9] Little more than a year before that American organist was admiring the choir at Magdalen, its choirmaster, J. Varley Roberts, had published *A Treatise on a Practical Method of Training Choristers*. All his recommendations are directed towards the cultivation of 'pure' and 'sweet' tone, the qualities of the notes in what he describes as the head register. The chest register, 'the natural notes of a boy's voice', which some musicians call the 'shouting' notes, is rough and unpleasant, and these notes, according to Varley Roberts, 'should *never* be forced, but *always* sung *softly*', otherwise the head notes will be ruined.[10] A way to teach boys about the head register, he explains, is 'for the teacher, if he can sing falsetto, to give an illustration with his own voice, by singing notes with his "chest", and then with his falsetto voice'.[11]

Dr Moody, who was organist at Ripon from 1902 to 1954, insisted on 'unforced' singing not only to enable the desired tone quality to develop but also to allow the boys to give unsleeping attention to accurate intonation. He suggested that at practices very little accompaniment should be used.[12] At King's College, Dr Mann rehearsed '*everything* without accompaniment – as a systematic principle'. In the 1890s, according to Edward Dent, this was 'most exceptional'. He was punctilious about tuning and 'extremely sensitive to such things as the difference between a major and minor whole tone (C–D and D–E, 8:9 and 9:10)'.[13] To obtain the desired 'smooth and restful tone',[14] physical relaxation must be encouraged: the throat 'must be absolutely open and loose, there must be no stiffening of the jaws, breath pressure must be steady and light, and no more breath must be taken than is absolutely necessary'.[15] The resulting tone quality is commonly described as 'white' by both admirers and critics; those who dislike the sound seem to want to convey by this word what they consider to be its weakness and blandness, its 'colourlessness', its absence of 'character'; admirers want to stress its radiant whiteness, its silveriness, its sweetness, its resemblance to the pure tones of a tuning fork, and to the gentle, straight, penetrating timbre of the violin G string.[16] The timbre of the boys' voices is complemented by the translucent timbre of the English counter-tenor, whose 'beautiful thin flute-like tone . . . brightens the entire quality of the tone of the choir',[17] and in order to match the tone of boys and countertenors singing in this unforced style, restraint by tenors and basses was crucial. If any of the tenors and basses at King's College early in the century went to a singing teacher to try and learn how to throw the voice forward they were promptly checked by Dr Mann.[18]

The cathedral singer has to 'sink his personality, and become one of the many who offer their corporate praise', according to Terry at Westminster Cathedral.[19] Sir John Stainer, who played a crucial part in creating higher standards and suggesting new possibilities as organist at Magdalen College from 1860 and at St Paul's from 1872, once said that he felt the men of the St Paul's choir 'entirely subordinated their own wills to the general effect and beauty of the music' so that at the close of an anthem he more often 'felt inclined to say "Thank God" than to say "Thank you, gentlemen of the choir."' And he was sure, he added, that 'that is what should be the case.'[20]

It was clear what these choirmasters between the wars did not like. The tone of the boys in French and German choirs was, in Terry's opinion, 'raucous and horrible'. There are many things we might learn from the Continent and America, but choirboy training is not one of them.[21] In 1922 about seventy singers drawn from Roman choirs which included St Peter of the Vatican and the Sistine Chapel gave two concerts in the Albert Hall. The editor of the *Musical Times*, Harvey Grace, who was to become the organist and choirmaster at Chichester Cathedral, was not impressed:

these Vatican youngsters ... were harmless enough in the soft passages, but when power was required the quality was painfully shrill ... [the choirs'] gusty changes from *pp* to *ff*, sudden *pp*'s at points where neither text nor music seem to call for them, an almost entire absence of any degree of power between the extremes of soft and loud, and the trick of ending most works with a long-held whisper, do not appeal to us when applied to the Palestrina school.[22]

This English cathedral style was certainly shaped by a character-istically English predilection for understatement and for self-control, 'the true English style' that Jane Austen detected in the greetings between two friends whose real devotion was buried 'under a calmness that seemed all but indifference'.[23] It is a manner of singing that has its counterpart in the way of reading lessons and prayers long familiar in cathedral services, in speaking of 'seeing through a glass, darkly' or of 'the word made flesh' – in treating 'depths and immensities', as one of the cathedral organists put it – with a measured calm, without any theatrical extravagance.[24]

Who were these musicians who were alive to such nuances and shades of meaning, whose outlook and tastes moulded this style? Parratt, appointed to St George's Chapel, Windsor, in 1882, was one of the most influential. The objectivity of his approach was seen clearly in a simple sixteenth-century piece like the anthem ascribed variously to Farrant and Hilton *Lord, for thy tender mercies sake* which he insisted upon being sung 'without any nuance or variation of tone colour whatever in a perfectly impersonal style'.[25] When he was appointed at Windsor he wrote to his wife that this would be his life's work, to 'refine' the singing of the choir.[26] Any form of individuality in cathedral singing was to him 'anathema'. As a teacher his most pungent condemnation was for any form of showiness or vulgarity.[27] While these views reflect the values of a certain kind of Englishman in late nineteenth-century England, and of a class, this was not a class from which men who played musical instruments for a living or trained cathedral choirs had usually come. For Parratt's aims and outlook reflected a change in the social status of musicians in England. They derived in part from men like the devout Sir Frederick Ouseley, born in 1825 and the son of the ambassador to the courts of Persia and Russia, who took holy orders and used his private wealth to establish St Michael's College Tenbury as a model of cathedral worship; the 'reverent agnostic', Sir Hubert Parry, the son of a gentleman landowner, described by Elgar in 1905 as 'the head of our art in this country',[28] who was once said to repre-sent in music 'the essential sanity of the English genius: its mixture of strength and tenderness . . . its entire freedom from vanity and affectation'.[29] Among Parry's many achievements was the breaking down of social barriers; he made it possible for the leading musicians in England to mix with the 'governing classes'; it inevitably meant that something of the manners and tastes and aspirations of educated, intelligent, serious, sensitive and artistic members of the upper-middle class were diffused among these men. For all these men egotism, vanity, conceit of any kind were to be deplored. When any piece by Parratt was sung in St George' Chapel, no composer's name was given on the chapel music-lists, nor was a name given against the chants he wrote for the chapel's own chant-book.[30]

Reserve, reticence, and an avoidance of flamboyance had been fundamental qualities in the spiritual and devotional life of the Tractarians, and their characteristic emphases had gradually affected the quality of public worship throughout the English church. 'Religion and poetry are akin', John Keble had written, 'because each is marked by a pure reserve, a kind of modesty or reverence . . . Beauty is shy, is not like a man rushing out in front of a crowd.' In the work of a quintessentially English poet, Walter de la Mare – who was himself a choirboy under the reforming Stainer at St Paul's in the 1880s – W. H. Auden perceived at its heart a sense of wonder, awe and reverence, which represented 'the most favourable soil in which goodness can grow'.[31] From this sense of wonder, according to Auden, can be learnt

> a style of behaviour and speech which is no less precious in art than in life; for want of a better word we call it good-breeding, though it has little to do with ancestry, school or income. To be well-bred means to have respect for the solitude of others, whether they be mere acquaintances, or, and this is much more difficult, persons we love; to be ill-bred is to importune attention and intimacy, to come too close, to ask indiscreet questions and make indiscreet revelations, to lecture, to bore.[32]

The singing of the choir of Magdalen College, Oxford, when it was directed by Bernard Rose – he was *informator choristarum* between 1957 and 1981 – which seems in many ways to epitomise the style, was described in a review of a recording released in 1979 as being characterised by 'gentle but clear articulation and . . . fine balance' in which no attempt was ever made 'to cheapen the music by exaggerated phrasing or tempi', and in which everything was always 'in its place and well controlled'; 'a gentle serenity' informed all the performances.[33] In comparison to which the recordings made by R. R. Terry with members of the Westminster Cathedral Choir and of the choir of St George's Chapel, Windsor, directed by E. H. Fellowes – the successor of Sir Walter Parratt, who appears to have made no recordings – come as something of a shock. Inevitably these early recordings mislead. Boys' voices were more difficult to record on both the acoustic and early electrical processes, and this is likely to be the main reason why the balance is always wrong, why the boys sound fainter and more distant than they should, or than they actually did.

Neither is the impersonality so much stressed by Terry and others a feature of these recordings. Rather the listener today is struck by the individuality, sometimes the rather unfortunate characterfulness, of the lower voices in these old recordings. This is evidently not because of the inadequacies or failings of the singers themselves. Fellowes emphasised that the lay clerks at Windsor in the years he directed the choir were the equal of any in England.[34] For the early electrical recordings, made after 1925, a single microphone was placed a few feet above the singers' heads, and it was not possible to capture much sense of a building's acoustic until the development of the long-playing record. These were not performances produced for the microphone; the men phrase and articulate and project as they would have done for a congregation standing forty or fifty feet or more away from them. Fellowes and Terry might well have wished their singers not to sustain the lines too smoothly, but to give the notes power and strength of attack, allowing the building to play its part in depersonalising the voices with its resonance, which effect is simply not caught by the microphone of the time.

It is also not likely that excessive smoothness and unanimity in attack and polish in execution would have been considered particularly desirable, certainly by the lay clerks. The editor of *The Musical Times* had to concede in 1889 that there was a prejudice among the general public that 'musicians are as a class wanting in the manlier qualities'.[35] In the 1890s 'Is he musical?' like 'Is he earnest?' was used as code for 'Is he homosexual?' It may not be fanciful to guess that aspects of the assertive, no-nonsense delivery of these early twentieth-century lay clerks are deliberately cultivated. Neither would these lay clerks all have shared these new views on interpretation of such a man as Parratt. A successor at St George's Chapel, Windsor, who endeavoured to emulate his style, knew that he achieved the style 'under much protest' and regarded his achievement as 'remarkable ... seeing that he had some very fine solo voices among his lay clerks'.[36]

As a result of the introduction of new terms of employment and because of changed economic conditions, singing in a cathedral choir is not the full-time job it was in many of these choirs a century ago. In collegiate choirs lay clerks have been replaced partly or wholly by choral scholars, undergraduate members of the college, so the average age of the men in the choirs is much lower. An advantage of this is that it has become possible to exclude voices that have deteriorated, have become looser and less focused, with a wide vibrato, and so to approach more closely currently held ideals concerning blend and balance.

Everyone agrees that standards of singing have been raised through broadcasting and recording, not only by the activities of the choirs themselves but also by the standards set by secular choirs of great expertise exploring the repertoire. Performances have acquired greater buoyancy and confidence through the increased use of unaccompanied Tudor and Elizabethan music. In recent years the acquisition of pre-Reformation repertoire has been encouraged by the widespread use of the Latin text of the Mass. The long-playing record in particular created opportunities for cathedral choirs, or at least some of them, to widen their repertoire and rehearse intensively the kind of works hitherto rarely tackled. During the 1960s David Willcocks did not aim deliberately to modify the style of the choir at King's College, Cambridge (see Fig. 5), but he noticed at the end of the decade that changes had undoubtedly occurred: a bigger, brighter and more penetrating sound had developed and a rhythmically more pungent style, the results chiefly, he thought, of working with orchestras (in the making of recordings of Bach's *St John Passion*, Vivaldi's *Gloria*, Handel's Chandos anthems, and Masses by Haydn).[37] New music taken up by cathedral choirs after the Second World War was written in idioms requiring greater rhythmic incisiveness and a different kind of sureness about pitching and intonation, music like Britten's *Ceremony of Carols*, and *Rejoice in the Lord*, and the setting of the Evening Canticles specially written for the choir of St John's College, Cambridge, by Michael Tippett, and later music by Richard Rodney Bennett and Maxwell Davies.

All musical performances since the 1920s have reflected the twentieth century's anti-Romantic and formalist aesthetics. It would certainly have been true that cathedral singers a hundred years ago were less indulgent over tempo changes (as we should now think) than solo singers or chamber musicians or orchestral players of the time. Parratt's successor at Windsor, E. H. Fellowes, may not have been quite as strict a 'classicist', but even so the very emphatic rallentandos he imposes in Gibbons's *Hosanna to the Son of David* may not have been excessive or eccentric to his own contemporaries.[38] They simply belong to the stylistic world of Elgar, of which the improvisatory sweep and 'useless nuances' and 'inaccurate rhythms' were mocked by Stravinsky in the 1920s and answered with a stylistic plainness in which Elgar could detect 'no soul & no romance & no imagination'. When in 1922 the Ripon organist drew attention to 'one of the most remarkable frailties of singers', namely 'the universal tendency to slacken the tempo when diminishing the tone, and to hurry it when making a crescendo',[39] he was merely reflecting a general tendency towards a greater fidelity to the letter of the score. Recording itself, everyone agrees, has encouraged this tendency towards meticulous observance of the text. Walford Davies, Fellowes's successor at Windsor, who was renowned as a broadcaster, realised very early that the microphone required different techniques, that singers must cultivate 'the purest and most conversational tones of which they are capable', that they

Figure 5 King's College Chapel, Cambridge: the choir viewed from the screen

will fail if they sing in their customary manner, that for an actor to use his stage demeanour in front of the microphone is as if he were to make up his face to sit and talk with just one other person.[40] In order to achieve the greatest possible accuracy and precision it is usual now for cathedral organists to direct the choir themselves most of the time with the assistant accompanying. This was rare even after the Second World War. Walter

Parratt considered the conducting of the cathedral choir 'unnecessary and unsightly'. Even if it were possible to obtain some extra expressive nuance, he thought 'the loss of spontaneity' too great a sacrifice.[41]

But as well as these evolutionary changes there were what might be termed revolutionary ones that appeared to deny the critical importance of the traditional timbre of the boy's voice. That a highly distinctive style had evolved and was widely recognised was clear in the 1950s when two cathedral choirmasters set out to create contrasting styles with quite different characteristics. George Malcolm was appointed organist at Westminster Cathedral in 1947. He was not brought up in the tradition; he was admitted to the Royal College of Music as a violinist at the age of seven, and subsequently trained as a concert pianist and became best known as a harpsichordist. He thought that English choirboys produced what he termed 'an artificial and quite unnatural sound'. The boy's singing voice, according to Malcolm, should develop the natural timbre of the voice which is heard when boys 'talk, or laugh, or cheer at a football match, or recite poems, or even sing songs round the camp fire'.[42] Instead the boy's voice is trained to become a 'tuneful little instrument which will echo back sweetly from the Gothic vaulting and never crack a stained-glass window'. This tone quality results from the boys being taught to exclude or at least underemploy 'those resonating-agents whose function it is to amplify the human voice, to colour it, and to give clarity and definition to its vowel-sound', and to use 'a very light breath-pressure'.[43] The tone quality Malcolm developed with his boys at Westminster was quickly dubbed 'continental', though in fact his starting point was the sound made by the boys at the Catholic church of Farm Street, Mayfair, before the War.[44]

A little later new sounds – there were some similarities with those produced by Malcolm's trebles – were created by George Guest at St John's College, Cambridge, who was choirmaster there between 1951 and 1991.[45] Unlike Malcolm, Guest did know the tradition from the inside; he had been a choirboy at the cathedrals of Bangor and Chester, and an organ scholar at St John's. The technical standards achieved by the choir at King's College were revelatory to him; but he was not 'moved', he has said.[46] At any rate with his own choir, just five minutes down the road from King's, he wanted to do something different. Guest considered that a boy had two voices, a flute tone but also an oboe tone, and that both should be developed. He was impressed by the sound of the boys at Montserrat Abbey near Barcelona whom he had heard singing Victoria on a recording released in 1953[47] and also by the Copenhagen Boys' Choir who had come to the Aldeburgh Festival in 1952 and had then made a recording of Britten's *Ceremony of Carols* with the composer conducting released in 1954.[48] Guest aimed to give the boys 'much bigger, more dramatic voices than most', developing in each boy 'a range extending over three octaves, from E flat or D below middle C to the G above top C' – earlier choirmasters had considered a boy's range extended to two octaves – and encouraging them when singing top notes not to maintain a relaxed physique but 'to adopt something of the poise of an all-in wrestler'.[49]

One of the reasons for not using girls in cathedral choirs has been the assumption that because of physiological differences they cannot produce the clear white impersonal tone quality that boys are uniquely capable of. The 'greater emotional appeal' of the woman's voice may appeal to some people, as an organist of Westminster Abbey put it in the 1920s, just as some prefer the 'colourful effects and tremolo of the cinema organ'. But this particular repertoire, these centuries of English church music, can never produce the effect intended unless it is sung by the voices for which it was intended.[50] Nicholson's views were deeply entrenched even if they weren't quite universally shared, but they were to some extent disproved by the gradual emergence after the Second World War, and especially from the 1970s onwards, of secular choirs singing the repertoire in concert performances and in broadcasts and recordings. The girls' timbre of the Clerkes of Oxenford may not have been indistinguishable from trebles' – though it was often mistaken for it – but it certainly embodied the hallmark qualities of the cathedral choir's male voices. In 1991 Salisbury Cathedral choir school admitted girl choristers and others have quickly followed.

A timbre, a tone colour, the quality of a crescendo, a particular manner of enunciating consonants, all such details are components of a style which is itself part of a constellation of values, and not just aesthetic ones but also social and spiritual and moral ones. The cathedral choirs sing of 'eternal changelessness', but the history even of their dignified art can illustrate only the fleetingness and impermanence of all things earthly.

11 Sacred choral music in the United States: an overview

NEELY BRUCE

The Continental Congress, which had governed thirteen British colonies while they were becoming the United States of America, adjourned in 1789. The first Congress then took office, elected under the recently adopted Constitution. After fifteen years of subversion, rebellion, war, divided loyalties and conflicting visions, a hard-won consensus had been reached. A new chapter in political and social history was beginning. A new chapter in cultural and artistic life was beginning as well. The young Timothy Dwight, contemplating 'war's dread confusion' during the Revolution, envisioned an unprecedented order of peace and prosperity in the emergent country, when

> New bards and new sages, unrivaled, shall soar
> To fame unextinguished when time is no more . . .
> Columbia, Columbia, to glory arise,
> The queen of the world, and the child of the skies. [1]

A momentous event in the history of sacred choral music took place shortly before Dwight penned these stirring words. William Billings (1746–1800), a tanner by trade, published his 'opus one', *The New England Psalm Singer*, in 1770, just in time for the Revolution. Approximately a dozen sacred pieces by American composers had been published in the thirteen colonies before Billing's collection appeared. In a single stroke Billings, with his original volume containing 120 new works, increased this repertoire a thousand per cent. Also, in the book's remarkable preface, he issued what amounts to a Declaration of Independence of the American composer. His emphatic and well-argued case for compositional flexibility (he observes that everyone knows what 'Poetical License' is, and 'I don't see why with the same priority there may not be a Musical License') culminates in his often-quoted exhortation to the composer of the future.

> for my own Part, as I don't think myself confin'd to any Rules for Composition laid down by any that went before me, neither should I think (were I to pretend to lay down Rules) that any who came after me were any ways obligated to adhere to them, any further than they should think proper; So in fact, I think it is best for every *Composer* to be his own *Carver*.[2]

Billings shows a decided preference for polyphonic music in the style of the English composers whose work he knew, particularly William Tans'ur. Tans'ur is credited with inventing the fuguing tune, a brief composition in two distinct sections. The first is homophonic; after a clear cadence a second section of imitative or non-imitative counterpoint begins. The order of entries is usually either from bottom to top – bass, tenor, alto, soprano – or, more often, bass, tenor, soprano, alto, reflecting the spatial disposition of the parts in the galleries of New England churches. Billings is a master of variety in his treatment of this simple structure. He frequently uses non-imitative counterpoint, a decidedly modern touch. He plays with the order of entrances and the number of beats elapsed between them; sometimes he changes tempo in the fuguing section; he introduces additional contrapuntal passages after the initial entrances. These and other techniques enliven these brief, colourful works; 'Creation' from *The Continental Harmony* is an excellent example.

He is fond of similar contrapuntal excursions in his anthems, the most successful lengthy compositions of an early American composer. Billings's finest anthems include 'Psalm 42', 'An Anthem for Thanksgiving: Psalm 148', the ever-popular 'An Anthem for Easter', and three settings of verses from the Song of Solomon. His contemporaries defined an anthem as an extended composition with words taken from scripture; Billings took liberties with biblical texts, cutting and pasting or even rewriting. His setting of Psalm 149 boldly paraphrases the text. For example, verse 7 in the King James Bible is simply 'Praise the Lord from the earth, ye dragons, and all deeps'. Billings sets to music the following flight of fancy:

> Ye dragons whose contageous breath
> Kindle the dark abodes of death,
> Change your dire hissings into heav'nly songs,
> And praise your maker with your forked tongues.[3]

The young William Billings is the prototypical American composer. His music is original, but clearly grows out of its own time and place. And he did not just write his own music; he sang it, published it, and taught other people how to sing it. His music and his career have been a model for a remarkably diverse group of composers for over 200 years.

Literacy was low and musical literacy lower still in colonial America during the seventeenth century. A few tunes sufficed for singing metrical psalms. By an act of Parliament in 1640, in all churches in England the parish clerk was required to read each line of the psalm before it was sung, as an aid to the illiterate. This practice, known as lining-out, spread immediately to the colonies, and took root with particular vigour in New

England. Over time the practice expanded; hymn texts were lined-out as well as psalms, and song leaders (not necessarily the parish clerk) chanted the lines instead of reading them.

Lining-out proved to be amazingly popular and resistant to change. It continued long after the literacy rate had risen, rendering the practice unnecessary. It came to dominate the sacred musical landscape, with important and unforeseen consequences. By the end of the seventeenth century most congregations were satisfied with singing very few tunes. The tempo of this limited repertory became slower and slower; by the early 1700s it was reported that some congregations sang 'Old Hundred' so slowly that a single note lasted two seconds. Compensating for the developing uniformity of repertory and tempo, singers ornamented tunes in highly individualistic ways.

The resulting sound was described by contemporary observers in totally negative terms. Thomas Walter in 1724 is typical; he describes a lined-out psalm as 'a confused Noise, made up of Reading, Squecking [*sic*] and Grumbling, [rather] than a decent and orderly Part of God's worship'.[4] In the view of Walter, and contemporaneous New England clergy, the public liturgy of the church was being subverted by the introverted vocal meditations of individuals. If we can trust that twentieth-century survivals of lining-out have something in common with seventeenth-century New England, to modern ears the sound is jarring at first, but it is also exhilarating, an intense, joyous musical anarchy unlike any other Christian music. It is certainly not 'a confused Noise', but rather something quite beautiful. It is no wonder that those who practised it resisted change for so long.

A 'long-overdue reform' of church music was instituted by the clergy, who made an enthusiastic push towards greater musical literacy and an enlarged repertoire. Teachers of singing in schools were mentioned in Virginia as early as 1710; by the end of the century they operated throughout the country, especially in New England, where Billings and his composer-tradesmen contemporaries taught singing schools. These itinerant singing masters had the complete support of the clergy, at least at first. Throughout the eighteenth century congregations and choirs learned more and more hymn tunes; by the 1750s fuguing tunes and anthems had been introduced. Most composers of this imported music were English (William Tans'ur, Aaron Williamson, Joseph Stephenson); two native-born composers, James Lyon (1735–94) and Francis Hopkinson (1737–91), published a small number of original pieces.

The 'old way of singing', as the slow heterophonic style of lining-out came to be known, declined markedly.[5] In its place a new style arose. Late eighteenth-century singing teachers taught the rudiments of musical notation; scholars were expected to sing from the written page rather than singing by ear. Agreement on pitch, dynamics and pronunciation was expected. The singing school movement succeeded in creating a large body of singers capable of handling a repertory of increasing complexity and variety. Compositional activity was stimulated in many levels of society. Daniel Read (1757–1836) of Connecticut (who ran a general store) was the first to follow Billings with an original tunebook. Supply Belcher (1752–1836) of Maine (tavern keeper, school teacher and politician) also wrote and published an original tunebook. Justin Morgan (1747–98) of Vermont (a farmer, among other things) wrote only a handful of excellent tunes and one anthem. Dozens of others followed suit, writing a little or a lot.

It must not be assumed that the original compositions of New England amateurs constituted the entirety of sacred choral music in the United States at the end of the eighteenth century. On the contrary, major urban centres of the East Coast boasted professional music-making in at least some churches from mid-century onwards. Charles Pachelbel (1690–1750), whose father composed the famous canon, was organist at St Philip's Church, Charleston, from 1737 until his death. William Selby (1738–98), a well-known organist and composer active in London, emigrated to the United States, where he served as a church musician in Anglican churches in and around Boston (he crossed musical paths with Billings several times). And in 1793 the young Benjamin Carr (1768–1831), formerly of London, arrived in Philadelphia, where he was to become a major force in the musical life of that city. These and other emigrant composer-performers gradually established a base for professional music-making in urban American churches.

Many of the finest immigrant musicians were Moravians, who established their own religious communities, the principal one being in Bethlehem, Pennsylvania. Moravians of all social classes and occupations were skilled performers, especially on bowed strings. They brought with them fine instruments and collections of music by Haydn, Stamitz and the sons of Bach. The extensive music-making of these communities and the large number of anthems generated for worship by both emigrant and native-born composers typify eighteenth-century American musical life in many ways; the lack of prejudice towards the home-grown product and the fundamentally democratic nature of the Moravian musical enterprise are American to the core.

Moravian music is even strangely prophetic. After Billings the first drastically original American composer, Anthony Philip Heinrich (1781–1861), was from Bohemia – very close to being from Moravia. The Moravian composers' reliance on German models is precisely analogous to the New England composers' reliance on English ones. In the nineteenth century more and more composers were educated in Germany, abandoning English models for German ones. And in the middle of the twentieth century, through the efforts of the Moravian Music Foundation, the compositions of these German-speaking American composers captured the imagination of a broad concert-going public indoctrinated with a sense of the greatness of German music, a public which quickly recognised Moravian excellence.

Throughout most of the young republic, the German composer most admired was not one of the ones emulated in Bethlehem. George Frideric Handel, as much an Englishman as a German, was the most popular foreign composer in eighteenth-century America. (The highest praise Billings received in his lifetime was to be called, by an anonymous reviewer in Philadelphia, 'the rival of Handel'.) While it appears that a complete performance of *Messiah* was not heard in America until 1817, excerpts from it and other Handelian oratorios were common from the middle of the eighteenth century onwards.

European music is not unique in its influence on the development of the art in the United States. The music of the indigenous Indian population, while certainly in evidence throughout the eighteenth century, received little attention and had little effect on the country's musical life until the turn of the twentieth century. The music of Africans, however, both slave and free, was to have a profound effect, a crescendo of influence running through the entire nineteenth century and continuing throughout the twentieth. The end of the eighteenth century saw the first organised efforts to convert slaves to Christianity; earlier informal attempts were only moderately successful. With organisation and determination, however, missionaries from England and various northern states began to convert southern plantation blacks in ever larger numbers, preparing for the mass conversions of the early nineteenth century.

Before the Civil War the religious music of American black people received only scant attention, primarily in private correspondence and diaries. The excellent singing of slaves, especially their singing of hymns, is noted by several clergymen from the 1750s onward. The practice of lining-out, vigorously opposed by northern clergy in the eighteenth century, was recommended by the same group at the turn of the nineteenth, as a method of teaching slaves,. The distinctive qualities of black singing were only hinted at in these early sources; more detailed descriptions of vocal style and production would follow in the 1840s and 1850s. However, at least some eighteenth-century observers intimated that the slaves sang in a distinctive manner. James Meacham, a Methodist preacher, wrote in 1789 that he was awakened in the middle of the night, in raptures of Heaven by the sweet Echo of Singing in the Kitchen among the dear Black people (who my soul loves.) I scarcely ever heard anything to equal it upon earth.

Two weeks later, on a Sunday, he wrote,

the dear black people was filled with the power & spirit of God and began with a great Shout to give Glory to God . . . this vexed the Devil. He entered into the cruel whitemen with violence [who] eagerly ran into the Church with sticks clubs and caines . . . abeating and abusing the poor Slaves the outcast of Men for praise of God . . . O America how she groans under the burden of Slavery . . .[6]

Meacham's diary, reading between the lines, tells us much about the singing of slaves in Virginia. It was beautiful, original, without parallel. It was an intense spiritual experience for the participants and those who listened with a sympathetic ear. It was a music of extreme dynamic contrast. And the singing was powerful enough to arouse an angry, even violent, response, as well as an enraptured one.

American sacred choral music at the end of the eighteenth century may be summarised as follows. There is a strong, vibrant and original outpouring of newly composed, self-consciously American music by Billings, Read and other New England composers. Typically it is found in Congregational churches, but increasingly in other denominations as well. There is also a vibrant but not so original body of music imported from Europe and performed both by persons born in America and by recent immigrants. Many people compose in this style, particularly immigrants working in large Episcopal churches and members of the Moravian Church. Outside of these 'parallel mainstreams' there were two important dissenting traditions. One was a deliberate dissent, an old-fashioned hold-out from the seventeenth century; white congregations who continued to line-out hymns in a slow, highly ornamented, dissonant, even cacophonic manner. At first isolated congregations in many denominations preserved this music; eventually it is found almost entirely in small groups of Baptists. The other dissent is the religious song of slaves, a 'dissent by default' of which the infant United States is barely aware; it is the music of the future. Many Christian slaves at this time had no denominational affiliation. Other southern black people, slave and free, were Anglicans, Methodists, Baptists and Presbyterians; in New Orleans there were many black Catholics. The distinctive black denominations of the north were in their infancy and did not become established in the south until after the Civil War.

Each of these four traditions cultivated a distinctive method of vocal production. The wild and primitive 'old way of singing', once ubiquitous, was preserved in isolation as a thing in itself. The singing of Billings and his contemporaries was an educated and refined version of the 'old way', with distinct vocal characteristics but still crude by professional standards. The vocal ideal of the immigrant composer, sometimes realised, sometimes not, was the professional voice, trained according to European methods. And the voice of the slave was different from all three: full-voiced, even strident, and capable of an extraordinary range of vocal colour. These four voices continue to be heard throughout the history of American music.

By the 1820s a profound change was well underway in American sacred music. William Billings had been dead for over two decades and the enthusiasm of the late eighteenth century was giving way to self-doubt. Even Daniel Read expressed the opinion that the rough-hewn psalmody of his youth was not so fine as he once believed. A new generation stood ready to educate and elevate. The most important agent for musical change was the bank clerk-turned-composer/compiler Lowell Mason (1792–1872). Mason composed many hymns which remain in use at the end of the twentieth century. He is also the composer of lovely anthems which deserve modern performance; many of these are contained in *The Boston Anthem Book* (1856). While travelling in Europe (his first visit was in 1837) he amassed a vast library of music, now housed at Yale University. He was the first American composer to earn his living exclusively from musical activities. In spite of these worthy accomplishments, his music, while not devoid of charm, lacks the spontaneity and originality of the best early New England composers. In his zeal to reform American church music Mason changed the ground rules. Where Billings sought to be vivid and expressive Mason sought to be correct. The correct can also be beautiful of course, and there is no arguing with the success of Mason and his programme. However, to have replaced something vital and indigenous with something derivative and imported does not seem, after 150 years, to have been the 'progress' which Mason and his contemporaries thought it was.

The reform movement in church music in the early nineteenth century was so successful that by the 1850s the music of New England in earlier times seemed totally forgotten. However, just as the 'old way of singing' did not completely disappear but was preserved by a dedicated minority of enthusiasts, the plain tunes, fuguing tunes and anthems of Billings and his contemporaries were similarly preserved. Some of the old tunes were so popular that they even remained in Mason's collections; one such is 'China' by Timothy Swan (1758–1842), 'improved' of course. More obscure northern publications such as *Ancient Harmony Revived* (1847) and *The American Vocalist* (1848) reprinted several of the most popular old tunes, more or less in their original form.

Dozens of fine pieces by early New England composers are contained in southern tunebooks of the period, the most important of which are William Walker's *Southern Harmony* (1836), and what has proved to be the most long-lived collection in the entire tradition, *The Sacred Harp* (1844). Benjamin Franklin White (1800–79), the principal compiler of this collection, was also a particularly interesting composer. It is difficult to assess his output in its totality. The 1991 edition of *The Sacred Harp* contains twenty-five compositions and arrangements attributed to him.[7] Other editions of the book are still in use; in these another dozen pieces by White may be found. Nineteenth-century editions of the book which have fallen out of use contain still more White tunes. There are many unattributed compositions in all of these volumes, some of which are certainly by White, just as many unattributed compositions in the collections of Lowell Mason are known to be by Mason himself. There are also pieces by White's students, relatives and unmusical associates, which may well bear the imprint of his editorial hand.

White's most bold compositional gesture, which concerns the work of others, was unprecedented. Composers and arrangers throughout the history of music have added obbligato parts or other passages to existing compositions; before White, however, no one wilfully subtracted a part from another's work. White admired the music of Billings and his contemporaries and included many of their pieces in his collection. However, he felt that it was unnatural for women to sing in the low part of the voice and as a consequence he wrote no alto parts himself. Being a man of high moral principle he removed most of the 'unnatural' alto parts from earlier compositions included in this book. So forceful was his personality that as long as he lived the alto parts of these pieces were not incorporated in *The Sacred Harp*, and living composers who contributed to the book wrote in three voices as White did. After his death alto parts were quickly supplied to the older New England pieces and most of White's as well; only a handful of the original three-part compositions survive in the 1991 edition.

The style of choral singing which has grown up around *The Sacred Harp* is rather different from that advocated by late eighteenth-century singing masters, and significantly different from that espoused by Mason. It is a loud, impassioned sound; the rare soft singing one hears is characteristically breathy in the extreme. Individual vocal timbres are tolerated, in view of the democratic nature of the musical enterprise, but they are not always considered beautiful. Blend is achieved by accumulating a large mass of people.

Sacred Harp singers sit in a square, the four parts facing the centre where the leader stands. It is not known at what point this spatial arrangement became standard; it was well established just before the Civil War. The historical precedent is clear, however. In Congregational churches in the late eighteenth century the choir stood in the front row of three-sided balconies, the singers grouped by vocal parts. As observed by several authors at the time, this arrangement caused the musical lines to seem to fly over the heads of the congregation. From singing on three sides of a room to singing in a square is a small step to take. Perhaps the square became popular in the 1840s when a similar enthusiasm for geometric shapes can be observed in other aspects of American life (the growing Sunday School movement, Masonic rites, public ceremonies, etc.). It is almost certain, however, that singing in a square occurred before this time. Early composers of fuguing tunes were well aware of the spatial implications of their work, and designed their pieces so that entrances would move around the square, mirror each other, reverse direction, etc.

The style of Billings and his musical descendants continues to thrive in the late twentieth century. A major revival of Sacred Harp singing is underway, and many composers have turned to this early American music for inspiration. Alice Parker (*b.* 1925) has drawn on the tradition to make excellent arrangements which blur the line between arranging and composing. 'And Sing Eternally' (1996) is a large work for orchestra and chorus which treats selected compositions of Billings and his contemporaries in a symphonic manner. Like so many late eighteenth-century composers, she is also an itinerant singing teacher.

William Duckworth (*b.* 1943) has taken twenty pieces from William Walker's *Southern Harmony* and used them as the basis of an extended work for chorus *a cappella*. Duckworth's eponymous cycle, composed in 1980, incorporates a number of avant-garde techniques, including process music which adds and subtracts rhythmic units, slowly changing repetitive fragments used in a minimalistic manner, random procedures, quasi-serial techniques, and harmonies made by piling melodies up on top of themselves.

The Bohemian immigrant Anthony Philip Heinrich is certainly the most original nineteenth-century composer in the United States. Known in his lifetime as 'the Beethoven of America', he preferred to be called 'the log-house composer from Kentucky'. A number of his compositions are designated 'Musica Sacra', including four hymns composed for Nathaniel Gould's collection *National Church Harmony* (1832) and 'Funeral Anthem'. There are also sacred solos and a beautiful vocal quintet, 'The Death of a Christian'. Most of his choral works are with orchestra. 'The Adieu of the Pilgrims' for five soloists and chorus (SATBB), with organ or piano accompaniment, is an excerpt from a massive oratorio entitled *The Jubilee*, which interweaves religious and patriotic themes, tracing the history of the British colonies from the Pilgrims through the Revolution. 'The Adieu' is a *tour de force* of vocal colour and chromatic complexity.

There are other large sacred choral works by nineteenth-century Americans. The finest is the Mass in D by John Knowles Paine (1839–1906). Unlike the Carr masses, which are attractive service music, the Paine Mass is a major concert work, dramatic in conception and bold in execution. It is composed in eighteen distinct movements; a complete performance lasts around an hour and forty minutes. While not so experimental as the music of Heinrich, this Mass is full of harmonic richness and fine orchestral and choral effects. Paine does not hesitate to use the colour of the organ by itself (most European composers of the nineteenth century use the organ merely to thicken the texture or to double the choral parts). An entire movement is written for chorus *a cappella*. The writing for solo voices is consistently gratifying, usually lyrical but occasionally dramatic or virtuosic as the musical situation demands.

The music of Paine, excellent and beautiful as it is, had little impact and today is known only to specialists. After the Civil War, however, a music was emerging from the newly freed southern slaves which would transform American music. These religious songs of black people were called spirituals almost from the beginning. Before the war a few writers had noted the beauty and originality of this music. Some even attempted to notate it, collecting isolated examples. Shortly after the beginning of the war one of these songs appeared in print: *The New York Tribune* published the words to 'Go Down Moses' in December 1861. Within weeks 'The Song of the Contrabands: O Let my people Go' appeared, a sort of slowed-down gigue in $\frac{6}{8}$ time, arranged by one Thomas Baker with singularly inappropriate harmonies. The tune bore a vague resemblance to the one known today. From such inauspicious beginnings the spiritual would conquer the world.

The first published collection of spirituals (which may be the first – no earlier private collection has survived) is entitled *Slave Songs of the United States*. It appeared in 1867, the work of editors William Francis Allen, Charles Pickard Ware and Lucy McKim Garrison. Most of the songs were collected on or near the island of Port Royal, South Carolina. When Port Royal was captured early in the war the white residents fled, leaving the luxuriant island to former slaves and occupying Union forces. Schools were set up, and idealistic young intellectuals from the north came to teach and observe the newly liberated blacks. These teachers remained on Port Royal for extended periods of time – months, even years – which allowed the leisure for hearing music and writing it down.

Slave Songs contains the first printed version of many familiar spirituals, including 'Roll, Jordan, Roll', 'Michael Row the Boat Ashore', 'Rock O' My Soul (in the bosom of Abraham)' and 'Nobody knows the trouble I've had'. Neither the words nor the music of any song in the book is identical with a spiritual as commonly sung today; the four just mentioned are close, compared to the earliest versions of 'O Daniel' (a variant of 'Didn't my Lord deliver Daniel') and 'No Man Can Hinder Me' (now sung as 'Ride on, King Jesus'). Other tunes are little known, or have fallen out of use entirely; all of them are interesting and worthy of modern performance.

This pioneering volume was eagerly read by former abolitionists and others interested in the culture and welfare of the freedmen. The press reviewed it politely. It reached no wider audience and had no effect on popular culture. The beautiful spirituals Allen, Ware and Garrison collected seemed destined to remain in black churches, on southern farms, and in specialised libraries. Had this remained the case, the spiritual would be an interesting footnote in the history of American music. However, in 1872 this music would begin to reach a far wider audience.

After the end of the Civil War the federal government established in the south seven universities for newly freed blacks. One of these, Fisk University in Nashville, Tennessee, encouraged a white employee to work with a few students who were particularly talented in music. George L. White was himself a gifted amateur musician; the treasurer of the university, he was also acutely aware of its financial problems. In the course of teaching standard hymns and classical pieces to his students White heard them sing 'their own music', spirituals remembered from their former state of slavery. Struck with the beauty of this music, and the ardour and excellence of the singing, White envisioned a way of earning money for the embattled university. He took his singers on the road, hoping to raise a fortune. After a lacklustre start in 1871, White renamed the ensemble the Fisk Jubilee Singers and their meteoric rise to fame began. Performing before enthusiastic crowds in Boston, New York, other major cities in the northern states and Europe, in seven years of touring the Fisk Jubilee Singers raised $150,000 for their alma mater and left the whole world singing spirituals.

Writers in the mid-nineteenth century frequently observed that black singers sang spirituals in groups. Occasionally a particular slave or freeman would sing a religious solo, and of course soloists were frequently heard in call-and-response songs. But the distinctive sound of the spiritual was a choral sound. In some areas the slaves sang in harmony, in other areas they did not. (Slaves were heard singing in harmony in the Caribbean as early as 1782.) The editors of *Slave Songs*, and most early collectors, focused almost entirely on writing down tunes, not whatever accompanying parts may have been sung. The collection of 112 songs of the Fisk Jubilee Singers is quite different. There are thirty-four tunes (30 per cent) which are unharmonised. The remaining 70 per cent have harmony parts, ranging from a second part (usually the bass) moving in thirds or sixths below the tune, to solo–chorus alternations (the chorus in four parts) to chorale-style harmonisations of entire tunes. It is not known whether these harmonisations are the work of White and/or his students, or cleaned-up versions of folk arrangements.

Virtually every black composer in the United States between 1870 and 1970 was influenced by the spiritual. These composers include the finest arrangers of spirituals, Harry Thacker Burleigh (1866–1949), Hall Johnson (1888–1970) and William Levi Dawson (1899–1990). Some also produced extended choral works based on spirituals; the most important of these are by R. Nathaniel Dett (1882–1943).

Dett's fascination with spirituals took many forms. Throughout his life he wrote impassioned prose statements about their importance. His first significant choral piece was 'Listen to the Lambs', which treats the spiritual as raw material, generating wonderful choral textures. He continued to write elaborate anthems and motets based on 'spiritual folk songs', as he called them. In 1927 and 1936 he produced five volumes of standard four-part arrangements of spirituals (236 titles). And he was the first to use a spiritual as the basis of an extended composition.

In 1919 Dett published 'The Chariot Jubilee', a work of considerable contrapuntal and textural ingenuity, based on 'Swing low, sweet chariot' and 'Ride up in the chariot'. Twelve years later Dett would compose another major choral work based in large measure on a single spiritual, 'Go down, Moses'. *The Ordering of Moses* was his master's thesis at the Eastman School of Music; not since Charles Ives (1874–1954) wrote his First Symphony – his senior project at Yale – had such a masterpiece been produced as an academic requirement.

Ives is certainly one of the truly original figures in the history of music; yet, like Dett's, his work is rooted firmly in the American past. His sacred choral music falls into four categories. The first is service music written for various denominations which employed young Charlie as an organist. Second, there are songs on sacred texts or sacred subjects, which exist in versions for chorus, including 'Serenity', 'General William Booth Enters Into Heaven', and 'The Collection' (which has a phrase in four-part harmony marked 'response by the village choir'). The 'Four Songs on Hymntune Themes' all sound good performed by a unison chorus (Ives himself said that 'Autumn' sounded better that way). In a third category are two lengthy choral works, *The Celestial Country* and the set of three 'Harvest Home Chorales'. Finally, the meat of Ives's work as a choral composer, and his most remarkable sacred music, is a series of psalm settings, beginning in 1892 with Psalm 42 and concluding in 1924 with Psalm 90.

Amy Beach (1867–1944), a somewhat older contemporary of Dett and Ives, attended the Congregational church as a child, but as an adult was baptised and confirmed an Anglican. Her first major work was a Mass in E♭ major, written in 1890 and premièred soon afterwards by the Boston Handel and Haydn Society. This is an ambitious but not particularly original work, in which beautiful passages alternate with rather bombastic ones.

Mrs Beach produced several collections of service music and approximately thirty anthems; much of this music is attractive and all of it is well crafted. With the passage of time her harmonic vocabulary became richer and her contrapuntal writing more ambitious. The gorgeous sense of line which characterises her solo songs is frequently in evidence in these choral works. Her last work for chorus and orchestra, *The Canticle of the Sun*, is a setting of Matthew Arnold's translation of the famous poem by St Francis of Assisi. It contains wonderful solo passages as well as fine choral and orchestral effects. While no one would mistake Beach's harmony for that of Schoenberg, it is original enough for her purposes and easily holds the listener's attention.

Dett and Ives were absorbed in the popular music of the past; out of this raw material they constructed an original, visionary art music. Beach was completely involved with the world of art music, as practised by the mainstream composers and performers of her time. But during the 1920s, as these three masters were writing some of their finest works, a different music was emerging which drew on vernacular traditions quite removed from the concert stage. Dett's elegant spiritual arrangements and choral fantasias evoked the past; the emerging music, known almost from the beginning as black gospel, was very much of the present.

The use of the term 'gospel music' to refer to a distinctive body of hymns and choruses can be traced to the collection *Gospel Songs* (1874) by Philip P. Bliss (1838–76) and *Gospel Hymns and Sacred Songs* (1875) by Bliss and Ira Sankey (1840–1908). Early gospel music was associated with urban evangelistic Protestantism and was strongly influenced by American popular music. The first gospel hymns were the work of white composers; white evangelists and their musical sidekicks took these hymns all over the world.

Black urban churches quickly appropriated white gospel hymns and made them a part of regular worship. The revival spirit of the Sankey-style hymns, the rhythms of ragtime, the vocal style of the blues, improvised percussion parts (handclapping, various small drums, above all the tambourine), other instrumental accompaniment (piano, guitar, later the Hammond organ) – congregations and choirs freely mixed all of these elements with traditional black folk elements to produce something new and exciting.

The origins of black gospel are shrouded in mystery. By the first years of the twentieth century it was well established in certain urban churches in Philadelphia, New York and Chicago. In Philadelphia the Reverend Charles A. Tindley wrote the first published black gospel songs in 1901; his most famous compositions have retained their popularity for almost a century. Tindley's tunes include '[Take your burden to the Lord and] Leave It There', 'Stand By Me', and 'I'll Overcome Someday', which is one of the sources (modified by five decades of oral tradition) of 'We Shall Overcome', the most important song of the mid-century civil rights movement.

Chicago is often considered the birthplace of black gospel because the first major composer specialising in this music was based there. Thomas A. Dorsey (1899–1993) was born in Villa Rica, Georgia. His family, upwardly mobile, moved to Atlanta when he was six years old; at the age of sixteen Dorsey left Atlanta for Chicago. He established himself as a professional musician, playing the piano and writing arrangements for the celebrated blues singer Gertrude 'Ma' Rainey. Southern black people who migrated to Chicago in the first quarter of the twentieth century encountered large mainstream black churches quite unlike the black congregations of the rural south. These so-called 'old-line' churches boasted well-educated ministers, spacious well-equipped buildings, active social outreach programmes designed to help newly arrived southerners, and music programmes which shunned traditional black music – near-professional choirs of splendid voices performed the music of Beethoven, Schubert, Rossini and other white Europeans. Dorsey became convinced that the spiritual needs of these large churches would be better served by another kind of music.

The National Baptist Convention and other mainstream black organisations had long recognised the value of gospel music; in 1921 the NBC published the first collection of gospel songs specifically for black churches, *Gospel Pearls*. But the songs in this seminal collection were rarely used as part of worship in old-line churches. Other churches used *Gospel Pearls* as a hymnal, but never as the basis of improvisatory music. Dorsey envisioned improvisatory music in church, music which would invite congregations to express themselves in the manner he remembered from his boyhood in Georgia. To this end he organised the first black gospel choir, at Ebenezer Baptist Church in Chicago. In a series of bold moves, upwardly mobile as always, Dorsey found himself in 1932 directing a gospel choir in one of the most prestigious of Chicago's old-line churches, Pilgrim Baptist.

Once Dorsey's choral 'gospel blues' was established in a major Chicago church it took the entire city by storm. A powerful way of reintroducing displaced rural blacks to their religious roots, the new gospel style captured the imagination of Americans of all races. The style, an inspired mixture of traditional and popular elements, eventually enriched virtually every aspect of American popular music and remains a vital force as the century draws to a close. Dorsey's own compositions became standards, including two of the finest and best-loved religious songs ever written, 'Precious Lord, take my hand' and 'Peace in the valley'. Always looking for appropriate singers to help promote his music, and the cause of gospel music in general, he had the great good fortune to 'discover' Mahalia Jackson, with whom he collaborated for fourteen years. Inspired by the blues singing of Bessie Smith and 'Ma' Rainey, Miss Jackson showed the potential of solo gospel singing as Dorsey had demonstrated its possibilities for choruses.

As the century progressed Dorsey's blues-and-jazz-based gospel style yielded to what is now known as contemporary gospel, heavily influenced by rock music and featuring electric instruments. Gospel soloists have become more and more professional, and gospel choirs have proliferated. Most black churches today have such choirs, many of them of professional or near-professional calibre; what was rare in the 1930s is now common. Many colleges, including predominantly white ones, have gospel choruses; there are even festivals of high-school gospel choirs and occasional hit singles by black gospel groups.

As Dorsey envisioned the blues in church, many others over the years envisioned various versions of sacred jazz. By far the most ambitious of these projects are the three Sacred Concerts of Duke (Edward Kennedy) Ellington (1899–1974). The composition and execution of these three mammoth projects were the principal undertakings of his last decade. The first, entitled 'In the Beginning God', was premièred in 1965 at Grace Cathedral, San Francisco. The Second Sacred Concert took place in 1968 at New York's Cathedral of St John the Divine; the Third Sacred Concert premièred in 1973 at Westminster Abbey. Ellington considered these sprawling, Ivesian conceptions his finest work.

Many Americans in the twentieth century have produced excellent Mass settings. The most individualistic of these is the notorious *Mass* of Leonard Bernstein (1918–90). Bernstein actually composed two masses; the other one, a charming *Missa Brevis* for double chorus *a cappella*, is quite appropriate for liturgical use. *Mass*, however, was never intended to be used in church. Nor is it a concert in the manner of the Paine Mass. Rather, *Mass* is a theatrical work which enacts Bernstein's own peculiar combination of a desire for religious ecstasy and compulsive doubt. The Celebrant is a non-liturgical, stagy presence who goes mad at the Fraction. The music is a melange of pop and symphonic styles, Christian and Jewish traditions, Beethoven quotes, and echoes of Bernstein the successful Broadway composer.

Bernstein's choral masterpiece, however, has a religious intention; perhaps, for all of his tortured posturing, he was a believer after all. 'Chichester Psalms', three movements based on psalm passages in Hebrew, are such good settings of the texts, so full of orchestral and choral colour, and so rhythmically exciting that they are surely among the finest choral music of the century.

There are many other settings of the psalms by American composers in the second half of this century, including a series of experimental settings by Edwin London entitled 'Psalm of These Days' (London has a great fondness for puns) which feature avant-garde vocal techniques. Other Jewish composers have looked to other parts of Hebrew scripture for texts. Henry Brant (*b.* 1913) uses verses from the Song of Solomon in his spatial composition 'Solomon's Garden', and the 'Four Love Songs from The Song of Songs' by Gerald Shapiro (*b.* 1942) are exquisite *a cappella* settings. Shapiro has also gone outside the Judeo-Christian tradition for religious texts; 'The Voice of the Dharma' and 'Prayer for the Great Family' are settings of the American Buddhist poet Gary Snyder. Lou Harrison (*b.* 1917) is the only major American composer to date to produce a large-scale sacred choral work not on a Christian or Jewish text. His most extensive choral composition is a setting of the Heart Sutra, an important Buddhist text, translated into Esperanto. He has other works directly inspired by Eastern religions, in addition to a fine mass in Latin. One can easily imagine that the increasing religious pluralism which characterises the United States at the end of the twentieth century will result in more Buddhist-, Hindu- or Muslim-inspired musical composition.

PART FOUR

Performance practices

12 Some notes on choral singing

HEIKKI LIIMOLA

There is a very large repertoire for choral societies and larger choirs ranging from the late Baroque of Bach and Handel, through the Romantics such as Mendelssohn, Reger and Brahms to composers of the present day. Although there are professional choir singers, the numbers involved usually mean that most people are singing for fun, though 'fun' in this case may mean a great deal of commitment and effort. Amateur singers are enthusiasts, often men and women who could have become professionals but for various reasons ended up pursuing singing as a hobby (which often begins after a hard day's work).

The singer

Singing in a large choir is very demanding for the singer. It may seem easy, with many singers on each part, but it is essential that the individual singer's resources are fully used in order for the complete ensemble to sound well as a choir. One of the most difficult problems is controlling your own voice when you may be sitting next to some one whose voice is very different from your own. It helps to think of a kind of mutuality of sound, each voice blending together, perhaps reducing the vibrato so that you can clearly hear each other's pitch. Consider the style of music that you are singing. Although the choir may have its own distinctive sound, the best choirs have a keen awareness of style: Bach, for example, will need to be approached with a straighter sound than the full-blooded singing appropriate for Richard Strauss. It goes without saying that you should watch the conductor, but do not become conductor-dependent. Be conscious that you are a line of singers trying to act as one: breathe and articulate together, think yourself into the voice of the person next to you. Basic singing technique is essential: breathe from your diaphragm, and remember that unless you open your mouth your contribution will not count for much. Don't coast along under the impression that no one can hear you: a good choir needs every ounce of energy from each of its members.

The conductor

The conductor should make sure that the choir rehearses in a big enough space. It is worth giving some attention to the psychology of the rehearsal space. Singers don't feel right if they have no room to enjoy the sound, and if they are not enjoying it fully they won't sing to the best of their ability. It is also impossible for the conductor to get an adequate idea of what the choir actually sounds like if he or she cannot get sufficiently far away to be able to hear the entirety of the sound. Perhaps the greatest difficulty for the conductor is the question of balance. In the first instance, the individual lines need to blend and balance within themselves. Rehearsing parts separately will help this, and perhaps changing the position of individual singers to maximise the opportunity to blend voices. Stronger voices can help and encourage weaker ones, but they should not dominate or inhibit them. Thought should also be given to how the forces should be disposed, according to what the music is and where it will be performed. If possible, rehearse in the same relative positions that will be used for the performance, so that the singers become familiar with the voices surrounding them. Normally the sopranos will stand in front, to the conductor's left, with the altos to his/her right; basses will stand behind sopranos and tenors behind the altos. This has the advantage that top and bottom will probably hear each other well, which will make tuning easier. Or you may find that your choir works better with the tenors behind the sopranos and basses behind the altos, which enables the high and low voices to support each other. Blocks of each voice can also work, and if you have an adventurous group of singers who want to try something interesting, ask them to sing in groups of solo lines so that each singer stands next to a different voice from his or her own. This can be good for confidence-building once the choir has got beyond a certain stage. Each choir has a position that it feels happy with, and it is worth experimenting for as long as it takes to find it.

Some basic instruction in good tuning is always helpful. It needn't be detailed and complicated, but should be sufficiently clear to enable the singers to rely less on a rehearsal pianist for pitch, and to have more confidence in their own ears. Getting singers to listen to each other is half the battle as far as pitch and blend are concerned. General basic rules are a good idea: encouraging singers to make sufficiently large tones when going up, and being careful not to overshoot descending semitones, for example. If the music is *a cappella*, dispense with piano doubling as soon as the singers know the notes, then serious attention can be given to tuning. On the other hand, if the music will eventually involve an orchestra it is essential that the singers get to know as much as they can as soon as they can about potentially useful orchestral cues that can be pointed up by the pianist. Make sure that your beat is clear, simple and easily read. An over-large beat can appear vague and be difficult to follow, and too much extravagance can lead to over singing. If you appear to be spoon-feeding your singers or driving them on they will become over-reliant on you, and you will never reach their creative centre.

A conductor must also be a psychologist. This instrument that you 'play' is unique and one of the most difficult in the world. You are dealing with people who *are* their instruments, so when you criticise someone's singing you may also seem to be criticising *them*. Singers have strong views about their voices and abilities, and they should be treated with respect. Conductors should have a comprehensive knowledge of singing technique so that they can argue from a position of strength. Don't try to blind singers with science: they may have as much knowledge of the metaphors used in describing singing (head/chest voice and so on) as you have.

Exercises

Warming up can be both vocally and psychologically useful. A singer uses many more muscles in singing than in speech, and like an athlete's these muscles work more efficiently if they are primed before the action begins. Exercises also help to concentrate people's minds and focus them on the physicality of singing (something they will probably want to forget about when enjoying the actual music). A warm-up is not an end in itself, simply a means to oil the wheels, so to speak, and facilitate the smooth running of the machinery. It should not take more than 15-25 minutes, and should be an enjoyable prelude to the music itself. Begin with breathing and relaxing: it is most important to disperse as much muscular tension as possible so that the appropriate muscles, and only the appropriate muscles, will be used for singing. No muscle works in isolation, and singers need to feel that their whole body is geared to the production of sound, becoming an instrument in itself. Every conductor will have his or her preferred way of warming up. Here are some singing exercises I use with my choirs, and which are suitable if you are singing *a cappella* or with an orchestra:

(1) Simple reaching and stretching make a good beginning, to which can be added gentle breathing exercises. Let the head and chest drop forward as the breath is exhaled, arms to sides, limbs loose. Inhale and raise the upper body to its upright position, being conscious of the breath filling the lungs. After doing this gently two or three times, which should be very relaxing, introduce a variation that will develop awareness of breath control. Having returned to the upright position with a comfortable lungful of air, keep upright and exhale in short bursts of a second or

so, keeping the throat open, with the air feeling as though it is supported on a column which extends right down to the stomach. Don't close the throat, but start each burst with a gentle push from the stomach. You are actually using a combination of stomach muscles and your diaphragm, the band of muscle that encircles the spinal cord and controls the pressure on the lungs. Keep the chest up and everything else relaxed.

(2) By now you should feel comfortably relaxed, aware of the breathing process and ready to make some sounds. Gentle humming of three-note descending scales is a good beginning, starting on C♯ (in the key of A) and rising in successive semitones, then returning to the starting point (correcting mistakes on the way down). Be conscious of how the breath relates to the sound; no forcing or pressing, just a natural extension of breath into sound. As the scales go higher feel the sounds going into your head, making an easy transition from chest to head voice. Think of an 'oo' sound, but with the lips gently closed. Be conscious of singing with your whole body, and remember that even exercises are real musical phrases:

(3) Moving to the next exercise, I try to keep something of what has already been achieved and transform it into the next stage. This one consists of descending major triads first hummed then repeated to /ng/ and again to /you-o/, the whole rising a step and beginning again, trying to keep the sound and the space in the mouth quite similar:

(4) Next we transform the /you-o/ into /tro/, thinking the 'oo' space in the mouth but with a feeling of 'oh' in the throat. These patterns can be extended higher than the previous exercises:

(5) Now, keeping the same feeling, open up the mouth a little more from the back, as though you are about to gasp (without actually gasping, of course). Use the /tro/ sound on the octave leap, then change to descending /tro/ arpeggios. If there are problems changing registers (opening the vowels too much or closing the throat, especially in altos and basses, for example) try thinking more 'oo' in the mouth (like the 'gasp' position mentioned above).

Fig. 6d

(6) We can now introduce 'mio'. The idea here is to make the /i/ sound well (especially difficult for Finns), and also to transfer some of the brightness of /i/ to /o/. I ask the singers to think of a /ü/ sound (or like French 'tu') as they sing the /i/, while still pronouncing it clearly as /i/.

Fig. 6e

(7) After this I move back to /o/ sounds, maintaining the clearer sound that thinking of /i/ has given us. Take care to keep the sound consistent, while opening up a little as you go higher. Don't let the /o/ move too much towards /a/ (keep thinking of the 'oo'-space in the mouth). When you reach the register break, change to /no/. The /n/ must be clear and fast, to give the maximum time on the /o/. Then try the same thing just with /no/, faster and higher:

Fig. 6f

(8) Next, begin some /tro/ arpeggios and then move to /nay/, trying to keep the sound consistent:

Fig. 6g

(9) We always end exercises the same way we started, by humming. This time we sing major triads gently, using the whole body as before. The sound must be rich and full, but of course soft, and not going too high:

Fig. 6h

Behind the scenes

Of course, choirs are not just about singing. Running such a performing community often requires tremendous sacrifices and involvement from the singers, and efficient organisation is essential. Rehearsal spaces have to be booked, rent has to be found, music hired, orchestras organised, publicity generated, soloists catered for, and everything has somehow to be paid for. Delegation of these duties is highly desirable, and the more choir members who are actively involved in their own administration, the better. It may even be possible for the choir to organise voice lessons for its members, or for different members to take charge of warm-up sessions. Above all, make sure that everybody has the maximum amount of information on the choir's activities. Choirs are full of artistically talented, creative people with vivid imaginations; if they have to invent information for themselves they may come up with vivid speculations.

Amateur singers often begin their choir work when everyone else is finishing theirs, and towards the end of a fifteen-hour day concentration may not be of the best. Good conductors will be aware of this and make allowances for singers taking a little longer to interpret their thoughts.

Orchestral conductors, accustomed to professional players, sometimes lack a certain psychological understanding of their singers. Sometimes when things go wrong this will result in the conductor blaming the choir, who may have done its very best. The conductor should perhaps look in the mirror: he should know the work, especially the text, in all its details, and he should know the choir, the human voice and its sensibility as an instrument.

Translated from the Finnish by Heikki and Katri Liimola.

13 Ensemble singing

JOHN POTTER

Since polyphony evolved out of plainchant sometime around the end of the first millennium there has been a tradition of people coming together to sing in harmony. The polyphony associated with the cathedral of Notre Dame in Paris specifically contrasts the singing of the chant choir with that of soloists who sing in up to four parts. These are likely to have been the best singers available, able to hold their own as soloists and yet sing with one another as a unit; they predate polyphonic choral singing by several generations and opera singing by hundreds of years. The successors of those early polyphonists are found today in all branches of Western music from barbershop to Berio's *A-Ronne*, from Corsican folk polyphony to the King's Singers. What all these musicians share is an ability to communicate with each other as well as with their listeners, and that is what this chapter is about. It will focus primarily on 'classical' ensemble singing, or consort singing as it is sometimes called, i.e. one voice to a part (usually no more than about eight parts, though larger groups are possible), but the same principles apply to any group of solo singers, whatever the music they are singing.

If you are getting together for the first time, the first thing you need to think about is how you are going to work together. Ensemble singing is a co-operative activity and it is very important that everyone's input is used to its fullest extent. This is one of the great differences between singing in a small one-to-a-part ensemble and singing in a choir. For obvious practical reasons choirs need conductors, who are expected to make creative decisions on their behalf, to motivate and inspire them. This is not the case when you have only one voice to a part: practical problems are easily resolvable and in a small ensemble you are, in effect, a very special kind of soloist with responsibility both to yourself and to your fellow singers, and the last thing you want to do is hand over creative control to one single person. Every group finds the way that is best for them, but having coached a very large number of ensembles over the years, I think it is possible to arrive at a few general principles which are helpful for most situations. Here are some suggestions:

(1) Think before you start, about your own pitch, but especially about tempo and how you are going to communicate it. Be aware that everyone is mentally 'tuning in' at this point. Everything you do from now on is

concerned with transmitting information to each other as well as to your listeners.

(2) Breathe together, listening to each other's intake of breath. You don't need arm waving or obvious eye contact to be able to start together. The breath has a shape to it, and this shape is full of enough tempo information to tell you how the first bar is going to go. By the time you reach the top of the breath you will, in effect, have agreed a tempo, which you must then have the courage to act on. Breathing is not just for survival – it is an important part of performance rhetoric, a carrier of essential signals.

(3) Start together, shaping the notes to give each other maximum information. Every note you sing contains information which is potentially useful to your fellow singers. No note is without a shape. Even the most sustained note will change before it ends, whether it is followed by another note or by a rest. This does not mean you have to make a swell on each note. It's analogous to the way speech works. Listen to your own speech: your voice is always in motion and every syllable has a unique rise and fall. So it is in singing, through what eighteenth-century Italians called the *messa di voce*, or placing of the voice.[1]

(4) Sing the text. In most music that you are likely to sing, the composer's aim was to heighten or illuminate the text in some way. Generally speaking, phrases of music will match phrases of text, which will have their own rhetorical shape. Within phrases, individual words and syllables have their own shapes, and reading these shapes (your own and the other parts') enables you to keep together. If the text occurs in someone else's part at the same time as yours, match your enunciation.

(5) The person with the moving part has control of the music. This is the really creative part: very few pieces are sung absolutely metronomically, and it is in tempo variation that singers have a chance to personalise their performance. If you have a part with more notes in it than the surrounding parts, then they have to listen to you in case you feel that something less than a strict movement is appropriate. Then when someone else has the faster part you have to support them. Negotiate: if you have the moving part, take expressive risks and trust the others to follow you. You'll probably find that for this to work effectively you have to keep the basic pulse moving. Being expressive often means slowing down, so remember to get back to tempo as soon as you can, or the piece will feel as though it's grinding to a halt.

(6) Read the whole score, following whoever has control of the music. Singing from single line parts (as from Renaissance part books, for example) can give a useful insight into early practice but has little to commend it to a modern performer. There are no advantages in not

knowing what is going on around you: information and its communication are basic requirements for everyone. It is sometimes said that singing from parts forces you to listen for what you cannot see. A good musician is not going to stop listening simply because she can see a score. Score reading can be enormously helpful in getting one's own notes: check what's going on around you, looking for cues in the other parts. This is especially helpful when learning a new piece. If someone in your group is a good sight-reader, or has a well-developed sense of pitch, then look out for their part in particular in case it's useful for you.

(7) Balance and blend: you should generally be able to hear your own voice and those of the singers on either side of you at approximately the same volume. This is something that you will monitor continuously, probably without being aware of it. Blend is a difficult subject, something that the Hilliard Ensemble is often asked about but which we rarely discuss. If you are listening and communicating (and keeping in mind the suggestions above) you will probably find, as we do, that the blend takes care of itself. You may have to fine-tune it occasionally (not always to make things more homogeneous; sometimes the voices need to be distinctly characterised).

(8) Tuning. Don't rehearse with a piano unless you really struggle with note learning, in which case you should abandon piano support as soon as you feel confident of the notes. The modern piano is tuned in equal temperament, which involves considerable compromise to make tuning work on every note of the scale in every key. Singers in effect have only one, moveable scale, so are able to sing in 'just' intonation based on intervals derived from the harmonic series. Relative to the piano, this means keeping major thirds very slightly lower, and minor thirds a little higher. You will also find yourself singing slightly wider fifths and slightly narrower fourths. Major and minor seconds should be wider, but chromatic semitones smaller; accidental flats should be thought higher, and sharps lower. But don't get obsessed with tuning, it's only a means to an end. The important thing is that everyone stays in the same 'parish'. Some music is undeniably difficult to tune (and in the case of Lassus's *Sibylline Prophecies*, for example, virtually impossible if you stick to the rules) but go with the flow: very few listeners will be able to tell that you are the only person singing in tune, and most will think quite the opposite.[2]

(9) End together. This is not difficult but needs the two most essential ingredients of ensemble singing, courage and trust. The information necessary for the placing of the last chord is contained within the chord before it, or in the composer's cadential formula. If there is, say, a suspension resolving at the cadence, the part doing the resolution has control of the music. Their rallentando (if they do one) is telling you where the final

chord will come. You must trust this information and act on it, otherwise you may get stranded on the penultimate chord with information that is no longer any use to you. Having arrived on it, you don't need to agree in advance the length of the last note, and it shouldn't be measured, as that gives the game away to listeners. In most Renaissance and medieval music the note given for the last chord simply means a note of an appropriate length. If a madrigal ends with a weak syllable, then it should be short (as in speech). If an Agnus Dei unravels on to a lush final chord, then you may want to hold it as long as you can.[3] The right place to end will depend on how things have gone immediately before. You will feel when the last chord is about to stop. Listen very carefully to all the voices. If one cuts out, perhaps having run short of breath, then that's when the piece ends and everyone must be aware of it (except the listener, for whom the whole process happens so quickly that they hear a simultaneous end). If there is a final consonant, listen for the tiny decay in the vowel that will happen as the mouth prepares itself to change from vowel to consonant. In that microsecond if everyone is listening, you communicate to each other exactly when the piece is going to end. Don't hold it on just because you think it should be longer: there is absolutely no point in being the only one 'right'.

Sound

Every group has its own distinctive sound. Don't try and imitate someone else's: exploit your own group characteristics. Professional soloists give considerable attention to their own personal tone colour. In ensemble singing your personal tone colour is used to colour the sound of the whole group, so you may have to hold back on the richness in the interests of an overall blend. You have to listen to your sound and sing it into that of your colleagues, so that your individual sounds become fused into one within nanoseconds of leaving your lips. The way to do this is to monitor the sounds as they leave your mouths, but listen to what happens to them in the acoustic space. The feedback from the acoustic tells you, if only sub-consciously, vital information about balance, blend and tuning, enabling you to make minute adjustments as you go along. Listening is a multi-stage process: you are aware of your own sound and are continuously blending it with the other voices, but an important part of listening is outside yourself altogether, almost as though part of you is at the back of the building. Think of the building (especially if it has interesting acoustics) as an exten-sion of the ensemble. The acoustic acts as both amplifier and speaker, and you should feel that you are singing the whole building.

Early music

A huge amount of repertoire for ensembles comes under the heading of early music. Whether you are attempting historically informed performances or simply singing it for fun, there are particular creative opportunities and problems that you will need to deal with.

Underlay and breathing

It's worth bearing in mind (for all sorts of reasons) that the idea of training singers to make beautiful sounds using well-supported breathing is not a concept that medieval and Renaissance singers would have been familiar with. Their singing voices would probably have been much more like their speech (accents and all). Without diaphragmatic breathing they would have needed to be very pragmatic. Change the underlay if to do so would make the breathing easier. In most pre-Baroque music underlay is the responsibility of the performers (not the dead composer or the – usually – unsinging editor) and it can be used creatively and pragmatically just as the original singers would have done. Don't breathe before a syllable in the middle of words, and you may find it satisfying to align the texts so that everyone sings on similar vowels for as long as possible.

Vibrato

In the early days of the early music revival reduced vibrato was thought to bring a cool objectiveness to performances. It was a semiotic antidote to all that was not early music. This is very clear in recordings from the 1970s and 1980s, where 'unvibrato' is applied in a rather unsystematic way. Later singing became far more text orientated and sometimes even made the leap to speech-song, with vibrato (which does not occur in speech) generally appearing only at moments of heightened emotion. It's a matter of taste, of course, but you will find it much easier to keep to the basic rules outlined above if you don't use too much of it.

Dynamics

Most choir trainers will go through a piece putting in dynamic markings, or hope that an editor will have done the job for them. In ensemble singing we have little use for markings of any kind. There are two main reasons for this. Firstly, the basic reason that you don't find markings in Medieval and Renaissance music is that singers, poets and composers all shared a common rhetorical and oratorical education which gave them a common attitude to text. The rhetorical rules that guided composer and poet were the same as those applied to performance, so dynamic markings would have been redundant as everyone knew what to do with texts.

This can generally be seen quite clearly in the way Renaissance pieces are constructed. In English and Italian madrigals, for example, the music will often rise in pitch as important sentences move to their climax. It feels quite natural to let the music grow at these points, and you will instinctively sing louder. You may also find yourself getting faster as the rhetoric becomes more urgent. The same process works in reverse: towards the end of a sentence the music may well descend in pitch and you will feel yourself getting softer, and possibly slower. These are rhetorical patterns that occur in speech, which the composer was seeking to heighten and extend into music. The second reason for not over-marking the score is that you may want to do things differently next time.

Rehearsal

Rehearsals are exploratory, the time to learn notes and feel what the expressive possibilities of a piece might be. Any given piece has a potentially infinite number of possible 'interpretations'. I enclose this in quotes because it's not really the ideal word for the realisation of an ensemble piece. Learning and performing a piece can be a very creative and spontaneous process and you should never feel that you have found the ideal way to do it, even when you're singing a piece for the hundredth time. People have often drawn parallels between the Hilliard Ensemble and a string quartet. Although we can, on a good day, move and think as one person, we never aim at an ideal interpretation of a piece. Many string quartets rehearse to achieve a kind of perfection, which they then try to reproduce in performance. This is a rather parsimonious use of creative energy. Discussing the music is often helpful, but it isn't the only way to decide how things go. Everyone will absorb and communicate various ideas about the piece simply by singing it, and it is generally perfectly obvious when someone is making a musical point. In the performance some, all or none of these ideas will emerge, as we continue to explore the possibilities as the performance goes along. When we can find nothing new to say, then it's time to replace the piece.

Of course it helps if you have spent literally thousands of hours singing with the same group of singers. You learn each others' instincts and idiosyncrasies; you learn how to relate your collective experience to your personal thoughts on how you want the music to go, how to influence your colleagues even while they are actually performing and when to support the things they like. For these parameters there is no substitute for covering a lot of musical mileage together. One rehearsal technique that can be helpful in developing communication skills is to sit in a circle facing away

from each other. In this position you have to have all your antennae operating at maximum sensitivity (a similar effect can be achieved by shutting
your eyes). You cannot start properly unless you take an audible breath in
which you share tempo information, and the rhythmic information
implied in breathing becomes essential throughout the piece. You cannot
do without note shaping, which tells your fellow singers what you expect
to happen next (don't forget that every musical event contains information about the next one). You cannot use rubato unless you are listening
very carefully to the other parts. Reading the whole score becomes an
invaluable aid. Eventually you learn to think yourself into the other
singers' minds and voices, and become one creative unit.

Think about how best to arrange yourselves. This is very much a
matter of personal taste but it can have noticeable effects on tuning and
balance. You may find that the highest and lowest voices tune better if they
are together in the centre, where they can hear each other well and be
heard by everyone else. If someone has absolute pitch it can be useful to
position them fairly centrally so that everyone can tap into this resource.
If one voice is particularly weak or strong a better balance may be found if
you experiment with different positions. Don't be afraid to experiment
with positioning even if you have been singing together for some time.
Our listening habits can change imperceptibly over time and a change of
position can sometimes have dramatic results.

It is much more impressive for listeners if everything appears to
happen by magic. Don't give the game away by obvious note giving (especially with a pitch pipe) and don't be tempted to conduct, especially at the
beginning and end of a piece. Arrange your programme so that you can
get the note for the next piece from the final chord of the piece before
(consider transposition if it makes it easier to get from one piece to the
next). If the pitch has gone a little astray don't worry too much: it can be
more stable to go with the slot into which you have slipped. All sorts of
extraneous things can affect the pitch (weather, central heating and
humidity, for example) and often you will find a level which may be either
side of a = 440 but which is comfortable and consistent. Go with this,
unless other problems arise as a result. The audience is likely to be far
more unsettled by your attempts to correct the pitch than by a mutually
agreed adjustment.

In the end, of course, you will find your own way. And that's what
counts. You can learn from listening to other groups (about what to do
and what not to do), but ultimately you have to make the music your own,
and develop something that is uniquely the sum (or more) of all your
parts. What works for you, is what works.

14 The voice in the Middle Ages

JOSEPH DYER

But of all musical instruments the human voice is the most worthy because it produces both sound and words, while the others are of use only for sound, not for a note and words.[1]

This quotation from an anonymous thirteenth-century treatise is not alone in testifying to the pre-eminent role occupied by the voice in medieval music. The Christian church from the very beginning had rejected the use of musical instruments in worship both because of their intimate associations with pagan cults and because of their connection with the profligate immorality of the Greco-Roman world. Christian liturgical music thus developed in a direction consistent with, and determined by, the capabilities of the singing voice. The organ, an instrument difficult to construct and constantly in need of maintenance, made only gradual headway towards its eventual status as the sacred instrument *par excellence*. Few medieval churches could hope to possess so extraordinary a treasure. Instruments were tangential to the performance of monophonic secular song of the Middle Ages, and they seemed to have played only the most minimal role in secular polyphony.

The 'early music' revival of the twentieth century was guided primarily by instrumentalists whose imaginations could roam freely in the absence of instruments surviving from the Middle Ages. The human voice did more than merely survive: its physiology has remained unchanged, yet as John Potter observed, there was no re-evaluation of singing techniques comparable to the re-examination of playing techniques applicable to 'period' instruments.[2] Instead, various twentieth-century vocal practices have competed for 'authentic' status, based more on the degree of aesthetic satisfaction they afford to twentieth-century ears than on their conformity with practices of the past.

The modest goal of the present chapter will be to gather up and interpret scattered references to the singing voice in medieval sources. Most of these references occur in theoretical treatises or the writings of ecclesiastical authors, but courtly literature preserves some allusions to the qualities most desirable in the singing voice. Theorists and churchmen – the two categories are not entirely distinct – sometimes rail against perceived abuses, and their colourful language tends to be quoted frequently, thus acquiring an authority that more objective, dispassionate reports might have supplemented or corrected. Medieval authors refer almost exclusively, moreover, to the mature male voice, a factor that needs to be kept in mind when evaluating the evidence. Women's and children's voices are rarely mentioned, generally serving as negative examples of weakness, and thus representative of qualities to be avoided. A genuinely sympathetic evaluation of the female voice occurs only in a late fourteenth-century treatise by Arnulf of St Ghislain but his praises may not be entirely free from subtle irony.[3]

Neither singly nor taken together do the aforementioned references and passing allusions amount to a reliable 'treatise' on the medieval art of singing.[4] Their authors were almost exclusively ecclesiastics concerned with the proper rendering of liturgical chant and the denunciation of abuses that threatened the attainment of that goal. The information they convey about performance outside this milieu consists largely of criticisms (often rhetorically embellished) that presumably reflect the practices of secular singers. More often than not, medieval treatises were addressed to real or potential *musici*, monks or secular clergy interested in understanding not only practical chant theory (notation, modes, solmisation, etc.) but also the recondite foundations of the art of music: its philosophical and historical-mythological background, the precise measurement of intervals and proportions. The cultivation and training of the voice was, on the other hand, an entirely practical matter within the purview of the cantor and thus outside the range of interests that pre-occupied medieval musical savants. A few medieval authors did, however, recognise the superior advantage of natural musical gifts when combined with an acquired profound knowledge of the scientific foundations of musical art.[5] In an age that equated definition with knowledge, one of the most eminent authorities was the encyclopaedist Isidore of Seville (*d.* 636), who transmitted to the Middle Ages the learning of late antiquity in his books of *Etymologies*. Although the terms he used to describe the 'perfect voice' are more suggestive than analytical, Isidore's description of the voice (summarised in the last sentence of the following quotation) continued to be repeated for centuries.

> Sweet voices are subtle and fine, clear and keen. Brilliant voices are those that possess great carrying power, so that they entirely fill a space, just like the sound of trumpets. Delicate voices are those with little breath, like the voices of children, women and the sick, or string instruments. Those with the most delicate strings emit delicate and fine sounds. Large voices are those produced with a considerable volume of breath, like those of men. Keen voices [are] fine and high, as we see in string instruments. A hard voice is one that produces sounds forcefully like thunder or like the sounds of an anvil whenever the hammer strikes hard iron. A harsh voice is one that is hoarse and produced as faint and equal pulsations. A 'blind' voice is one that, as soon as it is produced,

falls silent; having been suffocated, it can by no means be sustained for long, just as the case with earthen pots. An ingratiating ['vinola'] voice is soft and flexible, and it receives its name from *vinnus*, that is, a softly shaped curl. A perfect voice is thus high, sweet and clear: high, so that it might soar up to the highest pitches; clear, so that it might fill the ears; sweet, so that the spirits of the listeners might be charmed. If any of these qualities is missing, the voice is not perfect.[6]

The *perfecta vox* described by Isidore is akin to the lyric tenor – high, sweet and clear – an ideal that was both aesthetic and practical in the days before electronic amplification.[7] In this passage Isidore had in mind, not the choral singer, but the soloist, whose natural gifts qualified him to perform alone.

In another work, *De ecclesiasticis officiis*, Isidore described the ideal *psalmista* (i.e., solo cantor) in terms consistent with those in the passage quoted above, adding the admonition that the singer's voice must have 'a sound and melody suitable to holy religion, not one that cries out after the manner of tragedians but manifests Christian simplicity in its melody'.[8] The tension between singers' vanity and the inner dispositions of self-effacement in the discharge of a sacred office is a theme that continued to resonate in monastic and canonical literature throughout the Middle Ages.[9] The emphasis on flexibility and fluent voice production would seem to indicate that the church soloists of Isidore's day were called upon to execute music (which had not yet been committed to notation) of more than modest elaboration. Power was important, but not at the expense of 'sweetness', a word frequently encountered during the Middle Ages to describe optimally pleasing qualities in the performance of both vocal and instrumental music.[10] Isidore's endorsement of elegance and flexibility over force and roughness was repeated by music theorists from Aurelian of Réôme in the early ninth century to Marchetto of Padua and Walter Odington in the fourteenth.

Isidore's characterisation of the perfect voice as 'high, sweet and clear' was echoed even in secular literature for many centuries. In the *Roman de Troie* (*c.* 1165) '[Telamon] fu mout de grant valour. / Mout ot en lui bon chanter, / Mout aveit *la voiz haute et clere*, / Et de sonez ert bons trovere'.[11] The Isidorean ideal was also manifested in the contemporary Anglo-Norman *Roman de Horn* (*c.* 1170), in which the hero sings a *lai* with a voice 'loud and clear' (*haut et cler*).[12] The high regard for this characteristic expressed by clerical and lay authors alike suggests that no profound gap in the evaluation of the (solo) singing voice existed between the sacred and the secular world.

Isidore transmitted no information about the training techniques that would produce a 'perfect voice', but one would expect that they were in some measure traditional to the Mediterranean world.[13] This

Mediterranean ideal of the voice apparently encountered resistance from Franks and Germans, beginning in the late eighth century as Roman chant was transmitted north of the Alps. Different ideals of vocal tone and voice production – not just conflict over a new and older chant repertoire – must have figured in the contentiousness between Franks and Romans that is reported in contemporary chronicles. The northerners learned or adapted Roman chant, but they allegedly had a difficult time with the delicate ornamental effects known as *tremulae* and *vinnolae*, the latter term recalling one of the words used by Isidore in his description of a well-trained, flexible voice. The Franks and Germans allegedly 'broke' these notes in their throats, for they lacked the natural ability or training to sing them proficiently.[14] John the Deacon's biography of Gregory the Great (*c*. 844) heaped further ridicule on the crude singing of the Franks. As an Italian, John was not likely to have had much sympathy for the perceived shortcomings of northern tribes. Had we only these mutual invectives on which to rely, the northerners would come off poorly as singers. That they were far from insensitive to melodic refinement and rhythmic subtlety is attested by the notational systems developed to transmit the Frankish version of the melodies received from Rome. The neumatic notations developed at Laon and St Gall include a large number of special signs that denote dynamic nuances, subtle rhythmic differentiation and what have been called 'ornamental' tones.[15] If northern singers notated these nuances, does it not seem reasonable that they were capable of singing them?

Medieval understanding of the voice and vocal technique was limited by deficient conceptions of the physiology of vocal production and by an uncritical reliance on esteemed authorities of the past. Whatever could not be directly observed about the production of the singing voice seems to have remained essentially a mystery in the Middle Ages. Naturally, medieval authors recognised, even if only implicitly, the role of the lips, teeth, tongue, throat and lungs in vocal production. The thirteenth-century theorist Lambertus (also known as pseudo-Aristotle) added the epiglottis, assigning to it the principal role in vocal production.[16]

Most medieval authors who addressed the topic distinguished three 'voices': the *vox pectoris* (voice of the chest), the *vox gutturis* (voice of the throat) and the *vox capitis* (voice of the head), a nomenclature that still prevails to some extent in present-day vocal pedagogy. In a discussion of what was necessary for the proper singing of chant by two or more singers ('a duobus vel etiam a pluribus') Jerome of Moravia summed up the received opinion ('vulgariter loquendo') concerning the human singing voice:

We call those voices 'of the chest' that form notes in the chest, 'of the throat' those [formed] in the throat, and 'of the head' those [formed] in the head. Voices of the chest are best for the low register, of the throat for the high register, those of the head for the highest register. Large and low-pitched voices are of the chest; delicate and very high voices are of the head; the voices between these are of the throat. None of these [voices], therefore, is to be joined to the other in chanting, but the voice of the chest for the chest [tones], of the throat for the throat [tones], of the head for the head [tones].[17]

Jerome concluded that 'all voices draw their vigour from the chest [voice]', and he prescribed that all chant should be sung in a middle register, warning cantors not to intone pieces at too high a pitch level. A happy medium is to be sought: 'not too low, which is to howl, nor too high, which is to shout'.[18] Finally, for Jerome the supreme goal is singing the 'beautiful note' ('pulchra nota'). When once achieved, even if by accident, the singer should retain the conception until it becomes habitual. The greatest impediment to the production of 'beautiful notes' is sadness of heart: singers overwhelmed by melancholy, even if they have pleasing voices, will not be able to sing beautifully.

Jerome seems to use the same terminology both for individual voice types and for registers within a single voice. Not surprisingly, his vocal classification distinguishes among bass, baritone and tenor voices, a differentiation that rests on characteristics of human physiology that were the same in the thirteenth century as they are today. Marchetto posited a relationship between the vocal registers and the notes of the gamut. The chest voice sings the lowest seven tones (*graves*, A–G), the throat voice sings the next seven tones (*acutae*, a–g), and the head voice the final four pitches (*superacutae*, aa–dd). Marchetto and others maintained that the human voice, whether of wide or narrow compass, required a 'distinction' among the graves, acutes and superacutes.[19] He can hardly have meant, however, that differences in tone quality should be evident in the singing of a chant that might have covered only the range of an octave or less.

A late fifteenth-century author, Conrad von Zabern, proposed an analogy between the voice and the pipes of an organ – a comparison that 'anyone of any intelligence' would readily understand. Everyone knows, he says, that all organs have three sizes of pipes: large, medium and small. These produce three kinds of sound ('trivarius sit sonus'). Conrad recommended that the voice be used 'trivarie': resonantly on the lower pitches, moderately in the middle register, and with delicacy when negotiating the highest notes of the chant.[20] He acknowledged that the 'single wind-pipe' ('unam arteriam') that produces the human voice does not correspond to the multiple pipes of the organ. He implied, nevertheless, that singing should somehow reflect what he heard from the organs of his day, but that 'it would be mistaken to attempt to imitate [the organ's] diversity by uniform use of the voice'.[21] It might be that Conrad is here advising against a practice that is popularly known as 'belting', pushing the chest voice as high as possible without breaking.[22] He seems to recommend instead a smooth transition from one register to another, allowing for a change in vocal quality modelled on the sounds that would be made by the successive sounding of the pipes required to cover the medieval gamut.

The medieval *mensura fistularum* (measurement of organ pipes) treatises were not intended primarily as manuals for organ construction, but rather as theoretical exemplifications of musical proportions. They do not take pipe scaling into account, which would mean that, given a constant diameter, the progressively shortened pipes would yield a relatively thin tone quality in the bass compared to a flute-like quality in the treble. An organ with pipes of equal diameter over the two-octave range of the medieval gamut (*D–dd*) would have manifested noticeable, but probably not extraordinary, changes in tone quality.[23] An early twelfth-century practical treatise on the arts of the church by the monk Theophilus, *De diversis artibus*, includes instructions for the building of an organ. All of the pipes, made of thin copper, were turned on a single mandrel and were consequently of a constant diameter ('omnes unius mensure et eiusdem grossitudinis'). Theophilus divided the pipes into graves, acutes and superacutes, just as the medieval theorists of the gamut did.[24] Towards the end of the chapter on pipe-making Theophilus discusses the voicing of pipes in order to make the tone either larger ('grossam') or more graceful ('graciliorem') – exactly the kind of terminology encountered in medieval discussions of the voice.[25] Conrad might have known organs whose pipes were scaled, since his treatise was published only a few decades before Arnold Schlick's *Spiegel der Orgelmacher und Organisten* (1511), which gives clear evidence that pipe scaling was an accepted technique.[26] Conrad's analogy with the organ proves to be, nevertheless, a reasonable one that set a standard by which those who followed his teaching could model their voices.

The author of the *Summa musice* had a rather different concept of vocal physiology. He asserted that the tracheae, the cartilaginous tubes that carry air from the larynx to the lungs and vice versa, changed in size to produce low, high and very high pitches. When the tracheae were relaxed, low pitches (*graves*) were generated; when very tense, the highest pitches (*superacutae*). A state of tension between these two generated pitches in the 'high' range (*acutae*)[27], a concept not so far removed from what is now known about the action of the vocal cords. The author's terminology for the vocal ranges was borrowed from the three segments of the medieval gamut: grave, acute and superacute; he has no use for pitches higher or lower than these.

Important information about the voice and choral discipline in the high Middle Ages is contained in an early thirteenth-century Cistercian source known as the *Instituta patrum*.[28] The vocal ideal of the *Instituta* is no longer the 'suavis-alta-clara' voice of Isidore's model soloist, but a vocal quality and style of singing suited to choral psalmody. The psalms should be sung 'with an even voice, at a steady tempo that is not excessively drawn out, but at a moderate pitch, not too quickly, but with a full, virile, lively and precise voice'.[29] The specification about singing in the middle register, a range convenient to all voices (and one for which the adjective 'clear' might not be applicable), means that only one of Isidore's requirements survived the transfer from a solo to a choral orientation: that of 'sweetness'.

Towards the conclusion of the *Instituta* its author became quite exercised about certain kinds of vocalism that represented to him the abomination of qualities that should be cultivated by singers of sacred music. Some of these are basic flaws of vocal technique, but others are caricatures of the sounds he might have heard emanating from the throats of secular musicians. The author lumps together theatrical singing and chattering, 'mountain' (Alpine) voices, loud singing, hissing [lisping?], braying like a she-ass, growling or moaning like cattle, or (apparently worst of all!) singing with an effeminate voice.[30] Such singing was unacceptable from solo cantors (and he fears the worst when such morally suspect types aspire to musical leadership), nor could it be tolerated in choral singing. No longer are a high singing range, carrying power and intelligibility of the text the principal *desiderata*, but rather unanimity and moderation joined to an *apta flexibilitas* in the singing of neumes.

This text represents a certain shift in emphasis, which has been interpreted as the contrast between a southern ideal of vocalism and the Germanic preference for a fuller voice in the baritone range.[31] The shift can also be explained by the passage of time since Isidore's day, but more convincingly by the change of milieu from the public basilica of late antiquity to the medieval monastic choir. The *Instituta*'s preference for a *mezzo forte* dynamic level meant that Isidore's predilection for singing that would 'fill the ears' of the auditors had been replaced by a different aesthetic. It is inconceivable that one standard would be applied to choral singing and another, radically different, one to the rendition of the solo portions of the chants. Clearness of articulation was still demanded, but required more as reverence due the sacred text than as a necessity for the communication of that text to a listening audience. Intelligibility had been, nevertheless, an issue in the rule for canons by Chrodegang of Metz (*d.* 766), in which it is implied that the higher pitch acceptable for the *sonus cantilene* (solo singing) should be avoided in psalmody.[32]

The 'theatrical singing' ('histrionicas voces') denounced by the *Instituta patrum* apparently represented a catch-all for the vocal practices and singing mannerisms of secular performers, who probably performed polyphony. Secular performers might have preferred a tone quality with greater carrying power something akin to the Isidorean ideal. One hesitates, however, to draw more specific conclusions from a document of such polemical intent, or to equate the 'vanity and foolishness' condemned by the author exclusively with secular music. 'Theatrical' singers caused Aelred of Rievaulx (1110–67), abbot of the celebrated Cistercian abbey in Yorkshire, to become positively livid: the 'whole body is agitated by theatrical gestures, the lips are twisted, the eyes roll, the shoulders are shrugged, and the fingers bent in response to every note'.[33] The laity's reaction to these antics was, according to Aelred, nothing less than derision – exactly the opposite of what one ought to expect in a sacred place. Very likely Aelred was describing a performance of improvised organum or discant.

About a century after the *Instituta patrum* was written, Pope John XXII issued the bull *Docta sanctorum patrum* (1324) to condemn the musical practices of certain 'disciples of the new school', generally interpreted as adherents of the French Ars Nova. (John resided at Avignon.) After encouraging singers to 'sing with modesty and gravity melodies of calm and peaceful character' (either the traditional chants or melodies composed after them), the pope quoted the first responsory from the Office for the dedication of a church: 'and in their mouth resounded a *sweet* sound' ('et in ore eorum dulcis resonabat sonus').[34] In this case the 'sweetness' involved not only the manner in which the music itself was performed but the interior dispositions with which it was sung. The 'new school' erred in both respects and thus deserved censure.

There are indications that the aesthetic of 'sweetness' and moderate dynamic level was accepted outside the choir. A couplet from the madrigal *Useletto selvaggio* by Jacopo da Bologna implies that secular music also embraced a refined vocal aesthetic: 'loud shouting is not singing well, but with a sweet and pleasant melody' ('Per gritar forte non si cantar bene / Ma con soav'e dolce melodia').[35] Another critic of loud singing, the Bolognese rhetorician Boncompagno da Signa, witnessed the contention between Italian students and those from northern 'nations' in a university town. The 'Gauls' asserted that the Italians 'rave with constant fracturing of their voices', while the Italians (countrymen with whom the author would have sympathised) countered with the criticism that the French and Germans, 'like people suffering from fever, produce shaking voices ('tremulas voces'), and with an immoderate outpouring of sound strive to batter heaven itself, either because they believe that God is deaf or that he can be pleased with such wildness in singing'.[36]

Germans were often accused of loud and strained singing. Even Ornithoparchus had to confess that his countrymen were prone to excess in this matter.[37] They were not the only guilty ones, however. In the treatise *Scientia artis musice* (1274) Hélie Salomon ridiculed the canons of Lyons who sang so loudly that one might imagine that in their view the highest praise belonged to whoever made the greatest noise.[38] Two hundred years later, Conrad of Zabern was still excoriating stentorian singing. He mentioned two related 'rusticities' (as he was wont to call such defects) that mar fine singing: forcing the voice and loud singing, especially on high notes.[39] Forcing leads inevitably to fatigue and hoarseness, while excessive loudness disturbs the balance of the choir. Conrad recommended that his readers be guided by the prophet Micah: 'a song will be sung with sweetness' ('cantabitur canticum cum suavitate', Micah 2:4).

Proper balance among the voices was important in polyphonic music, but it could not be supplied by loud singing. In the penultimate chapter of his *Scientia* Hélie Salomon describes an actual choir rehearsal.[40] The 'rector' of the four singers preparing a four-voice parallel organum for performance is supposed to admonish a singer who sings either too loudly or too softly, sometimes joining the weaker performer to achieve a proper balance. (See Fig. 7.) Hélie permitted doubling of the lowest voice throughout, if necessary, in the interest of this balance. Doubling of the discantus and the tenor was also allowed in two-voice polyphony by Jacques of Liège, according to whom the two written vocal parts did not limit the number of singers.[41]

Some vocal practices perceived by medieval authors as offensive were excoriated both on aesthetic and on moral grounds. A passage from the *Instituta patrum* (quoted earlier) proscribes 'effeminate' singing as inappropriate for monks. Other references identify a vocal quality of a pronounced nasal character, sometimes called 'singing through the nose', with effeminacy. When Chaucer says of the prioress, Madame Eglentyne, in the *Canterbury Tales*, that 'Ful weel she soong the service dyvyne, / Entuned in hir nose ful semely', he can hardly have been paying her a compliment.[42] A mannerism that might be acceptable in the prioress because of her sex would certainly not be condoned in a monastery of male religious.

Conrad of Zabern included nasal singing among the 'rusticitates' that were to be avoided, a view that he assumed would be approved by

Figure 7 Fourteenth-century singing monks

everyone discriminating enough to judge.[43] He argued that, since the nose is never mentioned among the *naturalia instrumenta* that form the human voice, it would be a grave mistake to make use of it in vocal production. Nasal singing made the voice unpleasant or 'dissonant' ('absona'), and it contributed nothing to the 'sweetness' that Conrad and his contemporaries prized so highly.

In a sermon on the Canticle of Canticles, the Cistercian abbot Bernard of Clairvaux (1090/91–1153) encouraged his brethren to sing the office 'not as lazy, sleepy or bored creatures, not sparing your voices, not cutting off half the words or omitting some altogether, nor with voices broken or weak, neither singing through the nose with an effeminate lisp, but bringing forth with virile resonance and affection voices worthy of the Holy Spirit'.[44] For Aelred of Rievaulx, nothing was more detestable than witnessing monastic singers laying aside manly vigour for the artificial delicacy of a feminine vocal quality.[45] The connection between nasality, lisping and effeminacy was not accidental, for they were linked even in

Classical times. Presumably the author of the *Instituta patrum* referred to this idiosyncrasy when, in the long list of objectionable vocal qualities, he included 'voces . . . femineas'. John of Salisbury also took aim at the 'effeminate mannerisms . . . the harmony not of men but of sirens',[46] but John's extravagant portrayal of Parisian music-making in the mid-twelfth century is more of a literary exercise than an essay on performance practice.

Nothing suggests that the 'effeminate' voices were those of castrati, though nasal singing might possibly have been combined with the use of falsetto. That this mannerism was considered to lie outside the pale of normal church singing – though not beyond the pale in secular music – may be inferred from a rubric in the Office for the 'feast of fools' in an early thirteenth-century Beauvais antiphoner (London, British Library, Egerton 2615) instructing that all the antiphons were to be intoned 'cum falseto'.[47]

Particularly distasteful to several writers was singing that reminded them of the sounds made by animals. The *Instituta patrum* included among the detestable aspects of 'theatrical voices' their 'braying like a talking ass, bellowing or bleating like cattle', possibly a reference to nasal singing.[48] The unedifying sounds made by the voices of singers of polyphonic music which 'sound like the whinnying of horses' ('equinos hinnitus') in the house of God were intolerable to Aelred of Rielvaux.[49] These references to equine noises could also be interpreted as a reference to the strained vocal tone of singers attempting to reach pitches beyond their natural range.

Both vibrato and trills (short and long) were ornamental vocal resources in polyphony of the thirteenth century, judging from the remarks of Jerome of Moravia.[50] They were unnotated, but could be applied in certain circumstances and required an advanced vocal technique. The 'reverberatio' seems to have been a rapid ornament on a single pitch, like a mordent or a short trill. Another kind of 'reverberatio' was an appoggiatura which occupied one half of the value of the following note. In addition to these brief *agréments* (to borrow a term from the seventeenth and eighteenth centuries) there was another kind of ornament called by Jerome 'a harmonic flower, . . . a very swift and stormlike vibration'.[51] He distinguished several types of this longer ornament: (1) a steady oscillation that covers a semitone, (2) a steady oscillation no wider than a whole tone, and (3) a gradual acceleration of the trill, which can cover no more than a semitone. Such distinctions suggest an established practice, but Jerome also explains how the effect can be demonstrated to those unfamiliar with it on the keyboard of an organ.

Conrad of Zabern's treatise on chant singing has been mentioned several times previously. Despite its relatively late date (1474), it presents a thorough and methodical treatment of plainsong performance founded on medieval traditions. His six requirements for 'singing well' include: (1) singing of chant in perfect unison, (2) singing with equal note values and a consistent tempo, (3) pitching chants in the middle register so that all can participate, (4) adopting different tempi depending on the liturgical observance and singing in a way that reflects the sentiment of the words,[52] (5) singing with devotion and without the addition of improvised polyphony or the intrusion of secular melodies, and (6) avoiding the ten faults branded by Conrad as 'rusticities'. Only those that directly concern vocal quality or voice production are relevant to the present context.

Conrad opposed the practice of inserting an aspirate ('h') before the individual notes of a melisma, a fault he claimed was widespread among the clergy. (Can it have been entirely absent from the mannerisms of secular vocalists, who would have performed sacred music in princely chapels as part of their duties?) Incessant aspiration creates a harshness ('asperitas') that impairs the sweetness ('suavitas') appropriate to plainsong. A vocal production marked by forcing ('cum impetu sive violentia vocem emittere vel extorquere') can never be commended – additional proof, if such be needed, that the practice was not uncommon. Conrad is quite insistent about this point, claiming that 'innumerable ecclesiastics' make ignorance of this rule a common practice in their singing. Like Hélie Salomon two centuries earlier, he has his own story about some (unidentified) canons determined to shatter (or at least rattle) the windows of their choir with ear-splitting high notes.[53]

Recently, in *The Sound of Medieval Song* Timothy McGee has argued for a radical reconsideration of vocal quality and performance style in medieval music. He describes the 'repertory of sounds' in the medieval singer's repertoire as

> a clear (vibratoless) voice, rapid throat articulation and pulsation, slow, fast, and accelerating vibrato at variable intervals, and voice placement that alternates between a bright sound made in the front of the mouth and a dark tone from the throat. The sounds include fixed and sliding tones, diatonic and non-diatonic pitches, aspirated, gargled and sibilant sounds, and both clear and covered tone qualities.[54]

Some of these techniques might be applicable to secular music, though the conclusions drawn by McGee from the predominantly clerical theorists he cites do not always seem to warrant the interpretations placed on them. He argues that, even though most of the special signs in the nuance-rich chant notations of the ninth and tenth centuries utterly disappeared from the manuscript sources, the vocal style they represented (about which virtually nothing is known anyway) persisted through the centuries, though unrecorded in practice. He sees evidence for this in thirteenth-century theorists like Jerome of Moravia. He views contemporary Middle Eastern or Indian vocal production and singing styles as models for the singing of Western medieval music.

In the present essay (written before the publication of *The Sound of Medieval Song*) I have presented a more conservative assessment of what medieval documents tell us about the voice and how it was used. We can never satisfactorily re-create what medieval singing sounded like, but the material presented by McGee, once sifted historically and carefully distinguished according to sacred and secular venues, will enlarge our understanding of how medieval music was sung. Just how that understanding can be translated into sound depends, as it always will, on the sensitivity of talented modern performers.

15 Reconstructing pre-Romantic singing technique

RICHARD WISTREICH

Considering the tremendous breadth of musical activity throughout Europe and the range of its different social, technical and aesthetic contexts between the beginning of the sixteenth and the end of the eighteenth centuries, the sheer consistency of the information we have about the fundamentals of the art of singing during this time is remarkable. Some aspects of vocal performance which were constantly repeated throughout the period are as obviously necessary now as they were then. For example, the repeated demand that the words always be audibly and correctly pronounced, the text understood and intelligibly delivered by the singer, and that its meaning and poetics inform every aspect of the musical performance, suggests that in former times, just as in the present, singers needed regularly reminding of this fundamental principle. There are other aspects of vocal performance which were also reiterated in every generation, but which nowadays are either little understood and not seen as being as important as they once were (for example, the correct way to articulate *passaggi*), or which are quite simply not considered any more (for example, the differentiation of chest and falsetto registers and their proper joining together) and are therefore no longer part of the training of professional singers.

What, then, were the main preoccupations of singing teachers, writers of vocal treatises and singers themselves in the centuries under consideration and how might an awareness of the differences from current priorities in the teaching of singing technique affect the choices that performers of pre-nineteenth-century music might yet make, even in the current 'age of enlightenment' of historically aware music-making?

Bénigne Bacilly (1668) says that the three 'qualities necessary to sing well' are 'to wit: the voice, the disposition, and the ear, or intelligence'.[1] Taking the third quality to encompass both the sense of a 'musical' ear (especially the ability to sing in tune and improvise) and the intelligence to apply raw vocal skills to making performances, or, in Giulio Caccini's (1602) words, 'to be able to move the affect of the soul through that certain sense of where one should admit the use of the affects',[2] or perhaps those of Domenico Corri (1810), 'Quick perception; to give to every word its proper energy and pathos',[3] then we have a list of three basic headings under which to order the material.

Voice

Simply looking at any page of Renaissance vocal music, one can quickly see that very rarely does the notated music for any voice pass beyond the limits of the staff. Thus, although the clef may vary – and thus the absolute pitches of the notes may be higher or lower – the actual range required of any one voice is usually not much more than a tenth. Vocal music from the late sixteenth century onwards begins to change its appearance: notated ranges increase, sometimes dramatically. There is a song printed in 1620 which calls for a range from c^2 down to the Bb^1 three octaves and a tone below, which is definitely something extraordinary but is also evidence of an age that enjoyed extremes of expressivity and had the need to write them down.[4] The relatively narrow range of Renaissance vocal parts directly reflects the function of the human voice and the aesthetic preferences of the time. A comparison between these preferences and the ways voices work can in turn tell us much about how singing may actually have sounded.

Singers and composers understood, long before scientists confirmed the fact, that the voice has two registers: the modal or chest voice, and the falsetto. This is true for men and women and also for children. The upper register in children and women is normally referred to today as 'head voice', but this name has a different, specific meaning in the context of men's voices (see below). Although basses and tenors, and altos and sopranos have different lower limits to the tones they can reach, the point at which the chest register gives out at the top and the falsetto takes over (although normally with an area of overlap) is roughly the same in all broken voices, between d^1 and f^1. Children can extend the chest register upwards to about b^1 or c^2 and even further, and the evidence suggests that castrato singers retained the ability to take the chest register to this point. Likewise, adult men and women can also force the chest voice higher in a similar way to children, by pressuring the larynx upwards, and this is basically what most singers outside the relatively narrow confines of Western classical art-singing do today. Trained baritones and tenors can often carry the chest register relatively easily up to a^1 or even b^1 without forcing, if the tone is very lightly placed. This softer, sweeter sound, which almost all men can utilise to sing higher tones (often called 'head voice'), is nevertheless part of the chest register, although as early as the mid-eighteenth century it is regularly rather confusingly described as an 'intermediate vocal register' (for example, by Agricola, 1757[5]).

The technique by which singers can greatly increase the volume of the voice and carry the full chest voice higher still (at the expense of flexibility of articulation) by *depressing* the larynx was a development of the late eighteenth century, first described in a serious singing treatise by Manuel García in 1847.[6] It is thought-provoking that before the time of Rossini singers *raised* the larynx as the tone became higher – as rock, soul and folk singers do now – rather than consciously *lowering* it, as in modern classical technique. Marin Mersenne (1636), in an exhaustive investigation of the function of the human voice, states unequivocally that 'the larynx rises up when we sing the *Dessus* . . . the larynx goes down when singing the *Basse*'.[7] This is in essence repeated more than a century later by Jean Antoine Bérard (1755) who, in a mechanistic attempt to explain the way in which the voice changes pitches in the same way as stringed instruments, advises the student to place a finger on the larynx and to note how it rises by steps as the sung notes get higher.[8] However scientifically wrong his theory, the experiment demonstrates for us precisely the vocal technique of an eighteenth-century professional singer and teacher and reiterates Mersenne's own observation.

In the sixteenth and seventeenth centuries, there are regular reminders to singers in treatises to stick to the chest register as much as possible. Although the falsetto register was recognised early on as having special useful qualities, the chest (incidentally, the register in which we speak) is considered superior for singing. 'Since the low voice exceeds and surpasses and embraces all the others, it must be considered more perfect, more noble and more generous' states Maffei in 1562;[9] 'The falsetto voice cannot give rise to the nobility of good singing' says Caccini in 1602.[10] And what if the music you want to sing lies too high for the voice to reach without either straining the voice and being forced to sing too loud or having to change over into falsetto register for the odd note? Then simply change the pitch of the music: a practice that was clearly so often done that it usually went without saying throughout the period under consideration. Caccini says, 'let him choose a pitch at which he is able to sing in a full and natural voice, avoiding the falsetto, and at which he does not have to "cheat" or at least use force'. He makes the proviso that this is straightforward if one is singing alone 'without being constrained to accommodate himself to others'.[11] If singing in company, the simplest resolution of register problems is to sing another part (or perhaps use an instrument instead). Praetorius (1619) states, 'a singer . . . [needs] to choose a voice such as *Cantus, Altus* or *Tenor* etc. which he can hold with a full and clear tone without falsetto (that is half and forced voice)'.[12]

The falsetto voice was cultivated by certain singers in special situations, particularly because it could enable great flexibility and speed of articulation,[13] something especially prized in the sophisticated performances of certain repertoires for select audiences in small rooms. A good example is the Roman singer and composer Giovanni Luca Conforti, who was remembered by Pietro della Valle (1640) as 'the falsettist [he was not a castrato], great singer of *gorge* and *passaggi*, who could sing as high as the stars'.[14] This is confirmed by another writer who said that 'he usually sings soprano', but significantly, 'when he was in the papal chapel he always sang, so I understand, contralto [a chest register voice]'.[15] Likewise, Pietro della Valle recalls another Roman, Orazietto, 'excellent singer both as a falsettist and as a tenor'.[16]

The distinction between singing in church and in other places was marked. Gioseffo Zarlino (1588–9) expressed the difference succinctly: 'one sings in one way in churches and public chapels and another way in private rooms. In [the former] one sings in a full voice, but with discretion, nevertheless . . . and in private rooms one sings with a lower and gentler voice, without any shouting'.[17] In terms of vocal sound alone, here are challenging, maybe even uncomfortable, implications for present-day performers of Renaissance and Baroque music.

Right up until the late eighteenth century, church or chapel choirs throughout Europe were made up either from exclusively male or female singers. In a choir of males, boys would sing the soprano or cantus parts, men the tenor and bass parts (those notated in C4, F3 and F4 clefs), all using chest register as far as possible. In a few establishments, castrati sang the top part. But what of the middle-range parts, those usually notated in C3 clefs and called today 'alto' or 'high tenor' parts? With ranges generally from about d to g^1, but with a general tessitura in the upper part of this range, they create problems for modern choirs organised according to the nineteenth-century division of voices, lying too high for most tenors and too low for female altos and male falsettists. Tenors able to sing easily and lightly up to the highest notes of the chest register can be assigned to these parts, but even those with the necessary 'head-voice' facility (as it was first described by Agricola in 1757, see above) find it difficult to sing in such a high tessitura all the time.

If we start instead from what we know about church singers in the sixteenth and seventeenth centuries, a number of other possibilities become apparent. The vocal lines in Renaissance and Baroque church music notated in C3 clefs and going up to g^1 or higher could well be sung in chest register by broken voices, but perhaps with an intensity and hardness of timbre not now normally associated with this music. Likewise, the lines could have been sung by unbroken voices, whose chest registers were strong down to the lowest notes of the range through conscious exercise. It is worth remembering that much Renaissance polyphony is notated in *chiavette*, clefs which imply a degree of downward transposition.

Boys and men who sang the soprano and tenor parts in early seventeenth-century Germany were expected to change to falsetto when the notes became too high for the chest register, although not all of them could, sometimes leading to trouble: 'no less in error are those clumsy singers who, when they sing the *Discantus*, are unable to sing in falsetto and so have to take the octave below and make a tenor out of the *discant*, and no little damage results from fifths being made. Tenors also make crude errors when they sing an octave lower, going beneath the fundamental and making false consonances such as fourths and sixths below the bass.'[18]

Even taking into consideration the fact that much church polyphony in the Renaissance did not apparently require individual voices to sing especially high in their respective registers, the sound of boys and men singing in chest register at the top of the range would inevitably have produced a fairly strident sound (hopefully stopping short of Zarlino's 'shouting'). In all-male choral music, the singers could choose to perform the music at a low enough pitch to obviate the use of falsetto by any of the singers. References to *contrabassi* abound in Italy in the sixteenth century, as well as to *bassetti* and, occasionally, *baritoni*, who may have sung parts in F3 as well as C4 clefs. Late sixteenth- and seventeenth-century parts designated 'tenor' mostly span a range of about A–f^1, the range of the normal adult male voice (today usually called baritone); therefore it does not presuppose cultivation of the 'head voice'. We must assume that the bulk of notated music of the Renaissance and Baroque fitted the normal chest-voice ranges of most singers without recourse to special modifications such as 'head voice', and that the entire performance practice of Renaissance polyphony did not depend on the supply of extremely rare voice types.

In other churches, choirs of nuns could sing the same repertoire as male-voice ensembles by pitching the music higher, by putting bass parts up an octave, or by substituting instruments such as trombones for the lower voices. The upper voices made use of falsetto, whilst other women who took the lower parts would have used exclusively chest register. It is becoming clear that in numerous convents nuns did not deny themselves polyphonic music in five and more parts, nor were they constrained by modern definitions of voice types. Indeed there were nuns who were praised as tenors and basses.[19]

Singing in chambers and other non-ecclesiastical spaces needed a different kind of vocal technique. In intimate surroundings, vocal chamber music was often performed together with soft instruments like harps, viols, clavichords and lutes, and, having as its overriding priority the clear, flexible and affective conveying of texts, loudness was not only unnecessary, but highly undesirable: 'many learn to sing by singing softly and in rooms ['camere'] where loud singing is abhorred, and here sing those gentlemen and others who are not forced by necessity to sing in the churches and in the chapels where hired singers sing';[20] 'one [person] praises sweet and gentle singing, another church singing'.[21] Even allowing for the slightly more strident instruments such as violins, harpsichords and theorbos, and for the increasing size of the mixed vocal and instrumental ensembles required to perform concerted music for the courtly opera and the chamber cantatas of the Baroque period, a dynamic level close to normal speaking allowed for the flexibility, subtlety and expressiveness in which text could remain paramount. There is another technical consideration: the precision and sheer speed of throat-articulation as it was prized and practised from the sixteenth to the end of the eighteenth centuries functions optimally, as we shall see, at a surprisingly low dynamic level.

Amongst other things, this intimate chamber singing style favoured light voices, 'grace', 'discretion' and 'sweetness' of tone. What little we know about singing by adult women in the early sixteenth century suggests that in private chambers (which, until Venetian opera began in the late 1630s, were the only arena for women singers, with the exception of nuns and a very small number of exceptional *virtuose*) it was the lower part of the voice which was preferred, conforming to a general aesthetic which favoured softer, deeper voices to 'shrill' or 'raucous' ones, in polite conversation as well as in singing. Shakespeare summarises the prevailing ideal in his description of Princess Cordelia: 'Her voice was ever soft, / Gentle and low, an excellent thing in woman'.[22] Giovanni de' Bardi, a member of one of the famous Florentine Camerate in the 1570s and 1580s, summed up the way to sing chamber music as follows: 'whoever wants to sing well had better do so very sweetly, with a very sweet manner . . . and while singing, you will strive to behave in a seemly way, so similar to your normal [i.e. speaking] manner that people will be left wondering whether the sound issues from your lips or from someone else's'.[23]

The ability to sing in more than one voice category or register in the same piece of music was sufficiently rare to be the cause of comment in the sixteenth century, either admiring or scandalised, but it shows that some performers were singing notes beyond the written ranges of their parts as an aspect of the necessary improvised additions they made to the composed notation. At first, this appears to have been part of the performance of secular music in small rooms among select groups of aesthetes, but before the end of the sixteenth century, solo singers in more public venues, including theatres and churches, were demonstrating the expressiveness of the voice in the newer types of affective music, combining ever-increasing virtuosity of articulation with expanding vocal range. Songs published by Luzzasco Luzzaschi in 1601, but apparently representing performances by some of the famous women *virtuose* of the court of Ferrara in the 1580s, require solo singing well up into the falsetto range.[24] From the 1560s until the 1630s there are references to exceptional male performers who could sing not only bass and tenor but alto as well – able, as it were, to substitute for a whole ensemble in performances which look as impressive on paper as they must have been to hear. Published monodies, both secular and sacred, began to describe in their composed notation notes spanning more than one of the former voice categories or even of both registers – chest and falsetto – within one piece, and to require the singer to be able to pass from one to the other smoothly and at speed. By the early seventeenth century, Monteverdi was remarking of a singer hoping to be employed as a professional bass at San Marco in Venice, that the 'voice goes into the tenor with ease', implying that the proper connection of two separate vocal ranges, in this case perhaps even chest and falsetto registers, had already become a hallmark of a properly trained singer.[25] The mastery of this fundamental technique remained an essential and unchanging element of voice training until well into the nineteenth century.

The most detailed sources we have about singing teaching in the eighteenth century, by Tosi (1723) and Mancini (1774), give precisely detailed explanations of how to develop the two registers and how they should be joined. Tosi and Mancini were castrati, and their books are principally aimed at the education of castrato singers. Mancini, who acknowledges his debt to Tosi, makes it clear that their methods apply to all voices, although he too concentrates on the soprano voice. It seems logical that the need to develop both the chest and falsetto registers was particularly crucial for a castrato, whose voice would otherwise, in Tosi's words, make him 'constrained to sing within the narrow Compass of a few Notes'.[26] Tosi describes the upper limit of the chest register as around d$\sharp^2$, which, even allowing for regional pitch differences, is a considerably higher point than in the normal adult voice.[27] This pitch is repeated by Mancini, and suggests that castrati perhaps retained the ability of trained children to take the chest voice up high.[28] Neither mentions the lower limit of the soprano castrato voice, but existing repertoire puts it at not much lower than a. The techniques described by Tosi and Mancini reflect a long tradition of voice training, passed on from one generation to the next in the master–apprentice system of professional voice training; there is no reason why it should not still form the basis of singing teaching today.

Mancini tells us that the voice is first purged of any constrictions, either nasal or throaty, by the singing of long tones on each of the pure vowels or *sol-fa* syllables. This echoes numerous similar urgings from the previous century and a half, which reiterate the desirability of a 'natural' voice, and one completely free of unnecessary vibrations or shakings: 'The *fermo* or holding steady of the voice is required on every note which does not require a *trillo* or cadential trill';[29] 'the sound should not be formed in the midst of a rasping throat, by the tongue or between the cheeks and lips'.[30] Although Praetorius, in a much quoted comment, says that a good singer should have a pleasantly 'trembling' voice (but which he strongly tempers by insisting that it not be in any way extreme),[31] there is no doubt that purity and precision of tone were prized throughout the period under discussion.

Absolutely precise intonation is vital: 'the first and most important is the intonation of all notes, not simply so that nothing is too low or too high but also to have good *maniera*'.[32] Domenico Corri (1810) still regards it as necessary to devote a whole chapter of his method (essentially aimed at amateurs) to teaching the differences between the major and minor semitone.[33] Corri may have been fighting a rearguard action by this time, but it confirms a totally consistent preoccupation with tonal purity and precise intonation: 'Voices . . . must be *justes*, *égales* and *flexibles*; *justesse* consists in taking the given tone without allowing it to rise too high or fall too low . . . *égalité* is the firm and stable holding of the voice on one unchanging note without allowing it to vary either upwards or downwards'.[34] The evidence leads to the conclusion that any extraneous element in the vocal sound, be it simply vibrato or perhaps other acoustical complexes which the modern ear might describe simply as vocal timbre or 'grain', would have been regarded as undesirable.

Next, the singer learns to join one note to the next, literally to carry one tone to the other with a perfect legato: 'I remind the teacher that he should take care that the student's tones are audibly joined one to another. This occurs when one lets the previous tone last until the next one starts, so that no gap can be heard between them'.[35] This element of good singing is consistently reiterated: '*portar della voce*'[36] or '*porger la voce*';[37] 'à bien soutenir la voix; à bien porter';[38] 'the Manner to glide with the Vowels, and to drag the Voice gently from the high to the lower notes';[39] 'gutes Tragen der Stimme';[40] '*Portamento di voce* is the perfection of vocal music; it consists in the swell and dying of the voice, the sliding and bending of one note into another with delicacy and expression'.[41] Then comes a strengthening of the lower notes of the falsetto and the notes of the chest voice, especially in younger singers (Mancini talks of students starting their studies aged twelve, thirteen or fourteen), through the daily repetition of solfège exercises. 'After the Scholar has ascertained the compass of the Natural [i.e. chest] Voice, his great study should be to contrive to unite the Natural to the first Note of the Falsetto, to blend them with such nicety, that the union be imperceptible'.[42] And so, finally, the registers are very gradually connected through the agency of the *messa di voce*. This is an exercise particularly on notes common to the chest and falsetto registers, in which the voice is gradually swelled from a *pianissimo* tone in falsetto to a *forte* in chest voice, returning with a diminuendo to the softest of falsetto tones, all perfectly graduated and disguising the change of register. Like other vocal exercises (see the *trillo*, below) it was also deployed as an ornament in itself, and became a benchmark of the finest vocal technique.[43]

The 'finished voice', then, differs considerably from its modern, trained equivalent. First, instead of beginning by strengthening the voice through power-building exercises and aiming at unity of vocal timbre throughout the entire range of the voice, as today's opera singers learn, the emphasis was on clear differentiation of registers, strength in the lower and lightness in the upper (tenors, for example, sang notes above f^1 in pure falsetto until the late eighteenth century, and thereafter the change-over to producing higher tones in chest register was gradual and often strongly resisted).[44] Second, in contrast to the modern technique of vowel modification and depressing of the larynx at the upper ends of the registers, singers worked at achieving a consistency of pure unmodified vowels in all parts of the range and, above all, singing without any hint of force or pressure. Variations of loudness and 'colour' in different parts of the voice were thus accepted and expected. Mancini warns, for example, of the danger of being tempted to force the chest voice in a large theatre or church when trying to be heard above the audience ('il mormorio della gente'). 'Be absolutely clear, that forcing the voice is always one of the greatest errors which it is possible for a singer to commit'.[45]

Disposition

After *justesse* and *égalité*, Marin Mersenne names *flexibilité* as a basic requirement of a good voice, which he defines as 'nothing else than the facility and the disposition that [the voice] has to pass through all kinds of progressions and intervals, both rising and falling and the making of all kinds of passages and diminutions'.[46] There can be no doubt that the precise singing of melismas (*passaggi*) and rhetorical ornaments (*accenti*), which are an enduring feature of vocal music from the Renaissance to the nineteenth century, required and requires mastery of throat articulation, which in turn appears to be the technical essence of that elusive precondition of good singing: *disposition*. The ability to control rapid opening and closing of the glottis to make very fast and precise note articulation goes against normal modern vocal technique, dependent as the latter is on depressing the larynx. Nevertheless, the sources are absolutely clear on the matter, and without a flexible, swift and accurate disposition, no singer in the Renaissance, Baroque or Classical periods could hope to be taken seriously as a professional. 'I say that such a voice [that sings the *gorgia*] is nothing other than a sound caused by the minute and orderly repercussions of air in the throat';[47] 'a smooth, round throat and larynx [*Gurgel*] for diminutions';[48] '*Cadences*... which consist of "rattlings" of the throat... are the most difficult part of singing because they must be made only [by] beating the air in the throat';[49] '*Disposition* is a certain facility in the performance of everything having to do with singing. It has its location in the throat... a certain imperceptible repetition of notes';[50] 'it is vital that the teacher instructs the pupil in the art of making *passaggi* with effortless speed and true intonation, so that when the pupil performs them well in public he receives applause and [they] provide the singer with an all-round ability in all aspects of singing'.[51]

The principal way that disposition is displayed in singing is in the perfect execution of the *trillo*, which is the exercise used to learn it in the first place (in the same way that *messa di voce* and *portar della voce* gave rise to their own exemplary ornaments). '[A singer can] simply have a beautiful voice, an easy execution and also good taste; nevertheless if these are not combined with the sweet grace of the Trillo, his singing will always be imperfect, arid and impoverished ... O Trillo! sustenance, beauty and life of singing!'[52]

Praetorius gives a very clear description of the *trillo*: 'when many fast notes are repeated one after the other'.[53] In the eighteenth century, the *trillo* as an ornament gave way to the shake, or trill between two notes (the two types of trill had already been described by Praetorius), but the articulation exercises to achieve it vary little from those of the late Renaissance. That the *trillo* itself is not just an ornament to be added as a finishing touch to a vocal line, but is rather part of the very substance of singing technique, is already clear in one of the earliest and most detailed descriptions of it, by Caccini (1602). His singing treatise includes a musical example labelled 'trillo', and it shows a series of repetitions of the same tone, gradually increasing in speed from crotchets to demi-semi-quavers, followed by a breve. This has led to generations of 'Baroque' singers reproducing this exercise as it stands, in the belief that this *is* the *trillo*. If they read a little further in the treatise, they would see that Caccini explains: 'The *trillo* written by me on a single note is demonstrated in this way for no other reason than that, in teaching it to my first wife and now to the [other] one... I observed no other rule than that which is written out: that is... to begin with the first crotchet and then restrike each note with the throat on the vowel *a*, up to the final breve'.[54] In other words, it is an *exercise* in speeding up the repercussions of the glottis. The *trillo* itself is in fact the fastest possible repetition of the tone, and once mastered, it opens the door to all the other types of articulation figures in the singer's

armoury: *gruppo, tirata, cascata, ribattuta di gorgia, tremolo*, the diminutions of the Renaissance, and the *accenti* and *passaggi* of the Baroque, the
latter still being prescribed by Corri in 1810. French singers had their own
versions of many of these ornaments, painstakingly described in a
number of treatises. The rapid and precise double repercussion of the
glottis is a vital element in the performance of a specifically French
Baroque ornament: the *port de voix*, a gliding liaison between two notes
lying next to each other and considered the apogee of refined vocal technique throughout the seventeenth and eighteenth centuries.[55]

So how is it done? Several sources which try to describe the technique
in print confess that it can only really be learned by imitating someone
who can demonstrate it, 'just like a bird learns by observing another'.[56] I
am inclined to believe that this is not simply the usual evasive language of
singers, but rather a recognition of the special problem of describing
throat articulation in words alone. Francesco Rognoni (1620) published a
page of graded vocal exercises (probably the earliest we have, see Fig. 8).
The first, entitled 'Modo di portar la voce', shows a very simple ascending
and descending scale, in which each tone is divided into a dotted minim
tied over to a crotchet. The rubric explains: 'The *portar della voce*, which
should be [done] with *gratia*, is made [by] reinforcing the voice on the
first note little by little, and then making a *tremolo* on the crotchet';[57] he
might have added: 'before passing to the next note'. We have already seen
how the *portamento* from one note to the next is the basic building-block
of singing technique; here we see that from the very first exercise it is associated with gently increasing the intensity of the note until it is energised
sufficiently, then releasing it with a glottal articulation as the voice passes
up or down.[58] 'The *tremolo*, that is, the trembling voice, is the true door
for entering into the *passaggi* and for mastering the *gorgie*, because a ship
sails more easily when it is already moving than when it is first set into
motion'.[59]

The second exercise, interestingly labelled 'Accenti' (the name given to
short articulatory ornaments directly linked to text expression in early
Baroque vocal music), is very closely related to the 'modo di portar le
voce'. Out of these two emerge all the other basic ornaments and expressive articulations: the *gruppo*, simple and double, which is the equivalent
to the later shake or trill, and the 'tremolo', clearly a *trillo*-like note repetition of limited duration that arises out of a dotted-note movement, itself
a useful re-animator of the flexibility of the glottis during a melismatic
phrase.

Just getting the glottis into motion can be difficult for singers used to a
heavy kind of vocal production. Bacilly suggests 'when studying the performance of *passages*, one must beat the throat as heavily and as slowly as

Figure 8 Rognoni's vocal exercises from *Selva di varii passaggi* (1620)

possible at first so that by means of this deliberate slowness and solidity of accent one masters *justesse* and avoids singing through the nose and with the tongue',[60] once again demonstrating the interconnectedness of the basic elements of Baroque singing technique: purity of voice, precision of intonation and disposition itself. The 'trillo articulation' in the throat can only work if the voice is not pressured in the larynx, the mouth is relaxed and the dynamic level of sound not too high. When treatises describe faults they often reveal more about the right way to do things than 'how-to-do-it' instructions: 'Here we are in general to be reminded that each figure [ornament] must have its appropriate *Apulsus gutturalis*, that is an attack which must be made in the throat with a natural skilfulness and not with a nasty pressure, hard thrust, bleat, or whinny, so that the singer opens the mouth moderately without making the cheeks hollow, but leaving them as nature has given them, and does not lift the tongue high, or bend it, but leaves it straight and low, so that the free passage of the sound is not hindered'.[61] In the commentary on his translation of Tosi into German, Agricola suggests in a remarkably accurate description of the mechanism of disposition, that 'one should swiftly say as many 'a's one after the other as there are notes in the *Passagie*' that one is learning, so that 'when singing . . . air will come out of the lungs and be divided up into as many little interruptions as there are notes necessary for the *Passagie*, and they will be clear and articulated'.[62]

Once the glottis is freely moving comes perhaps the hardest part of all: to keep the *portamento* going whilst articulating fast in the throat. Many would say that this is a contradiction in terms, but in fact it merely needs a careful balance between freedom in the larynx and continuous legato tone. Rognoni sums it up perfectly: 'Two things are necessary to whoever wishes to practise this profession – chest [the abdomen, rather than the voice register] and throat; chest in order that a great quantity and number of figures can be carried through to the proper end; throat to be able to control them with facility'.[63] Other kinds of articulation of coloratura and *gorgie*, for example the so-called 'diaphragm articulation', do not meet the requirements.[64]

The intelligence

Singers must strive to grasp the sense of what it is they have to sing, especially when singing alone, so they can understand it in themselves and make it their own, in order to be able to bring their listeners to the same understanding, which is their principal purpose. They must take care to sing in tune, to sing *adagio* (that is, with great freedom of rhythm), to give forth the voice with *gratia* and to pronounce the words distinctly in order to be understood, and if they want to add *passaggi* they should remember that not every *passaggio* is suitable for good *maniera* in singing.[65]

Master: A singer, like an orator, will form to himself a peculiar distinguishing manner, but the command of good style can only result from taste, aided by judgement and experience, which will teach you to introduce embellishments with propriety.
    Scholar: What are the embellishments of singing?
Master: I see that you, like all other beginners, are impatient for the ornaments and graces, and are more inclined to direct your attention to the superficial than the solid, but the substance should be well formed before you think of adorning it.[66]

These two quotations, selected from a great number of possible others, can serve to provide a glimpse into the world of pre-nineteenth-century singing. Both lay total responsibility for all the principal performance decisions on the singer. Neither makes reference to the 'composition' being sung at all, or, for that matter, to a conductor or director, illustrating clearly how important it is for the singer to be able to act independently. This requirement of self-determination based on an innate fund of understanding, *gratia, maniera*, taste and sense of style, is perhaps the defining quality of the art of singing in the period under discussion. Furthermore, it is no less part of the technique of the singer than mastery of *portamento* and *disposizione*.

In contrast to the norms operating in most modern classical singing culture, a singer's individuality was expressed not so much through personal sound or timbre but rather by the often spontaneous choices he or she made from a vast palette of learned technical elements based on a precise understanding of the nature, function, place and social structure of the performance moment itself and of his or her position within these parameters – choices which still, in theory, allowed every singer a 'peculiar distinguishing manner'. The structures themselves have gone and are not to be recovered, but the notation remains and our ever-changing understanding of past techniques and parameters requires singers pretty well continuously to reinvent their ways of performing. Thus the informed performance of vocal music of the past involves the singer in having always to 'understand in herself' anew what a particular song consists of, with particular attention to those aspects of performance not in themselves notated but nevertheless required, and thus also to 'bring her listeners' to an ever-changing 'same understanding – which is her principal purpose'.

16 Alternative voices: contemporary vocal techniques

LINDA HIRST AND DAVID WRIGHT

Composers very often write music with specific performers in mind. Performers' particular gifts, perhaps an outstanding technique or an individual quality of interpretation, can stimulate and open up a composer's imagination. The written-out ornamentation Monteverdi supplied for Orpheus's central aria 'Possente spirto' in *Orfeo* poses a technical challenge which suggests why its likely first singer, Francesco Rasi, was so admired by his contemporaries. In our own century, Poulenc's intuitive response in setting the difficult poetry of Apollinaire and Eluard was also shaped by his experience of Pierre Bernac's sensitive projection of texts. The genesis of these examples, both of which belong firmly to the 'traditional' rather than the 'alternative' vocal tradition, only reinforces the point that very many alternative developments come out of the creative nexus between composer and intended interpreter. So even though most of today's alternative voices sound more radical to an audience's ears than does the Monteverdi (despite its stunningly wacky quality) or the Poulenc, artistically there is common ground in the shared concern to exploit the expressive possibilities of the musical situation, both vocally and compositionally. But the particular experience of the twentieth century is the move away from defining mainstream singing in terms only of *bel canto*. Certainly the rich, almost bewildering, variety of written and improvised styles that has now been opened up, as well as the opportunities for these styles to interact in new and fertile ways, point to the fact that vocal quality can be just as freshly or differently expressive, away from the constraints of the *bel canto* style.

Two experiences of preparing works, both from the avant-garde end of the compositional spectrum, illustrate how the contemporary composer and performer can work collaboratively in different ways to achieve a deeper quality of interpretation. James Dillon's *A Roaring Flame* (1982), a ten-minute piece for Voice and Double Bass, is written in Gaelic, a language whose unfamiliarity to most listeners gives it a sonorous, rather than a semantic, quality. When I sang the piece to the composer in preparation for the first performance, I found that Dillon silently communicated a strong sense of guidance as he assimilated the actuality of this realisation measured against his own original conception.[1] The opposite was the case when I worked with the composer Helmut

Lachenmann on *temA*. Here, every sound was discussed, repeated, practised endlessly and discussed again, with the composer exemplifying what he intended as best he could, I following, initially imitating and then advancing it in terms of my own experience and technique. Lachenmann is fascinated by the minutiae of the beginnings and ends of vocal sounds, and the infinite variations it is possible to impose on a breath. In *temA* (1968), written for Ivana Loudova, the voice rarely sings in the traditional sense, but the singer's breathing and the ritual associated with that particular physical action, has the central role in the theatricality of the piece. For example, the sound and gesture of breath: as it is taken; expelled sharply; breath held (to the point of being compelled to release it noisily); exhalation through the teeth (with or without the voice); humming; slow, sleep-based breathing; vowels changed by the sound of voiceless inhaling.

In their different ways, these two approaches, although polar opposites in terms of their composers' method of collaboration, performed the same essential function, which was of working to secure the boundaries of a performance convention. This in turn freed me and I was then able to work creatively on my performance within the field of that convention, and on the basis of an authentic sense of the composer's musical identity and points of reference. This is an ideal first stage in establishing the performance tradition of any new repertoire. The continuation or second stage comes when other singers create their own relationship with the music outside any direct contact with the composer. Their view of a work may have been partly formed on the basis of being taught it, or through other forms of transmission, particularly through recorded performances, in which constituent elements can be separately isolated and either imitated or reappraised and done slightly differently. A striking example of new music traditions being generated within the boundaries of convention as part of a living, creative process is evident with the recorded legacy of Cathy Berberian, particularly with the music of Berio written expressly for her. Berberian's interpretations of pieces such as Berio's *Sequenza III* are authoritative statements which no performer can ignore. But as a new generation of vocalists take up that work, so too the individual sensibility and technical command which each new performer brings to its interpretation and the realisation of the vocal symbols means an enlargement of the original tradition. Of course, some musics survive only through an evolving performance tradition. Any repertoire that has its identity on the basis of oral transmission relies on that as its central means of renewal. One such is the Portuguese *Fado*, whose form is well defined but whose special emotional charge comes from the projection and intensity of the individual artist. The *Fado* tradition relies on the expressive urgency of the vocalist while lying well outside the *bel canto* conception, and reinforces how important it is that new-music singers should be able to identify and situate the expressive nature of each work within its own performance convention. How revealing it would be to hear the unique voices of Annie Lennox or Gary Stringer from Reef singing new music composed for them outside their own traditions, and then to see how a performance convention might be established that takes full account of their individual vocal qualities.

A brief look at twentieth-century alternatives to the *bel canto* shows the capacity of singers outside the mainstream to engage with other vocal traditions in which there are fewer constraints on the vocabulary of sounds and vocal gestures which the singer can use expressively. What has remained constant in all this have been the innovative ways in which superb performers of whatever tradition have always made interesting things happen out of familiar material. What has changed, of course, is technology, which has opened up to all the experience of singing traditions previously known only to ethnomusicologists or folklorists, dating from the primitive recordings made by Grainger, Bartók and Kodály (and mainly transmitted through notational approximations) to digitally based investigations of African, Indian and Far Eastern musics. But now the irony is that what technology has made ubiquitous has also threatened the special individualism of traditions such as these through cross-contamination with imported styles. Nevertheless, where previously Western classical music was about one mainstream style of singing, awareness of the expressive spectrum that is now available across the range of styles – written and improvised, high art and vernacular, Western and world musics – has had a fundamental creative stimulus on both performer and composer. This means that 'non *bel canto*' voices tend naturally to gravitate towards the concept of an inclusive music, and away from any single prescriptive ethos.

So what exactly are some of these creative responses, and are they so radical as to suggest new definitions of performance practice? As we have seen, the use of non-standard vocal techniques often comes from the conscious wish to widen the lexicon of vocal gestures and its constituent vocabulary of sound. This means incorporating a new range of sounds, not always previously associated with singing and drawn from all aspects of life. The results of this vernacular inclusivity can seem perverse at times, particularly when the sounds are graphically onomatopoeic. But then, the excited stutter of a Monteverdi *trillo* is a striking means of conveying urgency. This stimulus to vocal exploration opens up for singers a more consciously proactive approach as interpreters, with greater emphasis on generating or creating appropriate responses to the score rather than falling back on established formulae in the more usual re-creative role. This new type of engagement is likely to use improvisation as an essential creative tool to home in on the sound or gesture best suited to the particular need, and for devising the mental or vocal exercises that may be needed to secure it. Sometimes the act of improvising can itself unlock the appropriate vocal responses a singer requires to meet the need of a new performance situation.

The mental expectations Karlheinz Stockhausen has of singers in *Stimmung* (1968) and the technical demands of the piece illustrate some of these points. The title *Stimmung* translates as 'tuning', but as Jonathan Harvey points out, it can also mean 'mood', 'frame of mind' or 'voicing'.[2] Lasting some seventy minutes, the work consists of a single harmony, the second to seventh harmonics of the B♭ below the bass clef, producing the pitches B♭, f, b♭, d^1, a♭^{1}, c^2. The singers are required to produce, very clearly, the individual overtones belonging to each of these. The emphasis therefore is on the precision of fine tuning, combined with individual command of microscopic intonation and balance. The actual process is described in some detail by Robin Maconie.[3] But in a text that Stockhausen originally intended to be declaimed to the audience, the composer defines his own understanding of a singer's unity of voice and personal experience: 'Close your eyes / climb into this sound as if into an aeroplane you had booked for, that you are paying for with your time / ... be – like the sound itself – notes, noises, mixtures, harmonic spectra / ... let yourself be transported across the boundaries of your accustomed *I*-domain'.[4] These demands of technique and concentration obviously call for very careful preparation, not least in the discipline of depersonalisation the score demands of its performers, who are required to effect the role of a collective resonating board, subsuming their individual vocal personality entirely within the group. The paradox of *Stimmung* is that participation becomes an individually compelling experience.

The opportunities opened up by technology continue to add new dimensions to today's performer. Any brief glance at music composed in the last part of the twentieth century will show different repertoires that have either been created out of electronic means or which rely on being modified electronically in performance. A singer needs to be aware of the many possibilities that can be used to put electronics to creative use in transforming the sound of the voice or to create complex textures using multi-tracking or sequencing techniques. It is now as easy (and far more creative) to use a microphone to change or inflect vocal timbre as it is just to make the voice louder; and the results of picking up and juggling with minute inflections or enhanced particles of a singer's vocal spectrum offer intriguing possibilities to the composer as well as to an improvising performer.

It was probably inevitable that the initial thrill of having these electronic devices available, together with their often crude use, meant that the microphone became a kind of 1960s icon, and a throat or stage microphone something of a sound cliché. In the 1970s pioneering work was done by the Extended Vocal Techniques Ensemble of San Diego,[5] and groups like the French *Swingle Singers* and composers such as Berio were particularly significant in popularising this technology in a range of contexts, from close-harmony textures to Berio's collaboration with Cathy Berberian. Of the singers of the time, it was perhaps Berberian who did most to use the microphone as a means to exploit and amplify individual vocal colours instead of just increasing the volume. Her pioneering of close-miking techniques encouraged their use by more composers and singers. Another impetus was given by the vocal ensemble *Electric Phoenix*, a four-voice group that evolved from Ward Swingle's English group but represented a radical departure from it. As its name suggests, *Electric Phoenix* was founded on the basis of this applied technology, taking as its starting point the technical vocal accomplishment of the *Swingles* but with the intention to explore the expressive potential offered by electronics. Beginning in 1978, *Electric Phoenix* provided a forum for composers' use of technology, and so created for itself a tailor-made repertoire in which the number of singers was fixed but the electronic means (and thus the effect) continued to expand and diversify as the technology developed. One major contributor to the group's repertoire was the Belgian composer Henri Pousseur, whose *Tales and Songs from the Bible of Hell* for four voices and tape provides a particularly telling use of these resources. Another was Trevor Wishart, whose extraordinary *Vox* series of five individual pieces used what Wishart refers to as 'the human repertoire' ('the fund of possible sonic objects and their articulations which is available to the human utterer') as its sound-world.[6] While each piece employs a variety of electronic devices to slow or speed the process, *Vox II* has individually structured click tracks or counted tapes. This means that each singer inhabits his or her own rhythmic world and syllabic landscape while relating to the others. Oriental singing, Japanese bun-raku, saliva noises, lip flabber, among many others, are all co-existing vocal aspects that come alive in these scores. But as with Berberian, *Electric Phoenix*'s use of electronic resources meant considerably more than mere amplification. It gave the opportunity to be minutely specific in producing particular vocal sounds: for example, the ability to make a distinction between the effect of a diacritic /r/ in terms of 'mouth air', 'throat air' or 'chest air'. The use of a delay line, ring modulator or a filter enabled alternatives to what had previously been the compulsory or 'natural' synchronisation of physical action and the vocal sound it produced. The fact that it was now possible to separate off the sound from the means of its production offered immense possibilities. These included the ability for one singer to create intricate multi-voice textures as well as the opportunity for alternative types of musical discourse, in which gestures could be taken out of their original physical sequence and reordered.[7]

In the face of such new demands on singers' attitudes and techniques alike, how adequately does the phrase 'extended vocal technique' suggest the real basis of 'alternative voices'? The danger of what is an almost automatically cited portmanteau term lies partly in its overuse (with any slight deviation from the *bel canto* norm being labelled as 'extended technique') and partly in the nature of the term itself. For instance, when examined in this context, what exactly is extended? A refined voice, beautifully produced and supported, can only come from someone who possesses a consummate and expressive vocal technique, that is complete or whole in itself. Such a singer is already equipped to respond to any vocal challenge. But the use of a non-standard technique extends the expressive purpose, and it is this aim which may require an extension of traditional means into new configurations. In other words, it is the artistic goal that has been redefined, and which needs to be complemented by the appropriate vocal means. So in the case of Schoenberg's *Pierrot lunaire*, the composer's own term 'Sprechgesang' accurately captures the combination of two half-techniques – speech and song – into one suggestively evocative hybrid. The singing inflects and shapes the vocal line far beyond the capabilities of normal or declaimed speech. And as is typical of Schoenberg, the 'Sprechgesang' component in *Pierrot* serves both a practical and an artistic purpose in the way that the speech, strongly inflected by the singing, projects the text across a complex and intense-sounding instrumental fabric. The result, somehow sounding both disembodied and primordial, conjures up an expressionistic atmosphere that corresponds to the visual and metaphysical worlds of Schiele, Kokoschka, Kandinsky and Nolde which so fascinated Freud.[8]

Moving in a very different direction, vocal sounds from everyday life and culture can be incorporated within a composer's expressive palette. In a work for male voice that vividly unites expressive means and purpose, HK Gruber's *Frankenstein!!* has all the musical exaggeration – cliché, onomatopoeia, rumbustiousness – of the medium of the contemporary comic strip from which it takes much of its subject matter. Indeed in certain respects, this 'pan-demonium' suggests itself as a postmodernist cultural counterpart to *Pierrot lunaire*. *Pierrot* originated as a cycle of melodramas for cabaret entertainment, commissioned by an actress, Albertine Zehme, and based on expressionist poems by Albert Giraud (in Otto Hartleben's translation) that dwell on grotesque images of crime, punishment and death. *Frankenstein!!* offers revisionist, gothic inter-pretations to icons of vernacular culture such as James Bond and Goldfinger, Batman and Robin, Superman, John Wayne and the epony-mous Frankenstein himself. For just as *Pierrot* went to extremes in gener-ating its expressionist atmosphere, so too *Frankenstein!!* achieves its cartoon effect by the up-front nature of its slabs of garish material and the primary colours of its musical gestures. The vocal soloist, described as a 'chansonnier', projects these texts across a wide vocal spectrum, involving different combinations of declaiming and singing, vocal mimicry and acting. The expressive effect of each of these works would be unimagin-ably the poorer without the extended vocal palette, rather than technique *per se*, that each demands. Together they emphasise the point that what is at issue is the expansion of vocal resources in order to realise a particular expressive goal.

As these new expressive resources began to be tapped, so they raised questions of notation. There are obvious constraints on the application or adaptation of traditional notational forms to new sounds, whether they be technologically driven, or have been caught out of improvised ges-tures. Composer-invented symbols may seek to convey musical gestures visually with some element of onomatopoeic equivalence, but because these symbols tend to be individual, potentially they can set up an engage-ment between composer and interpreter in a personal way that has obvious differences to that which is generated by conventional notation. The effect of such new symbols (which may not necessarily be graphic) can serve as a goad to the performer's imagination. However, the symbols themselves are not likely to be self-sufficient, and some further annota-tion or commentary is nearly always necessary, such as the detailed observations that Ligeti provides to assist performers in the preparation of *Aventures* and *Nouvelles Aventures*, which underline the limitations of notation alone for some types of work. Working from a facsimile of the composer's manuscript can be another point of contact: the visual impact of a composer's own layout may have the capacity to convey something of the sense of the music, or in other ways to catch a performer's imagination and so prompt from them a personal response that is another comple-mentary reflection of the composer's creative impulse. Of course that sort of response says something about that particular performer's visual sensibilities as much as it may reflect a composer's beautiful or idiosyn-cratic script.

Berio's *Sequenza III* testifies to the ingenuity of the notational solu-tions that he adopts to capture on the page the sound-image of the work. It also highlights the problems that such notation poses in the transmis-sion and conveying of meaning to the performer. Much of what Berio does in this score has become accepted as standard practice in this area, and his presentation of the text is based on the alphabet drawn up by the International Phonetic Association. But the inexperienced singer will be reliant on the instructions and explanatory material with which Berio prefaces the score, and may also want to listen for guidance to different recordings of the work in order to hear how other performers match the vocal realisation to the notated page. Berio uses an enormously wide gamut of vocal resources in this challenging score. He uses the text more as a vehicle for the performer and only intermittently for its semantic impact. In this he is assisted by the mobility of Kutter's text into phrases which are able to be freely ordered and reordered, coming into the listener's consciousness and moving out again, with some words (such as 'sing') given a momentary emphasis. This approach to the text sets up the means by which the singer is able to explore the expressive nature of her voice in ways that draw in the audience to share this essentially emotional journey as it moves from one state to another. These emotional states are articulated with kaleidoscopic variety, through sharp contrasts and mutational change; from ultra short sounds, some breathy, very high, very low, gasping, sobbing, seducing and whimpering, to more sustained sounds of laughter and crying, of pitched and unpitched notes. The mood jump-cuts continuously, through the frantic, tense, dreamy, ecstatic and relaxed. In preparing this piece, it is important to be aware of the strengths that Cathy Berberian (see Fig. 9), its first interpreter, brought to it. It is not just a question of vocal agility and flexibility and her willingness to experiment, but of her deep sense of drama through music, a quality that sustains even minimally notated pieces such as her own *Stripsody*.

The late 1950s and the following two decades were rich in works which demanded special expressive effects and new sorts of notational conventions to match them. Two of the most important of these are a pair of stage pieces by Ligeti, *Aventures* and *Nouvelles Aventures*, his vivid deconstruction of types of operatic *scena* which he termed 'anti-operas'. Both meticulously notated, each pushes its singers to the limits of range and invention, using some aleatoric passages, others which are rigorously prescribed. Ligeti's play on stock-in-trade operatic conventions is also a means of questioning their continued relevance into the second half of the twentieth century. For example, his portrayal of a mad scene in *Aventures* consists of just six vocal gestures, set at an emotional extreme despite their vocal restraint. As the scene unfolds around its central female protagonist, so the mood (alone and getting colder) intensifies, with growing elements of silence that underline others' lack of responsiveness to her plight. The fact that these two pieces could together

Figure 9 Cathy Berberian performing *Stripsody*

be understood as the constituent parts of a basic concept is indicated symbolically by *Aventures* beginning with a sharp inhalation of breath, and its companion concluding with the opposite gesture of a choking exhalation. Istvan Anhalt writes extensively about *Sequenza III* and *Nouvelles Aventures* in his book *Alternative Voices* and addresses a range of issues bound up with composing for the voice, including the question: why does the composer destroy his text? [9] Perhaps what Ligeti does is not so much a destruction as a revelation, for as with the disappearance of a conventional syntax and semantic framework, so an alternative theatre emerges, based upon the unconventional juxtaposition of phonemes and vocal gestures, all depending upon the performers' ability to set out this alternative communication and the quality of his or her engagement with its vocalisation. Anhalt opens up a psychological exploration of both pieces, also suggesting the gender of certain vowels and phonemes, and the ways in which the story without plot of *Nouvelles Aventures* sparks empathy and aversion in an audience. In this context it is interesting that Ligeti should have referred to those works as 'semantically without meaning'.[10] An amusing gloss is added in his reference to his 'grand opera' *Le Grand Macabre* as an anti-anti-opera, in which the two successive 'antis' cancel each other out.

Maxwell Davies's *Eight Songs for a Mad King* provides another example of the generation of a music-theatre work based on mental disintegration coupled with images of despair and isolation, this time the well-documented historical madness of King George III. King George's descent is used as a vehicle for extremes of vocal pyrotechnics and a melange of stylistic allusion which incorporates sudden switches, as when the Handel quotation 'Comfort ye, my people' from *Messiah* is, with a reference by the king to sin, transformed into a foxtrot. The music for the third movement is written in the score in the shape of an elaborate birdcage, a visual reference to the king's attempt to teach captive bullfinches to sing. Across this raft of symbolic representation moves the singer, tracing the progress of King George's madness through the extremes of the vocal range and its expressive resources to create an experience which is as harrowing in its violence as it is ultimately moving in its poignancy.

Turba (1972) by Miklos Maros initially disconcerted the John Alldis Choir with a notational symbol which some described as looking like a Christmas pudding. The composer's intention was to produce the effect of the eponymous crowd, and he did this (expressed notationally by the pudding shape) by requiring the sixteen singers to make individual blips of sound, articulated as 'di(p)', 'do(p)', and 'da(p)', with the idea of stopping the sound almost as it began by closing the mouth on to the silent 'p'.

This effect produces a series of extremely short sounds separated by gaps, which, when produced in the unsystematic, unsynchronised manner specified by the composer, proved an ingenious means for only sixteen singers to suggest the impact of a crowd.

Most singers would argue that composers have a responsibility to make their music possible to vocalise or else to accept practical suggestions that make performance feasible. The fact that some composers choose not to make a particularly idiomatic distinction between the music they write for voices and for instrumental forces can generate tension. At its extreme, composers may sometimes claim that what they have written can be done, and that singers' primary excuse for not delivering this is more an artificial concern to conserve the beauty of their vocal instrument at the expense of the composer's artistic goal. Set against this are those specialist singers who point to the impractical, even destructive, nature of some alternative vocal writing devised by composers. This situation can be exacerbated because some composers do find the very limits of vocal possibility to be precisely the most interesting field in which to work. Xenakis's *N'shima* uses female voices in an aggressive vocal duet, in which the sound-quality he wants requires the singers to accent each note by beginning the attack from below it with a fierce glottal stop and concluded with an upward glissando. The resulting sound is close to a bark, and its extreme nature (in vocal terms) places it close to the composer's instrumental works.

Given this context, it is perhaps surprising that John Cage has often used the voice in particularly simple ways. Taking a range of his pieces for voice, such as *The Wonderful Widow of Eighteen Springs* (1942), *A Flower* (1950), *Mirakus* (1984), *Selkus* (1984) and *Sonnekus* (1985), all ask for an untrained, folk-song singing style, with, in *Sonnekus*, a mixture of church and cabaret, an instruction which is a key guideline for vocal production. In *Aria* (1958) the score merely stipulates ten different vocal styles, in a gesture of simplicity that poses immense challenges to the singer. The ten vocal styles may perhaps be best attained through ten imaginary people who each in turn are inhabited rather than imagined by the singer, the composite effect producing a kaleidoscope, or flicker book, element of changing voice styles that gives the piece its character. Cage leaves his performer remarkably unfettered by instruction, stipulating only that all aspects of the performance, such as dynamics, volume, etc., be freely determined by the singer. It is an opportunity for the performer to exploit to the utmost the vocal possibilities involved in portraying this diversity of character, with no noise – 'musical' or 'unmusical' – being excluded. In this, Cage is perhaps presenting his interpreter with the ultimate challenge posed by the 'alternative voices' philosophy. For the voice, by its very nature, is always expressive of the human condition. Cage's gauntlet is a challenge liberating the performer to harness that potential across the vocal spectrum, in which each of its extremes – 'musical' and 'non-musical' – is as viable as the other in generating an expressive moment.

17 The teaching (and learning) of singing

DAVID MASON

Basic approaches

For the singer of today, especially when starting out on a career, finding the right teacher, or the perfect 'method', can be fraught with difficulty. One teacher may seem to have some secret that will perfect the student's breathing technique, another may claim to have found the secret of the old Italian *bel canto*. Add to this the vagaries of what or who is fashionable and it is not surprising that many singers prefer to rely on their own instincts. Many mainly self-taught singers have considerable success in working out an approach that works for them, while others may embark on a career harbouring a sense of insecurity caused by unsolved problems. I hope that this overview of teaching precepts, past and present, will provide an objective framework for the singer, whatever his or her particular needs, thus helping him or her to contribute his own informed input to the complex process involved in the study of singing.

Every singing teacher brings his own individual personality, a different cultural and intellectual background, and different tastes to the teaching/learning situation. In a sense therefore, one could say that there are as many ways to teach singing as there are teachers and students. However, one can locate most approaches on a scale that ranges from the 'non-technical' to the overtly scientific. The existence of a 'non-technical' approach demonstrates the unusual nature of the singing voice, compared with other musical instruments. Although the finest instrumental teachers show an understanding of psychology and the importance of motivation, inspiration and so on, it is not possible to avoid some actual discussion of the physical nature of the skill being taught. The singing voice, however, is actually *part* of the person who is to 'play upon it', and therefore the psychological state of the singer can have the most profound effect on the quality of sound that emerges. Indeed, the voice of the depressed singer may cease to function at all, and many singers have let a lack of confidence, often in respect of high notes, affect their chances of a successful career. The ability of teachers to give encouragement and motivate their students is clearly of no small significance, and there are teachers whose main skill is the ability to 'psych' their pupils into 'letting go' of themselves and their voices. Another, closely related, 'non-technical' approach is to concentrate almost entirely on interpretation, in the belief that vocal freedom and control will follow; and it is true that a complete technique cannot be attained without regard for the expression of the ideas or emotions inherent in the text. If the singer does not 'say something' with every vocal utterance, and allow his imagination to be stimulated beyond a mere mechanical realisation of the notes, then it is unlikely that he will ever activate all the colours of the voice. Most singers, however, need at some point to work specifically to improve their vocal skill. Many find that as their voice changes with age, or if they tackle a new repertoire, some intense technical work may be necessary. As for the young singer, to have mastered a number of basic principles early on can prevent problems arising later, and may thus extend his or her career. What follows describes some of the approaches that have been used in voice training since the seventeenth century. Although presented historically, according to when certain ideas originated or were dominant, the spectrum of ideas is also intended to be viewed synchronically, as a range of possible approaches that are still practised today.

The seventeenth century

It is very likely that singing in the seventeenth century bore little relationship to modern Western classical singing. In fact, modern popular and jazz singers, or Mediterranean folk singers, with their natural tone quality, are possible models. The jazz singer analogy is also relevant in a consideration of musical style, with the importance of the text and subtly nuanced rubato, forgetting the nineteenth-century 'super-legato'. But the seventeenth-century sources are not merely of relevance to the 'early music' specialist. A consideration of the writings of the late sixteenth and early seventeenth centuries should remind any singer (and singing teacher) that the art of singing is not merely a question of unleashing torrents of sound. Apart from the ability to express a text by using all the colours of the voice, a most important aspect of seventeenth-century technique is coloratura, which requires a throat articulation. Just to talk in terms of using the throat may be worrying to some singers. After all, a lot of singing teaching is geared to avoiding any mention of this area. However, there need not be anything harmful in *using* the throat (avoiding, of course, any glottal stops, or excessive breath pressure) which is quite different from the voice being *stuck* in the throat, or producing a throaty tone. Indeed the voice (and throat) likes to be used athletically, and the practice of this type of coloratura (known variously as *passaggi*, *gorgie* or *gorgheggi*) can be of great technical benefit in developing an immediacy of vocal onset, preventing overloading with the breath, and encouraging greater flexibility. Also of interest are the ten rules Maffei gives for the mastering of the *gorgie*. The modern reader may well have heard such suggestions in the course of his studies. These include not making any movement in any part of the body apart from the '*cimbalare* cartilage' (the glottis), because 'if those people appear ugly to us who, when they sing, shake their heads, tremble in their legs, or move their feet, we must be sure that we appear ugly to others'.[1] Similar advice is to be found in a large number of the treatises up to this day. Maffei advises the singer to extend the tongue so that the tip touches the base of the lower teeth, and that the singer should open the mouth no wider than when conversing with friends. This important aspect of vocal technique recurs throughout the history of vocal training, and is still relevant today. Another rule states that the breath should be let out a little at a time, taking care 'that it does not go out through the nose or through the palate, for each would be a great mistake'. The result of this is, of course, a nasal tone, evidently as undesirable then as it is now.

The eighteenth century

By the eighteenth century a more legato style had developed, and a more powerful vocal production. The registers of the voice were fully exploited, as we can see in Handel's operatic roles, as well as in Mozart's roles such as Elektra and Fiordiligi, to name two particularly striking examples. High notes were delivered in a more powerful and brilliant manner, as noted by the theorist William Jackson, who wrote in 1791, 'Instead of developing their voices so as to be soft at the top and full at the bottom, singers are now achieving the opposite effect'.[2] And, of course, the castrati brought a previously unattained brilliance and virtuosity into the opera theatre, which was emulated by the *prime donne* of the age. Probably the most comprehensive guide to the sort of training that helped bring about such a high level of vocalism is *Practical Reflections on the Art of Florid Song* by Giambattista Mancini. As representative of a period which was both a high point in the history of singing, and one which saw the composition of operas as being still central to the modern singer's repertoire, this work is indispensable in any discussion of vocal pedagogy.

Much of what Mancini writes will be familiar to modern students of singing. He stresses the importance of the singer's posture and also mouth position. This is with the aim of allowing the throat 'to let the voice come out with great ease.' As Mancini says,

> As for myself, I always acted with my pupils like a dancing master. I used to call
> my pupils one by one in front of me, and after having placed them in the right
> position, I was telling them, 'Boy, look ... raise your head...don't lean on the
> chest ... no ... not in the back either ... there, that's right, straight and natural.
> In that position the vocal organs remain relaxed and flexible; because if you lean
> your head forward on to your chest, your side muscles of the neck area tense,
> and they are also tense if you lean your head back'.[3]

Similar ideas are expressed in nearly all contemporary treatises. Mancini
devotes a section of his treatise to 'The correct opening of the mouth'. As
with the posture, the main aim is to adopt a mouth position that will allow
the freest emission of the voice. The teeth and jaws should not be gripped,
or the mouth opened so much that the voice falls back into the throat.
Similarly, care should be taken to keep the tongue relaxed. Like other
authorities of the period (and well into the nineteenth century) he recommends that the singer should position his mouth as he positions it
when he smiles, that is in such a way that the upper teeth be per-
pendicularly and moderately separated from those below. He also suggests that the same position be maintained for the different vowels except
for U and O which require more rounded lips. Although some modern
teachers recommend this sort of position, modern practice is to adopt a
generally more open mouth and rounder lips.

As for actual vocalising, Mancini's approach is to strengthen the voice
gradually, but always maintaining an ease of production, an ease of
breathing, neither taking too much nor giving too much. He recommends
the practice of *solfeggi*, short at first, but gradually increasing in length,
but insisting on a perfect legato without ever forcing. By means of these
solfeggi the registers are to be perfectly joined, thus ensuring the quality
and strength of the voice, as well as gradually increasing breath control.
Throughout the eighteenth and nineteenth centuries the singers of the
Italian school gained a reputation for their breath control, and indeed one
of the generally held notions concerning the so-called *bel canto* tradition
is the importance of breathing technique, as expressed in the statement
attributed to Maria Celloni, 'Chi sa respirare sa cantare'.[4] However, one
searches in vain for any specific breathing exercises that one might do as a
preparation for singing (although the importance of having a strong
chest is acknowledged). The control of the breath is to be learnt by actually singing. The classic exercise which was used to teach the co-ordination of the voice and breath, and which occupies an important position in
all the famous vocal treatises, is the *messa di voce*. Apart from taking up a
chapter in Mancini's reflections, the *messa di voce* features as the first exercise in Corri (see Fig. 10)[5] and is also discussed in great length in Isaac
Nathan's *Musurgia Vocalis* of 1836 (see Fig. 11).

Figure 10 'The Soul of Music' (Corri, *The Singers Preceptor*, 1810)

ON THE SWELLING AND DYING OF THE VOICE.

The voice must gradually increase in magnitude or volume of tone, and dissolve again into softness, as the following characters open and close :

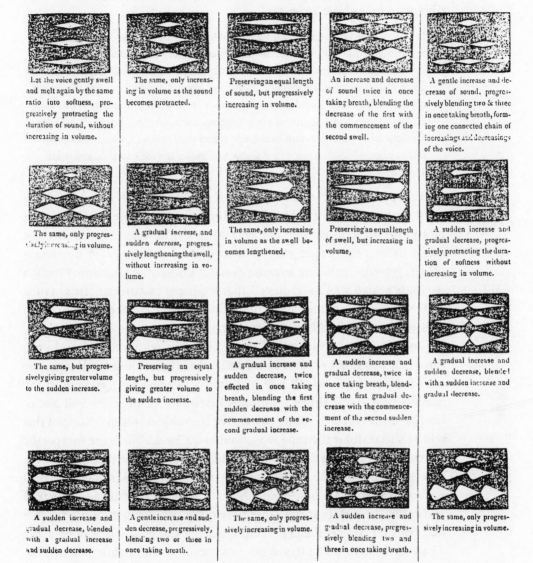

Figure 11 'On the swelling and dying of the voice', *Musurgia Vocalis* (Nathan, 1836)

The term *messa di voce*, not to be confused with *mezza-voce* (which means half-voice), might be translated as the 'putting forth of the voice', or simply 'placing the voice'. This placing of the voice, a much-used concept in teaching today, is achieved by making a long crescendo–diminuendo. As Nathan writes,

> Let every note be begun as softly as possible, by swelling gently and immediately returning to the first piano, as the voice increases in power and quality let the swell be increased, yet with caution, the slightest irregularity or roughness being a sign that the singer has exceeded the development of which his organ is as yet capable. This swelling and dying of the voice is the most important to practice ... on it depends the principal art of Singing, for it sweetens, enriches, and gives the delicious roundness and fullness to the tone. It is this ... which makes the music respond to the various passions, and passes the feeling of one mind to another.[6]

The practice of *messa di voce* demonstrates the essence of the eighteenth-century way of voice teaching, which to those singers trained in a more prescriptive manner may seem a little vague. In executing a *messa di voce* the singer can learn to control a number of important things, yet without losing any ease or naturalness of production. Firstly, a perfectly poised attack is required, that is centred and precise. This in turn will require a certain tonicity in the abdominal muscles if excessive breath pressure is not to be allowed to spoil the precision of the attack. In learning to crescendo to maximum strength, either without holding in the throat, or pushing breath into the tone, the singer will learn the precise use of the muscles, which will maintain a steady tone. Likewise in the diminuendo, if the singer maintains his 'noble' posture, he will notice how his body reacts to subtle changes of colour and volume. None of this will be successful if the tone is allowed to go 'back'. There are no specific instructions of where to 'put' the sound or to use this or that muscle: the precise placing and use of different muscles is discovered rather than prescribed. Although all these elements are to be perfected with a certain trial and error, the task is at the same time quite specific, with a predictable outcome. Of course, the experienced teacher can guide the singer, using whatever images and metaphors may occur to him, thus helping the development of a strong yet subtle connection between aural and physical sensations.

Also important in eighteenth-century training was the mastery of agility. Mancini writes that coloratura should be supported by a robust chest, assisted by graduation of the breath and a flexible 'fauces' (where the pharynx opens into the mouth). This last piece of advice is repeated several times in connection with legato singing. The idea of deliberately manipulating or 'opening the throat' had not yet been adopted, and today there are many teachers who avoid the suggestion, for fear of making the voice heavy or unwieldy.

Nineteenth-century voice training: Manuel García

Vocal treatises written well into the nineteenth century do not differ very much from Mancini and other eighteenth-century works. The vocal technique of the castrati, based on the study of *messa di voce*, still forms the basis of many of the important sources. Indeed, much of what Nathan writes in 1836 is indistinguishable from Mancini. Times had changed, however. When Nathan published his *Musurgia Vocalis*, Bellini had already been dead a year, and the opera world had seen the emergence of a new type of *prima donna*, as much recognised for dramatic ability as for perfect vocalism. The three most famous were Colbran, Pasta and Malibran, the last of whom became an icon of this new Romantic age. It is notable that none of these three produced the effortless and faultless vocalism for which the castrati were renowned, demonstrating a recurring problem for singers (which still exists today): to reconcile a perfect vocal delivery with emotional and dramatic demands, especially in heavily scored Romantic operas. The new developments are reflected in the most famous treatise of the nineteenth century, Manuel García's *Traité complet de l'art du chant* (1842/1847).[7] The nineteenth century saw important advances in science and technology, with practical and philosophical repercussions still felt today. The belief that science held the key to understanding many previously unexplained phenomena in various areas of human activity pervades García's treatise. He attempts to present a comprehensive method of voice training based on his observations and scientific studies of the voice. For the first time, through his invention of the laryngoscope, the larynx could actually be observed. The belief that one could exercise some direct control upon it represented quite a radical change of philosophy in vocal pedagogy.

A significant new idea was García's advocacy of the *coup de glotte*. García states that,

> it is necessary to prepare for the stroke of the glottis by closing, which stops and momentarily accumulates some air in the passages; then, much as a rupture operates as a means of relaxation, one opens it with an incisive and vigorous stroke, similar to the action of the lips in pronouncing the consonant P.[8]

Even though García does caution the singer against a *coup de poitrine*, which 'resembles a cough or the effort of expelling something which is obstructing the throat', his description of the *coup de glotte* does seem perilously close to that of the glottal plosive common in English, and particularly strongly identified with an east London accent. Though it is unlikely that García would have recommended a manner of attack that is universally regarded today as potentially harmful, his description of the *coup de glotte* caused a lot of confusion and controversy. Hermann Klein, the editor of García's *Hints on Singing* of 1894, attempts to dispel this confusion in a footnote:

> The meaning of the term 'stroke of the glottis' [*coup de glotte*] which was invented by the author has been seriously misrepresented, and its misuse has done a great deal of harm. To the student it is meant to describe a physical act of which there should be merely a mental cognisance, not an actual physical sensation. The 'articulation' which gives the precise and clean start to a sound is not felt in the throat of the singer. It is the sound itself, the attack of the note, beginning clean, clear and true, upon the middle of that note, without preliminary movement or action of any sort beyond the natural act of singing.[9]

This footnote is significant in that, while apparently defending García, it rather contradicts his scientific approach. It also highlights a recurring problem in vocal pedagogy, namely just how anatomically specific one should be. In the case of García the problem arose because viewed by means of his newly invented laryngoscope the action of the larynx appears as he described, whereas the actual attack is softer than the glottal plosive, which is really a cough. Whatever García's intentions there is no doubt that he required an attack that would activate all the ringing power of the voice from the start. This is in contrast to his father who, in the seventh of eight rules which precede his vocal exercises, advocated the practice of tones that begin 'as gently as possible'.[10] The first of these exercises is for *messa di voce*. García the younger, however, introduces this exercise some way into his treatise, as a way of refining and polishing the tone, after mastering the lungs and the pharynx.

Mastering the action of the pharynx was part of García's use of the different timbres, the *voix claire* and *voix sombre*. He considered the open Italian vowels A, E and O to be modifications of the clear timbre, and the closed Italian vowels E, O and U as modifications of the dark timbre. The darker colours of the *voix sombre* are produced with a lower position of the larynx. In this timbre the open vowels are modified: A approximates to O, E to EU in French, I to U in French, and U approximates to U in Italian. This *voix sombre* is almost universal in today's opera houses, with the demand for a tone quality that will provide the most constant resonance that will carry over the orchestra in large theatres. It will also be clear from the above that in producing a consistently dark quality the clarity of vowel sound is often compromised, giving ammunition to those who criticise, and even denounce, modern operatic performances because of the impossibility of distinguishing the text. To consciously lower the larynx and to manipulate the pharynx to alter the resonance of the voice are concepts that are quite foreign to eighteenth-century teaching precepts. However, in many ways García's teaching was quite traditional, although presented in more systematic way, in keeping with his 'modern' approach. Preceding his actual vocal exercises, García outlines the various ways the student should vocalise (i.e. sing on vowels). He lists five manners of vocalisation:

> Carrying the sounds (*Portamento di voce*)
> Tying them (*Agilità legata e granita*)
> Marking them (*Martellata*)
> Staccato (*Pichettata, staccata*)
> Aspirating them (a rarely used manner).

These different kinds of vocalisation are to be practised:

> On all vowels in turn
> In the three registers
> In the two timbres
> In the entire compass of the voice
> In all degrees of force
> At all degrees of velocity
> Marking all the different inflections
> By combining all these means.[11]

The vocal exercises that follow fill some fifty or so pages and a large number are devoted to the practice of agility (see Fig. 12).

The question often arises today of how the coloratura in Rossini should be sung, especially by tenors and baritones. There is little doubt that to perform the sort of exercises that García writes (and by implication Rossini's coloratura) a technique not that far removed from that of the seventeenth century is required. García's teaching may therefore be seen as a bridge between the classical *bel canto* and modern practice, and much of García's basic approach is still used by teachers today.

Towards the twentieth century

As we reach the late nineteenth century there is less and less emphasis on agility, and more on resonance. In studying early sources the modern singer will often be surprised by the absence of any explicit discussion of resonance. However, in the desire for greater power, the teaching of the late nineteenth century aimed for a more direct control of this aspect of voice production. Such aims were encouraged by the study of acoustics

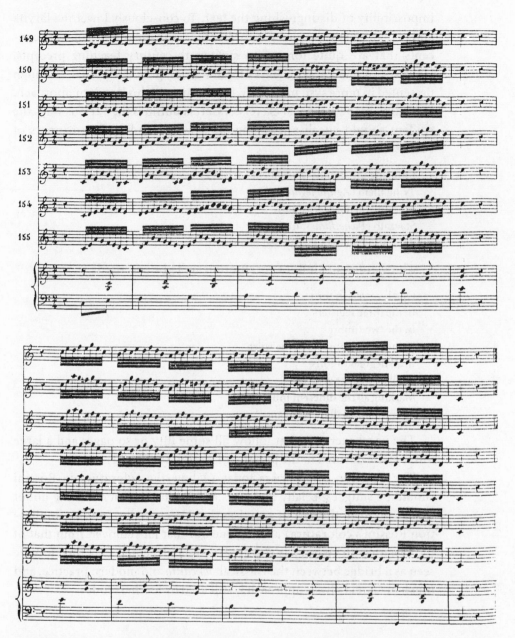

Lorsque la voix se maintiendra inaltérablement pure sur la voyelle A, il sera tems de parcourir les autres voyelle E È, O Ò, (voyez de l'articulation 2ª Partie.) Les voyelles I et U s'étudieront plus tard, et seulement autant qu'il ser nécessaire pour que la voix y soit habituée.

Figure 12 Exercises from García (*Traité complet de l'art du chant*, 1847)

and phonetics, applied to both speech and singing, a major influence being the work of Helmholtz (1821–94), whose *On the Sensations of Tone* was first published in German in 1863, and in English in 1875.[12] Helmholtz was one of the first to investigate the 'singers' formant', a vibration in the region of 3000Hz, which gives the 'ring', as well as carrying power, to the voice. In the gentle attack of the *messa di voce* this ring is not immediately present, unlike in the more vigorous attack recommended by García and many of the teachers who followed him. Of course the singer's, or indeed speaker's, awareness of the properties of resonance and vowel sounds was not a totally new phenomenon. Isaac Newton wrote in about 1665 (when he was around twelve years old), that 'the filling of a very deep flaggon with a constant stream of beare or water sounds ye vowels in this order w, u, ʊ, o, a, e, i, y.'[13] But in the last quarter of the nineteenth century many teaching concepts came directly from the rapidly developing science of acoustics and phonetics, and indeed modern research in these fields continues to have an important influence on the teaching of singing. One teacher who made direct use of Helmholtz's researches was Enrico delle Sedie, who, in his *Aesthetics of the Art of Singing and of the Melodrama* (1885), notated a scale which showed how the resonances (the term 'formant' had not yet been adopted) of vowels might be subtly modified so as to be tuned as to the ideal resonance for each pitch. Register changes were also to be effected by changes in resonance and vowel quality. All these ideas incorporated and built upon García's concepts of the timbres. Singers became more aware of the need to open the pharynx, and keep the larynx fairly low in order to maximise the ring in the voice. This was, and still is, described by singers and teachers in different ways. 'Inhalare la voce' ('Breathe in the tone'), a sensation described by Caruso, is a commonly met instruction; Tito Schipa said he felt that an egg could be slipped into his throat while he was singing. The idea of yawning or sighing is often used to help 'open the throat', though many teachers advise against this last idea because of the danger of the voice going back.

When the singers' formant is produced the singer will have the feeling that the voice is forward, or 'in the mask'. One of the great advocates of singing 'dans le masque' was Jean de Reszke, who used nasal consonants to help place the sound. One sentence supposedly used by de Reszke was 'Pendant que l'enfant mange son pain, le chien tremble dans le buisson'. Of course, it will be obvious that such an approach could cause a voice to become nasal, and most readers will be able to name at least one singer who sings down his nose (see also Maffei's comments above). By the end of the nineteenth century these two aspects of singing technique, the 'open throat' and 'focus', or 'forward placement', had become central to

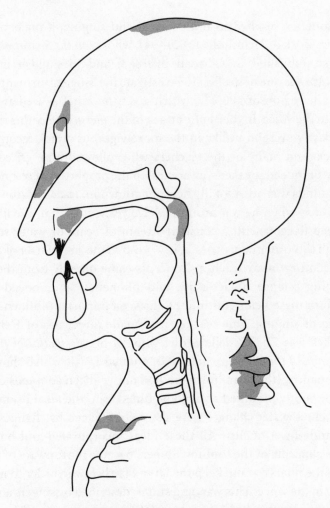

Figure 13 Types of placing: singers are often encouraged to feel (or at least imagine) sensations of vibrations in various places such as those above. Different teachers may stress different locations according to the tone quality required. Others discourage any specific 'placing' in favour of a more general 'letting go of the sound' (drawing after Hussler and Rodd-Marling, *The Physical Nature of the Vocal Organ*, 1976).

the singer's training, and indeed for many teachers still are (see Fig. 13). W. J. Henderson, who knew the singing of Caruso, Ponselle, Patti, Flagstad and Sembrich to name a few of the best known, writing at the end of last century, described placing in a manner that will be familiar to many present-day teachers and students of singing. After a warning about the fault of nasal singing of which he says the French are guilty, he writes,

> The singer must use some art in focusing the tones in the mouth . . . a proper conception of the point at which one should aim to focus tone leads to a correct position of the organs employed in the formation and thus prevents the taking of unnatural positions certain in the long run to injure the voice.[14]

According to Henderson this point is at the front of the hard palate just above and behind the front teeth. Many teachers of today teach such a placing. Important in finding this focus is the recurring question of how one should open the mouth. Henderson writes,

> Some teachers and some singers believe that the secret of good tone lies in pushing forward the lips. The mouth is resolutely opened in the form of the letter O. Sbriglia of Paris is the most ardent advocate of this style, and yet Jean de Reszke ... discarded it in the very beginning. Madame Nordica employs it and is a firm believer in it. Madame Sembrich, on the other hand, employs the horizontal oval ... This lip formation, the old masters asserted, gives the tones a beautifully soft sonority, suitable for the expression of feeling.[15]

A skilful teacher will help each student find his or her most suitable position. The degree to which one has the lips somewhat smiling or rounded depends on the age of the student and also on the intrinsic nature of his or her voice. More dramatic voices will tend towards a more rounded position, as will the lower voices. Observing most of the baritones and basses in Romantic opera, one will see an almost constant use of a rounded mouth position. This is not to say, however, that every young aspiring baritone should slavishly imitate this; to over darken too young will often mean an unfocused, if not wobbly voice when the singer should be in his prime.

Perhaps the other single aspect of singing technique that causes most concern for singing students is breathing, and its elusive relation, support. We read time and time again that the secret of good singing is breath control, and students are frequently criticised for a lack of vocal support. Indeed, this last comment is heard so often without further elaboration that it is difficult to escape the suspicion that its use often merely reflects a lack of anything else to say. The teaching of breathing ranges from the 'totally natural', to attempts to control almost every muscle involved. The muscular control methods may include pushing out either the lower abdomen, or upper abdomen (*epigastrium*), sometimes against a tight belt. Singers may be instructed to clench the buttocks, or to bear down as though they were about to give birth. Very common advice is to keep the ribs expanded, even fixed. Other muscles to be used include the upper muscles of the back (*latissimus dorsi*) and the side abdominals (*obliques*). In total contrast to such instructions, some teachers choose to say nothing about breathing and support, believing it to be a totally natural process, perhaps mentioning the precepts of the eighteenth century to back up their assertion. Some singers respond well to having something specific to control, while others feel merely hampered by thinking of tensing this or that muscle. It also has to be taken into account that the support may function naturally during a lesson or during practice, but may well desert the singer when on stage and under pressure. Nearly all the writers from the end of the nineteenth century up to the present day state that breathing should be easy, and never strenuous, even when carrying out a rapid half-breath. It is often suggested that one should breathe in reaction to an imagined stimulus, as in the 'pleasant surprise breath', or as if one 'were smelling a rose' (attributed to the great baritone Mattia Battistini). Crucial to an efficient manner of breathing and support (known in Italian schools as *appoggio*) is the maintaining of an erect posture, the 'noble posture' of the traditional Italian *bel canto*. Any heaving or lifting of the shoulders during inspiration is to be avoided. Correspondingly, letting the chest drop during singing is to be avoided. This advice has been summarised as 'Breathe in the position of singing and sing in the position of breathing'. Many traditional sources mention the importance of breathing silently, advice which is reiterated in scientific sources. In the 'noble posture' there will be a certain tonicity in the *epigastrium* and lower abdomen. As singers begin a phrase, they will find it necessary to contract the lower abdomen in order not to let the chest collapse, often described as a 'tuck'. At the same time it is useful to imagine that the body is still breathing in, as during phonation the inspiratory muscles help control the pressure of breath. This balance of inspiratory and expiratory forces has been described by Lamperti as 'la lutte vocale',[16] or 'vocal contest'. Proctor, after several chapters of tortuous descriptions of physiology, measurements of airflow and the like, recommends the practice of a long crescendo–diminuendo, the traditional *messa di voce,* as the best exercise for controlling a function over which we only have indirect control. It would seem that a combination of traditional ideas allied to an imaginative use of modern physiological knowledge can provide a solid foundation for every singer. With trial and error the singer can begin to use the sensations of the 'lutte vocale' to provide a real support. Proctor defines this last term rather neatly as 'the correct use of the abdominal muscles to provide the control of subglottic pressure in the most effortless manner'.[17]

The German school

With the general rise of nationalism in music and opera at the end of the nineteenth century there was the development of national styles of singing and, correspondingly, of vocal pedagogy. Although the singing of each nation will demonstrate different tendencies, the German school might be seen as the major alternative to the Italian. German teachers will tend to favour a softer attack, perhaps to counter the hard glottal stop that figures so strongly in the spoken language. The same is true in much

English teaching, not only to counteract the English glottal stop, but perhaps also influenced by the English choral sound. This soft attack can be clearly heard, for example, in the singing of Elisabeth Schwarzkopf, and Dietrich Fischer-Dieskau, especially if compared to singers from the Latin countries such as Freni, Tebaldi or Cappucilli. The tendency in German teaching is to aim to maintain a low larynx, resulting in a somewhat covered tone. There is also a tendency to aim for roundness rather than brilliance and 'forwardness', with the U vowel often favoured for vocalising. In the treatment of the different vowels, whereas the singer schooled in the Italian manner may sacrifice the clarity of the vowels for an even vocal line, the German-trained singer may well sacrifice the legato line for the clarity of the vowels. This is not so surprising if one considers the importance of the text in the Lieder repertoire, or in the music of Bach (apart from the fact that German has nineteen vowel phonemes, including three diphthongs, compared with seven in Italian). Other phonetic factors are also relevant. In Italian the onset of a vowel is direct, yet not as hard as the glottal plosive. The cut-off of the vowel is also direct, unlike the cut-off of the vowel in German and English, which consists of a more gradual relaxation, often with breath coming in. Italian speech therefore has a more consistent bodily energy than German and English. In the performance of the dramatic repertoire, especially Wagner, a very low breathing may be allied to a very muscular use of support. It might be added that in the Wagnerian repertoire a rather slow rate of vibrato is often heard, sometimes down to five oscillations per second, in contrast to the archetypal Italian singer such as Caruso, whose vibrato was around seven per second. French singers tend to favour a fast vibrato, whereas many Russian singers produce a slow vibrato rather like some of the heavier Wagner singers. It is difficult to make an objective judgement on these matters; after all, one man's vibrato is another's wobble, though one might venture to suggest that as soon as the listener is unable to distinguish the pitches, or recognise which language is being sung, then the vibrato is excessive and the tone too covered.

Towards a pedagogic ideal

While the particular requirements of every singer are going to be different, it is possible to outline a number of principles that are important to all. The first is the need to adopt the optimum posture, as advised throughout the history of singing. The position of the head and freedom of the neck are particularly important. Many singers find the practice of Alexander technique or *Tai ch'i* of considerable benefit. In the ideal posture, breathing should not be such a big issue. The best approach is perhaps to discover what the voice asks of the body. Different attacks, different consonants, crescendos and diminuendos all cause different bodily reactions. These can then be used by the singer. It may be that in heavier repertoire a little more direct muscular control is desired; the teacher may then find it necessary to be more prescriptive.

Every singer should be able to execute a clean start of the note, both strong and gentle. Apart from being indicative of the co-ordination of the breath and the larynx it is an indication of vocal health. It is particularly important to maintain this cleanness as the singer's voice grows and he or she sings heavier roles in bigger theatres. Any roughness or pushing with the breath may eventually cause a deterioration of the condition of the instrument.

The question of whether singers should be taught to deliberately lower their larynx frequently arises today. While nobody would suggest that the larynx should be high, to recommend a young singer to push his larynx down may overweight the voice. It is unlikely that with good breathing technique that this would be necessary, and again it is perhaps better to be guided by the demands of the music, and the required colours. The same holds with regard to vowels and resonance. Rather than forcibly 'open the throat' it should be kept loose along with the jaw so the shape of the mouth and pharynx can be altered so as to find the ideal colour of vowel and mix of overtones that will bring about the best vocal quality (though the singer of a more dramatic repertoire may sometimes need a more 'muscular' approach).

In all the above matters, the teacher may well be guided by scientific knowledge (and the teacher should have this knowledge) but there is much that scientific analysis does not explain. If we run to catch a ball, there is an equation that expresses the relation between the speed we run at and the curve of the ball's flight. However, the cricketer who executes a spectacular catch has not actually made those calculations, and if he did it probably wouldn't help him. The cricketer relies on his visual faculty, and leaves his unconscious mind free to do whatever calculating it needs to do. Just as the cricketer's main guide is his eyes, the singer and singing teacher's main tools are the ears. Whatever the approach finally adopted by the singer or teacher, it will not be effective without a highly sensitive aural faculty, allied to imagination, and a not inconsiderable degree of patience.

18 Children's singing

FELICITY LAURENCE

There are certain basic, practical things we can do with children which will enable the vast majority to sing pleasantly and tunefully in a group, and to improve individually. In the description of these ideas, the focus will be on how to convey them in a group situation – a choir, or in the classroom – within a wider context of a general understanding of children's actual musical and vocal possibilities, and the assumption that (barring exceptional physiological impediment): *all* children can sing, learn to sing better, and have the right to do both.

Each child, being unique, has also a unique voice, with its own special colour, and dynamic and vocal range, as with adults, although usually a lighter instrument than a fully formed adult voice, and lacking its power. As children grow, so does the strength of their voices. Many investigations of children's vocal range give a general picture of about c^1–c^2 at five to six years, increasing to a–g^2 by nine to ten years, and further to a–c^3 by eleven to twelve years. However, most studies omit any mention of head or chest register, when in fact each is available even to tiny children, as confirmed by observation of very young children's spontaneous, improvised singing, which shows that they can manifest a very high voice. Each register yields its own vocal range, and while the lower chest-voice range tends to be very limited in small children, many of whom find it difficult to reach tones below c^1, the head-voice range extends in most children rather higher than indicated in conventional studies and than commonly believed. Some singing teachers differentiate between the range where children can comfortably sing a melody and where they can do singing exercises.

Children react to rhythm, tonal colour and melody when still babes-in-arms, and during their first five to six years they learn to distinguish their singing from their speaking voices. Their ability to perceive and reproduce rhythmic and melodic patterns develops both earlier than the perception of, and ability to sing in, harmony, and also far further than generally acknowledged in a Western context. This is what can be expected of most 'ordinary', 'normal' children aged around seven to fourteen years: they have a wide vocal range within which they are able to move their voices rapidly and from the smallest to very wide intervals; they are potentially able to cope with complex tunes and rhythms by the age of nine to ten years, while the ability to sing in harmony may only then be properly ready to work with; they are potentially able to sing with good intonation by this stage, and remain free enough of culturally imposed musical ideals and traditions to be able to sing and appreciate music of many styles and cultures; they have a particularly strong response to timbre, and will be capable of and interested in distinguishing different qualities of tone in instruments and in voices; their voices in the head register tend to a characteristic lightness and clarity, and are potentially capable of great flexibility; they are well able to achieve beauty of tone and a high level of musical expressiveness in their singing; and, finally, they have an inherent motivation to sing, which may endure, or wither, largely according to the behaviour of the prevailing adults.

As indicated, most people in Western society are not aware of the real capacities of children and their voices. This is lamentable, but unsurprising when one considers, for example, a recent British survey which concluded that 85 per cent of secondary schools provided no vocal curriculum at all,[1] while most of the (albeit few) didactic texts and singing curricula insist still on limiting younger children to pentatonic tunes and restricted vocal ranges, and older ones to pallid and rather anaesthetic arrangements of pop songs. Clearly the perpetrators have never heard an 'ordinary' class of ten-year-olds whizz through a scat version of 'Take Five', after ten minutes or so of vocal games, and managing the vocal dartings-about (not to mention the rhythmic aspects) pretty well. Or any group of children you might meet in a South African township . . .

This, then, is our context; now comes the question: if this is what children are intrinsically capable of, *how* best may we help them learn, and *what* can we best teach them in order to realise their potential?

First the *how*.

Headtone

I have found in my work with children at all stages (pre-school to tertiary) and backgrounds, that a headtone-based approach is effective. While my eventual aim is to enable all children to explore their voices and to use them however they wish as expressive instruments, and while I do not think children must always sing in head voice (nor that it is necessarily the 'ideal' sound for children), I would suggest that in headtone children can best hear the sound they are making, and also, in general, have the best possibility of making what they themselves consider to be a beautiful sound. A detailed description of head and chest registers and voices is to be found elsewhere in this volume; suffice it here to assure the reader that even tiny children have no problem in locating and using their 'high' and their 'low' voices.

When children sing a note in headtone with neither 'pushing' nor 'shouting', but in an unforced and natural way, they seem to experience a direct connection with the 'inner ear'; they can hear the sound they are making very clearly, so that their perception of pitch becomes extremely focused. This enables them to achieve in-tune singing far more quickly, and better, than in chest voice, which seems harder for them to hear. Launched into headtone, most children can achieve good accuracy of pitch, where before they may have tended towards flatness when singing in their chest voices. The effect can be instantaneous, and can (and has many times in my presence, always a miraculous moment) allow a 'droner' suddenly to find and sing the right notes. Through working in headtone, children can develop optimally the aural awareness and brain–voice connection required in singing. I have worked with African children who sing in rich harmony and mostly with a full and ravishing chest-voice production. But where there arose problems of intonation, we found together that it was through singing lightly in a head voice that they could best hear and then correct these faults. Some years ago, I received the most dramatic confirmation of this effect when working with a group of deaf children: I sang a tone in a high and very focused head voice, emphasising a forward and rounded lip formation, in order for them to sing any tone and thus form together a cluster chord. Nearly all of the children sang exactly my note back to me – somehow, the vibrations had penetrated, and somehow, they could also immediately find the 'right' tone with their minds and voices.

With this brief introduction to (one possible) method, we move now to the *what*.

Many people will be familiar with the basic rudiments – Posture, Relaxation, Intonation, Breathing, and Articulation; what is not so widely understood is that children are indeed capable of learning about these concepts and of putting them into practice from pre-school age. I have heard countless numbers of times from musically educated people that they just don't know which parts of singing technique they can usefully and safely teach children; I would like to state quite clearly: these are they!

Posture
Just by sitting or standing with a 'long' feeling from toe to top, an 'open' feeling around the chest and neck area, head balanced and straight, tilted neither up nor down, feet slightly apart and sharing the body's weight – children (like all of us) can gain immediate and significant improvement

in the sound of their singing. All the various muscles involved throughout the body will be able to function optimally; appropriate, natural breathing will be facilitated and the tone will emerge more clearly. When children are sitting on the floor, or on low chairs, they tend to rest their heads back on to their shoulders in order to peer up at a teacher; this puts strain on their voices, and 'cuts off' the sound. No matter what else the teacher then does, this unfavourable posture will impede and even hurt the children's voices. So if the children must sit on the floor, so too must the teacher, trying to keep at the children's eye level while reminding them to look ahead rather than upwards. In any case, it is good to swap between standing and sitting.

Relaxation

It is as important for children to be relaxed in the appropriate parts of the body as it is for adults, for children, too, build up bodily tensions and many live stressful lives. A common source of tension is the lower jaw, which many children tend to stick out and forwards when singing, or seem unable to open widely: it should be loose, the chin 'dropped'. The shoulders should also be loose and 'down' – there is often a tendency to hunch shoulders up when taking a breath.

Intonation

The fundamental prerequisite to being able to sing in tune is the ability to listen to the sound one is making. Good singing in children is as much about aural as vocal development, and using the head voice, as described above, can facilitate both. The children need firstly to listen to the notes they are to sing (given preferably by a voice rather than by a piano or other instrument), and then to listen acutely to what their own voices are actually doing. Whenever they sing a note, a line, a phrase . . . they should visualise it in their minds, so that they make a sort of mental map to follow, rather than having to find the right pitch as they go, by sliding their voices around. I ask them to 'think' the tone before they sing it. It is particularly important to pitch the first note of any entry accurately, otherwise it can be difficult, and for some children impossible, to find the rest of the tune, having, for example, started off a little low. It is also vital to give constant feedback, response and reference points so that the children can build up their ability and confidence.

With this combination of listening, mental imaging and the concomitant concentration, together with the use of the head voice, virtually all children with normal faculties and undamaged voices can learn to sing in tune, sooner or later. In a group, it may be only a few weeks before most of the children are singing in tune most of the time, and probably all of them at least some of the time.

Breathing

While children cannot and need not undertake the intensive training in breath control required by adult singers in certain musical genres, they can be encouraged to be aware of their breathing, and that it is important in their singing. I find it helpful to draw their attention away from the chest area, to minimise the chance of tightness in the neck and shoulders, and to help maintain a relaxed feeling in those areas. They can instead focus upon their abdominal region, and picture the air being drawn downwards 'to fill the bottom of the lungs'.[2] With upper and lower jaws separate and loose (see Relaxation) they can take in a breath with a little gasp – as if in response to a 'happy surprise'.[3] Such a breath will provide plenty of air and, if they have their hands on their abdomens or around the sides of their rib cages, they should be able to feel the movement as they breathe in. They can also be asked to expand their rib cages, all around; or they can 'drink in a breath', or imagine that they are breathing in a pleasant smell. These simple ideas can help prevent the very common phenomenon of children trying to take huge breaths with resulting raised shoulders and much tension all through the chest and neck regions. Children can also understand and practise 'keeping the breath in', and using it bit by bit, saving enough to sing the last note of the phrase right to its end.

Articulation

Forming words as clearly as possible, with clarity and precision in both vowels and consonants, contributes enormously to the quality of the sound, and is an aspect of singing which children can do brilliantly. They can learn to 'prepare' each vowel (and/or consonant) with lips and tongue immediately before singing it. This resembles the visualisation process described above (see Intonation). In the same way, it allows the brain to get all the relevant head and throat muscles poised to make exactly the right sound – by always 'thinking ahead'.

These rudiments can be usefully caught in a 'five-point plan'[4] – which can help children to recall them each time they are about to sing.

(1) Check that there is a *long, open and relaxed feeling* throughout the body.
(2) *Think* the note to be sung (i.e. its pitch).
(3) Form the vowel with lips and face.
(4) *Breathe in* (as described).
(5) And . . . *Sing!*

While there is general agreement among children's singing specialists that these are indeed the basic concepts and techniques which can and should be taught to children, there are differences of opinion about how best to convey them. In Germany, for example, there is a complete acceptance of a separation between *Stimmbildung* (vocal technique) and *Gesang* (actually singing), and 'serious' children's choirs will have distinct sessions, often with different teachers, on each. By contrast, in Sweden, particularly in the field of singing with young, or 'ordinary', children, there has been a strong move to a holistic approach, with suggestions that the technical aspects should be camouflaged, in order that the children's spontaneity and joy in singing be preserved. One American children's singing specialist believes that the teacher should know much more than s/he actually says, and that the children should not be made too aware of the technique involved: 'They should sing well because you know how to get the quality of sound you want from them'.[5]

My own position is derived from the knowledge that children learn best and are happiest where they recognise that there is understanding of and respect for their *actual* capacities, in an affectionate atmosphere which resonates with explicit feedback and honest praise. To this end, I integrate the technical work fully, and in fact, present all the activity as 'musicking',[6] where the children know (because I tell them) that we are making music together. I also focus the children's attention constantly upon the aesthetic nature of our work, in 'technical' activity no less than in 'singing'.

> Sing this scale . . . chins loose . . . smooth tone . . . lips forward and rounded . . . a long line . . . make it beautiful . . . listen to each other and together find the moment to let the sound die away . . .

By explaining the technical aspects, which one can do through games or in other compelling, interesting and relevant ways (technique can be exciting!), you can empower the children, so that in the end they can choose and control the way they sing. Of course teachers should try to elicit what they consider to be good singing from the children, but the children's own understanding of what they are doing can only enrich and enable them, and the singing activity becomes part of their general exploration of the world, of their own abilities, and of themselves.

There follows now a picture-in-words of how a session of singing with children might go. To illustrate a little further the mention already made of headtone, I have sketched a typical 'first-ever' lesson, as it is at this point that I would introduce this concept, along with other foundations.

There you are, surrounded by expectant, curious (or possibly sceptical) young faces, watching and waiting to see what you will do . . . so how do you start? I invite the children to sit in a semicircle (single, double or even triple if they are many), so that we can all see each other and I can retain eye contact with everyone, and am also able to move around and come into close proximity to any child. Just this circular arrangement helps the feeling of co-operative and shared activity, facilitating the aims outlined in the preceding paragraph. The most important single thing for me at this stage is to make, with the children, a very positive, warm and safe atmosphere. Singing involves self-exposure, and many children may not feel free to sing out unless they perceive an entirely non-judgemental situation (in the sense of adult or peer criticism). At the same time, I try to persuade them as soon as possible of their own musical and vocal possibilities, so that they feel also a sense of what they have to contribute, and that this is going to be a two-way process where they will have something to give and to say. With the idea that they all have beautiful voices (let's find them!) and the understanding that you and the children are partners in an interesting and pleasurable quest, you can move right away from a feeling of authoritarian imposition of adult whim and 'wisdom'.[7]

Now, a minute or so to introduce myself and my intentions, and then we make sure we are sitting straight, tall, elegant! relaxed, loose hands, loose neck; imagine our heads wafting very gently as if attached by a thread to a hot-air balloon on an almost-calm day . . . and bring the heads to stillness and balance, chins neither up, nor down.

Lips forward and rounded, not very loudly and using my head voice, I sing 'loooo', around the note a^1 or b^1. I ask them to try it, and they do, producing a much duller, less resonant and less focused sound. So there is an obvious difference in my sound and in theirs, and the children can spot this straight away. We try again, this time concentrating very hard on listening to the difference. What is it? I ask. A hand waves in the air. 'Your sound is clearer' . . . or 'purer' or 'echoey' . . . or 'our sound is . . . rougher . . . not very clear . . .' Perhaps we sing a line or verse from a familiar song, just with this 'looo' vowel. More comments: 'your voice is better . . . higher . . . lower . . . rounder . . . we sound fuzzy. . .'

Here it is, that innate and universal sense of quality, with which we discern for ourselves what seems good, what seems better.

With the help of some Socratic questioning and more demonstration from me, they work out that their combined sound is less clear because of their slight (or otherwise) variations of pitch ('we're not all singing exactly the same') and because they are letting lots of air come out with their voices.

At this point I show them how I make the 'looo' sound (like 'aw' but lips more rounded), moving my lips very slowly forward so that they can hear the sound grow more resonant as the lips become more rounded. Now they can say what they saw, and what they heard, and then they can try it themselves. The change in the tone is always very obvious as it suddenly becomes focused and resonant, and is often quite dramatic. I direct their attention to the vibrations they may feel in various parts of their heads, and explain that what they are making is 'head tone', where the voice feels centred in the head, and I point out how clearly they can hear their own voices (or one of them might point this out to me). They can experiment a bit now, moving their lips into different shapes as they sing, feeling the sound grow as they come back to the 'looo', and enjoying this rather magical effect.

The die is now cast. They themselves have identified a sound as being pleasant and 'better' (my tone), and have already contributed much, and motivation now comes from them as they realise that they can both understand what to do, and physically do it, with immediate and tangible results. All of the subsequent activity rests now on the basis of a 'model sound' or reference point ('looo') and the way of working is established – with a sense of challenge on the one hand, of fun on the other, and that we are acting musically together and are interested in beauty and quality of sound from the first moment and throughout.

I might then teach a catchy tune, just using the 'looo' syllable to help the children become familiar with this new sound, and pitching high enough to maintain the singing in head voice; then we could tackle some factors which tend to muffle the tone, such as their breathing.

'Everyone lie on the floor . . . breathe gently and naturally with hands resting, one above the other, on your abdomen (one hand at the level of the rib cage, the other below it). Feel the rising and falling movement as the air is taken in, and then breathed out again. After a minute or two, when you have become familiar with this feeling and its slow rhythm, sit up, very carefully, very slowly, keeping your hands where they were. Concentrate, and try to keep that gentle feeling of expansion as you breathe in, and the falling back movement as the breath leaves the body. Again, wait until you feel confident, and then carefully get up and stand. With a hand still on your stomach, keep the breathing going, and feel the motion – as you breathe in and then out' (the exact terminology used will vary according to the children's ages).

After this rather contemplative interlude, perhaps a game. All of the activities in fact can be games, at least as far as the children are concerned: games in which their skills are extended, their minds challenged, their limits explored.

Simon says; when the leader (first me, later one of the children) announces 'Simon says do this', the children must copy whatever he or she does, but when the leader says only 'Do this', they must ignore the command and remain still.

When the children already know the 'model sound' as described above, you can play with it in this and other ways.

Simon says do this:

Fig. 14a

Simon says do this:

Fig. 14b

Simon says do this:

Fig. 14c

Do this:

Fig. 14d

Simon says do this:

Fig. 14e

And so on. In a simple game like this, the children can explore all kinds of possibilities in their voices, practise their head voice, and other tones they can make, play with rhythms – and all this with necessarily intent listening too.

To round off the session, some subtle recapitulation, and through the new song again – perhaps introduce the words now, to continue next time. With a bit of luck, the children will leave the room singing quite nicely, and happy in their singing. In subsequent work, sessions should always begin with at least a short warm-up, to protect the children's voices from any sudden strain, to help them recall previous learning and to re-establish concentration.

This, then, is a glimpse into the world of children's singing. The very way in which it is done will determine not only the quality of the singing and the actual learning achieved, but, most profoundly, the ultimate significance of the act of singing for the children. Thousands of years ago, the first Australians sang their world into existence; more recently, I listened and watched South African children singing themselves into existence. In New Zealand, I have witnessed the affirming power of song throughout a multi-cultural school where singing is entirely functional, where it is the 'glue' which holds everyone there together.[8] Nevertheless, singing for children throughout the Western world seems too often a monotonous and meaningless thing, and, sadly, there are cultures elsewhere where it is proscribed altogether.[9] For singing, like language, should be for every child a primary source of their awareness of their humanness.

19 Where does the sound come from?

JOHAN SUNDBERG

Singing is rightfully regarded as fine art, producing musical experiences for listeners and performers. However, a substantial amount of research has been devoted to singing in recent decades, which allows a complementary scientific view of singing. A system of solid information about singing has emerged which offers the possibility of supplementing the understanding of singing by physical, tangible facts. These facts may facilitate the use of the voice and make listening to singing more profound and rich. This chapter provides an overview of this research, explaining how voice sounds are generated and controlled by breathing patterns, laryngeal adjustment and resonance phenomena.

Voice production

Three major factors are involved in the production of voiced sounds: the *respiratory system*, the *vocal folds* and the *vocal tract* (the cavity formed by the pharynx and the mouth, which is sometimes complemented by the nasal cavity). Each of them serves a purpose of its own as shown in Figure 15.

The respiratory system compresses the lungs, thus causing an overpressure of air which generates an air stream, if the airways are open. This airstream sets the vocal folds vibrating, and the vibrations chop the airstream into a pulsating airflow, which is a sound called the *voice source*. It is controlled by two main factors, the air pressure in the lungs (the *lung pressure*) and the vocal folds, which are themselves controlled by a number of laryngeal muscles. The voice source consists of a chord of simultaneously sounding simple tones, or *partials* of different frequencies and strengths. This sound is filtered by the *vocal tract*, which has a frequency curve characterised by peaks and valleys reflecting resonances enhancing and suppressing partials (depending on their frequencies). The vocal tract has the function of acoustically forming the output sound, so we call the vocal tract resonances *formants*. Vowel sounds contain a number of partials of varied strengths reflecting the formants. The properties of the voice source plus the frequencies of the formants determine the vowel quality and the personal timbre that we perceive in a voice.

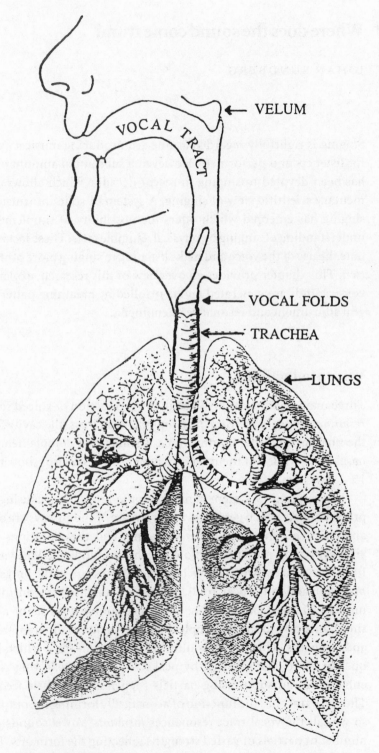

Figure 15 The voice organ.

The voice organ

The vocal folds are made up of muscles shaped as folds and covered by a mucous membrane. They are approximately 3 mm long in newborn infants and grow during puberty to about 9 to 13 mm and 15 to 20 mm in adult women and men, respectively. The vocal-fold length is crucial to the pitch range of the voice: the longer the vocal folds, the lower the pitch range. The fold length does not significantly depend on body length but is more related to the circumference of the neck. The slit between the vocal folds is called the *glottis*. The vocal folds originate at the back of the thyroid cartilage near the thyroid angle. The front angle of this cartilage is referred to as the Adam's apple and marks the location of the vocal folds in the throat. The folds run horizontally from front to back, and each fold is inserted into a tiny cartilage, known as the arytenoids. The arytenoid cartilages can be moved very quickly. They open and close the glottis by *abducting* (spreading) or *adducting* (bringing together) the posterior ends of the vocal folds. In order to pronounce a voiced sound, the vocal folds must be adducted; and in order to pronounce an unvoiced sound, they must be abducted. Thus, adduction and abduction enable us to shift from unvoiced to voiced and from voiced to unvoiced sounds, respectively. When we pronounce a word such as 'voicing', the vocal folds are adducted until the unvoiced /s/-sound is reached, then they are abducted during that sound and again adduct for the remaining voiced sounds. Clearly, the arytenoid cartilages are very quick and precise.

A few millimetres above the vocal folds there is another pair of folds, also covered by mucous membrane. These are called the *false vocal folds* (an unduly moralistic name) or the *ventricular folds*. Between the vocal folds and the ventricular folds there is a small cavity known as the laryngeal ventricle. The glottis serves as the bottom of a small tube-shaped cavity, the larynx tube. At the back, this tube is limited by the arytenoid cartilages, at the front by the thyroid cartilage and the lower part of the epiglottis, while the lateral parts of the larynx tube consist of the tissues that join these structures. The larynx tube is narrow and short, about one or two centimetres long, and is inserted into the bottom part of a much wider and longer tube, the pharynx, which partially surrounds it. At the bottom of the pharynx, just behind the arytenoids, there is an opening to the stomach system. This is normally closed, but opens when we swallow, closing the entrance to the airways. The back wall of the pharynx is determined by the cervical vertebrae, and the side walls by constrictor muscles. The front wall consists of the larynx tube at the bottom, then the epiglottis, which is a cartilage shaped somewhat like a spoon, and, higher up, the tongue. The tongue, which originates in the hyoid bone, is composed of a number of muscles. The root of the tongue goes well below the upper tip of the epiglottis, so that there is a cavity between the root of the tongue and the upper part of the epiglottis. The ceiling of the pharynx cavity is called the soft palate, which also serves as the gateway to the nose cavities. In the ceiling of the nasal cavity narrow channels lead up to other cavities, the maxillary and frontal sinuses, which are located in the bone structure of the skull (and which, when suppurated, cause sinusitis).

Breathing

The lungs are elastic, spongy structures suspended in vacuum in a sac within the rib cage. Because of the vacuum, their volume is enlarged. They contain a great number of small cavities linked by a system of air pipes which join in the trachea, a tube ending at the vocal folds. Inhalation and exhalation correspond to decompression and compression of the lungs which is performed by the respiratory system, containing forces generated by muscles, elasticity and gravitation. By muscle contraction we can expand and contract the rib cage, and as most of the lung surface is covered by the rib cage, small rib cage movements result in substantial compression and decompression. A large inspiratory muscle sheet, the diaphragm, constitutes the boundary between the rib cage and the abdomen. It originates along the lower edge of the rib cage and is vaulted into it. When contracting, it lowers the bottom of the rib cage by pushing downward the abdominal content, which in turn expands the abdominal wall. By contracting the abdominal wall muscles the abdominal content can be pushed back into the rib cage, thus compressing the lungs. The elasticity forces can be either exhalatory or inhalatory and vary depending on lung volume. At high lung volumes they are exhalatory and vice versa. This means that elasticity provides an overpressure of air in the lungs. This pressure, however, gradually decreases as air is consumed for phonation thus causing lung volume to decrease. At a certain lung volume, generally near 40 per cent of maximum lung volume, the expiratory and inspiratory elasticity forces are equal. In tidal breathing, inhalations are started from this lung volume, which is called the Functional Residual Capacity, or FRC. After a completely relaxed sigh, lung volume typically reaches FRC. In singing and speech alike, we usually phonate at lung volumes above FRC, and phonating below FRC can feel uncomfortable. When trained singers learn new songs, they learn how to breathe and sing so as to avoid lung volumes below FRC. Small lung volumes are

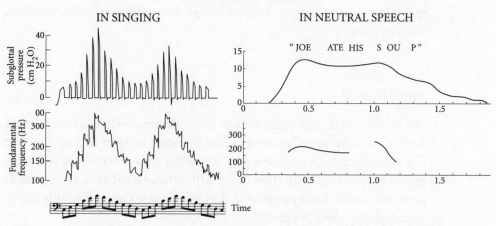

Figure 16 Subglottal pressure (upper panels) and pitch contours (lower panels) in singing a melody (bottom left) and in speech (right).

generally used in speech, whereas in classical singing phrases are often initiated at very high lung volumes. Classical singers tend to repeat their breathing patterns very consistently when they sing the same phrase. They seem to use the rib cage mainly for controlling lung volume, though some singers seem to rely also on the abdominal wall.

The overpressure of air in the trachea generates an air stream through the *glottis*. The pressure just below the glottis, the *subglottal pressure*, provides the driving force of the voice and is the main tool for controlling vocal loudness: the higher the pressure, the louder the voice. It can be measured in the unit kiloPascal, or kPa, a unit equal to 1 dm of water column, approximately. In neutral speech it generally remains in the vicinity of 0.5 kPa. In singing it varies not only with loudness but also with fundamental frequency of phonation, and is much more varied, reaching 2 kPa or even more (see Fig. 16).

This pressure variation in singing needs to be quite accurate as pressure affects pitch, and failure to match a target pressure may result in fundamental frequency errors (singing out of tune). The classical singing exercise with staccato performance (short tones interleaved with short silent intervals) of ascending and descending triad patterns seems particularly appropriate to train the singer's subglottal pressure control. During the silent intervals the vocal folds part, leaving the airways open, so lung pressure must then be reduced to zero to avoid waste of air. Additionally, each tone usually needs a renewed pressure. Singers also use subglottal pressure to demarcate the tones in rapid sequences such as legato coloratura singing. Then each tone receives its own pressure pulse, so that one pressure pulse is produced for each note in synchrony with the fundamental frequency pattern. In quick tempi, these pressure pulses may be as short as 150 ms.

Voice source

In voiced sounds the voice source is a pulsating airflow as mentioned above. It can be described in terms of the wave form of this airflow (see Fig. 17), which is characterised by triangular pulses occurring when the glottis is open in its vibration cycle, with interspersed zero or minimum airflow sections corresponding to the closed phase (when the folds nearly or completely close the glottis).

As the voice source consists of a chord of simultaneously sounding *partials* of different frequencies and strengths it is also relevant to describe it in terms of the spectrum showing the frequencies and the amplitudes of the different partials. The partials are *harmonic*, implying that their frequencies are integer multiples of the frequency of the lowest partials, called the *fundamental*. Thus, if the fundamental frequency is 110 Hz, the frequencies of the subsequent partials are 2 times 110, 3 times 110, 4 times 110, and so on. Musical intervals appear between the lowest partials: an octave between numbers 1 and 2, a fifth between 2 and 3, a fourth between 3 and 4, a major third between 4 and 5 and a minor third between 5 and 6. Above this, the intervals become narrower and gradually deviate from common musical intervals. The highest overtones tend to appear somewhere between 5 and 8 kHz. At normal vocal loudness the spectrum envelope typically falls off at a rate of about 12 dB per octave as measured in flow units, but the spectrum characteristics vary depending on the phonatory conditions. The voice source can be varied in several different ways, according to fundamental frequency, overall amplitude of the spectrum partials, and the dominance of the fundamental. The fundamental frequency is the vibration frequency of the vocal folds and corresponds to the pitch perceived. Thus, the fundamental frequency is 440 Hz when the pitch of A4 is being sung. The main determinant of fundamental frequency is the length and vibrating mass of the vocal folds: the longer and thinner the folds, the higher the pitch. These properties are controlled by the laryngeal musculature. The approximate ranges covered by the main singer classifications are bass singers 80 Hz–330 Hz (pitch range E–e^1), tenors 123 Hz–520 Hz (c–c^2), altos 175 Hz–700 Hz (f–f^2), and sopranos 260 Hz–1300 Hz (c^1–c^3). Fundamental frequency is also influenced by subglottal pressure. For each tenth of a kPa pressure increase the frequency rises by a few Hz. Therefore, to stay in tune while

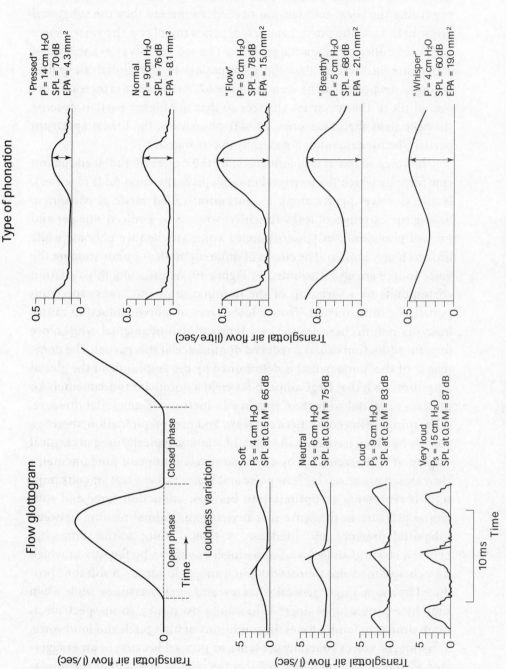

Figure 17 Transglottal airflow waveforms in different phonatory conditions. Top left shows a stylized waveform with open and closed phases of the glottal vibratory cycle. The four lower panels (left) show effects of loudness variation. Right panels show waveforms of different types of phonation. Ps = lung pressure; SPL = sound pressure level at 0.5m; EPA = maximum estimated glottal area.

Type of phonation

"Pressed"
P = 14 cm H_2O
SPL = 70 dB
EPA = 4.3 mm^2

Normal
P = 9 cm H_2O
SPL = 76 dB
EPA = 8.1 mm^2

"Flow"
P = 8 cm H_2O
SPL = 78 dB
EPA = 15.0 mm^2

"Breathy"
P = 5 cm H_2O
SPL = 68 dB
EPA = 21.0 mm^2

"Whisper"
P = 4 cm H_2O
SPL = 60 dB
EPA = 19.0 mm^2

Transglottal air flow (litre/sec)

Flow glottogram

Open phase   Closed phase

Time

Loudness variation

Soft
Ps = 4 cm H_2O
SPL at 0.5 M = 65 dB

Neutral
Ps = 6 cm H_2O
SPL at 0.5 M = 75 dB

Loud
Ps = 9 cm H_2O
SPL at 0.5 M = 83 dB

Very loud
Ps = 15 cm H_2O
SPL at 0.5 M = 87 dB

Time

10ms

Transglottal air flow (l/sec)

Transglottal air flow (l/sec)

producing a crescendo a singer needs to reduce the activation of the laryngeal muscles that regulate fundamental frequency as the subglottal pressure increases. This may partly explain why less-skilled singers cannot sing high notes softly: their laryngeal muscles are not capable of producing the vocal-fold tension needed, so instead they use subglottal pressure to raise the pitch. *Loudness* depends mainly on the voice source and is controlled by subglottal pressure. The acoustically relevant effect of a pressure increase is that the termination of the glottal air pulses becomes steeper, as can be seen in Figure 17. As loudness is increased the overall tilt of the spectrum changes so that the higher partials become stronger than the lower ones. In soft phonation, the lowest spectrum partial (the fundamental) is generally the strongest.

The voice source is also influenced by the degree of glottal adduction (the force by which the laryngeal muscles press the vocal folds together). It affects voice quality along a continuum called *mode of phonation*, having the extremes of leaky (breathy) voice as in a voiced whisper and pressed phonation, or tense/strangled voice as when we phonate while lifting a heavy burden. The effects of different modes of phonation on the voice source are also illustrated in Figure 17. Acoustically this variation corresponds to a variation of the dominance of the lowest spectrum partial, the fundamental. Thus, a low degree of glottal adduction causes leaky phonation characterised by a dominating fundamental, while more forceful adduction causes a reduced dominance of this partial. The dominance of the fundamental is determined by the amplitude of the glottal air pulses, such that large amplitudes yield a dominant fundamental. An increase of glottal adduction requires an increase of subglottal pressure, other things being equal. Between leaky and neutral phonation, there is a voice type which has been called *flow phonation*, typically used in classical singing. It is characterised by a comparatively dominant fundamental, a clear closed phase, a large flow pulse and hence rather great air consumption. It represents an optimisation between adduction force and subglottal pressure in the sense that it yields an optimal relation between subglottal pressure and loudness. A typical voice source difference between classical singers and non-singers seems to be the way in which they change the voice source with pitch and/or loudness. A soft tone produced by a non-singer generally has few and weak overtones, while when sung by a professional singer it has more overtones, so its spectrum is more similar to louder tones. In conditions of high pitch and loud voice, non-singers' voices generally get tense or pressed because of an exaggerated glottal adduction which reduces the relative strength of the fundamental. It seems to be essential for classical singers to retain the possibilities of varying the voice source for purposes of musical expression even under conditions of extreme pitch and loudness. By and large, the voice source seems rather independent of the vocal tract (i.e. it is not affected by changes in articulation). However, in female singing at very high pitches, the fundamental frequency is close to the first formant. In such cases a strong interaction between voice source and vocal tract has been assumed. The result is claimed to be that the transglottal airflow is reduced or even reversed during a short period of the open phase.

In unvoiced sounds the vocal folds do not vibrate. Instead, the voice source is noise, a signal lacking pitch. It is generated when the airstream from the lungs is forced to pass through a narrow slit with quite rigid walls, which makes the airstream turbulent. The slit is located at different places along the vocal tract in different consonants. For example, in the consonant /f/, the slit is formed between the lower lip and the front teeth, and in /s/ between the tongue tip and the hard palate. In voiced consonants the noise is complemented by vocal-fold vibrations. In whispering and in the consonant /h/, the voice source is noise created when the airstream passes through a slightly opened glottis, but the vocal folds are so tense that the airstream fails to make them vibrate.

Another type of voice source variation corresponds to different modes of vocal-fold oscillation. These modes are called *vocal registers*. There are at least three registers, generally referred to as vocal fry, chest (or modal), and falsetto. In vocal fry, which frequently occurs at phrase endings in conversational speech, the vocal folds are thick and lax, and the glottal air-pulses appear in groups of two or more with a long interspersed closed phase, presumably because the two vocal folds vibrate asynchronically. Therefore fundamental frequency is low, generally well below 100 Hz for male voices. In modal register, the folds are less lax and vibrate symmetrically. Adjacent glottal pulses appear at rather constant time intervals and tend to occupy 50 per cent or more of the period. Also in falsetto the folds vibrate symmetrically, the vocal folds are thin and stretched and rarely close the glottis completely. The pulses are longer than in modal register. According to Titze, these register breaks depend on an interaction between subglottal resonances and vocal-fold vibrations.[1] While in conversational speech all three registers are occasionally used, only the modal register is used by classical tenors, baritones and basses. Countertenors appear to sing mainly in the falsetto register, but with a complete closure of the glottis during the closed phase. In female voices the situation is less clear: there are reasons to assume that female singers use chest register in the lower part of their range and a falsetto-like register in the upper part. The latter is often referred to as middle register.

A voice source characteristic of the trained singing voice is the *vibrato*. There seem to be at least two types of vibrato, which are produced and sound differently. The vibrato used in classical singing is normally produced by pulsations in the pitch-raising cricothyroid muscle and is a *frequency vibrato*. In popular music a different kind of vibrato is often used which is generated by variations in subglottal pressure imposing an undulation of voice-source amplitude. It corresponds to an amplitude modulation of the voice source and is really an *intensity vibrato*. Frequency vibrato corresponds to a slow, nearly sinusoidal fundamental frequency modulation. Typically, the rate is somewhere between 5.5 and 7 undulations per second and the extent varies between +/− 50 and +/− 150 cents. Both rate and extent are important. If the rate goes below 5 undulations per second, which may occur in old and/or strained voices, no clear single pitch can be perceived; it sounds as if the pitch is swaying around. If it is faster than 7 undulations per second, the tone sounds nervous. Also, the acceptable range of modulation depth is limited. If the extent surpasses ±6 per cent of the mean fundamental frequency (about 100 cents), it tends to sound exaggerated. In choral and in pop singing vibrato is typically much smaller than in classical singing. As a secondary effect, a frequency vibrato is accompanied by an amplitude modulation. The reason is that partials close to a formant frequency vary in amplitude depending on their distance from that formant, so the frequency modulation induces an amplitude modulation (which is not easy to hear). Similarly the amplitude vibrato contains a frequency modulation as a byproduct of the underlying modulation of subglottal pressure because of the effect of subglottal pressure on fundamental frequency mentioned above. No thorough research has been carried out on this type of vibrato, but it seems likely that the modulation of fundamental frequency is very small, perhaps subliminal.[2]

Formants

A formant is a vocal-tract resonance. There are generally five formants relevant to singing. Each of them produces a peak in the frequency curve of the vocal tract. This curve can be thought of as an account of the vocal tract's ability to transport sounds of different frequencies; the peaks represent frequencies which are transported more easily than other frequencies. If tones of various frequencies are transmitted through the vocal tract simultaneously, those appearing at the peaks of the frequency curve are radiated from the lip opening with a greater strength than others, so the formants appear as peaks in the spectrum of the radiated sound. The resonance frequencies of the vocal tract depend on its length and shape. These parameters are controlled by the positioning of the lips,

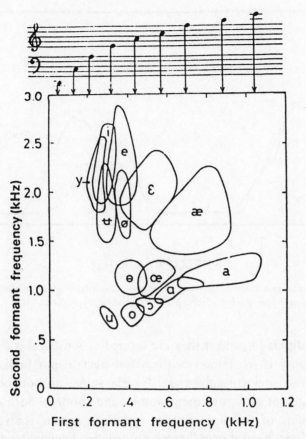

Figure 18 Frequency values of first and second formants characterising different vowel sounds (from Sundberg, *The Science of the Singing Voice*, 1987).

the jaw, the larynx, the velum (soft palate) and the pharyngeal side walls, i.e. by articulation. There is a close relation between vocal-tract shape and certain formants. A shortening of the tract, caused by retracting the corners of the mouth or by raising the larynx, increases all formant frequencies more or less, and a narrowing of the pharynx and a widening of the mouth cavity increases the first formant. Moreover, a lengthening of the pharynx by a lowering of the larynx decreases the second formant in vowels produced with a forward position of the tongue, such as /i/ (as in heed). Formant frequencies are decisive for vocal timbre. There are two distinct aspects to the timbre of vocal sounds: one is the *vowel quality*, which determines which vowel is perceived (e.g. an / i/ or an /a/), another is the personal *voice quality*, which determines whether the voice sounds as if it is Pavarotti or your neighbour pronouncing the vowel. We have developed an acoustic code system for vowels. It mainly concerns the frequencies of the lowest two formants, as illustrated in Figure 18. If the first and second formants are located at 600 and 1000 Hz, respectively, the

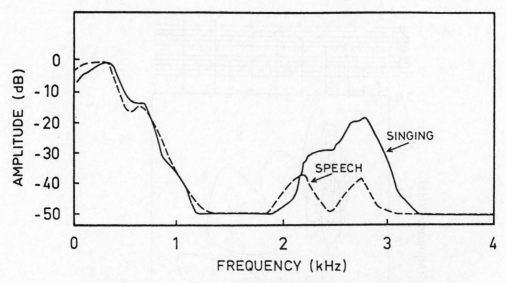

Figure 19 Spectrum contours of the vowel [u:] as pronounced by an operatic baritone singer in neutral speech and singing (after Sundberg, *The Science of the Singing Voice*, 1987).

vowel quality is /a/, and if they are located at 300 Hz and 2000 Hz the vowel quality is /i/. However, the vocal-tract length (and hence the formant frequencies of a given vowel) varies somewhat both between and within different groups of men, women and children. Such differences explain some of the voice timbre variations among individuals. For example, it has been shown that for a given vowel, tenors tend to possess higher formant frequencies than bass singers. Relatively high formant frequencies are thus typical for the tenor voice timbre.

A characteristic feature of classical bass, tenor and alto singers' voices is an exceptionally high spectrum envelope peak occurring somewhere between about 2 and 3.5 kHz. Figure 19 shows a typical example. This peak has been called the *singers' formant*. It appears in all voiced sounds and is a consequence of a clustering of the third, fourth and fifth formant frequencies. An important articulatory means for achieving such a clustering is the shape of the larynx tube and a wide pharynx, often produced by a lowering of the larynx. The amplitude of the singers' formant varies with vocal loudness since vocal loudness affects the slope of the source spectrum (as mentioned above).

Appearing in a frequency range where the ear is particularly sensitive, the singers' formant contributes to making the voice timbre more distinct and 'brilliant'. Also, the overtones of an accompanying orchestra are, on average, much softer in this frequency range than near 500 Hz, where they are generally loudest. This is illustrated in Figure 20, which compares the averaged level of sound energy in different frequency bands occurring

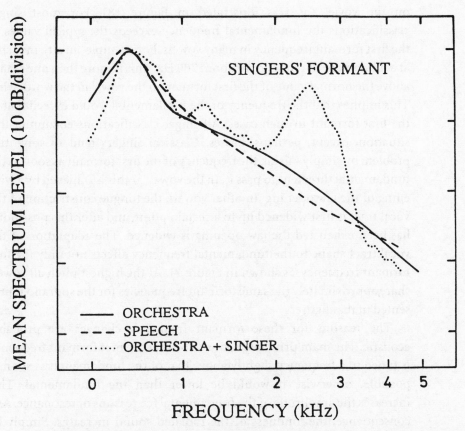

Figure 20 Mean sound level of an orchestra playing with and without a singer soloist (dotted and solid curves); the singers' formant can be clearly seen as the major difference between the two contours. The dashed curve shows the corresponding data for neutral speech (from Sundberg, *The Science of the Singing Voice*, 1987).

when an orchestra plays with and without a singer soloist; the singers' formant seems to contribute to making the singer's voice easier to hear even when the orchestral accompaniment is loud. An important advantage is that this effect can be achieved without excessive vocal effort.

The centre frequency of the singers' formant seems to have real significance for voice quality. In synthesis of singing voices, a typical bass voice quality can be obtained if the centre frequency is near 2.2 kHz and a tenor timbre is obtained with a centre frequency near 2.9 kHz. Alto voices seem to have a still higher centre frequency. These variations can be assumed to reflect differences in vocal tract length and pharyngeal shape. The wide pharynx needed for clustering the higher formants brings changes in the first two formants as well. For example, the second formant in front vowels such as /i:/ is considerably lower in classical singing than in neutral speech, a phenomenon associated with what singers call 'covering'. The first formant varies between about 250 and 1000 Hz depending on the vowel (as was illustrated in Figure 18). For most singer classifications the fundamental frequency exceeds the typical values of the first formant frequency in many vowels. For example, an alto may sing at a fundamental frequency of about 700 Hz. This is more than one octave above the normal value of the first formant in the vowel in the word 'who'. This implies that the frequency of the fundamental would exceed that of the first formant in such cases. All singer classifications encounter this situation, except, perhaps, basses. Classical singers tend to solve this problem by simply raising the frequency of the first formant as soon as the fundamental threatens to pass it. In the vowel /a/ this is achieved by a widening of the jaw opening. In other vowels, the tongue constriction of the vocal tract is first widened up to a certain point, and after this possibility has been exhausted the jaw opening is widened. The adaptation of the vocal tract shape to the fundamental frequency affects not only the first formant frequency, as shown in Figure 21. At the highest pitch all vowels share approximately the same formant frequencies for the soprano represented in that figure.

The reasons for these formant frequency changes are probably acoustic. The main principle seems to be that the first formant frequency is tuned to a frequency slightly above that of the fundamental as soon as possible, otherwise it would be lower than the fundamental. This increases the amplitude of the fundamental for reasons of resonance. As a consequence, the loudness of the radiated sound increases. Simply by opening her mouth to an appropriate extent, a classical soprano may increase her sound level by 20 dB or more at high pitches with no increase of vocal effort. Since vowel quality is determined mainly by the two lowest formant frequencies one would expect disastrous consequences for vowel intelligibility when singing at high pitches. Faced with a choice between inaudible tones with normal vowel quality or audible tones with modified vowel quality, singers generally choose the latter. The vowel quality of sustained vowels survives these pitch-dependent formant frequency modifications surprisingly well, except for fundamental frequencies above about 700 Hz, where no formant frequency combination seems to help, and below it the vowel quality would be no better if normal formant frequencies were chosen. The amount of text intelligibility that occurs at very high pitches relies almost exclusively on the consonants preceding and following the vowel.

Formants are resonances of the vocal tract and are generally sufficient to explain the vowel sounds produced by classical singers. It is often said that singers have special types of resonances in addition to the vocal tract and the nose cavity (in the chest and in the various bone cavities of the

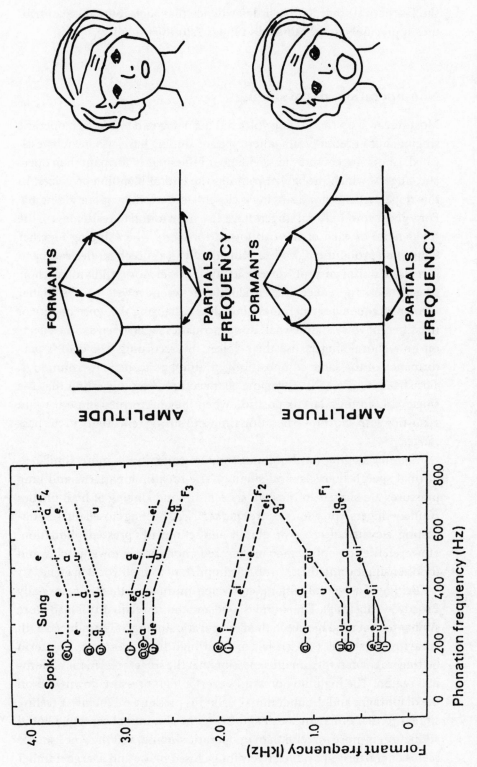

Figure 21 Left panel: four lowest formant frequencies (F1–4) as produced at different fundamentals by a soprano. The circled vowels represent spoken vowels, the non-circled represent sung vowels (from Sundberg, *The Science of the Singing Voice*, 1987). Right panel: schematic illustration of the spectrum resulting from a higher fundamental than the first formant (upper diagram) and when the first formant has been raised to the neighbourhood of the fundamental (lower diagram).

skull structure) but there is little evidence that such resonance contributes appreciably to the radiated sound (i.e. to voice quality).

Non-operatic styles of singing

Most research on the singing voice has been devoted to Western operatic singing, but in recent years other types of singing have also been investigated. Choir singers show less evidence of the singers' formant than operatic singers, which probably promotes the choral blending of voices. In this respect, then, choral singing is closer to speech than operatic singing. For a given vowel, choral singers have also been found to scatter less in the frequencies of each of the two lowest formants when singing together than when pronouncing vowels individually in a speech mode, leading to increased uniformity of vowel quality. Furthermore, individual choir singers tend to reduce the variability between vowels of the higher formant frequencies when they sing, thus equalising the voice quality of the different vowels somewhat. Room acoustics seem to have some effects on how choral singers use their voices. By recording one choir's performance of the same compositions in different acoustic surroundings, Ternström showed that formants changed in a way suggesting that the singers raised their larynx position when they performed in poor room acoustics with short reverberation time and strong reflectivity in the bass range.[3]

Country singing (and popular singing generally) is more similar to normal speech than classical singing. The breathing patterns and lung pressures are similar to those in speech. In loud singing at high pitches country singers' voice sources are characterised by long closed phases suggesting elevated degrees of glottal adduction, i.e. pressed phonation. However, they do not seem to use pressed phonation at lower pitches and in softer singing and this is probably important to their vocal hygiene.

Belting is a type of singing cultivated in musical theatre (especially Broadway musicals). The sound is loud and the vowel quality is also more similar to that used in speech than in operatic singing. It is produced with a narrow pharynx, a raised larynx, and high lung pressures. The term belting might derive from the sensation that the singers feel in the abdominal region. The high lung pressures exert a high pressure downward on the diaphragm and the abdominal wall; this pressure might give a feeling similar to that of having a belt squeezing the abdominal content. Glottal adduction is more forceful than in operatic singing, and the voice source seems characterised by a relatively long closed phase and a large number of high overtones. Belting is sometimes described as the use of loud chest

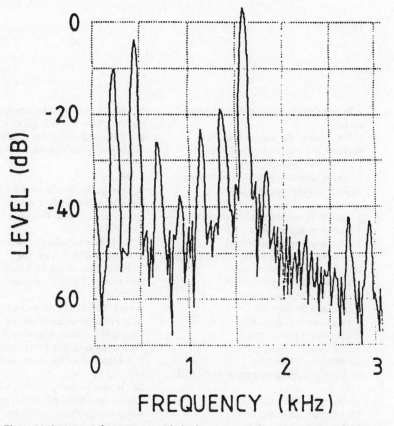

Figure 22 Spectrum of a tone sung with the formants tuned so as to enhance an individual spectrum partial, which is heard as a clear pitch in addition to the fundamental.

register phonation, also at pitches that would be produced in the middle register in classical singing. When used habitually it is considered detrimental to voice function, although some singing teachers have developed varieties of belting which can be used without harmful effects.

Overtone singing was first mentioned by García in the nineteenth century.[4] In our time it can be found in several Asian cultures. Here the fundamental frequency is kept constant while the frequencies of the second and third formants are tuned to enhance specific spectrum partials, creating melodic patterns where the pitches correspond to those of the particular (and strongly enhanced) overtones in the spectrum. Figure 22 offers an example, where the 7th partial is so enhanced that it is actually the strongest in the entire spectrum.

Notes

1 Introduction: singing at the turn of the century

1 For example, the volume *Voice*, ed K. Faulkner, in the series of Yehudi Menuhin Music Guides (London, 1983).

2 See my *Vocal Authority: Singing Style and Ideology* (Cambridge, 1998), ch. 2.

2 'Songlines': vocal traditions in world music

1 Interview, 26 July 1989.

2 Interview, 11 September 1997.

3 John Schaefer, *New Sounds: The Virgin Guide to New Music* (London, 1990).

4 Interview, 12 November 1993.

5 Interview, 13 March 1991.

6 Interview, 28 July 1993.

7 Interview, 30 August 1996.

8 Interview, 1 March 1995.

9 Interview, 13 February 1987.

10 Interview, 2 May 1995.

11 Correspondence with the author, 23 July 1997.

12 Interview, 6 February 1997.

13 Interview, 18 March 1993.

14 Interview, 19 June 1990.

15 Interview, 14 December 1989.

16 Interview, 12 April 1990.

17 Interview, 17 July 1989.

18 Interview, 17 February 1998.

19 To begin to appreciate the depth and subtleties of the concept of singing along a songline, you can't do any better than the remarkable book by the late Bruce Chatwin, *Songlines* (London, 1988).

20 Interview, 3 June 1991.

(Note: All interview material was broadcast and copyright by WNYC Radio in New York and is used here by permission.)

3 Rock singing

1 J. Savage, *Time Travel: Pop, Media and Sexuality, 1977–96* (London, 1996), pp. 332–3.

2 I am defining 'rock' here as the whole body of 'pop music' which stems stylistically from rock 'n' roll. This is unsatisfactory – but less so than attempting to separate out a more limited pop genre called 'rock' and policing its (inevitably fuzzy) boundaries.

3 Quoted in S. Chapple and R. Garofalo, *Rock 'n' Roll is Here to Pay: The History and Politics of the Music Industry* (Chicago, 1977), p. 46.

4 S. Frith, *Music for Pleasure: Essays in the Sociology of Pop* (Cambridge, 1988), pp. 121, 120.

5 *Ibid.*, p. 119.

6 A particularly good source is S. A. Floyd Jnr, *The Power of Black Music: Interpreting its History from Africa to the United States* (New York, 1995).

7 The Presley recordings mentioned below can be found on Elvis Presley, *The Complete Sun Sessions*, RCA PD 86414, and Elvis Presley, *The All Time Greatest Hits*, RCA PD 90100.

8 See R. Middleton, 'All Shook Up? Innovation and Continuity in Elvis Presley's Vocal Style', in *Elvis: Images and Fancies*, ed. J. Tharpe (Jackson, MS, 1979), pp. 151–61.

9 G. Marcus, *Mystery Train* (London, 1977), p. 185.

10 On gender codings of timbre in rock singing, see J. Shepherd, 'Music and Male Hegemony', in *Music and Society: The Politics of Composition, Performance and Reception*, ed. R. Leppert and S. McClary (Cambridge, 1987), pp. 151–72. The Joplin recordings mentioned below can all be found on Janis Joplin, *Anthology*, Columbia 467405 9 (1980) (original issues: 1968–71).

11 E. Willis, 'Janis Joplin', in *The Rolling Stone Illustrated History of Rock & Roll*, ed. J. Miller (London, 1981), p. 275.

12 *Ibid.*, p. 277.

13 G. Marcus, 'Anarchy in the U.K.', in *The Rolling Stone Illustrated History of Rock & Roll*, ed. J. Miller (London, 1981), p. 453.

14 All to be found on Sex Pistols, *Kiss This*, Virgin CDV 2702.

15 This is discussed by Dave Laing in *One Chord Wonders: Power and Meaning in Punk Rock* (Milton Keynes, 1985), pp. 63–73.

16 Marcus, 'Anarchy', p. 462.

17 All recordings mentioned can be found on James Brown, *Star Time*, 4 CD set, Polydor 849 108–2 (1991).

18 See, for instance, D. Brackett, 'James Brown's "Superbad" and the Double-Voiced Utterance', in *Interpreting Popular Music* (Cambridge, 1995), pp. 108–56.

19 Except where indicated, all songs

mentioned are contained on Madonna, *The Immaculate Collection*, Sire 7599–26440-2 (1990).

20 *Music from the Motion Picture 'Evita'*, Warner Brothers 9362-46432-2 (1996).

21 Of course, video plays a big part as well. Music video performance, a key constituent of 1980s pop/rock, was nowhere more important than for Madonna.

22 For an interesting analysis of 'Live to Tell' from this perspective, see S. McClary, 'Living to Tell: Madonna's Resurrection of the Fleshly', in her *Feminine Endings: Music, Gender and Sexuality* (Minneapolis, MN, 1991), pp. 148–66.

23 See Laing, *One Chord Wonders*, pp. 63–73.

24 S. Cubitt, '"Maybelline": Meaning and the Listening Subject', *Popular Music*, 4 (1984), pp. 207–24.

25 R. Barthes, 'The Grain of the Voice', in *Image–Music–Text*, trans. S. Heath (London, 1977), pp. 179–89, here p. 182.

26 S. Frith, *Performing Rites: On the Value of Popular Music* (Oxford, 1996), pp. 210–12.

4 The evolving language of rap

1 Paul Winley interview with the present author, February 1984.

2 Bobby Robinson interview with the present author, February 1984.

3 Grandmaster Flash interview with the present author, January 1984.

4 Dennis Wepman, Ronald Newman, Murray B. Binderman, *The Life: The Love and Folk Poetry of the Black Hustler* (Los Angeles, 1976), p. 5.

5 Irene Jackson, *Afro-American Religious Music* (Westport, CT, 1979).

6 Roger D. Abrahams, *Deep Down in the Jungle* (New York, 1970), p. 129.

7 T. Cripps, *Black Film as Genre* (Bloomington, IN, and London, 1979), p. 128.

8 Quoted in Edwin Pouncey, 'The Man Who Sold the Underworld', *The Wire*, 161 (July 1997), p. 28.

9 Abrahams, *Deep Down in the Jungle*, pp. 44–5.

10 *Ibid.*, p. 3.

11 R. Finnegan, *Oral Literature in Africa* (Oxford, 1970).

12 Grandmaster Flash interview with the present author, January 1984.

13 Danny Glover and Grandmaster Flash interview with the present author, December 1984.

14 Interview with the present author, December 1984.

15 J. Baugh, *Black Street Speech: Its History, Structure and Survival* (Austin, TX, 1983), p. 1.

16 See 'Abroad Rap Speaks Up', *New York Times* (23rd August 1992).

5 Jazz singing: the first hundred years

1 Stacey Kent, quoted in Bruce Crowther and Mike Penfold, *Jazz Singing: The Singers and Their Styles* (London, 1997) p. 14. Crowther and Penfold also quote many other singers who struggle to define their art. The formative elements that musicologists customarily associate with the birth of jazz traditionally include pre-Columban African chants, Afro-American work songs, white American presbyterian choirs, nineteenth-century European drawing room music and vaudeville, among others.

2 Quoted in *Hear Me Talkin' to Ya: The Story of Jazz by the Men Who Made It*, ed. Nat Hentoff and Nat Shapiro (New York, 1966), p. 408. The same chapter also features various other jazz musicians attempting to answer the same question.

3 From *Bring on the Night* (A&M Films, 1984).

4 Gunther Schuller's *History of Jazz*, published in two parts (so far) is among the most comprehensive: *Early Jazz: Its Roots and Musical Development* (New York, 1968) and *The Swing Era: The Development of Jazz 1930–1945* (Oxford and New York, 1991).

5 See Schuller *The Swing Era*, pp. 223–5, and Appendix II, pp. 855–9, for a graphic account of 'swing'.

6 See Will Friedwald, *Jazz Singing: America's Greatest Voices from Bessie Smith to Bebop and Beyond* (London, 1991), p. 28n for various alternative origins of scat.

7 For the scatting of Leo Watson and Ella Fitzgerald see Friedwald, *Jazz Singing*, pp. 140–4; for scat and wordless singing in general see Crowther and Pinfold, *Jazz Singing*, pp. 128–35.

8 For the Armstrong–Crosby relationship see Friedwald, *Jazz Singing*, pp. 23–49.

9 Holiday's first recording coincided with Smith's last and was witnessed by Waters, in a curious historical conjunction in November 1933 (Crowther and Pinfold, *Jazz Singing*, p. 71).

10 *Hear Me Talkin' to Ya*, p. 405.

6 Stage and screen entertainers in the twentieth century

1 H. Pleasants, *The Great American Popular Singers* (New York, 1974).

2 C. Osborne, 'The Broadway Voice: Just Singin' in the Pain', *High Fidelity* (January–February 1979), pp. 57–65 and 53–6.

3 R. Philip, *Early Recordings and Musical Style:*

Changing Tastes in Instrumental Performance, 1900–1950 (Cambridge, 1992).

4 See the Discography at the end of this chapter for full details of abbreviated references to compilation and original cast recordings. UB/II/16, for instance, indicates the CD *Ultimate Broadway*, volume II, track 16.

5 Osborne, 'The Broadway Voice', p. 61.

6 *Ibid.*

7 'Plagal' describes a basic dominant-to-dominant (soh-to-soh) melodic range, 'authentic' a tonic-to-tonic (doh-to-doh) one.

8 D. van Leer, 'Putting It Together: Sondheim and the Broadway Musical', *Raritan*, 7 (1987), p. 121.

9 Mordden, *Make Believe: The Broadway Musical in the 1920s* (New York and Oxford, 1997), p. 60.

10 The caret (ˆ) above a figure indicates the scale degree that figure represents. $\hat{1}$ is the tonic, $\hat{3}$ the mediant, and so on.

11 H. Pleasants, 'Crosby, Bing (Harry Lillis)', *The New Grove*, V: 60.

12 J. Potter, *Vocal Authority: Singing Style and Ideology* (Cambridge, 1998), pp. 110–12.

13 R. Rastall, 'Vocal Range and Tessitura in Music from York Play 45', *Music Analysis*, 3 (1984), p. 190.

14 G. Block, 'The Broadway Canon from "Show Boat" to "West Side Story" and the European Operatic Ideal', *Journal of Musicology*, 11 (1993), pp. 525–44.

15 H. Prince, *Contradictions: Notes on 26 Years in the Theatre* (New York, 1974), p. 165.

16 P. O'Connor, 'Music for the Stage', in *Music in Britain: The Twentieth Century*, ed. Stephen Banfield (Oxford, 1995), p. 119.

17 V. Ellis, *I'm on a See-Saw* (London, 1953; repr. Bath, 1974), pp. 233–4; see also pp. 224–5.

18 Prince, *Contradictions*, p. 165.

19 Osborne, 'The Broadway Voice', p. 62.

7 Song into theatre: the beginnings of opera

1 To his father Leopold Mozart, 5 April 1778, in *The Letters of Mozart and his Family*, ed. and trans. Emily Anderson, 3rd edn (London, 1985), p. 522.

2 C. Burney, *The Present State of Music in France and Italy* (London, 1771), pp. 16–17, 25–7, 31–2, 50.

3 L. Bianconi and T. Walker, 'Dalla *Finta Pazza* alla *Veremonda*: storie di Febiarmonici', *Rivista Italiana di Musicologia*, 10 (1975), pp. 379–454; L. Bianconi, *Music in the Seventeenth Century* (Cambridge, 1987); E. Rosand, *Opera in Seventeenth-Century Venice: The Creation of a Genre* (Berkeley, 1991).

4 N. Pirrotta, *Music and Theatre from Poliziano to Monteverdi* (Cambridge, 1982), and 'Commedia dell'arte and Opera', in *Music and Culture in Italy from the Middle Ages to the Baroque* (Cambridge, MA, 1984), pp. 343–60; J. R. Anthony, *French Baroque Music from Beaujoyeulx to Rameau* (London, 1973).

5 Bianconi, *Music in the Seventeenth Century*, pp. 165–7.

6 B. de Bacilly, *Remarques curieuses sur l'art de bien chanter* (1679; repr. Geneva, 1971). The work was conceived and in part written in the 1660s. Cf. L'Ecuyer, *Principes de l'art du chant* (Paris, 1769; repr. Geneva, 1972), and Raparlier, *Principes de musique: Les agréments du chant* (Lille, 1772; repr. Geneva, 1972).

7 Bacilly, *L'art de bien chanter*, pp. 92–9, 116.

8 J.-A. Bérard, *L'art du chant* (Paris, 1755; repr. Geneva, 1972), p. 50.

9 J.-B. de Laborde, *Essai sur la musique ancienne et moderne*, 4 vols. (Paris, 1780), I: 349, III: 496.

10 E. Hehr, 'How the French Viewed the Differences Between French and Italian Singing Styles of the Eighteenth Century', *International Review of the Aesthetics and Sociology of Music*, 16 (1985), pp. 73–85; see also M. Cyr, 'Eighteenth-Century French and Italian Singing: Rameau's Writing for the Voice', *Music & Letters*, 61 (1980), pp. 318–37.

11 Burney, *Present State of Music*, p. 18.

12 Bérard, *L'art du chant*, p. 35.

13 W. Weber, 'La musique ancienne in the waning of the ancien régime', *Journal of Modern History*, 56 (1994), pp. 58–88; R. M. Isherwood, *Music in the Service of the King* (Ithaca, NY, 1973).

14 J. A. Hiller, *Anweisung zum musikalisch-zierlichen Gesange* (Leipzig, 1780; repr. Leipzig, 1976), p. xiii; Burney, *Present State of Music*, p. 71.

15 R. Donington, review of G. Moens-Haenens, *Das Vibrato in der Musik des Barock* (Graz, 1988), in *Early Music*, 16 (1988), pp. 571–3.

16 P. F. Tosi, *Opinioni de' cantori antichi e moderni* (Bologna, 1723), pp. 49–56; reprinted in A. Della Corte, *Canto e bel canto* (Turin, 1933); Eng. trans. by J. E. Galliard as *Observations on the Florid Song* (London, 1742; facs. repr. London, 1967).

17 Bacilly, *L'art de bien chanter*, pp. 206, 224.

18 F. Chrysander, 'Ludovico Zacconi as Lehrer des Kunstgesanges', *Vierteljahrsschrift für Musikwissenschaft*, 7 (1891), pp. 337–96; 9 (1893), pp. 249–310; H. Goldschmidt, *Die italienische Gesangsmethode des XVII. Jahrhunderts und ihre Bedeutung für die Gegenwart* (Breslau, 1890), pp. 28–33.

19 V. Manfredini, *Regole armoniche, o sieno Precetti ragionevoli per apprendere la musica* (Venice, 1775), p. 5n.; P. Petrobelli, 'Un cantante fischiato e le appoggiature di mezza battuta:

cronaca teatrale e prassi esecutiva alla metà del '700', in *Studies in Renaissance and Baroque Music in Honor of Arthur Mendel*, ed. R. L. Marshall (Kassel, 1974), pp. 363–76.

20 Bianconi, *Music in the Seventeenth Century*, pp. 6–7, 15–20.

21 Luzzasco Luzzaschi, *Concerto delle dame di Ferrara*, Harmonia Mundi France recording, HMA 1901136, 1985. See A. Newcomb, *The Madrigal at Ferrara 1579–1597*, 2 vols. (Princeton, 1980), I: 7, 21–2, 59–62, 90–2; I. Fenlon, *Music and Patronage in Sixteenth-Century Mantua*, 2 vols. (Cambridge, 1980), I: 127–8, 130–3.

22 Among the many recordings of Monteverdi's madrigals, those few with Italian singers enjoy a distinct advantage, in particular those by the Concerto Italiano under Rinaldo Alessandrini (sixth book, Arcana, A66 942066, 1992; fourth book, Opus 111, HM90 OPS 30–81, 1993; eighth book, Opus 111, HM90 OPS 30–187, 1997). A now old-fashioned LP of *Il combattimento di Tancredi e Clorinda* with mainly Italian singers (Turnabout, TV 34018S, no date) has the virtue of immediate dramatic communication.

23 J. Rosselli, 'The Castrati as a Professional Group and a Social Phenomenon, 1550–1850', *Acta Musicologica*, 60 (1988), pp. 143–79.

24 M. Benoit, *Versailles et les musiciens du Roi 1661–1733* (Paris, 1971), pp. 269–70, 324–9, 362; L. Sawkins, 'For and Against the Order of Nature: Who Sang the Soprano?', *Early Music*, 15 (1987), pp. 315–24.

25 L. Sawkins, 'Haute-contre', *The New Grove Dictionary of Opera* (London, 1992).

26 A. Zorzi, *Cortigiana veneziana: Veronica Franco e i suoi poeti* (Milan, 1986); A. Newcomb, 'Courtesans, Muses, or Musicians?' and E. Rosand, 'The Voice of Barbara Strozzi', in *Women Making Music*, ed. J. Bowers and J. Tick (Urbana, IL, 1986), pp. 90–115 and 168–90; E. Rosand, 'Barbara Strozzi, virtuosissima cantatrice: The Composer's Voice', *Journal of the American Musicological Society*, 31 (1978), pp. 241–81.

27 C. Sartori, 'La prima diva della lirica italiana: Anna Renzi', *Nuova Rivista Musicale Italiana*, 2 (1968), pp. 430–52.

28 The leading teacher Bartolomeo Nucci wrote of his nephew and pupil Biagio that he could sing all Masses and Vespers provided he already knew the psalms in use, 'but in a full motet, as he is scarcely able to read handwriting, he will run into trouble unless he has studied the words beforehand' [to Padre G. B. Martini], 20 May 1774, Bologna, Civico Museo Bibliografico Musicale, I.3.165.

29 Case *of Antonio Palella v. Flavia Muzzillo*, Rosselli, *Singers of Italian Opera: The History of*

a Profession (Cambridge, 1992), p. 98 (where – I am grateful to Sergio Durante for having pointed out – I misunderstood the term 'modi cantabili', used of the accomplishments offered by the second teacher).

30 See E. J. Dent, *The Rise of Romantic Opera*, ed. W. Dean (Cambridge, 1976).

31 R. Celletti, *A History of Bel Canto* (Oxford, 1991), ch. 4.

8 Grand opera: nineteenth-century revolution and twentieth-century tradition

1 A. Caswell, 'Mme Cinti-Damoreau and the Embellishment of Italian Opera in Paris: 1820–45', *Journal of the American Musicological Society*, 28 (1975), pp. 459–92.

2 J. Rosselli, *The Life of Bellini* (Cambridge, 1997), p. 129.

3 R. Hahn, *On Singing and Singers*, trans. I. L. Simoneau (London and Portland, OR, 1990), p. 53.

4 E. V. Foreman, 'A Comparison of Selected Italian Vocal Tutors of the Period circa 1550 to 1800', DMA dissertation, University of Illinois (1969), p. 5.

5 Elizabeth Grant of Rothiemurchus, *Memoirs of a Highland Lady*, ed. A. Tod, 2 vols. (Edinburgh, 1988), II: 84–6.

6 Crescentini to Emanuele Imbimbo, 26 Dec. 1826, Milan, Museo Teatrale alla Scala, CA4307. Cf. similar opinions reported in G. Cecchini Pacchierotti, *Ai cultori ed amatori della musica vocale: cenni biografici intorno a Gaspare Pacchierotti* (Padua, 1844), pp. 14–15, and S. Maguire, *Vincenzo Bellini and the Aesthetics of Early Nineteenth-Century Italian Opera* (New York and London, 1989).

7 P. Metastasio, *Tutte le opere*, ed. B. Brunelli, 5 vols. (Milan, 1943–54), IV: 172–3, 179, 195.

8 G. Morelli and E. Surian, 'Come nacque e come morì il patriottismo romano nell'opera veneziana', in *Opera e libretto*, 2 vols. (Florence, 1990), II: 101–35, esp. p. 106n.

9 Adelaide Carpano to Duke Sforza-Cesarini, 28 May 1814, in E. Celani, 'Musica e musicisti in Roma 1750–1850', *Rivista Musicale Italiana*, 18 (1911), pp. 1–63; 20 (1913), pp. 33–88; 22 (1915), pp. 1–56, esp. pt 3, pp. 28–9; R. Celletti, *A History of Bel Canto* (Oxford, 1991), pp. 163–7.

10 [J. E. Cox], *Musical Recollections of the Last Half-Century*, 2 vols. (London, 1872), I: 171–2, II: 84–5. Monteverdi's advice to Alessandro Striggio, 24 July 1627, *The Letters of Claudio Monteverdi*, rev. edn, ed. D. Stevens (Oxford, 1995), p. 346.

11 L. Quicherat, *Alphonse Nourrit*, 3 vols. (Paris, 1867), I: 401–2.

12 Mercadante to Francesco Florimo, 26 Nov. 1838, S. Palermo, ed., *Saverio Mercadante:*

biografia, epistolario (Fasano, 1985), p. 189. The tenor originally engaged, Domenico Reina, was replaced by Alphonse Nourrit, but the lover's part still went to the baritone Paul Barroilhet.

13 All contraltos wanted to become sopranos, an experienced observer reported in 1770, 'women especially, though they should burst [in the attempt]': G. M. Ortes to J. A. Hasse, 22 Dec. 1770, Venice, Civico Museo Correr, Cod. Cicogna 2658 no. 193.

14 W. Ganz, *Memoirs of a Musician* (London, 1913), p. 14.

15 Bellini to Giuditta Pasta, 1 Sept. 1831, F. Lippmann, ed., 'Belliniana', in *Il melodramma italiano dell'Ottocento: Studi e ricerche per Massimo Mila* (Turin, 1977), pp. 281–317, esp. pp. 283–4.

16 Costa to Giuditta Pasta, 10 Oct. 1849, New York, Library of Performing Arts, Pasta Collection; E. Imbimbo, *Observations sur l'enseignement mutuel appliqué à la musique* (Paris, 1821), pp. 35–44; F. Lamperti, *Guida teorico-pratica-elementare per lo studio del canto* (Milan, *c.* 1864), pp. vii–viii; E. Panofka, *Voci e cantanti, Sala Bolognese*, 1984 (1st edn 1866), pp. 77–9, 84–6.

17 J. Gourret, *La technique du chant en France depuis le 17e siècle*, 2nd edn (Paris, 1976), p. 52. On teachers' conservatism, see R. Donington, *The Interpretation of Early Music*, 3rd edn (London, 1974), p. 516.

18 M. García, *Traité complet de l'art du chant*, 3rd edn (Paris and London, 1851); B. Marchesi, *Singer's Pilgrimage* (London, 1926), p. 17; J. -A. Bérard, *L'art du chant* (Paris, 1755; repr. Geneva, 1972), pp. 19, 39–40.

19 E. Eames, *Some Memories and Reflections* (New York, 1927), pp. 50–6; M. Marchesi, *Aus meinem Leben* (Vienna, 1889), inadequately rendered in *Marchesi and Music* (London, 1897).

20 Italo Campanini to Ippolito Canedi, 29 Aug. 1877, Milan, Museo Teatrale alla Scala, Coll. Casati 233.

21 Arimondi to Carlo D'Ormeville, 25 Dec. 1902, Milan, Museo Teatrale alla Scala, Coll. Casati 34.

22 R.- A. Mooser, *Annales de la musique et des musiciens en Russie au XVIII.me siècle*, 3 vols. (Geneva, 1948–51), I: 241; II: 157–8, 176, 186–7.

23 Kaschmann to Carlo D'Ormeville, 4 Aug. 1894, Milan, Museo Teatrale alla Scala, Col. Casati 698. Cf. similar comments in Bernard Shaw's reports from Bayreuth between 1889 and 1894, *Shaw's Music*, ed. D. H. Laurence (London, 1981).

24 I. Kolodin, *The Metropolitan Opera*, rev. edn (New York, 1966), pp. 106–9.

25 A. Scalaberni to G. Marchetti, November 1889, Forlì, Biblioteca Comunale, Autografi Piancastelli *s.v.* Marchetti; J. and A. Bèges, *Mémoire d'un théâtre* (Béziers, 1987), pp. 109–10, 115.

26 Kolodin, *Metropolitan Opera*, pp. 118, 128.

27 *Ibid.*, pp. 92, 98, 135, 207, 217, 246; F. Litvinne, *Ma vie et mon art* (Paris, 1933), p. 38.

28 G. B. Mancini, *Practical Reflections on Figured Singing*, trans. E. Foreman (Champaign, IL, 1967), p. 13. Cf. similar comments in – among many others – the treatises mentioned in note 16.

29 J. B. Steane, *The Grand Tradition: Seventy Years of Singing on Record* (London, 1974), p. 6.

9 European art song

1 *Tag- und Jahreshefte*, February 1801, in A. Einstein, *Schubert* (London, 1951), p. 53.

2 Letter to Friedrich Wieck, November 1829, in H. Gal, *The Musician's World: Letters of the Great Composers* (London, 1965), p. 130.

3 P. J. Pirie, *The English Musical Renaissance* (London, 1979), p. 99.

4 Von Uffenbach, quoted in E. D. Mackerness, *A Social History of English Music* (London, 1964), p. 88.

5 Mackerness, *A Social History*, p. 110.

6 Letter to Albert Grzymala, October 1848, quoted in Gal, *The Musician's World*, p. 150.

7 S. Banfield, *Sensibility and English Song* (Cambridge, 1985), p. 12.

8 *Musik und Gesellschaft*, April 1930, quoted in Ian Kemp, 'Hindemith' *The New Grove Dictionary of Music and Musicians*, 20 vols. (London, 1980), VIII: 579.

9 See Jane Manning's *New Vocal Repertory: An Introduction* (Oxford, 1994), and *New Vocal Repertory*, vol. 2 (Oxford, 1998) for lists of recent songs graded by technical difficulty.

10 English cathedral choirs in the twentieth century

1 Peter Phillips, 'The Golden Age Regained', *Early Music*, 8/1 (January 1980), p. 4.

2 George Dyson, 'Of Organs and Organists', *The Musical Times*, 93 (1952), p. 492; the tone quality the author has in mind is exemplified perhaps on the opening of side 1 of ARGO RG 190/ZRG 5190 (12″ 33⅓ rpm disc, mono/stereo, issued 1959).

3 Christopher Page, 'The English *a cappella* Renaissance', *Early Music*, 21/3 (August 1993), pp. 461, 463.

4 *King's College Chapel: Services* (Cambridge, 1989), p. 3.

5 C. V. Stanford, *Pages from an Unwritten Diary* (London, 1914), p. 307.

6 Donald Tovey and Geoffrey Parratt, *Walter*

Parratt: Master of the Music (London, 1941), pp. 144–5.

7 See Frederic Hodgson, *Choirs and Cloisters – Sixty Years of Music in Church, College, Cathedral and Chapels Royal* (London, 1988), pp. 68–71.

8 S. S. Wesley, *A Few Words on Cathedral Music* (London and Leeds, 1849), p. 72.

9 *The Musical Times*, 41 (1900), p. 464.

10 J. Varley Roberts, *A Treatise on a Practical Method of Training Choristers* (London, 1898), p. 4.

11 *Ibid.*, p. 5.

12 Charles H. Moody, *The Choir-Boy in the Making* (London, 1922; repr. 1939), pp. 13, 14.

13 H. F. Andrews, *Westminster Retrospect: A Memoir of Sir Richard Terry* (London, 1948), pp. 10–11.

14 George Dyson, *The Progress of Music* (London, 1932), p. 3.

15 Moody, *The Choir-Boy in the Making*, p. 7.

16 Walter S. Vale, *The Training of Boys' Voices* (London, 1932), pp. 73–4.

17 Roberts, *A Treatise*, p. 12.

18 S. J. A. Evans, 'A Victorian Choirmaster – Dr. A. H. Mann', *Church Music Society Annual Report* (1959), p. 11.

19 R. R. Terry, 'The Essential Fitness of the Old Music', *Catholic Church Music* (London, 1907), p. 47.

20 Sir John Stainer, *The Musical Times* (August 1888), quoted in Peter Charlton, *John Stainer and the Musical Life of Victorian Britain* (Newton Abbot, 1984), pp. 83–4.

21 R. R. Terry, 'Why is Church Music so Bad?', *A Forgotten Psalter and Other Essays* (London, 1929), p. 105.

22 Harvey Grace, *The Musical Times*, 63 (1922), p. 419; a glimpse of the style on which Grace is commenting may perhaps be had from a recording of the Cappella Sistina singing Palestrina's *Sicut cervus* made in June 1931, HMV DB 1570 (12″ 78 rpm electrical disc; side 1: *matrix no:* 2F 501ᴵᴵΔ).

23 Jane Austen, *Emma*, pp. 99–100.

24 Vale, *The Training of Boys' Voices*, p. 72.

25 Hodgson, *Choirs and Cloisters*, pp. 68–71.

26 Tovey and Parratt, *Walter Parratt*, p. 149.

27 *Ibid.*, p. 142.

28 Edward Elgar, *A Future for English Music and Other Lectures*, ed. Percy M. Young (London, 1968), p. 49.

29 Sir Henry Hadow quoted in Charles L.Graves, *Hubert Parry: His Life and Works* (London, 1926), II: 165.

30 Tovey and Parratt, *Walter Parratt*, p. 141.

31 W. H. Auden, 'Walter de la Mare', in *Forewords and Afterwords* (London, 1973), p. 393.

32 *Ibid.*, p. 394.

33 David Fallows, *Gramophone*, 56/672 (May 1979), p. 1926.

34 E. H. Fellowes, *Memoirs of an Amateur Musician* (London, 1946), p. 94.

35 'Manliness in Music', *The Musical Times*, 30 (1889), p. 460.

36 Sir William Harris, in his Presidential Address to the Royal College of Organists in July 1947, quoted in Hodgson, *Choirs and Cloisters*, p. 69.

37 Sir David Willcocks, 'The Choir of King's College, Cambridge', BBC Transcription Service disc 134648 (issued 1974).

38 Columbia 4211 (10′ 80 rpm electrical disc; side 1: *matrix no:* A 4564, issued 1927).

39 Moody, *The Choir-Boy in the Making*, pp. 27–8.

40 Walford Davies, 'Both Sides of the Microphone', *BBC Handbook 1929* (London, 1929), pp. 130–1.

41 Tovey and Parratt, *Walter Parratt*, p. 67.

42 George Malcolm, 'Boys' Voices', *Fifteenth Aldeburgh Festival Programme-Book* (Aldeburgh, 1962), p. 14; the article was reprinted in *Tribute to Benjamin Britten on his Fiftieth Birthday*, ed. Anthony Gishford (London, 1963), pp. 100–3, and in *English Church Music* (1967), pp. 24–7.

43 'Boys' Voices', p. 15.

44 Few recordings of the choir under Malcolm were made; the two most characteristic are: Victoria: extracts from the *Officium Hebdomadae Sanctae*, ARGO RG 149/ZRG 5149 (12″ 33⅓ rpm mono/stereo disc, issued 1960); Britten: *Missa brevis* Op. 63 recorded in the cathedral on 22 July 1959, DECCA CEP 654 [7″ 45 rpm mono disc].

45 A complete list of the choir's commercial recordings under Guest is given in George H. Guest, *A Guest at Cambridge* (Orleans, MA, 1994), pp. 86–107.

46 In an interview with Bernard Keefe, BBC Radio 3, 12 December 1991, National Sound Archive Tape B8899.

47 Victoria: *O Domine Jesu* in *The History of Music in Sound*, vol. IV, side 6: HMV HMS 34 (12″ 78 rpm electrical disc; side 2: *matrix no*: 2KA 1559–2).

48 DECCA LW 5070 [10″ 33⅓ rpm mono disc].

49 Peter Phillips, 'The Golden Age Regained, 2' *Early Music*, 8/1 (January 1980), p. 181.

50 Sir Sydney Nicholson, 'Of Women's *versus* Boys' Voices', *Cathedral Music Today and Tomorrow* (The report of a sub-committee appointed by the Cathedral Organists' Association and the Church Music Society) (London, 1941), p. 46.

11 Sacred choral music in the United States: an overview

1 *The American Musical Miscellany* (1798, repr. with a new introduction by H. Wiley Hitchcock, New York, 1972), pp. 207–11.

2 *The Complete Works of William Billings*, ed. Karl Kroeger, 4 vols. (The American Musicological Society and The Colonial Society of Massachusetts, Virginia, 1981), I: 32.

3 Billings, *The Continental Harmony*, ed. Hans Nathan (Cambridge, MA, 1961), pp. 35–47.

4 Jeoffry Chanticleer, 'To Old Master Janus', *The New England Courant* (17–24 February 1724), quoted in Charles Hamm, *Music in the New World* (New York, 1983), p. 33.

5 For more information on the 'old way' and its survival into the present, see S. Wicks, 'A Belated Salute to the Old Way of Singing on its (ca) 345th birthday', *Popular Music*, 8/1 (January 1989), pp. 59–96.

6 The two passages from the diary of James Meacham are quoted in Dena J. Epstein, *Sinful Tunes and Spirituals: Black Folk Music to the Civil War* (Urbana, IL, 1977), p. 110.

7 *The Sacred Harp*, ed. Hugh McGrae *et al.* (n.p.: Sacred Harp Publishing Company, Inc., 1991).

13 Ensemble singing

1 For a brief introduction to the relationship between singing and speech, see my 'Reconstructing Lost Voices' in *Companion to Medieval and Renaissance Music*, ed. Tess Knighton and David Fallows (London and New York, 1992; repr. Oxford, 1998), pp. 311–16.

2 I am indebted to my Hilliard Ensemble colleague Rogers Covey-Crump for this summary of basic tuning principles. For further (and quite readable) information on the subject, I can recommend his articles in the booklets accompanying the first four *Hilliard Live* CDs, and his 'Pythagoras at the Forge: Tuning in Early Music', in *Companion to Medieval and Renaissance Music*, ed. Tess Knighton and David Fallows (London and New York, 1992; repr. Oxford, 1998), pp. 317–26.

3 In my *Vocal Authority: Singing Style and Ideology* (Cambridge, 1998), pp. 178–82, I analyse (from the performers' point of view) a notional performance of an Agnus Dei by Antoine Brumel.

14 The voice in the Middle Ages

1 'Sed inter caetera instrumenta musicalia instrumentum vocis humane est dignissimum, eo quod profert et sonum et verba, cum caetera de sono tantum serviant, non de voce, et verbis'. *Summa musice* 4, ed. and trans. Christopher Page, *Summa musice: A Thirteenth-Century Manual for Singers* (Cambridge, 1991), pp. 62–3 and 152.

2 John Potter, 'Reconstructing Lost Voices', in *Companion to Medieval and Renaissance Music*, ed. Tess Knighton and David Fallows (London and New York, 1992; repr. Oxford, 1998), pp. 311–16. See Christopher Page, *Voices and Instruments of the Middle Ages: Instrumental Practice and Songs in France, 1100–1300* (London, 1987); *idem*, 'Machaut's "Pupil" Deschamps on the Performance of Music: Voices or Instruments in the 14th-Century Chanson', *Early Music*, 5 (1977), pp. 484–91.

3 Christopher Page, 'A Treatise on Musicians from ?*c* 1400: The *Tractatulus de differentiis et gradibus cantorum* by Arnulf of St Ghislain', *Journal of the Royal Musical Association*, 117 (1992), pp. 1–21, especially pp. 16 and 20.

4 A curious passage in the *Scientia artis musice* of Hélie Salomon seems to offer a 'singing lesson' of exercises on alternative grouping and separation of notes ('Rubrica de doctrina cantandi'); Martin Gerbert, ed., *Scriptores ecclesiastici de musica sacra potissimum*, 3 vols. (St Blaise, 1784), III:24–6 (hereafter GS). The question of medieval instruction in singing has been addressed in two recent studies: Michael Walter, '*Sunt preterea multa quae conferri magis quam scribi oportet*: Zur Materialität der Kommunikation im mittelalterlichen Gesangsunterricht', in *Schule und Schüler im Mittelalter. Beiträge zur europäischen Bildungsgeschichte des 9. bis 15. Jahrhunderts*, ed. Martin Kintzinger, Sönke Lorenz and Michael Walter, Beihefte zum Archiv für Kulturgeschichte 42 (Cologne, 1996), pp. 111–43; and Pia Ernstbrunner, 'Fragmente des Wissens um die menschliche Stimme: Bausteine zu einer Gesangskunst und Gesangspädagogik des Mittelalters', in *Mittelalterliche Musiktheorie in Zentraleuropa*, ed. Walter Pass and Alexander Rausch, Musica Mediaevalis Europae Occidentalis 4 (Tutzing, 1998), pp. 21–50. Timothy McGee, *The Sound of Medieval Song: Ornamentation and Vocal Style According to the Treatises* (Oxford, 1998) proposes radically new theories about the use of the voice in medieval music, based on his conviction that improvised ornamentation was ubiquitous in the Middle Ages. He does not cite some of the treatises on which I have relied and his argumentation links notational and literary evidence from widely scattered times and regions.

5 Arnulf of St Ghislain has unreserved praise for the singer whom 'nature scilicet et artis beata felicitas decorat' (the blessed felicity of art and nature adorns); Page, ed., 'A Treatise on Musicians', pp. 16 and 20.

6 'Suaves voces sunt subtiles et spissae, clarae atque acutae. Perspicuae voces sunt, quae longius protrahuntur, ita ut omnem inpleant continuo locum, sicut clangor tubarum. Subtiles voces sunt, quibus non est spiritus, qualis est infantium, vel mulierum, vel aegrotantium, sicut in nervis. Quae enim subtilissimae cordae sunt, subtiles ac tenues sonos emittunt. Pingues sunt voces quando spiritus multus simul egreditur, sicut virorum. Acuta vox tenuis, alta, sicut in cordis videmus. Dura vox est, quae violenter emittit sonos, sicut tonitruum, sicut incudis sonos, quotiens in durum malleus percutitur ferrum. Aspera vox est rauca, et quae dispergitur per minutos et indissimiles pulsus. Caeca vox est, quae, mox emissa fuerit, conticescit, atque suffocata nequaquam longius producitur, sicut est in fictilibus. Vinola est vox mollis atque flexibilis. Et vinnola dicta a vinno, hoc est cincinno molliter flexo. Perfecta autem vox est alta, suavis et clara: alta, ut in sublime sufficiat; clara, ut aures adinpleat; suavis, ut animos audientium blandiat. Si ex his aliquid defuerit, vox perfecta non est.' *Isidori Hispalensis episcopi Etymologiarum sive Originum libri xx*, III.xx, ed. W. M. Lindsay (Oxford, 1911), lines 11–14.

7 Obviously, Isidore experienced none of the problems that tortured Augustine two centuries before, lest the pleasure taken in a 'suavis et artificiosa vox' prove a hindrance to genuine devotion (*Confessions*, 10.33).

8 'Vox eius non aspera, vel rauca, vel dissonans, sed canora erit, suavis, liquida atque acuta, habens sonum et melodiam sanctae religioni congruentem, non quae tragica exclamat arte, sed quae christianam simplicitatem et in ipsa modulatione demonstret.' Isidore, *De eccl. off.* ('De psalmista'), 2.12 (*Patrologia Latina* 83: 792).

9 The eighth-century rule for canons by Chrodegang of Metz requires that 'a singer, as the holy Fathers tell us, should be outstanding and eminent in both voice and artistry, so that the pleasures of sweetness might rouse the souls of the listeners ('Cantorem autem, sicut traditum est a sanctis patribus, et voce et arte praeclarum illustremque esse oportet, ita ut oblectamenta dulcedinis animas incitent audientium'), *Regula canonicorum* 50 (*Patrologia Latina* 89: 1079). I have used the edition published in A. S. Napier, ed., *The Old English Version of the Enlarged Rule of Chrodegang Together with the Latin Original*, Early English Text Society 150 (London, 1916), p. 56. The text is dependent on Isidore's 'De psalmista' (see previous note).

10 F. Alberto Gallo has published reproductions of two leaves from an illustrated

Latin translation of the Arabic medical treatise known as the *Tacuinum sanitatis*. One shows three instrumentalists (portative organ, vielle, shawm), the other two instrumentalists (vielle, portative organ) and a singer. In both cases the captions speak of singing sweetly and without hurrying; *Music in the Castle: Troubadours, Books, and Orators in Italian Courts of the Thirteenth, Fourteenth, and Fifteenth Centuries*, trans. Anna Herklotz (Chicago, 1995), figs. 2 and 5.

11 As quoted in Page, *Voices and Instruments*, p. 29 (emphasis added); cf. the description of two fiddlers singing 'a haute voix mout cler' in the thirteenth-century romance *Gille de Chym* (*ibid.*, p. 30).

12 As quoted in Page, *Voices and Instruments*, p. 92.

13 Ancient methods of vocal culture were described by the Roman author Quintilian and others; see Franz Müller-Häuser, *Vox Humana: ein Beitrag zur Untersuchung der Stimmästhetik des Mittelalters* (Regensburg, 1963), pp. 45–67.

14 'Et omnes Franciae cantores didicerunt notam Romanam, quam nunc vocant notam Franciscam, excepto quod tremulas vel vinnolas sive collisibiles vel secabiles voces in cantu non poterant perfecte exprimere Franci, naturali voce barbarica frangentes in gutture voces pocius quam exprimentes.' *Annales Lauressenses* [i.e., of Lorsch], *Monumenta Germaniae Historica* I: 170 and IV: 117.

15 For a valuable survey of chant notation see David Hiley, *Western Plainchant: A Handbook* (Oxford, 1993), pp. 340–61 and 373–85.

16 'Sed principaliter factor vocis est epiglotus'. *Tractatus de musica*, ed. Edmond de Coussemaker, *Scriptorum de musica medii aevi nova series*, 4 vols. (Paris, 1864–76), I: 253 (hereafter CS).

17 'Non naturaliter sed vulgariter loquendo, quedam voces sint pectoris, quedam gutturis, quedam vero sint ipsius capitis. Voces dicimus pectoris que formant notas in pectore, gutturis que in gutture, capitis autem que formant notas in capite. Voces pectoris valent in gravibus, gutturis in acutis, capitis autem in superacutis. Nam communiter voces grosse et basse sunt pectoris, voces subtiles et altissime sunt capitis, voces vero inter has medie sunt ipsius gutturis. Nulla igitur ex his alteri iungatur in cantu, sed vox pectoris pectorali, gutturis gutturali, capitis autem capitali'. *Tractatus de musica* 25, ed. Simon Cserba (Regensburg, 1935), p. 188. Cf. John of Afflighem: 'Naturale autem instrumentum humanum dicimus illas gutturis cavitates, quas arterias vocamus; ipse enim naturaliter apte sunt recipere aerem et reddere, unde sonus naturaliter procreatur' ('The

natural human means [for making musical sound] I call those hollow places in the throat that we name the windpipes; they are naturally suited to take in or give forth air, so that a natural sound is created'). GS II: 234; *Hucbald, Guido, and John on Music: Three Medieval Treatises*, trans. W. Babb (New Haven, 1978), p. 106. Jerome quotes this passage in ch. 9 of his *Tractatus*. Cf. also John of Garland, *Introductio musice* (CS I: 158); Marchetto of Padua, *Lucidarium musice plane* 14, ed. Jan Herlinger (Chicago, 1985), pp. 540–1.

18 'Nec nimis basse, quod est ululare, nec nimis alte, quod est clamare, sed mediocriter quod est cantare.' Ed. Cserba, p. 188.

19 'Et notandum est quod in unaquaque humana voce, quantumcumque ascendere possit et descendere, vel quantumcunque ascensus et descensus penuriam patiatur, hec voces, graves, acute, et superacute, necessario distinguuntur.' *Lucidarium*, ed. Herlinger, p. 542.

20 'Quilibet discrete et bene cantare volens debet sua voce uti trivarie, hoc modo silicet: grossius sive tubalius in gravibus, id est inferioribus notis, et medio modo in mediis, et subtilius in acutis, id est altioribus notis.' Conrad von Zabern, *De modo bene cantandi* (Mainz, 1474), ed. Karl-Werner Gümpel, *Die Musiktraktate Conrads von Zabern* (Wiesbaden, 1956), p. 132; Joseph Dyer, 'Singing with Proper Refinement from *De modo bene cantandi* (1474) by Conrad von Zabern', *Early Music*, 6 (1978), pp. 207–27, here pp. 216–17.

21 'Quanta indiscretio erit hoc [emulation of the organ's many pipes] velle facere uniformi vocis suae usu, cum tamen sic nullam correspondentiam habeat vox hominis ad tam diversarum cannarum organi sonum trivarium.' *De modo bene cantandi*, ed. Gümpel, p. 277.

22 Though it might seem out of place in an essay on medieval music, I would nevertheless recommend Conrad L. Osborne, 'The Broadway Voice: Just Singin' in the Pain', *High Fidelity Magazine* (January and February 1979), pp. 57–65 and 53–6.

23 K.-J. Sachs, *Mensura fistularum: die Mensurierung der Orgelpfeifen im Mittelalter* (Stuttgart, 1970); Peter Williams and Barbara Owen, *The Organ*, The Grove Musical Instruments Series (New York, 1988), pp. 53–72.

24 'Facturus organa primum habeat lectionem mensurae, qualiter metiri debeant fistulae: graves, acutae, et superacutae.' C. R. Dodwell, ed. and trans., *Theophilus: De diversis artibus* (London, 1961), p. 142; J. G. Hawthorne and C. S. Smith, *On Divers Arts: The Treatise of Theophilus* (Chicago, 1963), p. 158 (English translation only). The generally excellent translation of Dodwell misses the connection with the terminology of the gamut.

25 'Si eam vult esse grossam, foramen [between the languet and the lip of the pipe] fiat latus; si vero graciliorem, fiat strictius' ('If one wishes it to be fuller in tone, the space is made wider; and if more graceful, narrower'). Dodwell, ed., *Theophilus: De diversis artibus*, p. 144. An extraordinary medieval conjunction of organ pipes and wind pipes is the fragment of Gerlandus printed by Gerbert in the second volume of the *Scriptores*. A brief instruction in the measurement of pipes and the making of bells concludes with recipes for vocal potions; GS II: 277–8.

26 Williams and Owen, *The Organ*, pp. 80–2. I would revise my comments at the close of the introduction of 'Singing with Proper Refinement' (p. 213) in light of this information.

27 'Inventores itaque cantus et primi doctores consideraverunt trachiam arteriam, id est organum vocis humanae, secundum triplicem dispositionem triplicem cantum posse proferre.' *Summa musice*, ed. Page, pp. 152 and 64. Cf. also Isidore of Seville: 'Vox est aer spiritu verberatus, unde et verba nuncupata' ('the voice is air that is struck [from "verbero" to beat] by the breath, and for this reason "words" [verba] are thus named'. *Lib. Etym.* III.xx. Though Marchetto of Padua had a very different conception of how the voice was produced, he divided its range into the same three registers: *Lucidarium musice plane* 14, ed. Herlinger, pp. 540–1.

28 Ed. Michael Bernhard, *Clavis Gerberti: Eine Revision von Martin Gerberts Scriptores ecclesiastici de musica sacra potissimum (St. Blasien 1784)*, Bayerische Akademie der Wissenschaften, Veröffentlichungen der Musikhistorischen Kommission 7 (Munich, 1989), pp. 3–8; this is a revised version of the edition in Gerbert's *Scriptores* I: 5–8. A not entirely satisfactory English translation of the *Instituta patrum* was published in the appendix to Alphege Shebbeare, *Choral Recitation of the Divine Office: A Guide to Choir Directors*, The Church Musician's Bookshelf 1 (Toledo, OH, 1954). Several passages found in the *Instituta* were borrowed from a text attributed to St Bernard of Clairvaux; see S. J. P. van Dijk, 'Saint Bernard and the "Instituta patrum" of St. Gall', *Musica Disciplina*, 4 (1950), pp. 99–109.

29 'Psalmodia semper pari voce, equa lance, non nimis protrahatur; sed mediocri voce, non nimis velociter, sed rotunda, virili, viva et succincta voce psallatur.' *Instituta patrum* 7, ed. Bernhard, *Clavis Gerberti*, pp. 5–6. This is a very

different set of values from the ones proposed by McGee, *The Sound of Medieval Song.*

30 'Histrionicas voces, garrulas, alpinas, sive montanas, tonitruantes, vel sibilantes, hinnientes velut vocalis asina, mugientes seu balantes quasi pecora; sive femineas, omnemque vocum falsitatem, iactantiam seu novitatem detestemur, et prohibeamus in choris nostris, quia plus redolent vanitatem et stultitiam quam religionem.' *Instituta patrum* 33, ed. Bernhard, p. 8.

31 Müller-Häuser, *Vox Humana*, p. 96.

32 'Psalmi namque in ecclesia non cursim aut in excelsis atque inordinatis seu intemperatis vocibus ... recitentur, ut ... audientium aures illorum pronuntiatione demulceantur, quoniam quamvis cantilene sonus in aliis officiis excelsa soleat fieri voce, in recitandis tamen psalmis huiuscemodi vitanda est vox.' *Regula canonicorum* 50 (*Patrologia Latina* 89: 1079); ed. Napier, *The Old English Version*, p. 56.

33 *Patrologia Latina* 195: 571; there is a translation in Robert F. Hayburn, *Papal Legislation on Sacred Music, 95 A.D. to 1977 A.D.* (Collegeville, MN, 1979), pp. 19–20.

34 Translated in Hayburn, *Papal Legislation*, pp. 20–1.

35 The New Oxford History of Music, III: *Ars Nova and the Renaissance*, ed. Anselm Hughes and Gerald Abraham (London, 1960), pp. 75–6.

36 'Asserunt Gallici quod Ytalici semper in crebra vocum fractione delirant, unde illos dedignantur audire; Ytalici e contrario perhibent quod Gallici et Teutonici ad modum febricitantium tremulas voces emittunt, et cum per immoderatam vocum emissionem celum propulsare nituntur, aut arbitrantur Deum esse surdum, aut illum posse aliqua vocum rabiditate placari.' *Rhetorica antiqua* (1215) 3 ('Notula in qua doctrina datur de consuetudinibus et naturis cantorum'), as quoted in Giuseppe Vecchi, 'Musica e scuola delle Artes a Bologna nell'opera di Boncompagno da Signa (sec. XIII)', in *Festschrift Bruno Stäblein zum 70. Geburtstag*, ed. Martin Runke (Kassel, 1967), p. 270. Germans always suffered from a bad reputation for 'howling' ('ululare'). Matthew Herbenus observed that, when he crossed over the Mosel and the Rhine, his entire manner of singing changed: 'my voice becomes germanicised – perhaps others might say: he is howling' ('vox mea teutonizat – dixerunt alii fortasse: ululat'), *De natura cantus ac miraculis vocibus* (1496) 1.5, ed. Joseph Smits van Waesberghe, Beiträge zur rhenischen Musikgeschichte 22 (Cologne, 1957), p. 31.

37 'Germani vero (quod pudet dicere) ut lupi ululant' ('but the Germanes – which I am ashamed to utter – doe howle like Wolves').

Musice active micrologus (Leipzig, 1517), cap. 8. The treatise is reproduced in facsimile with the translation of John Dowland (quoted) as *A Compendium of Musical Practice*, ed. Gustave Reese and Steven Ledbetter (New York, 1973), pp. 105 and 208.

38 'Et tunc illorum iudicio plus laudatur, qui maiori clangore astra ferit, velut possent sanctos angelos superius excitare.' *Scientia artis musice* 30; GS III: 59. Hélie might well have been in Lyons with the papal court at the time he wrote his treatise.

39 *De modo bene cantandi*, ed. Gümpel, pp. 131–2; Dyer, 'Singing with Proper Refinement', pp. 216–17.

40 See Joseph Dyer, 'A Thirteenth-Century Choirmaster: The *Scientia Artis Musicae* of Elias Salomon', *The Musical Quarterly*, 66 (1980), pp. 83–111. The theorist's first name was almost certainly 'Hélie', a favourite name in his native Dordogne until the nineteenth century.

41 'Sed aliud est esse duos cantus et duos cantantes. Nihil enim prohibet in duobus cantibus simul esse cantantes plures, tam in tenore quam in discantu.' ('But it is one thing to have two voices and another to have two singers. For nothing forbids that with two vocal parts there can be more [than two] singers performing together, on the tenor as well as on the discantus.') Jacques of Liège, *Speculum musice*, ed. Roger Bragard, Corpus Scriptorum de Musica 3, 7 vols. (American Institute of Musicology, 19XX), VII: 8.

42 See Richard Rex, *'The Sins of Madame Eglentyne' and Other Essays on Chaucer* (Newark, DE, 1995), especially ch. 7 ('Why the Prioress Sings through Her Nose').

43 *Die Musiktraktate Conrads von Zabern*, ed. Gümpel, p. 130; Dyer, 'Singing with Proper Refinement', p. 215.

44 'Non pigri, non somnolenti, non oscitantes, non parcentes vocibus, non praecidentes verba dimidia, non integra transilientes, non fractis et remissis vocibus, muliebre quiddam balba de nare sonantes, sed virili, ut dignum est, et sonitu et affectu voces Sancti Spiritus depromentes.' *Sancti Bernardi Opera*, ed. J. Leclercq, C. H. Talbot and H. M. Rochais, 7 vols. (Rome, 1957–74), II: 66. Bernard's citation of the Roman satirist Persius's criticism of the sound of a rival poet's voice ('quiddam balba de nare locutus') has been noted on more than one occasion.

45 'Aliquando virili vigore deposito, in feminee vocis gracilitates acuitur [vox].' *Speculum charitatis* 2.23 (*Patrologia Latina*, 195: 571). The chapter is translated in Hayburn, *Papal Legislation*, pp. 19–20. *The Mirror of Charity: The Speculum Charitatis of St Aelred of Rievaulx,*

trans. Geoffrey Webb and Adrian Walker (London, 1962), pp. 72–4, offers only an abridged paraphrase of this important chapter of a treatise that Aelred wrote early in his career, when he was master of novices at Rievaulx.

46 Joannis Sarisburiensis Episcopi Carnotensis, *Policratici sive de nugis curialium et philosophorum libri VIII*, ed. Clement Wood (Oxford, 1909), 1.41; the passage is translated in Janet Knapp, 'Polyphony at Notre Dame of Paris', in The New Oxford History of Music, II: *The Early Middle Ages to 1300* (new edition), ed. Richard Crocker and David Hiley (Oxford, 1990), p. 557.

47 'Omnes antiphone psalmorum incipiuntur cum falseto.' *Ein Festoffizium des Mittelalters aus Beauvais in seiner liturgischen und musikalischen Bedeutung*, 2 vols., ed. Wulf Arlt (Cologne, 1970), II: 7.

48 *Instituta patrum* 33, ed Bernard, p. 8. Hélie Salomon reproved singers who howled 'miau miau', an activity that allegedly secured for them a monetary reward likely to be turned to illicit purposes. *Scientia artis musice*, prologue (GS III: 17).

49 *Speculum charitatis* 2.23 (*Patrologia Latina* 195: 571). For an English translation of the section on music see Hayburn, *Papal Legislation*, p. 19.

50 Hieronymus de Moravia O. P. *Tractatus de musica* 25, ed. Cserba, pp. 179–89. Passages in italic in this edition represent Jerome's transmission of earlier works of medieval music theory. The chapter in question ('De modo cantandi et formandi notas et pausas ecclesiastici cantus') is original to Jerome, who is quoted extensively in McGee, *The Sound of Medieval Song, passim*.

51 'Est autem flos armonicus decora vocis sive soni celerrima procellarisque vibratio. Florum autem alii longi, alii aperti, alii vero existunt subiti. Longi flores sunt quorum vibratio est morosa, metasque semitonii non excedit. Aperti autem sunt quorum vibratio est morosa, metasque toni non excedit. Subiti vero sunt quorum quidem vibratio in principio est morosa, in medio autem et in fine est celerrima, metasque semitonii non excedit.' The passage is translated in Carol MacClintock, ed., *Readings in the History of Music in Performance* (Bloomington, IN, 1979), pp. 3–7.

52 A similar thought occurs in the final chapter (19) of the *Musica Enchiriadis*. Though apparently directed to composers of new melodies, it would apply very well to all chant interpretation. *Musica et Scolica Enchiriadis una cum aliquibus tractatulis adiunctis*, ed. Hans Schmid (Munich, 1981), pp. 58–9; trans. Raymond Erickson, *Musica enchiriadis and Scolica enchiriadis* (New Haven, 1995), p. 32.

53 *Die Musiktraktate Conrads von Zabern*, ed. Gümpel, pp. 131–2; Dyer 'Singing with Proper Refinement', pp. 216–17. See also Müller-Häuser, *Vox Humana*, pp. 105–16.

54 McGee, *The Sound of Medieval Song*, pp. 119–20.

15 Reconstructing pre-Romantic Singing Technique

1 Bénigne de Bacilly, *Remarques curieuses sur l'art de bien chanter* (Paris, 1668), p. 33: 'Il y a trois choses pour parvenir à bien chanter . . . à sçavoir, la Voix, le Disposition & l'Oreille, ou l'Intelligence'. Translations are by the present author unless otherwise credited.

2 Giulio Caccini, *Le nuove musiche* (Florence, 1602), 'Ai lettori' (n.p.): 'à poter muovere l'affetto dell'animo, in quei concetti di vero ove più si conviene usare tali affetti'.

3 Domenico Corri, *The Singers Preceptor, or Corri's Treatise on Vocal Music* (London, 1810), p. 1.

4 Ottavio Valera, 'Sfogava con le stelle', in Francesco Rognoni, *Selva di varii passaggi* (Milan, 1620), pp. 72–3.

5 Johann Friederich Agricola, *Anleitung zur Singkunst* [commentary on Pier Francesco Tosi, *Opinioni de' cantore antichi e moderni* (1723)] (Berlin, 1757), pp. 22ff. Agricola wrestles with the continuing problem that Tosi used the words *voce di testa* (literally 'head voice') to describe the falsetto. Lodovico Zacconi, *Prattica di musica* (Venice, 1592), I: 77v, describes (disparagingly) singers who produce notes which are (apparently) partly *di petto* and partly *di testa*.

6 Manuel García, *Traité complet de l'art du chant* (Paris, 1847), p. 10.

7 Marin Mersenne, *Harmonie universelle* (Paris, 1636), I: 6: 'le larynx monte en haut quand nous chantons le Dessus . . . le larynx descend en bas en chantant la Basse'.

8 Jean-Antoine Bérard, *L'art du chant* (Paris, 1755), pp. 19, 21: 'Les Observations apprennent que le Larinx monte tout entier dans les Sons aigus, & qu'il descend dans les Sons graves . . . & que les degrés d'abaissement sont exactement dans les mêmes proportions, que les degrés d'élévation dans les Sons aigus. On peut se convaincre de la verité & l'exactitude de ces proportions, en portant le doigt sur le Larinx, lorsqu'on rend des Sons aigus ou graves.'

9 Giovanni Camillo Maffei, *Lettere* (Naples, 1562), ed. Nanie Bridgman, 'Giovanni Camillo Maffei et sa lettre sur le chant', *Revue de musicologie*, 38 (1956), p. 17: 'Onde poi che la voce grave eccede, e sopera, e tutte l'altre abbraccia, si deve più perfetta, più nobile, e più generosa riputare.' Translation by Candace Smith and Bruce Dickey.

10 Caccini, *Le nuove musiche*, 'Ai Lettori': 'Ma dalle voce finte non può nascere nobilità di buon canto'.

11 *Le nuove musiche*: 'senza essere forzato acommodarsi ad altri, ... se elegga un tuono, nel qual possa cantare in voce piena e naturale per isfuggire le voci finte, nelle quali per fingerle, o almeno nelle forzate. ...'.

12 Michael Praetorius, *Syntagmatis musici*, III: 231: 'ein Sänger [muß] ... eine Stimm als *Cantum*, *Altum* oder *Tenor &c*. erwehlen / welche er mit vollem und hellem laut / ohne Falsetten / (das ist halbe und erzwungene Stimme) halten könne'.

13 Bacilly, *Remarques*, p. 46; Tosi, *Opinioni*, pp. 24–5.

14 Pietro della Valle, 'Della musica dell'età nostra' (1640), ed. G. B. Doni, *Lyra Barberina* (Rome, 1763), II: 255: 'Mi ricordo di Gio: Luca Falsetto, gran Cantore di gorge, e di passaggi, che andava alto alle stelle'. Translation by Candace Smith and Bruce Dickey.

15 Letter of Scipione Gonzaga to the Duke of Mantua, 29 March 1586. Quoted in Murray C. Bradshaw, *Giovanni Luca Conforti 'Salmi passaggiati' (1601–1603)* (Neuhausen-Stuttgart, 1985), p. xviii.

16 Della Valle, 'Della musica', p. 255.

17 Gioseffo Zarlino, *Le istitutioni harmoniche* (Venice, 1558; edn of 1588–9), III: 253: 'ad altro modo si canta nelle Chiese & nelle Capella publiche; & ad altro modo nelle private Camere; imperoche ivi si canta à piena voce; con discrezione però ... & nelle Camere si canta con voce più sommessa & soave, senza fare alcun strepito'.

18 Daniel Friderici, *Musica figuralis* (Rostock, 1649), p. 47: 'Irren derowegen die ungeschickten *Cantores*, nicht wenig, Welche, wenn Sie bey den *Discantisten* nicht können *ficta voce* singen, alsbald zur *Octava* greiffen, und einen *Tenorem* auß dem *Discant* machen, und nicht wenig *vitia* von *quinten* einführen. Die *Tenoristen* aber irren in dem gröblich, wann Sie die *Octavam* singen, daß sie das Fundament umbstossen, und falsche *Consonanten*, als *Quarten* und *Sexten* unter den Baß bawen.'

19 At the convent of S. Vito, Ferrara in 1621 there were, among other distinguished composers, singers and instrumentalists, 'Cassandra Pigna tenori buoni, Alfonsa Trotti di basso singolare, e di stupore'. Marcantonio Guarini, *Compendio historico dell'origine, accrescimento, e prerogative delle chiese, e luoghi pii della città, e dioscesi di Ferrara* (Ferrara, 1621), p. 376.

20 Lodovico Zacconi, *Prattica di musica* (Venice, 1592), I: 52v: 'molte imparano di cantare per cantar piano & nelle Cammere, ove s'abborisce il gridar forte, & non sono dalla necessità astretti a cantar nelle Chiese, ò nelle Capelle ove cantano i Cantori stipendiati.' Translation by Candace Smith and Bruce Dickey.

21 Maffei, *Lettere*, quoted in Bridgman, 'Maffei', p. 9: 'un lodar il cantar dolce, e soave, un'altro il cantar nella capella'.

22 *King Lear*, Act V, scene 3, lines 271–2.

23 Giovanni de' Bardi, *Discorso ... sopra la musica antica, e 'l cantar bene*, ed. and trans. in Claude Palisca, *The Florentine Camerata* (New Haven and London, 1989), pp. 128–9: 'E che chi cantar ben vuole, conviene che con dolcissima maniera et dolcissimi modi ... Et v'ingenerete ancora cantando di star in modo acconcio, et al vostro ordinario si somigliante. Che si dubiti se 'l suono della voce dalla vostra esca, o, dall'altrui bocca.'

24 Luzzasco Luzzaschi, *Madrigali* (Rome, 1601; facs. edn Florence, 1979).

25 Letter to Alessandro Striggio of 20 June, 1627: 'La voce sua ariva ad un tenore *con* gratezza del senso'. See Richard Wistreich, 'La voce è grata assai, ma ... Monteverdi on singing', *Early Music*, 22 (1994), pp. 13–14.

26 Tosi, *Opinioni*, ed. Luigi Leonesi (Naples, 1904), p. 38; English translation by J. E. Galliard: Tosi, *Observations on the Florid Song* (London, 1742), p. 23: 'un Soprano senza falsetto bisogna che canti fra l'angustie di poche corde'.

27 *Opinioni*, p. 36. Tosi specifies the 'higher' pitch of Lombardy in preference to that of Rome. Galliard gives the pitch as c^1 or d^1, *Observations*, p. 24.

28 Giambattista Mancini, *Pensieri e riflessioni pratiche sopra il canto figurato* (Vienna, 1774), p. 44.

29 Christoph Bernhard, *Von der Singe-Kunst, oder Maniera*, ed. J. Müller-Blattau, *Die Kompositionslehre Heinrich Schützens in der Fassung seines Schülers Christoph Bernhard* (Kassel, 1926; repr. 1999), p. 31: 'Das *fermo* oder Festhalten der Stimme, wird bey allen Noten erfordert, ausgenommen, wo das *trillo* oder *ardire* gebraucht wird'.

30 Johann Mattheson, *Der volkommene Capellmeister* (Hamburg, 1739), p. 79: 'daß der Klang nicht mitten in der schnarrenden Gurgel, mittelst der Zunge, oder zwischen den Backen und Lippen seine Form bekommen möge'.

31 Praetorius, *Syntagmatis musici*, III: 231: 'Die *Requisita* sind diese: daß ein Sänger erstlich eine schöne liebliche zittern- und bebende Stimme (doch nicht also/ wie etliche in Schulen gewohnet seyn/ sondern mit besonderer *moderation*)'. Praetorius would appear to be specifically ruling out the artificial suppression of the natural vibrancy of some voices. For a fuller discussion of vibrato see Peter

Reidemeister, 'Zur Vokalpraxis', *Historische Aufführungspraxis: eine Einführung* (Darmstadt, 1988), pp. 91ff.

32 Caccini, *Le nuove musiche*, 'Ai Lettori': 'i primi e più importamenti fondamenti sono l'intonazione della voce in tutte le corde, non solo, che nulla non manchi sotto, ò cresca di vantaggio, ma habbia la buona maniera'.

33 Corri, *The Singers Preceptor*, Lesson 3, pp. 22–3.

34 Mersenne, *Harmonie universelle*, II: 353: 'elles doivent estre justes, égales, & flexibles; dont la justesse consiste à prendre le ton proposé, sans qu'il soit permis d'aller plus haut, ou plus bas... L'égalité est la tenuë ferme, & stable de la voix sur une mesme chorde, sans qu'il soit permis de varier en la haussant ou en la baissant'.

35 Agricola, *Anleitung zur Singkunst*, p. 50: 'Hier gebe ich dem Sangmeister nun noch die nöthige Erinnerung, daß er ja Acht habe, damit die Töne, von dem Schüler, gehörig mit einander verbunden und zusamme gehängen werden mögen. Dieses geschieht, wenn man den vorgehenden Ton so lange klingen läßt, bis der folgende anspricht: damit nichts Leeres dazwischen vernommen werde.'

36 Rognoni, *Selva di varii passaggi* (Milan, 1620), p. iv.

37 Francesco Anerio, dedication to Giovanni Domenico Puliaschi, *Gemme musicale* (Rome, 1618), n.p.

38 Bacilly, *Remarques*, p. 5.

39 Tosi, trans. Galliard, *Observations*, p. 29.

40 Johann Adam Hiller, *Duetten zur Beförderung des Studium des Gesanges* (Leipzig, 1781) quoted in John Butt, *Music Education and the Art of Performance in the German Baroque* (Cambridge, 1994), p. 168.

41 Corri, *The Singers Preceptor*, p. 3.

42 *Ibid.*, p. 66.

43 Corri calls the *messa di voce* 'The Soul of Music' (*ibid.*, p. 14). See also Tosi, trans. Galliard, *Observations*, pp. 27–8; Mancini, *Pensieri*, pp. 99–107.

44 Will Crutchfield, 'Voices: The Classical Era', *The New Grove Performance Practice: Music after 1600*, ed. Howard Mayer Brown and Stanley Sadie (London, 1989), pp. 294–5.

45 Mancini, *Pensieri*, p. 86: 'Resti dunque per deciso, che lo sforzare la voce è sempre uno dei maggiori errori, che possa commettere un Cantante'.

46 Mersenne, *Harmonie universelle*, II: 353: 'Et la flexibilité de la voix n'est austre chose que la facilité & la disposition qu'elle a à se porter par toutes sortes de degrez & d'intervalles tant en montant, qu'en descendant, & en faisant toutes sortes de Passages, & de diminutions'.

47 Maffei, *Lettere*, p. 18: 'Dico, che tal voce, non è altro, ch'un suono caggionato dalla minuta, et ordinata ripercussione dell'aere nella gola'.

48 Praetorius, *Syntagmatis musici*, III: 230: 'einem runden Halß unnd Gurgel zum diminuiren'.

49 Mersenne, *Harmonie universelle*, II: 355: 'les cadences, qui consistent aux roulemens de la gorge... sont les plus difficiles à faire de tout ce qu'il y a dans les Chants, à raison qu'il faut seulement battre l'air de la gorge'.

50 Bacilly, *Remarques*, p. 48: 'Disposition... est une certaine facilité d'executer tout ce qui consiste la Maniere de Chanter, & qui a son siege dans le gosier'.

51 Tosi, *Opinioni*, p. 60: 'è di somma urgenza, che il Maestro ne istruisca lo Scolaro, acciò con facile velocità e giusta intonazione lo possega, che quando in sito proprio è ben eseguito esige il suo applauso, e fa il Cantor universale, cioè capace di cantare in ogni stile'.

52 Mancini, *Pensieri*, pp. 108, 109: 'Abbia pure un Cantante bella voce, abbia facile esecuzione, ed abbia ancor buon gusto; nondimeno il suo canto, se non sarà unito alla dolce grazia del Trillo, sarà sempre imperfetto, arido, ed asciutto ... Oh Trillo! Sostegno, decoro, e vita del canto!'

53 Praetorius, *Syntagmatis musici*, III: 237: 'Wann viel geschwinde *Noten* nacheinander *repetiret* werden'.

54 Caccini, *Le nuove musiche*, 'Ai Lettori': 'Il trillo descritto da me sopra una corda sola non è stato per l'altra cagione dimostrato in questa guisa, se non perchè nello insegnarlo alla mia prima moglie ed ora all' altra ... non ho osservato altra regola, che l'istessa, nelle quale è scritto ... cioè il commiciarsi dalla prima semiminima e ribattere ciascuna nota con la gola sopra la vocale 'a' sino all' ultima breve'.

55 For a comprehensive guide to the *port de voix*, see Frederick Neumann, *Ornamentation in Baroque and Post-Baroque Music* (Princeton, 1978), pp. 52–8.

56 Praetorius, *Syntagmatis musici*, III: 237: 'gleich wie ein Vogel vom andern *observiren* lerne'.

57 Rognoni, *Selva di varii passaggi*, I: 2: 'El portar della voce, vuol esser con gratia, il che si fà rinforzando la voce su la prima nota à poco, à poco, e poi facendo il tremolo sopra la negra'.

58 The similarities between this and the *port de voix* are clear. In the French ornament a *doublement de gosier* is a vital component of the sliding motion from one note to the next. See also Stewart Carter, 'Francesco Rognoni's *Selva di varii passaggi* (1620): Fresh Details Concerning Early-Baroque Vocal Ornamentation', *Performance Practice Review*, 2 (1989), pp. 14–17.

59 Zacconi, *Prattica di musica*, I: 60: 'il tremolo, cioè la voce tremante è la vera porta d'intrar

dentro a passaggi, & di impataonirse [*sic*] delle gorgie: perchè con più facilità se ne và la Nave quando che prima è mossa'.

60 Bacilly, *Remarques*, p. 228: 'Il faut s'accoustumer en étudiant l'execution des Passages, à marquer du gosier le plus grossierement que l'on peut, & mesme assez lentement d'abord, afin que par cette lenteur, & cette solidité, on se rende maistre de la justesse, & que l'on évite le Chant du nez & de la langue'.

61 Wolfgang Caspar Printz, *Musica modulatoria vocalis* (Schweidnitz, 1678), p. 43, quoted and translated in Butt, *Music Education*, pp. 132–3: 'Hier erinnern wir ins gemein daß jede *Figur* ihren manierlichen *Apulsum gutturalem* haben müsse das ist eine Anschlagen welches in der Kehle gemacht werden soll mit einer natürlichen Geschickligkeit nicht mit einem garstigen Drücken harten Stossen Meckern oder Wiehern so daß der Sänger den Mund mittelmässig eröffne die Backen nicht hohl mach sondern sie bleiben lasse wie sie die Natur gegeben und die Zunge nicht in die höhe hebe noch krömme sondern gerade und niedrig liegen lasse damit sie den Schalle nicht den freyen Durchgang verhindere'.

62 Agricola, *Anleitung*, p. 124: 'man muß so viele *a* nach einander geschwinde aussprechen, als Noten in der Passagie sind ... beym Singen ... wird ... aus der Lunge heraus getriebene, Luft in so viele kleine Absätze zertheilet, als Noten sind, welche denn dadurch articuliret und deutlich werden'.

63 Zacconi, *Prattica di musica*, I: 58v: 'Due cose si ricercano à chi vuol far questa professione: petto, & gola; petto per poter una simil quantità, & un tanto numero di figure à giusto termine condurre; gola poi per poterle agevolmente sumministrare'.

64 Note for example the following warning from Johann Quirsfeld, *Breviarum musicum* (Dresden, 1675; repr. 1688), p. 28: 'Wenn geschwinde Läuffer kommen soll er nicht die Noten heraus hauchen sondern eine jede mit ihrem Tone ausschlagen. Doch nicht mit der Brust welches der Lungen höchst schädlich ist sondern zwischen dem Schlunde und der Kehlen darzu der Gaumen etwas gebraucht wird' (If there are fast runs, he should not only touch on the notes, but attack each and every one with its own sound. Not with the chest, however, which is highly damaging to the lungs, but between the pharynx and the throat so that the palate is used somewhat.) Quoted and translated in Butt, *Music Education*, p. 81.

65 Ottavio Durante, *Arie devote, le quali contengono in se la maniera di cantar' con gratia, l'imitation' delle parole, et il modo di scriver passaggi, et altri affetti* (Rome, 1608), 'Ai Lettori': 'I Cantori devono procurar di capir bene in se stessi, quel che hanno da cantare, massime quando cantano soli, accio intendolo e possendendolo bene, lo possino far intender all' altri, che li stanno a sentire, che questo è il loro scopo principale, e devono avertire di intonar bene, e di cantar adagio, cioè con la battuta larga, porgendo la voce congratia e pronuntiando le parole distintamente, acciò siano intese, e quando si vorrà a far passaggi, si avertisca, che non ogni passaggio è approvato nella buona maniera di cantare'.

66 Corri, *The Singers Preceptor*, p. 1.

16 Alternative voices

1 First person refers to Linda Hirst.

2 J. Harvey, *The Music of Stockhausen: An Introduction* (London, 1975), p. 110.

3 R. Maconie, *The Works of Karlheinz Stockhausen* (London, 1976), pp. 239–43.

4 Liner notes to the Singcircle recording (Hyperion CDA66115) by Gregory Rose and Helen Ireland.

5 The Extended Vocal Techniques Ensemble, based at the Center For Music Experiment, San Diego, compiled a comprehensive Lexicon of vocal sounds in 1974.

6 *On Sonic Art* (York, 1985), ch. 12. For further repertoire from the period see Karen Jensen, 'Extensions of Mind and Voice', *Composer*, 66 (Spring 1979), pp. 13–17.

7 See John Potter, 'Electronics and the Live Performer', *Composer*, 66 (Spring 1979), pp. 19–21, for some contemporary thoughts on working with live electronics.

8 Schoenberg's own description of 'Sprechgesang' can be found in his foreword to the score of *Pierrot*, a translation of which is given in Egon Wellesz, *Arnold Schoenberg: The Formative Years* (London, 1971), pp. 138–9.

9 *Alternative Voices* (Toronto, 1984), pp. 25–92.

10 *Ligeti in Conversation* (London, 1983), p. 111.

17 The teaching (and learning) of singing

1 G. C. Maffei, *Delle lettere del Sor Gio. Camillo Maffei da Solofra*, Libri Due Napoli. 1562, Letter 1, as printed in N. Bridgeman, 'Giovanni Camillo Maffei et sa lettre sur le chant', *Revue de Musicologie*, 38 (July 1956), pp. 10–34, quoted in C. MacClintock, *Readings in the History of Music in Performance* (Bloomington and London, 1979), p. 45.

2 Cited in R. Fiske, *English Theatre Music in the Eighteenth Century* (Oxford, 1973), p. 270.

3 Giambattista Mancini, *Pensieri e riflessioni pratiche sopra il canto figurato* (Vienna, 1774; rev. 1777), English translation: E. Foreman, *Practical Reflections on Figured Singing* (Champaign, IL, 1967), p. 30.

4 'He who knows how to breathe knows how to sing.' This well-known maxim is attributed to Maria Celloni in M. García, *Hints on Singing* (London, 1894), p. 13. Similar statements have been attributed to the famous castrato Pacchierotti and others, sometimes as: 'He who knows how to breathe and pronounce well, etc.' Gigli summed up his singing in such terms. Most singing students probably wish it were that easy!

5 D. Corri, *The Singers Preceptor* (London, 1810). Corri writes that the 'swelling and dying of the Voice, the most important qualification in the vocal art . . . may be learnt in a few days by moderate, regular, and frequent practice' (p. 11).

6 I. Nathan, *Musurgia Vocalis* (London, 1836), p. 145. This was a revision of the earlier *Essay on the History and Theory of Music, and on the Qualities, Capabilities and Management of the Human Voice* (London, 1823).

7 García's first important work is the *Mémoire sur la voix humaine*, submitted to the French Academy of Sciences in 1840. This formed the basis for Part 1 of his *Traité complet*, which appeared in 1841. Part 2 came out in 1847. In 1854 García invented the laryngoscope, and produced his *Nouveau traité sommaire de l'art du chant* in 1856, which was reprinted in 1872. The 1856/1872 revision is more advanced as regards vocal physiology, though it omits some of the sections concerned with musical style. There is a facsimile edition of the 1847 edition (Geneva, 1985), and an English translation, which collates the editions of 1847 and 1872: *Manuel García II: A Complete Treatise on the Art of Singing*, collated, edited and translated by Donald V. Pashke, 2 vols. (New York, 1984).

8 García, *A Complete Treatise*, trans. Pashke, p. 42.

9 García, *Hints on Singing*, p. 13.

10 M. García I, *Exercises and Method for Singing* (London, 1824).

11 García, *Traité complet de l'art du chant*, p. 29.

12 H. Helmholtz, *Die Lehre von den Tonempfindungen als physiologische Grundlage für die Theorie der Musik* (Brunswick, 1863); A. J. Ellis (trans.), *On the Sensations of Tone* (London, 1875).

13 Cited in P. Ladefoged, *A Course in Phonetics* (New York, 1993), p. 194.

14 W. J. Henderson, *The Art of Singing* (New York, 1938; repr. 1978), p. 61.

15 *Ibid.*, p. 63.

16 F. Lamperti, *A Treatise on the Art of Singing*, trans. J. C. Griffith (New York, 1890).

17 D.F. Proctor, *Breathing, Speech, and Song* (Vienna and New York, 1980), p. 110.

18 Children's singing

1 British Federation of Young Choirs, *Survey* (1991) quoted in *Music File* Series 9/3 (1997), Editorial.

2 Helen Kemp, *Of Primary Importance* (Dayton, OH, 1991), II: 9.

3 Esther Salaman, *Unlocking Your Voice – Freedom to Sing* (London, 1989), p. 21.

4 I was first introduced to the 'five-point Plan' by Tor Skauge at a workshop given in Bergen, Norway, in 1976.

5 *Of Primary Importance*, II: 12.

6 The verb 'to music' was coined by Christopher Small, *Music of the Common Tongue* (London, 1987), p. 50.

7 You can teach singing in this authoritarian way, and plenty of people do, but I believe that children's interests are not best served by this.

8 'Music is the glue of the modern multiracial, multilinguistic city, holding it together more effectively than any political or social system'. R. Murray Schafer, *Voices of Tyranny, Temples of Silence* (Indian River, Ont., 1993), p. 77.

9 For those interested in finding out more about children's singing, the following may be of some help:
Jean Ashworth-Bartle, *Lifeline for Children's Choir Directors* (Gordon V. Thompson, distributed Oxford University Press, 1988); Nicholas Bannan, 'Voice–Sound–Music', *Music File*, Series 2, issue 1 (1989); Nicholas Bannan, 'Singing Towards KS3', *Music File*, Series 9, issue 2 (1997) (*Music File*, pub. Stanley Thornes); Nicholas Bannan, A series of four articles in *Music Teacher* (Jan.–May 1988); Inga Olsson Ekström, *Sjung på lågstudiet* (Bromma, 1980); Gunnel Fagius and Katharina Larsson, eds., *Barn i Kör, Ideer och metoder för barnkörledare* (Stockholm, 1990); Robert Göstl, *Singen mit Kindern* (Regensburg, 1996); Helen Kemp, *Of Primary Importance – A Practical Guide for Directors of Younger Elementary Choristers* (Texas, 1989; distributed by The Lorenz Corporation 501 E.Third Street, Box 802, Dayton, OH 45401); *Of Primary Importance – A Practical Guide for Directors of Young Choristers* vol. 2 (1991, publisher as above). These volumes contain much information about how to teach children to sing, with detailed suggestions for helping those with intonation problems. They also include repertoire for Christian worship, and accompanying suggestions about exactly how to tackle it. Helen Kemp has also produced two video recordings: *Body, Mind, Spirit, Voice: Developing the Young Singer*, and *Sing and Rejoice: Guiding Young Singers*, both by Concordia Publishing House, 1985. Also relevant are Felicity Laurence, *Birds, Balloons and Shining Stars – A Teacher's Guide to Singing with Children* (London, 1994); Andreas Mohr,

Handbuch der Kinderstimmbildnung (Mainz, 1997); Paul Nitsche, *Die Pflege der Kinder- und Jugendstimme I Theoretische Teil* (Mainz, 1970); *Die Pflege der Kinder- und Jugendstimme II Stimmbildung am Lied* (Mainz, 1969); Doreen Rao, *Choral Music Experience, Volume 5: The Young Singing Voice* (Boosey and Hawkes, TXB66, 1987); Helen Willberg, *Sing Together* (Wellington, 1993) and Graham F. Welch, *et al.*, *Singing Development, Childhood and Change: An Overview* (London: ASME (The Centre for Advanced Studies in Music Education), Roehampton Institute, n.d.). This last publication contains five articles (1995–7) concerning recent research on singing development in children of different age groups.

The following publications, although not solely about children's singing, include relevant material: Mike Brewer, *Kickstart Your Choir* (London, 1997); Colin Durrant and Graham Welch, *Making Sense of Music: Foundations for Music Education* (London, 1995) includes two chapters on children's vocal work; David Hill, Hilary Parfitt and Elizabeth Ash, *Giving Voice: A Handbook for Choir Directors & Trainers* (Rattlesden, Suffolk, 1995).

For those interested in pursuing recent and current research into children's singing, the following will be of interest: D. M. Howard and G.F. Welch, 'Microcomputer-Based Singing Ability Assessment and Development', *Applied Acoustics*, 27/2(1989), pp. 89–102; 'Visual Displays for the Assessment of Vocal Pitch Matching Development', *Applied Acoustics*, 39/3 (1993), pp. 235–52. These articles describe the system SINGAD (Singing Assessment amd Development). Further articles by Howard, Welch, *et al.*, describing results can be found in *Psychology of Music* (1989 and 1991), *Proceedings of the Institute of Acoustics* (1994) and *Logopedics Phoniatrics Vocology* (1998). The work of the Canadian composer and educator Nancy Telfer is comprehensive, including publications and recordings specialising in warm-ups for choirs, vocal technique for children, diagnosis and remedies for vocal problems, as well as programmes to develop sight-singing. Information and material is available from the publishers Neil A. Kjos Music Company, 4380 Jutland Drive, San Diego, CA 92117. The Voices Foundation is developing programmes and written material not only for optimal development of children's singing in schools and in choirs, but also focusing upon the sociological implications of good individual singing ability and group singing in a positive context. Further information is available from The Voices Foundation (founder Susan Digby), The Poets' House, 21 Earl's Court Square, London SW5 9BY.

19 Where does the sound come from?

1 I. Titze, *Principles of Voice Production* (Englewood Cliffs, NJ, 1994).
2 P. H. Dejonkere, M. Hirano, and J. Sundberg (eds.), *Vibrato* (San Diego, 1995).
3 S. Ternström, 'Acoustical Aspects of Choir Singing'; unpublished dissertation, Royal Institute of Technology, Stockholm (1989).
4 M. García, *Traité complet de l'art du chant* (Paris, 1847).

Select bibliography

Abraham, G., The New Oxford History of Music, vol. IX: *Romanticism 1830–1890* (Oxford, 1990).

Abrahams, Roger D., *Deep Down In the Jungle* (New York, 1970).

Agricola, J. F., *Anleitung zur Singkunst* (Berlin, 1757; facs. repr. Leipzig, 1998, English trans ed. J. A. Baird, Cambridge, 1996).

Allen, W. F., C. P. Ware and L.M. Garrison (compilers), *Slave Songs in the United States* (New York, 1867).

Allgood, R. Dexter, 'Black Gospel in New York City and Joe William Bostic, Sr.', *The Black Perspective in Music*, 18/1–2 (1990), pp. 101–15.

Anderson, E. (ed.), *The Letters of Mozart and his Family*, 3rd edn (London, 1985).

Andrews, H. F., *Westminster Retrospect: A Memoir of Sir Richard Terry* (London, 1948).

Anhalt, I., *Alternative Voices* (Toronto, 1984).

Anthony, J. R., *French Baroque Music from Beaujoyeulx to Rameau* (London, 1973).

Ardoin, J., *The Callas Legacy*, 2nd edn (London, 1982).

Armstrong, W. (ed.), *Lillian Nordica's Hints to Singers* (New York, 1923).

Ashworth-Bartle, Jean, *Lifeline for Children's Choir Directors* (Gordon V. Thompson, distributed Oxford University Press, 1988).

Auden, W. H., 'Walter de la Mare', in *Forewords and Afterwords* (London, 1973), pp. 384–94.

Austen, J., *Emma* (Oxford, 1933), pp. 99–100.

Babb, W., trans., *Hucbald, Guido, and John on Music: Three Medieval Treatises* (New Haven, 1978).

Bacilly, Bénigne de, *Remarques curieuses sur l'art de bien chanter* (Paris, 1679; facs edn Geneva, 1971). English trans. ed. Austin, B. Caswell as *A Commentary upon the Proper Art of Singing* (New York, 1968).

Bailey, Ben E., 'The Lined-Hymn Tradition in Black Mississippi Churches', *The Black Perspective in Music*, 6/1 (Spring 1978), pp. 3–19.

Banfield, S., *Sensibility and English Song* (Cambridge, 1985).

'Popular Song and Popular Music on Stage and Film', in *The Cambridge History of American Music*, ed. David Nicholls (Cambridge, 1998), pp. 309–44.

Bannan, Nicholas, 'Voice–Sound–Music', *Music File*, Series 2, issue 1 (1989).

'Singing Towards KS3', *Music File*, Series 9, issue 2 (1997).

A series of four articles in *Music Teacher* (Jan.–May 1988).

Bardi, Giovanni de, *Discorso . . . sopra la musica antica, e 'l cantar bene*. Ed. and trans. Claude Palisca, The Florentine Camerata (New Haven and London, 1989).

Barthes, R., 'The Grain of the Voice', in *Image-Music-Text*, trans. S. Heath (London, 1977), pp. 179–89.

Baugh, J., *Black Street Speech: Its History, Structure and Survival* (Austin, TX, 1983).

Bèges, J. and A., *Mémoire d'un théâtre* (Béziers, 1987).

Benoit, M., *Versailles et les musiciens du Roi 1661–1733* (Paris, 1971).

Bérard, J.-A., *L'art du chant* (Paris, 1755, repr. Geneva, 1972).

Bernard, J., 'Abroad Rap Speaks Up', *New York Times* (23 August 1992) pp. 1 ff.

Bernhard, C., *Von der Singe-Kunst, oder Maniera*, ed. J. Müller-Blattau, *Die Kompositionslehre Heinrich Schützens in der Fassung seines Schülers Christoph Bernhard* (Kassel, 1926; repr. 1999).

Bianconi, L., *Music in the Seventeenth Century* (Cambridge, 1987).

Bianconi, L., and T. Walker, 'Dalla *Finta pazza alla Veremonda*: storie di Febiarmonici', *Rivista Italiana di Musicologia*, 10 (1975), pp. 379–454.

'Production, Consumption and Political Function of Seventeenth-Century Opera', *Early Music History*, 4 (1984), pp. 209–96.

Blackburn, B. J., and E. E. Lowinski, 'Luigi Zenobi and his Letter on the Perfect Musician', *Studi musicali*, 23 (1994), pp. 61–107.

Block, A. F., *Amy Beach: Passionate Victorian* (New York and Oxford, 1998).

Block, G., 'The Broadway Canon from "Show Boat" to "West Side Story" and the European Operatic Ideal', *Journal of Musicology*, 11 (1993) pp. 525–44.

Bloothooft, G., E. Bringmann, M. van Cappellen, J. van Luipen, and K. Thomassen 'Acoustics and Perception of Overtone Singing', *Journal of the Acoustic Society of America*, 92 (1972) pp. 1827–36.

Bowers, J., and J. Tick (eds.), *Women Making Music* (Urbana, IL, 1986).

Boyer, Horace Clarence, 'Contemporary Gospel Music', *The Black Perspective in Music*, 7/1 (Spring 1979), pp. 5–58.

Brackett, D., 'James Brown's "Superbad" and the Double-Voiced Utterance', in *Interpreting Popular Music* (Cambridge,1995), pp. 309–24.

Bradbury, W. B., *The Jubilee: An Extensive Collection of Church Music* (Boston, MA, 1858).

Bradshaw, M. C. (ed.), *Giovanni Luca Conforti 'Salmi passaggiati' (1601–1603)* (Neuhausen-Stuttgart, 1985).

Brewer, M., *Kickstart Your Choir* (London, 1997).

Broughton, Ellingham, *et al.*, *World Music: The Rough Guide* (London, 1994).

Brown, H. M., *Embellishing Sixteenth-Century Music* (Oxford, 1976).

Bunch, M., *Dynamics of the Singing Voice*, 2nd rev. edn (Vienna and New York, 1993).

Burgin, J. C., *Teaching Singing* (Metuchen, NJ, 1973).

Burkholder, J. Peter, *Charles Ives: The Ideas Behind the Music* (New Haven and London, 1985).

All Made of Tunes: Charles Ives and the Uses of Musical Borrowing (New Haven and London, 1995).

Burkholder, J. Peter (ed.), *Charles Ives and His World* (Princeton, 1996).

Burney, C., *The Present State of Music in France and Italy* (London, 1771).

Butt, J., *Music Education and the Art of Performance in the German Baroque* (Cambridge, 1994).

Caccini, Giulio, *Le nuove musiche* (Florence, 1602; facs. edn Rome, 1934), English trans. ed. H. Wiley Hitchcock (Madison, 1970).

Carter, S., 'Francesco Rognoni's *Selva di varii passaggi* (1620): Fresh Details Concerning Early-Baroque Vocal Ornamentation', *Performance Practice Review*, 2 (1989), pp. 14–17.

Caruso, Jr, E., and A. Farkas, *My Father and My Family* (Portland, OR, 1992).

Caswell, A., *A Commentary upon The Art of Proper Singing* (New York, 1968).

　'Mme Cinti-Damoreau and the Embellishment of Italian Opera in Paris: 1820–45', *Journal of the American Musicological Society*, 28 (1975), pp. 459–92.

Celani, E., 'Musica e musicisti in Roma 1750–1850', *Rivista musicale italiana*, 18 (1911), pp. 1–63; 20 (1913), pp. 33–88; 22 (1915), pp. 1–56.

Celletti, R., A *History of Bel Canto* (Oxford, 1991).

Chapple, S., and R. Garofalo, *Rock 'n' Roll is Here to Pay: The History and Politics of the Music Industry* (Chicago, 1977).

Charlton, P., *John Stainer and the Musical Life of Victorian Britain* (Newton Abbot, 1984).

Chatwin, B., *Songlines* (London, 1988).

Christiansen, R., *Prima Donna: A History* (London, 1984).

Chrysander, F., 'Ludovico Zacconi as Lehrer des Kunstgesanges', *Vierteljahrsschrifte für Musikwissenschaft*, 7 (1891), pp. 249–310.

Cleveland, T., 'Acoustic Properties of Voice Timbre Types and their Influence on Voice Classification', *Journal of the Acoustic Society of America*, 61 (1977), pp. 1622–9.

Cobb, Buell, *The Sacred Harp: A Tradition and Its Music* (Athens, GA, 1978).

Coffin, B., *Historical Vocal Pedagogy Classics* (Metuchen, NJ, 1989).

Cooper, W. M. *et al.* (eds.), *The B. F. White Sacred Harp* (Troy, AL, 1949).

Corri, Domenico, *The Singers Preceptor, or Corri's Treatise on Vocal Music* (London, 1810, facs. edn New York and London, 1995).

Coussemaker, Edmond de, *Scriptorum de musica medii aevi nova series*, 4 vols. (Paris, 1864–76).

Covey-Crump, R., 'Pythagoras at the Forge: Tuning in Early Music', in *Companion to Medieval and Renaissance Music*, ed. Tess Knighton and David Fallows (London and New York, 1992; repr. Oxford, 1998), pp. 317–26.

　'Pitch, Musica Ficta and Tuning Systems', liner note to *Hilliard Live* 1 (1996); 'Tuning Ockeghem', liner note to *Hilliard Live 2* (1997); 'Tuning Brumel', liner note to *Hilliard Live* 3 (1997); 'Tuning Dufay', liner note to *Hilliard Live* 4 (1998).

Cripps, T., *Black Film As Genre* (Bloomington, IN, and London, 1979).

Crocker, R., and D. Hiley (eds.), The New Oxford History of Music, II: *The Early Middle Ages to 1300*, new edition (Oxford, 1990).

Crutchfield, W., 'Voices: The Classical Era', *The New Grove Performance Practice: Music after 1600*, ed. Howard Mayer Brown and Stanley Sadie (London, 1989), pp. 292–319.

Cserba, S. (ed.), *Hieronymus de Moravia O. P. Tractatus de musica* (Regensburg, 1935).

Cubitt, S., '"Maybelline": Meaning and the Listening Subject', *Popular Music*, 4 (1984), pp. 207–24.

Cyr, M., 'Eighteenth-Century French and Italian Singing: Rameau's Writing for the Voice', *Music & Letters*, 61 (1980), pp. 318–37.

Daniel, Ralph T., *The Anthem in New England before 1800* (Evanston, IL, 1966).

Dejonkere, P. H., M. Hirano and J. Sundberg (eds.), *Vibrato* (San Diego, 1995).

Denson, T. J. (ed.), *Original Sacred Harp* (Bremen, GA, 1971).

Dent, E. J., *The Rise of Romantic Opera*, ed. W. Dean (Cambridge, 1976).

De Venney, David P., *American Masses and Requiems: A Descriptive Guide* (Berkeley, 1990).

  Source Readings in American Choral Music (Missoula, MT, 1995).

Dmitriev, L., and A. Kiselev, 'Relationship Between the Formant Structure of Different Types of Singing Voices and the Dimension of Supraglottal Cavities', *Folia Phoniatrica*, 31 (1979), pp. 238–41.

Dodwell, C. R. (ed. and trans.), *Theophilus: De diversis artibus* (London, 1961).

Doni, G. B., *Lyra Barberina* (Rome, 1763, facs. ed. Bologna, 1975).

Donington, R., *The Interpretation of Early Music*, 3rd edn (London,1974).

  Review of G. Moens-Haenens, *Das Vibrato in der Musik des Barock* (Graz, 1988), in *Early Music*, 16 (1988), pp. 571–3.

Drake, J. A., *Rosa Ponselle: A Contemporary Biography* (Portland, OR, 1997).

Duey, P., *Bel Canto in its Golden Age* (New York, 1980).

Durante, Ottavio, *Arie devote, le quali contengono in se la maniera di cantar' con gratia, l'imitation' delle parole, et il modo di scriver passaggi, et altri affetti* (Rome, 1608).

Durante, S., 'Theorie und Praxis der Gesangsschulen zur Zeit Händels: Bemerkungen zu Tosis *Opinioni de'cantori antichi e moderni*', in *Händel auf dem Theater* (Karlsruhe, 1986–7), pp. 59–77.

  'Il cantante', *Storia dell'opera italiana*, ed. L. Bianconi and G. Pestelli, 6 vols. (only vols. 4–6 published) (Turin, 1987–   ), pp. 349–41 [English translation of all 6 vols. forthcoming from University of Chicago Press].

Durrant, C., and G. Welch, *Making Sense of Music: Foundations for Music Education* (London, 1995).

Dyer, J., 'A Thirteenth-Century Choirmaster: The *Scientia Artis Musicae* of Elias Salomon', *The Musical Quarterly*, 66 (1980), pp. 83–111.

  'Singing with Proper Refinement from *De modo bene cantandi* (1474) by Conrad von Zabern' [introduction, translation, commentary], *Early Music*, 6 (1978), pp. 207–27.

Dyson, G., *The Progress of Music* (London, 1932).

  'Of Organs and Organists', *The Musical Times*, 93 (1952), pp. 491–2.

Eames, E., *Some Memories and Reflections* (New York, 1927).

Einstein, A., *Schubert* (London, 1951).

Ekström, Inga Olsson, *Sjung på lågstudiet* (Bromma, 1980).

Elgar, E., *A Future for English Music and Other Lectures*, ed. Percy M.Young (London, 1968).

Ellis, V., *I'm on a See-Saw* (London, 1953; rpt. Bath, 1974).

Epstein, Dena J., *Sinful Tunes and Spirituals: Black Folk Music to the Civil War* (Urbana, IL, 1977).

Erickson, R., *Musica enchiriadis and Scolica enchiriadis* (New Haven, 1995).

Eriksen, T. W., 'The New Northampton Collection of Sacred and Secular Harmony', unpublished Master's thesis, Wesleyan University (1993).

Ernstbrunner, Pia, 'Fragmente des Wissens um die menschliche Stimme: Bausteine zu einer Gesangskunst und Gesangspädagogik des Mittelalters' in

Mittelalterliche Musiktheorie in Zentraleuropa, ed. W. Pass and A. Rausch, Musica Mediaevalis Europae Occidentalis 4 (Tutzing, 1998), pp. 21–50.

Estill, J., 'Belting and Classic Voice Quality: Some Physiological Differences', *Medical Problems of Performing Artists*, 3 (1988), pp. 37–43.

Estill, J., T. Baer, K. Honda, and K. Harris, 'Supralaryngeal Activity in a Study of Six Voice Qualities', in A. Askenfelt, S. Felicetti, E. Jansson and J. Sundberg, *Proceedings of the Stockholm Music Acoustics*, 83/1 (1985), pp. 157–74.

Evans, S. J. A., 'A Victorian Choirmaster – Dr. A. H. Mann', *Church Music Society Annual Report* (1959).

Fagius, Gunnel, and Katharina Larsson (eds.), *Barn i Kör, Ideer och metoder för barnkörledare* (Stockholm, 1990).

Fant, G., *Acoustic Theory of Speech Production* (The Hague, 1960).
'Glottal Flow: Models and Interaction', *Phonetics*, 14 (1986), pp. 393–9.

Farkas, A., *Opera and Concert Singers* (New York, 1985).

Faulkner, K., *Voice* (London, 1983).

Fellowes, E. H., *Memoirs of an Amateur Musician* (London, 1946).

Fenlon, I., *Music and Patronage in Sixteenth-Century Mantua*, 2 vols. (Cambridge, 1980).

Finnegan, R., *Oral Literature in Africa* (Oxford, 1970).

Fiske, R., *English Theatre Music in the Eighteenth Century* (Oxford, 1973; 2nd edn 1986).

Floyd, S. A., *The Power of Black Music: Interpreting its History from Africa to the United States* (New York, 1995).

Foreman, E., *Masterworks on Singing* (Champaign, IL, 1967).
'A Comparison of Selected Italian Vocal Tutors of the Period circa 1550 to 1800', DMA dissertation, University of Illinois (1969).

Forte, A., *The American Popular Ballad of the Golden Era: 1924–1950* (Princeton, 1995).

Friderici, Daniel, *Musica figuralis* (Rostock, 1649).

Frith, S., *Music for Pleasure: Essays in the Sociology of Pop* (Cambridge, 1988).
Performing Rites: On the Value of Popular Music (Oxford, 1996).

Gal, H., *The Musician's World: Letters of the Great Composers* (London, 1965).

Gallo, F. A., *Music in the Castle: Troubadours, Books, and Orators in Italian Courts of the Thirteenth, Fourteenth, and Fifteenth Centuries*, trans. Anna Herklotz (Chicago, 1995).

Gammond, P., *The Oxford Companion to Popular Music* (Oxford and New York, 1991).

Ganz, W., *Memoirs of a Musician* (London, 1913).

Gänzl, K., *The Blackwell Guide to the Musical Theatre on Record* (Oxford, 1990).

García, M. (the elder), *Exercises and Method for Singing* (London, 1824).

García, M., *Traité complet de l'art du chant* (Paris, 1847; English edition by D. Paschke, *A Complete Treatise on the Art of Singing*, 2 vols. (New York, 1984)).
Hints on Singing (London, 1894).

García, W. B., 'Church Music by Black Composers: A Bibliography of Choral Music', *The Black Perspective in Music*, 2/2 (Fall 1974), pp. 145–57.

Gauffin, J., and J. Sundberg, 'Spectral Correlates of Glottal Voice Source Waveform Characteristics', *Journal of Speech and Hearing Research*, 32 (1989), pp. 556–65.

George, L. A., 'Lucie E. Campbell: Baptist Composer and Educator', *The Black Perspective in Music*, 15/1 (Spring 1987), pp. 25–50.

Gerbert, M. (ed.), *Scriptores ecclesiastici de musica sacra potissimum*, 3 vols. (St Blaise, 1784).

Goldschmidt, H., *Die italienische Gesangsmethode des XVII. Jahrhunderts und ihre Bedeutung für die Gegenwart* (Breslau, 1890; repr. 1997).

Göstl, Robert, *Singen mit Kindern* (Regensburg, 1996).

Gourret, J., *La technique du chant en France depuis le 17e siècle*, 2nd edn (Paris, 1976).

Gramming, P., 'Vocal Loudness and Frequency Capabilities of the Voice', *Voice*, 5 (1991), pp. 144–57.

Grant, Elizabeth (of Rothiemurchus), *Memoirs of a Highland Lady*, ed. A. Tod, 2 vols. (Edinburgh, 1988).

Graves, C. L., *Hubert Parry: His Life and Works* (London, 1926).

Greenlee, R., '*Dispositione di voce*: Passage to Florid Singing', *Early Music*, 15 (1987), pp. 47–55.

Guarini, Marcantonio, *Compendio historico dell'origine, accrescimento, e prerogative delle chiese, e luoghi pii della città, e dioscesi di Ferrara* (Ferrara, 1621).

Guest, G. H., *A Guest at Cambridge* (Orleans, MA, 1994).

Gümpel, Karl-Werner, *Die Musiktraktate Conrads von Zabern* (Wiesbaden, 1956).

Haas, R., 'Aufführungspraxis der Musik', *Handbuch der Musikwissenschaft*, 8 (Wildpark-Potsdam, 1931).

Hahn, R., *On Singing and Singers*, trans. I. L. Simoneau (London and Portland, OR, 1990).

Hamm, C., *Music in the New World* (New York, 1983).

Hampton, Marion, and Barbara Acker (eds.), *The Vocal Vision* (New York and London, 1997).

Harris, E. T., 'Voices: The Baroque Era', *The New Grove Handbooks in Music Performance Practice: Music after 1600*, ed. H. M. Brown and S. Sadie (London, 1989), pp. 97–116.

Harris, M., *The Rise of Gospel Blues: The Music of Thomas Andrew Dorsey in the Urban Church* (New York and Oxford, 1992).

Harvey, J., *The Music of Stockhausen: An Introduction* (London, 1975).

Hayburn, R. F., *Papal Legislation on Sacred Music, 95 A.D. to 1977 A.D.* (Collegeville, MN, 1979).

Hehr, E., 'How the French Viewed the Differences Between French and Italian Singing Styles of the Eighteenth Century', *International Review of the Aesthetics and Sociology of Music*, 16 (1985,) pp. 73–85.

Helmholtz, H., *Die Lehre von den Tonempfindungen als physiologische Grundlage für die Theorie der Musik* (Brunswick, 1863; English translation: A. J. Ellis, *On the Sensations of Tone*, London, 1875).

Henderson, W. J., *The Art of Singing* (New York, 1938; repr. 1978).

Henstock, M. E., *Fernando De Lucia* (London, 1990).

Herlinger, J. (ed.), *The Lucidarium of Marchetto of Padua* (Chicago, 1985).

Hiley, D., *Western Plainchant: A Handbook* (Oxford, 1993).

Hill, D., H. Parfitt, and E. Ash, *Giving Voice: A Handbook for Choir Directors and Trainers* (Rattlesden, Suffolk, 1995).

Hiller, Johann Adam, *Anweisung zum musikalisch-zierlichen Gesange* (Leipzig, 1780; repr. Leipzig, 1976).

Duetten zur Beförderung des Studium des Gesanges (Leipzig, 1781).

Hines, R. S. (ed.), *The Composer's Point of View: Essays on Twentieth Century Choral Music by Those Who Wrote It* (Norman, OK, 1963).

Hirst, L., 'Extending Singers', *Contact,* 32 (Spring 1988), pp. 57–8.

Hitchcock, H. Wiley, *Music in the United States: A Historical Introduction* (Englewood Cliffs, NJ, 1974).

Hitchcock, H. Wiley, and Stanley Sadie (eds.), *The New Grove Dictionary of American Music,* 4 vols. (London, 1986).

Hodgson, F., *Choirs and Cloisters – Sixty Years of Music in Church, College, Cathedral and Chapels Royal* (London, 1988).

Hollien, H., 'On Vocal Registers', *Phonetics,* 2 (1974), pp. 125–43.

'The Puzzle of the Singer's Formant', in D. Bless and J. Abbs (eds.), *Vocal Fold Physiology: Contemporary Research & Clinical Issues* (San Diego, 1983), pp. 368–78.

Hope-Wallace, P., *A Picture History of Opera* (London, 1959).

Horii, Y., 'Acoustical Analysis of Vocal Vibrato: A Theoretical Interpretation of Data', *Voice,* 3 (1989), pp. 36–43.

Howard, D. M., 'Quantifiable Aspects of Different Singing Styles: A Case Study', *Voice,* 1 (1992), pp. 47–62.

Howard, D. M. and G. F. Welch, 'Microcomputer-Based Singing Ability Assessment and Development', *Applied Acoustics,* 27/2 (1989), pp. 89–102.

'Visual Displays for the Assessment of Vocal Pitch Matching Development', *Applied Acoustics,* 39/3 (1993), pp. 235–52.

Hughes, A. and Gerald Abraham (eds), The New Oxford History of Music, III: *Ars Nova and the Renaissance* (London, 1960).

Hussler, F., and Y. Rodd-Marling, *The Physical Nature of the Vocal Organ* (London, 1976).

Huws Jones, E., *The Performance of English Song 1610 – 1670* (New York and London, 1989).

Imaizumi, S., H. Saida, Y. Shimura, and H. Hirose, 'Harmonic Analysis of the Singing Voice: Acoustic Characteristics of Vibrato', in A. Friberg, J. Iwarsson, E. Jansson and J. Sundberg (eds.), *Proceedings of the Stockholm Music Acoustics Conference 1993* (SMAC 93), Stockholm: Royal Swedish Academy of Music, publ. no. 79 (1994), pp. 197–200.

Imbimbo, E., *Observations sur l'enseignement mutuel appliqué à la musique* (Paris, 1821).

Isherwood, R. M., *Music in the Service of the King* (Ithaca, NY, 1973).

Itz, Wolfgang Caspar, *Musica modulatoria vocalis* (Schweidnitz, 1678).

Ives, Charles E., *Memos,* ed. John Kirkpatrick (New York, 1972).

Jackson, G. P., *White and Negro Spirituals* (New York, 1943).
  White Spirituals in the Southern Uplands (Chapel Hill, NC, 1933; repr. New York, 1965).
Jackson, Irene, *Afro-American Religious Music* (Westport, CT, 1979).
Jensen, K., 'Extensions of Mind and Voice', *Composer*, 66 (Spring 1979), pp. 13–17.
Johnson, A., *The Songmakers' Almanac (Reflections & Commentaries)* (London, 1996).
Kemp, Helen, *Of Primary Importance – A Practical Guide for Directors of Younger Elementary Choristers* (Texas, 1989).
  Of Primary Importance – A Practical Guide for Directors of Young Choristers, vol. 2 (Texas, 1991).
  Body, Mind, Spirit, Voice; Developing the Young Singer, and *Sing and Rejoice; Guiding Young Singers* (video recordings from Concordia Publishing House, 1985).
Kemp, I., 'Hindemith', *The New Grove Dictionary of Music and Musicians*, ed. S. Sadie (London, 1980), VIII: 573–87.
Knapp, J., 'Polyphony at Notre Dame of Paris', in The New Oxford History of Music, II: *The Early Middle Ages to 1300* (new edition), ed. Richard Crocker and David Hiley (Oxford, 1990).
Knighton, T., and D. Fallows (eds.), *Companion to Medieval and Renaissance Music* (London and New York, 1992; repr. Oxford, 1998).
Kolodin, I., *The Metropolitan Opera*, rev. edn (New York, 1966).
Kutsch, K. J. and L. Riemands (eds.), *Grosses Sängerlexicon*, 2 vols. (Bern-Stuttgart, 1987).
Laborde, J.-B. de, *Essai sur la musique ancienne et moderne*, 4 vols. (Paris, 1780).
Ladefoged, P., *A Course in Phonetics* (New York, 1993).
Laing, D., *One Chord Wonders: Power and Meaning in Punk Rock* (Milton Keynes, 1985).
Lambert, P. (ed.), *Ives Studies* (Cambridge, 1997).
Lamperti, F., *Guida teorico-pratica-elementare per lo studio del canto* (Milan, c. 1864).
  A Treatise on the Art of Singing, trans J. C. Griffith (New York, 1980).
Laurence, D. H. (ed.), *Shaw's Music* (London, 1981).
Laurence, Felicity, *Birds, Balloons and Shining Stars – A Teacher's Guide to Singing with Children* (London, 1994).
Leanderson, R., J. Sundberg, and C. von Euler, 'Role of the Diaphragmatic Activity During Singing: A Study of Transdiaphragmatic Pressures', *Journal of Applied Physiology*, 62 (1987), pp. 259–70.
  Vocal Fold Physiology: Laryngeal Function in Phonation and Respiration (Boston, MA, 1986).
Lehmann, L., *My Path through Life* (London, 1914).
Leppert, R., and S. McClary, *Music and Society: The Politics of Composition, Performance and Reception* (Cambridge, 1987).
Ligeti, G., *Ligeti in Conversation* (London, 1983).
Lippmann, F. (ed.), 'Belliniana', in *Il melodramma italiano dell'Ottocento: Studi e ricerche per Massimo Mila* (Turin, 1977), pp. 281–317.

Litvinne, F., *Ma vie et mon art* (Paris, 1933).

Locke, A. W., *Music and the Romantic Movement in France* (London, 1920).

Lovell, John, Jnr, *Black Song: The Forge and the Flame* (New York, 1972).

Luzzaschi, Luzzasco, *Madrigali* (Rome, 1601, facs. edn Florence, 1979).

MacClintock, C. (ed.), *Readings in the History of Music in Performance*
(Bloomington, IN, 1979; repr. 1982).

Mackerness, E. D., *A Social History of English Music* (London, 1964).

Maconie, R., *The Works of Karlheinz Stockhausen* (London, 1976).

Maffei, Giovanni Camillo, *Delle lettere del Sor Gio Camillo Maffei da Solofra*, Libri
Due (Naples, 1562); ed. Nanie Bridgman, 'Giovanni Camillo Maffei et sa lettre
sur le chant', *Revue de musicologie*, 38 (1956), pp. 3–34.

Maguire, S., *Vincenzo Bellini and the Aesthetics of Early Nineteenth-Century Italian
Opera* (New York and London, 1989).

Malcolm, G., 'Boys' Voices', *Fifteenth Aldeburgh Festival Programme-Book*
(Aldeburgh, 1962), pp. 14–16.

Mancini, Giambattista, *Pensieri e riflessioni pratiche sopra il canto figurato* (Vienna
1774; rev. 1777; English translation E. Foreman, *Practical Reflections on Figured
Singing*, Champaign, IL, 1967).

Manfredini, V., *Regole armoniche o sieno precetti ragionevoli per apprendere la musica*
(Venice, 1775).

Manning, J., *New Vocal Repertory: An Introduction* (Oxford, 1994).
New Vocal Repertory: Volume 2 (Oxford, 1998).

Mara, G. E., 'Eine Selbstbiographie von Gertrud Elisabeth Mara', *Allgemeine
Musikalische Zeitung* 10 (1875).

Marchesi, B., *Singer's Pilgrimage* (London, 1926).

Marchesi, M., *Aus meinem Leben* (Vienna, 1889; trans (abridged) as *Marchesi and
Music*, London, 1897).

Marcus, G., *Mystery Train* (London, 1977).
'Anarchy in the U.K.', in *The Rolling Stone Illustrated History of Rock & Roll*, ed. J.
Miller (London, 1981).

Marsh, J. B. T., *The Story of the Jubilee Singers; With Their Songs* (1881 edn, repr. New
York, 1969).

Marshall, R. L. (ed.), *Studies in Renaissance and Baroque Music in Honor of Arthur
Mendel* (Kassel, 1974).

Mattheson, Johann, *Der volkommene Capellmeister* (Hamburg, 1739).

McClary, S., 'Living to Tell: Madonna's Resurrection of the Fleshly', in her *Feminine
Endings: Music, Gender and Sexuality* (Minneapolis, MN, 1991).

McGee, T., *Medieval and Renaissance Music: A Performer's Guide* (Toronto, 1985).
*The Sound of Medieval Song: Ornamentation and Vocal Style According to the
Treatises* (Oxford, 1998).

McGee, T. (ed.), *Singing Early Music: The Pronunciation of European Languages in
the Late Middle Ages and Renaissance* (Bloomington, IN, 1996).

McGlinn, J., 'Settling Old Scores', *The Golden Age of Musicals, BBC Music Magazine
Special Issue* (January 1999), pp. 60–2.

McGraw, Hugh (ed.), *The Sacred Harp: 1991 Revision* (Bremen, GA, 1991).

McKay, David P., and Richard Crawford, *William Billings of Boston: Eighteenth-Century Composer* (Princeton, 1975).

Mersenne, Marin, *Harmonie universelle* (Paris, 1636).

Metastasio, P., *Tutte le opere*, ed. B. Brunelli, 5 vols. (Milan, 1943–54).

Middleton, R., 'All Shook Up? Innovation and Continuity in Elvis Presley's Vocal Style', in *Elvis: Images and Fancies*, ed. J. Tharpe (Jackson, MS, 1979).

Miller, J. (ed.), *The Rolling Stone Illustrated History of Rock & Roll* (London, 1981).

Miller, R., *English, French, German and Italian Techniques of Singing* (Metuchen, NJ, 1977).

The Structure of Singing (New York, 1986).

Mohr, A., *Handbuch der Kinderstimmbildnung* (Mainz, 1997).

Monahan, B. J., *The Art of Singing* (Metuchen, NJ, 1978).

Moody, C. H., *The Choir-Boy in the Making* (London, 1922; repr. 1939).

Mooser, R-A., *Annales de la musique et des musiciens en Russie au XVIII.me siècle*, 3 vols. (Geneva, 1948–51).

Mordden, E., *Make Believe: The Broadway Musical in the 1920s* (New York and Oxford, 1997).

Morelli, G., and E. Surian, 'Come nacque e come morì il patriottismo romano nell'opera veneziana', in *Opera e libretto*, 2 vols. (Florence, 1990).

Mori, R. M., *Coscienza della voce nella scuola italiano di canto* (Milan, 1970).

Müller-Häuser, Franz, *Vox Humana: ein Beitrag zur Untersuchung der Stimmästhetik des Mittelalters* (Regensburg, 1963).

Murray Schafer, R., *Voices of Tyranny, Temples of Silence* (Indian River, Ont., 1993).

Myers, M., *Modern French Music* (Oxford, 1971).

Napier, A. S. (ed.), *The Old English Version of the Enlarged Rule of Chrodegang Together with the Latin Original*, Early English Text Society 150 (London, 1916).

Nathan, I., *Musurgia Vocalis* (London, 1836).

Neumann, F., *Ornamentation in Baroque and Post-Baroque Music* (Princeton, 1978).

Newcomb, A., *The Madrigal at Ferrara 1579–1597*, 2 vols. (Princeton, 1980).

'Courtesans, Muses, or Musicians?' in *Women Making Music*, ed. J. Bowers and J. Tick (Urbana, IL, 1986), pp. 90–115.

Nicholson, S., 'Of Women's *versus* Boys' Voices', *Cathedral Music Today and Tomorrow* (report of sub-committee appointed by the Cathedral Organists' Association and the Church Music Society (London, 1941)).

Nitsche, P., *Die Pflege der Kinder- und Jugendstimme: I Theoretische Teil* (Mainz, 1970); *II Stimmbildung am Lied* (Mainz, 1969).

O'Connor, P., 'Music for the Stage', in *Music in Britain: The Twentieth Century*, ed. S. Banfield (Oxford, 1995), pp. 107–24.

Osborne, C., 'The Broadway Voice: Just Singin' in the Pain', *High Fidelity* (January and February 1979), pp. 57–65 and 53–6.

Pacchierotti, G. C., *Ai cultori ed amatori della musica vocale: cenni biografici intorno a Gaspare Pacchierotti* (Padua, 1844).

Page, C., 'Machaut's "Pupil" Deschamps on the Performance of Music: Voices or Instruments in the 14th-Century Chanson', *Early Music*, 5 (1977), pp. 484–91.

Voices and Instruments of the Middle Ages: Instrumental Practice and Songs in France, 1100–1300 (London, 1987).

'The Performance of Ars Antiqua Motets', *Early Music,* 16 (1988), pp. 147–64.

'Polyphony before 1400', in *Performance Practice: Music Before 1600*, ed. H. M. Brown and S. Sadie (New York, 1990), pp. 79–104.

Summa Musice: A Thirteenth-Century Manual for Singers (Cambridge, 1991).

'A Treatise on Musicians from ?*c.* 1400: The *Tractatulus de differentiis et gradibus cantorum* by Arnulf of St Ghislain', *Journal of the Royal Musical Association,* 117 (1992), pp. 1–21.

'The English *a cappella* Renaissance', *Early Music,* 21/3 (August 1993), pp. 452–71.

Palermo, S. (ed.), *Saverio Mercadante: biografia, epistolario* (Fasano, 1985).

Palisca, C., *The Florentine Camerata* (New Haven and London, 1989).

Panofka, E., *Voci e cantanti*, Sala Bolognese, 1984 (1st edn 1866).

Pass, W., and Alexander Rausch (eds.), *Mittelalterliche Musiktheorie in Zentraleuropa*, Musica Mediaevalis Europae Occidentalis, 4 (Tutzing, 1998).

Petrobelli, P., 'Un cantante fischiato e le appoggiature di mezza battuta: cronaca teatrale e prassi esecutiva alla metà del '700', in *Studies in Renaissance and Baroque Music in Honor of Arthur Mendel*, ed. R. L. Marshall (Kassel, 1974), pp. 363–76.

Philip, R., *Early Recordings and Musical Style: Changing Tastes in Instrumental Performance, 1900–1950* (Cambridge, 1992).

Phillips, P., 'The Golden Age Regained', *Early Music,* 8/1 (January 1980), pp. 3–16.

'The Golden Age Regained: 2', *Early Music* 8/2 (April 1980), pp. 178–98.

Pirie, P. J., *The English Musical Renaissance* (London, 1979).

Pirrotta, N., *Music and Theatre from Poliziano to Monteverdi* (Cambridge, 1982).

'Commedia dell'arte and Opera', in *Music and Culture in Italy from the Middle Ages to the Baroque* (Cambridge, MA, 1984), pp. 343–60.

Playford, J., 'Introduction to the Skill of Music', in O. Strunk, *Source Readings* (Madison, 1970), pp. 377–92.

Pleasants, H., *The Great Singers* (New York, 1966).

The Great American Popular Singers (New York, 1974).

'Crosby, Bing (Harry Lillis)', *The New Grove Dictionary of Music and Musicians*, ed. S. Sadie, 20 vols. (New York and London, 1980), V: 60.

Potter, J., 'Electronics and the Live Performer', *Composer*, 66 (Spring 1979), pp. 19–21.

'The Singer, not the Song: Women Singers as Composer-Poets', *Popular Music*, 12/2 (1994), pp. 191–9.

'Reconstructing Lost Voices', in *Companion to Medieval and Renaissance Music*, ed. Tess Knighton and David Fallows (London and New York, 1992; repr. Oxford, 1998).

Vocal Authority: Singing Style and Ideology (Cambridge, 1998).

Pouncey, Edwin, 'The Man Who Sold the Underworld', *The Wire,* 161 (July 1997), pp. 24–30.

Prince, H., *Contradictions: Notes on 26 Years in the Theatre* (New York, 1974).

Printz, W. C., *Musica modulatoria vocalis* (Schweidnitz, 1678).

Proctor, D. F., *Breathing, Speech and Song* (Vienna and New York, 1980).

Quicherat, L., *Alphonse Nourrit*, 3 vols. (Paris, 1867).

Quirsfeld, Johann, *Breviarum musicum* (Dresden, 1675; repr. 1688).

Rao, Doreen, *Choral Music Experience*, V: *The Young Singing Voice* (London, 1987).

Rastall, R., 'Vocal Range and Tessitura in Music from York Play 45', *Music Analysis*, 3 (1984), pp. 181–99.

Raymond, J., *Show Music on Record: From the 1890s to the 1980s* (New York, 1982).

Razzi, F., 'Polyphony of the *seconda prattica*: Performance Practice in Italian Vocal Music of the Mannerist Era', *Early Music*, 8 (1980), pp. 298–311.

Reese, G., and S. Ledbetter (eds.), *A Compendium of Musical Practice* (New York, 1973).

Reid, Cornelius L., *Bel Canto: Principles and Practices* (New York, 1971).

Reidemeister, P., 'Zur Vokalpraxis', *Historische Aufführungspraxis: eine Einführung*, (Darmstadt, 1988).

Rex, R., *'The Sins of Madame Eglentyne' and Other Essays on Chaucer* (Newark, DE, 1995).

Ricks, George Robinson, 'Some Aspects of the Religious Music of the United States Negro: An Ethnomusicological Study with Special Emphasis on the Gospel Tradition', unpublished Ph.D. dissertation: Northwestern University (1960).

Roberts, J. S., *Black Music of Two Worlds* (New York, 1982).

Rognoni, Francesco, *Selva di varii passaggi* (Milan, 1620 facs. ed. Bologna, 1970).

Rosand, E., 'Barbara Strozzi, virtuosissima cantatrice: The Composer's Voice', *Journal of the American Musicological Society*, 31 (1978), pp. 241–81.

'The Voice of Barbara Strozzi', in *Women Making Music*, ed. J. Bowers and J. Tick (Urbana, IL, 1986), pp. 168–90.

Opera in Seventeenth-Century Venice: The Creation of a Genre (Berkeley, 1991).

Rose, G., and H. Ireland, liner notes to the Singcircle recording of Stockhausen's *Stimmung* (Hyperion CDA66115).

Rosenthal, H., and J. Warrack, J. (eds.), *The Concise Oxford Dictionary of Opera*, 2nd edn (London, 1979).

Roß, Erwin, *Deutsche und italienische Gesangsmethode: erläutert auf Grund ihrer geschichtlichen Gegensätzlichkeit im achtzehnten Jahrhundert* (Kassel, 1928).

Rosselli, J., *Singers of Italian Opera: The History of a Profession* (Cambridge, 1992).

'The Castrati as a Professional Group and a Social Phenomenon, 1550–1850', *Acta Musicologica*, 60 (1988), pp. 143–79.

The Life of Bellini (Cambridge, 1997).

Sachs, K.-J., *Mensura fistularum: die Mensurierung der Orgelpfeifen im Mittelalter* (Stuttgart, 1970).

Sadie, S. (ed.), *The New Grove Dictionary of Opera*, 4 vols. (London, 1992).

Salaman, E., *Unlocking Your Voice – Freedom to Sing* (London, 1989).

Santley, C., *Student and Singer* (London, 1892).

Sartori, C., 'La prima diva della lirica italiana: Anna Renzi', *Nuova Rivista Musicale Italiana*, 2 (1968), pp. 430–52.

Sataloff, R. T. (ed.), *The Professional Voice: The Science and Art of Clinical Voice Care* (San Diego, 1997).

Savage, J., *Time Travel: Pop, Media and Sexuality, 1977–96* (London, 1996).

Sawkins, L., 'For and Against the Order of Nature: Who Sang the Soprano?', *Early Music*, 15 (1987), pp. 315–24.

'Haute-contre', *The New Grove Dictionary of Opera*, 4 vols. (London, 1992), II: 668–9.

Schaefer, John, *New Sounds: The Virgin Guide to New Music* (London, 1990).

Schmid, H. (ed.), *Musica et Scolica Enchiriadis una cum aliquibus tractatulis adiunctis* (Munich, 1981).

Schutte, H., and D. Miller, 'The Effect of F0/F1 Coincidence in Soprano High Notes on Pressure at the Glottis', *Journal of Phonetics*, 14 (1986), pp. 386–92.

Seeley, R., and R. Bunnett, *London Musical Shows on Record 1889–1989* (Harrow, 1989).

Seidner, W., and J. Wendler, *Die Sängerstimme*, 3rd edn (Berlin, 1997).

Shaw, G. B., *Shaw's Music*, ed. D. H. Laurence (London, 1989).

Shepherd, J., 'Music and Male Hegemony', in *Music and Society: The Politics of Composition, Performance and Reception*, ed. R. Leppert and S. McClary (Cambridge, 1987).

Shipp, T., 'CT-EMG & Vibrato', *Voice* 5 (1991).

Shipp, T., T. Doherty, and S. Haglund, 'Physiologic Factors in Vocal Vibrato Production', *Voice*, 4 (1991), pp. 300–4.

Shipp, T., and K. Izdebski, 'Vocal Frequency and Vertical Larynx Positioning by Singer and Nonsingers', *Journal of the Acoustic Society of America*, 58 (1975), pp. 1104–6.

Simpson, A. K., *Follow Me: The Life and Music of R. Nathaniel Dett* (Metuchen, NJ, 1993).

Small, C., *Music of the Common Tongue* (London, 1987).

Smith, H., K. Stevens, and R. Tomlinson, 'On an Unusual Mode of Chanting by Certain Lamas', *Journal of the Acoustic Society of America*, 41 (1967), pp. 1262–4.

Smith, L., and B. Scott, 'Increasing the Intelligibility of Sung Vowels', *Journal of the Acoustic Society of America*, 67 (1980), 1795–7.

Songs of Zion (Nashville, TN, 1981).

Southern, E., 'Hymnals of the Black Church', *The Black Perspective in Music*, 17/1–2 (1989), pp. 153–70.

The Music of Black Americans (New York, 1985).

Readings in Black American Music (New York, 1971).

Spencer, J. M. (ed.), *The R. Nathaniel Dett Reader: Essays on Black Sacred Music* (Durham, NC, 1991).

Stanford, C. V., *Pages from an Unwritten Diary* (London, 1914).

Steane, J., *The Grand Tradition: Seventy Years of Singing on Record* (London, 1974).

Voices, Singers and Critics (London, 1992).

Stevens, D. (ed.), *The Letters of Claudio Monteverdi* (Oxford, 1995).

Stevenson, R., *Protestant Church Music In America* (New York, 1966).

Stone, P. E., 'John Knowles Paine; Mass in D', article accompanying the New World Records recording of the Paine Mass (Recorded Anthology of American Music, Inc., New York, 1978).

Strunk, O., *Source Readings in Music History* (Princeton and London, 1950; repr. 1965, rev. edn New York and London, 1998).

Sundberg, J., 'What's So Special about Singers?', *Voice*, 4 (1990), pp. 107–19.

    The Science of the Singing Voice (DeKalb, IL, 1987; German translation, 1997: 'Die Wissenschaft von der Singstimme', Bonn, 1997).

    'Vocal Tract Resonance in Singing', *NATS Bulletin*, 44 (1988), pp. 11–19 and 31.

Sundberg, J., P. Gramming, and J. Lovetri, *Voice Source, Formant Frequency and Subglottal Pressure Characteristics in a Professional Female Musical Theatre Singer*, 7 (1993), pp. 301–10.

Taylor, T. D., *Global Pop: World Music, World Markets* (New York, 1997).

Ternström, S., 'Acoustical Aspects of Choir Singing', unpublished dissertation, Royal Institute of Technology in Stockholm (1989).

    'Physical and Acoustic Factors that Interact with the Singer to Produce the Choral Sound', *Voice*, 5 (1991), pp. 128–43.

Terry, R. R., 'The Essential Fitness of the Old Music', in *Catholic Church Music* (London, 1907), pp. 47–53.

    'Why is Church Music so Bad?', *A Forgotten Psalter and Other Essays* (London, 1929), pp. 105–25.

Tharpe, J. (ed.), *Elvis: Images and Fancies* (Jackson, MS, 1979).

Thomassen, K., 'Acoustics and Perception of Overtone Singing', *Journal of the Acoustic Society of America*, 92 (1992), pp. 1827–36.

Titze, I., *Principles of Voice Production* (Englewood Cliffs, NJ, 1994).

    'The Importance of Vocal Tract Loading in Maintaining Vocal Fold Oscillation', in *Proceedings of the Stockholm Music Acoustic Conference 1983* (SMAC 93), ed. A. Askenfelt, S. Felicetti, E. Jansson and J. Sundberg. Royal Swedish Academy of Music, publ. no. 46:1 (Stockholm, 1995), pp. 61–72.

Toop, D., *The Sugarhill Story: Old School Rap – To the Beat Y'all*, booklet notes to 3CD compilation, Sequel Records, 1992.

    Rap Attack 2 (London, 1991).

Tosi, P. F., *Opinioni de' cantori antichi e moderni* (Bologna, 1723), pp. 49–56; reprinted in A. Della Corte, *Canto e bel canto* (Turin, 1933); Eng. trans. by J. E. Galliard as *Observations on the Florid Song* (London, 1742; facs. repr. London, 1967).

Tovey, D., and Geoffrey Parratt, *Walter Parratt: Master of the Music* (London, 1941).

Upton, William Treat, *Anthony Philip Heinrich: A Nineteenth-Century Composer in America* (New York, 1939).

Vale, W. S., *The Training of Boys' Voices* (London, 1932).

van Dijk, S. J. P., 'Saint Bernard and the "Instituta patrum" of St Gall', *Musica Disciplina*, 4 (1950), pp. 99–109.

Van Leer, D., 'Putting It Together: Sondheim and the Broadway Musical', *Raritan*, 7 (1987) pp. 113–28.

Varley Roberts, J., *A Treatise on a Practical Method of Training Choristers* (London, 1898).

Wainwright, D., *The Piano Makers* (London, 1975).

Walford Davies, H., 'Both Sides of the Microphone', *BBC Handbook* 1929 (London, 1929).

Walker, F., *Letters of a Baritone* (London, 1895).

Walker, W., and Glenn C. Wilcox (eds.), *The Southern Harmony* (repr. of 1854 edn, Los Angeles, 1966).

Walter, Michael, '*Sunt preterea multa quae conferri magis quam scribi oportet*: Zur Materialität der Kommunication im mitteralterlichen Gesangsunterricht', in *Schule und Schüler im Mittelalter: Beiträge zur europäischen Bildungsgeschichte des 9. bis 15. Jahrhunderts*, ed. M. Kintzinger, L. Lorenz and M. Walter (Cologne, 1996), pp. 111–43.

Wang, S., 'Singing Voice: Bright Timbre, Singer's Formant, and Larynx Position', in *Proceedings of the Stockholm Music Acoustic Conference1983* (SMAC 93), ed. A. Askenfelt, S. Felicetti, E. Jansson and J. Sundberg. Royal Swedish Academy of Music, publ. no. 46:1 (Stockholm, 1985), pp. 313–22.

Webb, G., and A. Walker (trans.), *The Mirror of Charity: The Speculum Charitatis of St Aelred of Rievaulx* (London, 1962).

Weber, W., 'La musique ancienne in the Waning of the ancien régime', *Journal of Modern History*, 56 (1994), pp. 58–88.

Welch, Graham F., *et al.*, *Singing Development, Childhood and Change, An Overview* (London, ASME (The Centre for Advanced Studies in Music Education), Roehampton Institute, n.d.).

Wellesz, E., *Arnold Schoenberg: The Formative Years* (London, 1971).

Wepman, Dennis, Ronald B. Newman, and Murray B. Binderman, *The Life: The Lore and Folk Poetry of the Black Hustler* (Los Angeles, 1976).

Wesley, S. S., *A Few Words on Cathedral Music* (London and Leeds, 1849).

White, B. F., and E. J. King, *The Sacred Harp* (Spartanburg, SC, 1844).

White, E. D., *Choral Music by Afro-American Composers* (Metuchen, NJ, 1981).

Willberg, Helen, *Sing Together* (Wellington, 1993).

Williams, P., and Barbara Owen, *The Organ*, The Grove Musical Instruments Series (New York, 1988).

Willis, E., 'Janis Joplin', in *The Rolling Stone Illustrated History of Rock & Roll*, ed. J. Miller (London, 1981).

Wishart, T., *On Sonic Art* (rev. edn Amsterdam, 1998).

Wistreich, R., 'La voce è grata assai, ma . . . Monteverdi on singing', *Early Music*, 22 (1994), pp. 7–19.

Work, John W., *Jubilee* (New York, 1962).

Yeats-Edwards, P., *English Church Music: A Bibliography* (London, 1975).

Zacconi, Lodovico, *Prattica di musica* (Venice, 1592; facs. edn Bologna, 1983).

Zarlino, Gioseffo, *Le istitutioni harmoniche* (Venice, 1558; edn of 1588–9; facs. edn Bologna, 1966).

Zorzi, A., *Cortigiana veneziana: Veronica Franco e i suoi poeti* (Milan, 1986).

Journal of Voice, official journal of the Voice Foundation, Philadelphia, Pennsylvania, USA, contains a great number of articles on the voice in singing and speech.

Index